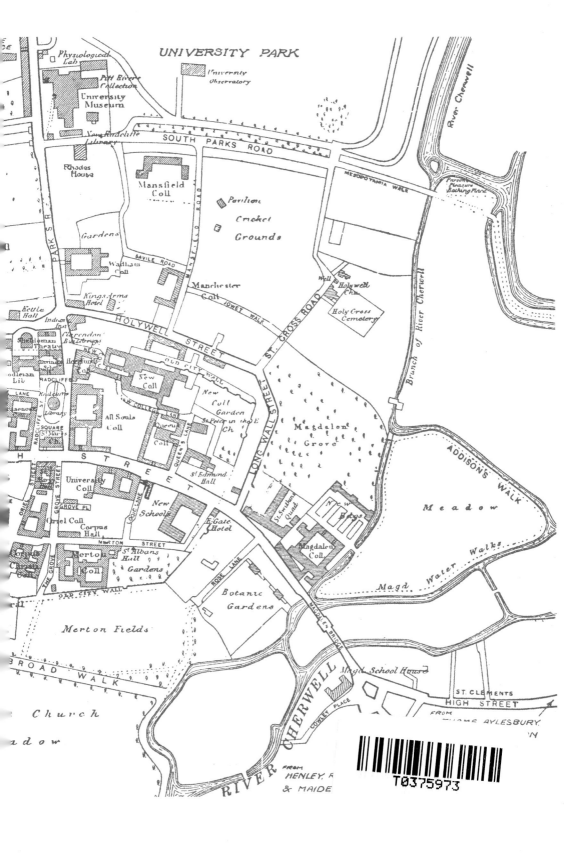

OXFORD'S WAR

OXFORD'S WAR
1939–1945

ASHLEY JACKSON

BODLEIAN
LIBRARY
PUBLISHING

Dedicated to the memory of
Sabre Badger Beetle Bungle Bagpuss Balrog Bandersnatch Basil Beastling
Buckbeak Centaur Crocodile Darkstar Emu Lion Mekon
Roo-legs Shark Sluglet Smaug Sunbeam Yoda Jackson,
otherwise known as His Badgesty Saberius Rex I
30 September 2013 to 6 October 2020
Sabre boy, you lit up our lives

First published in 2024 by Bodleian Library Publishing
Broad Street, Oxford OX1 3BG
www.bodleianshop.co.uk
ISBN 978 1 85124 613 7
Text © Ashley Jackson, 2024
All images, unless specified on p. 365, © Bodleian Libraries,
University of Oxford, 2024
Endpapers: author's collection
This edition © Bodleian Library Publishing, University of Oxford, 2024

Ashley Jackson has asserted his right to be identified as the author of this Work.

All rights reserved.

No part of this book may be reproduced, stored in a retrieval system, or
transmitted in any form or by any means, electronic, mechanical, photocopying,
recording, or otherwise, without the written permission of the Bodleian Library,
except for the purpose of research or private study, or criticism or review.

Publisher: Samuel Fanous
Managing Editor: Susie Foster
Editor: Janet Phillips
Picture Editor: Leanda Shrimpton
Cover design by Dot Little at the Bodleian Library
Designed and typeset by Lucy Morton of illuminati in Perpetua
Printed and bound in China by C&C Offset Printing Co., Ltd.
on 115 gsm Yulong Pure paper

British Library Catalogue in Publishing Data
A CIP record of this publication is available from the British Library

CONTENTS

	PREFACE	vii
	INTRODUCTION	1
ONE	A TOUR ROUND TOWN	7
TWO	OF UNIVERSITY AND COLLEGES	21
THREE	RISING FASCISM, APPROACHING WAR	43
FOUR	CONSCRIPTION AND REQUISITIONING	66
FIVE	LIVING UNDER REQUISITION	90
SIX	THREAT, WORRY AND EVACUATION	116
SEVEN	IN WARTIME OXFORD	149
EIGHT	UNDERGRADUATES AT WAR	175
NINE	DONS AT WAR	198
TEN	INTELLIGENCE, SCIENCE AND MEDICINE	226
ELEVEN	THE POST-WAR WORLD	261
	A NOTE ON SOURCES	290
	ABBREVIATIONS AND ACRONYMS	292
	NOTES	294
	BIBLIOGRAPHY	352
	ACKNOWLEDGEMENTS	363
	PICTURE CREDITS	365
	INDEX	366

PREFACE

This is a history of the University of Oxford and its constituent colleges during the Second World War. While profiling 'gown' as opposed to 'town', it embraces the city and the county in which this ancient seat of learning is set, contributing to the history of Oxfordshire and the British Isles during the conflict. It begins in the 1930s, as the menace of fascism and the prospect of war permeated British society.

Like other institutions and their environs, British universities were unavoidably affected by the actions of the dictators and the war they caused. As it approached, they mobilized in service of the state, the peril clear, the enemy in plain sight. Universities wanted to play their part in a struggle that, without recourse to hyperbole, was easily viewed as a battle for civilization as well as national survival. For its part, the state looked to them for a range of services. They could provide military officers and civil servants as armed forces and government ministries expanded. They were looked to for expertise – for codebreaking and translation, post-war reconstruction planning and topographical intelligence on regions where Allied forces fought. They were looked to for innovations – weapons, protective devices, and communication and detection technologies – as well as lifesaving drugs and medical treatments. They were looked to for explanations of the international situation that could inform public audiences and bolster propaganda campaigns. And they were looked to for real estate, as swollen ministries and multifarious military organizations came to roost in towns and cities away from the embattled capital. Up and down the country undergraduates marched off to war, and quadrangles, great halls, libraries and halls of residence became hospitals, evacuee centres, cadet schools and offices for government clerks. Amid the hyper-activity of national, institutional and communal endeavours to defend Britain, defeat its enemies and prepare for what would come after, Oxford played its part.

A note on usage

I've generally avoided using Oxford terminology – 'the High' for the High Street, 'the Turl' for Turl Street, 'the Bod' for the Bodleian Library and so on. Such terms are either seldom heard today, even in Oxford, or are very much confined to Oxford. Their use might cloud meaning for readers not familiar with the place. In this spirit, I've also eschewed acronyms and abbreviations that are common, even dominant, today such as 'LMH' for Lady Margaret Hall, 'Teddy Hall' for St Edmund Hall or 'Univ' for University College – even though using the proper names might jar with people familiar with the city and University (NB Manchester College changed its name to Harris Manchester College in 1996). Where I have used Oxford terms, such as 'going up' for 'to go to Oxford as a fresher', explanation is offered.

When referring to Oxfordshire I have in mind today's county boundaries, though readers will recall that until 1974 much of it was actually in Berkshire. This included the towns and environs of Abingdon, Didcot, Wallingford and Wantage, as well as places such as Uffington and the Vale of the White Horse. Surprisingly, it also included land abutting Oxford city itself, such as Boars Hill, Cumnor, Harcourt Hill and Hinksey – even Wytham!

A PEOPLE'S PEACE FOR TWO PERSONS

You and I must shortly sever
All the bonds of our endeavour
To be sharp and self-sufficient.
Was our coast-defence efficient
Or did truthful bombs endanger
Attempts by our reasons' governments to make us grow stranger?

We with pleasure masochistic
Learned each detailed death-statistic,
Due to my hot Bren guns – kinder
Than your accurate range-finder
Since more sudden, yet as certain
To mean the collapsed brick-shelter, the bleeding black-out curtain.

To replace these shared sensations
No romantic League of Nations
Or precise Federal Union,
No World Church's chaste communion:
Overturning our ruling-classes
Whose wars for abstract thinking's profits formed our lives of farces.

Flesh's frontier-forts demolished,
Racial rules by both abolished,
Each consumes without trade-fracture
Other's novel manufacture.
But, my dear, though slack peace plighting,
May not we who fought to love fight again for love of fighting?

DRUMMOND ALLISON, The Queen's College Oxford, December 1940,
killed at Monte Cassino with the East Surrey Regiment, December 1943[1]

INTRODUCTION

The blackout plunged the city into a 'stygian darkness' unknown since medieval days.[1] Static water tanks appeared in New College Great Quad, Radcliffe Square, Merton College Grove and other university and public spaces, intended to douse the flames should the Luftwaffe strike. A Home Guard rifle range opened in the Fellows' Garden at Wadham, and the Women's Auxiliary Air Force (WAAF) drilled on New Building Lawns in Magdalen. An enormous Ministry of Food grain silo arose at Water Eaton, and the factories and chimneys of the Cowley motor works were camouflaged, rooflines broken up with timber structures in an attempt to fox German reconnaissance flights.[2] Assessing the claims of conscientious objectors, the warden of New College was knocked over and killed on a blacked-out London street, his underwear subsequently worn by the corpse floated onto a Spanish shore as part of the 'Mincemeat' deception operation preceding the invasion of Sicily.[3] The New Bodleian provided bomb-proof storage for treasures from Oxford colleges and scores of national institutions, including the British Library, Parliament and the Royal Botanic Gardens. It also accommodated cartographers preparing D-Day invasion maps, a Red Cross team sending parcels to prisoners of war, and a blood transfusion centre supplying local hospitals, their bed capacity increased in order to cope with the expected level of civilian casualties.

War pervaded the city. The hushed, incensed precincts of Pusey House hosted Air Raid Precaution (ARP) classes; Wellington Square lost its iron railings, as did the University Parks and St Michael's at the North Gate on Cornmarket. Refugees from the Spanish Civil War and the Nazis came to form a distinct element of the city's population. Evacuees from blitzed London crowded into a cinema and a dance hall and were put up in colleges as they awaited lodgings, the well-to-do of Boars Hill and North Oxford accused of reluctance to take in children from less privileged areas. Magdalen fellow C.S. Lewis patrolled the streets with a Home Guard rifle and was inspired to write *The Chronicles of Narnia* by evacuee children berthed at his home in the east of the city, and an encounter with a wardrobe in Brasenose.[4] His brother Warnie, meanwhile, chugged along the Cherwell and the Thames aboard a cabin cruiser as part of the Upper Thames Patrol, a riverine 'Dad's Army' irreverently known as 'Up The Pub'.[5]

German bombers flew over Oxford as they made their way to the industrial Midlands, residents unaware that Hitler, as the story goes, had spared their city in order to make it his capital when he arrived in triumph. Instead, they were mindful of the destruction visited upon nearby Coventry – the inferno visible from Oxford – and the 'Baedeker raids' targeting historic cities like their own. They were mindful too of the fact that Oxford's factories, churning out military equipment and repairing hundreds of downed Spitfires and Hurricanes during the Battle of Britain, presented highly attractive targets for the Luftwaffe.

To meet the threat from the air, firewatchers and aircraft spotters took to the rooftops, at the Pressed Steel works in Cowley and the Ashmolean Museum, at St Hilda's and St John's and all the other colleges, town and gown in equal peril. There were ARP watchtowers atop Woolworth's on Cornmarket (today's Boots), All Saints on the High Street, New College's Muniment Tower and Trinity's chapel. People trained to use stirrup pumps, and fire engines were housed in quads and municipal buildings such as the Town Hall on St Aldate's. The prospect of ground attack was real too, Oxford squatting athwart potential routes for German forces advancing on London or the Midlands. With the British Army largely immobilized and disarmed following the Dunkirk evacuations, its heavy weapons abandoned on French beaches, thousands of Canadians troops massed in Oxford and surrounding towns and villages to meet the threat, flooding the city centre at night to drink and pinch unattended cars and bicycles. American service personnel were to follow, as Oxfordshire became a major base for Allied airpower and pre-D-Day preparations, the skies alive with RAF and US Army Air Force machines flying from the airbases that proliferated across the county. Americans jitterbugged in the Great Hall of Rhodes House and took over the Churchill Hospital, constructed by the Emergency Medical Services early in the war for the treatment of air raid victims, named for the prime minister, and opened by the Duchess of Kent.

Like every other British city, Oxford bore the hallmarks of home-front hardship, from gas masks to ration books, weakened beer and nightly blackouts. People suffered powdered egg, were denied bananas, and knitted balaclava helmets for merchant seamen. Tree trunks were stacked ready to block roads should the invader come, and air raid shelters appeared, even before the outbreak, in under-stairs cupboards and basements, including the cellar of The Grapes pub on George Street and the Norman crypt of St Peter-in-the-East on Queen's Lane. The war brought many more, in Broad Street and Rewley Road, in fellows' gardens and college cellars, and in schools such as St Thomas's in Osney Lane. There were 'dig for victory' allotments in the University Parks and Port Meadow and scores of plots on Oriel College's sports ground. Public and private spaces such as Southfield golf course and Cutteslowe Park were turned over to the patriotic production of vegetables. In the Provost's Lodgings of Worcester College, with views out over the lake, the wives of dons and vicars rolled bandages and made slings and swabs for the Red Cross, aided by undergraduates from Somerville.

Those too old or too young to join up, or in reserved occupations, as well as those of age but medically unfit for the regular forces, joined the Home Guard. Christ Church don Frank Pakenham (Baron Pakenham of Cowley from 1945) commanded a Home Guard company which prowled around Christ Church Meadow from headquarters in the college garages and Salter's Boatyard. Maurice Bowra, warden of Wadham, was his second in command, Magdalen historian A.J.P. Taylor one of his men. Armed with .22 rifles and large sticks, they patrolled the Broad Walk looking for enemy parachutists, under orders to 'give them stick' should they land.[6] Scientists from the University's chemical laboratories sought to perfect the Molotov cocktail in case it came to street fighting, throwing dozens of different mixtures against the rock face of a Headington quarry. They discovered that a 60:40 split using petrol and coal tar worked best, and that rope slings improved both accuracy and range.[7]

Students fit for active service took shortened degree courses and underwent military training while they studied. As the male undergraduate population plummeted, Oxford brimmed with military officers on short training courses accommodated in college buildings. Younger dons left for the forces or for government work in London or at the Government Code and Cypher School (Bletchley Park), which recruited university types able to help break and decipher codes and translate foreign languages. Academics and civil servants worked on 'post-hostility planning' under the auspices of the Royal Institute of International Affairs (commonly known as Chatham House) lodged at Balliol, influencing policy as government sought to address challenges such as growing Soviet influence in eastern Europe and the return of British rule to colonies conquered by the Japanese. By printed and spoken word – books, pamphlets, lectures and radio broadcasts – Oxford academics articulated ideas and explanations of the world crisis that boosted public morale and nurtured understanding and resolve.

University bigwigs advised ministers and conducted studies on post-war reconstruction and foreign and imperial policy. Sir William Beveridge, resembling 'a gargoyle thatched with white hair', performed his duties as master of University College while compiling the report on public welfare that would come to bear his name, known mischievously to SCR colleagues as *Mein Pamph*.[8] Sir Henry Tizard, president of Magdalen, was a major player in scientific work of national importance, while Sir Frederick Lindemann, Professor of Experimental Philosophy, fellow of Wadham, resident of Christ Church and head of the Clarendon Laboratory, became one of the prime minister's most trusted advisers. He coordinated Oxford's scientific contribution to the war, including work on the atom bomb and radar.[9] At the Radcliffe Infirmary on the Woodstock Road, Elva Akers and City of Oxford police constable Albert Alexander became penicillin's first human guinea pigs as revolutionary advances in the drug's development were made by a team led by Professor Howard Florey, head of the nearby Dunn School of Pathology.

Defining facets of Oxford life and tradition were suspended because of the war. There was no varsity match at Lord's and the annual Oxford–Cambridge Boat Race was cancelled, taking place unofficially on quiet stretches of the Thames instead.[10] All Souls stopped electing new fellows and St Edmund Hall suspended dinnertime sconcing – the Oxford tradition of obliging someone to take drink, or down a drink, for a breach of etiquette – 'the necessary beverage', as the college magazine put it, 'in strictly limited supply'.[11] There were no commemorative balls; affluent students lost the privilege of hosting extravagant lunches in their college rooms; and the unfortunate inhabitants of Magdalen's Deer Grove were culled, college fellows sent home with haunches of venison. War brought an end to the Queen's College's tradition of brewing its own beer, and import restrictions reduced St John's stocks of vintage port to such a level that consumption was confined to special occasions only.[12]

It wasn't just the degree courses and the privileged trimmings of university life that were affected by war; the very stones themselves were enlisted, as national emergency shrunk academic life and consumed buildings as well as people's time and energy. Students were ejected from their staircases as real estate across Oxford was requisitioned. Around half its colleges were occupied in whole or in part by officers on training courses and civil servants evacuated from London or forming part of the overflow of bureaucrats called forth by total war. In consequence, spaces that for centuries had been men-only preserves became the preserve of women too. The Ministry of Food, the Foreign Office, the Ministry of Home Security, the Ministry of Information, the Ministry of Labour and the Ministry of War Transport all had a presence in Oxford, as did the Admiralty, the War Office, the Air Ministry, MI5 and Bletchley Park.

Further swelling Oxford's population, thousands of military personnel passed through the city as patients hospitalized as a result of active service, including 13,000 head-injury cases treated in the pioneering military hospital established at St Hugh's. Others were treated in the Examination Schools, and Ruskin College, taken over as a maternity hospital, delivered around 2,500 war babies. The University's press – 90 per cent of its capacity devoted to war work – printed secret military documents, codebooks and invasion maps, as well as propaganda

INTRODUCTION 5

publications such as the 'Oxford Pamphlets on World Affairs' series, retailing at 6 pence and shifting over 6 million copies worldwide.[13]

Before chronicling the approach of war and the impact of hostilities upon the University and the city, we turn first to a study of what the place was like in the 1930s.

ONE

A TOUR ROUND TOWN

Oxford sits on a low-lying plain at the confluence of the rivers Cherwell and Thames. The Cotswolds lie to the north, the Berkshire Downs and Chilterns to the south and east.[1] What was the city like on the eve of the Second World War? Though not as outlandishly different as Lyra's Oxford – the recognizable yet phantasmagorical city of Philip Pullman's *Dark Materials* novels – 1930s' Oxford was very different to the city of today.[2] It was much smaller, a settlement of 80,000 souls in 1931 (compared to around 150,000 today).[3] Though in the midst of a transformational growth spurt, with houses spreading along the Botley Road and sprouting at Cowley, Cumnor and Cutteslowe, suburban sprawl was limited, the countryside much closer to the city centre. In *Brideshead Revisited*, Charles Ryder and Sebastian Flyte enter 'open country' in their borrowed Morris-Cowley two-seater once past the railway station.[4] Evidence of the county's agricultural activities was visible on the streets, and villages now enveloped by the city – Headington, Hinksey, Iffley, Marston, Wolvercote – remained separate and distinct.[5]

It was an insular place: great university it may have possessed, but great international city Oxford was not. Migrating Welsh workers formed a distinct element of its population as the car industry developed, and the student body contained a handful of Rhodes Scholars from America and the dominions and students from imperial territories such as India. But the city and the University were overwhelmingly British, not to say English, lacking the cosmopolitanism that the arrival of refugees from Nazism was beginning to stir and that was to become a hallmark of the place in later decades. The University dominated what was quintessentially a university town, though one with a growing industrial working class. Almost a quarter of the area within the City of Oxford was owned by the University and the colleges.[6] Many more Oxford residents lived in the city centre than do today, and they helped independent retailers hold their own against national chain stores. Shop awnings protruded onto pavements, adding to the colour and closeness of the streets, as did newspaper-sellers and kerbside handcarts selling fruit and veg. Victorian streetlights abounded, 95 per cent of them gas.[7] There was little of the street furniture and road markings – bollards, traffic islands, arrows, lines, and lettering – that were to proliferate from the 1960s.[8] Horse-drawn traffic could still be seen on the streets, vehicles of agricultural workers as well as waggons collecting luggage massed at porters' lodges as students headed for the railway stations at the end of term.[9] But the motor car was already king, and the first sections of what would become the ring road – Headington to the Banbury Road roundabout and Botley to South Hinksey – had been completed by 1938.[10]

Then, as now, Christ Church Meadow, the University Parks, Port Meadow and Magdalen meadows buffered the city centre, and there was a riparian Oxford that all could enjoy, 'Cherwell, willows, meadows, boathouses, tea gardens and punts moored close to the bank'.[11] Further afield the Cumnor Hills, associated with Matthew Arnold's 'Scholar Gipsy' and inspiration for Ralph Vaughan Williams's *An Oxford Elegy* (written shortly after the war), provided good walking. Though inwardly focused and often sedentary, some members of the University knew the towns and villages that lay beyond the golden mile at the city's heart.

Oxford's status as a university town was reflected in its retailers and hostelries as well as the extraordinary concentration of scholarly buildings dating back 700 years.[12] It was a town of university and college outfitters vying for the trade of undergraduates seeking gowns and mortar boards, establishments such as Walter's on Turl Street also flaunting their wares to those requiring formal attire or destined for the tropics and in need of baggy shorts and pith helmets.[13] It was common for businesses to identify themselves with the University for reasons of prestige, practitioners of this form of one-upmanship including Shepherd & Woodward on the High Street and Robert Alden & Son in the Covered Market, 'University and family butchers and makers of the finest Oxford sausages'.[14]

Oxford at the time of the war was a major centre for bookselling, printing and publishing. In addition to the University's own press, independent bookshops and stationers flourished. Thornton's stood opposite Balliol, a few doors down from F.A. Woods, a general bookseller and stationer offering its own series of Oxford etchings. Slatter & Rose, booksellers, stationers and newsagents, maintained two shops on the High Street and branches on the Banbury and Cowley roads. Blackwell's doubled its shelf space in 1938 when 48 and 49 Broad Street were added to its existing premises at 50–51. The Dolphin Bookshop in Fyfield Road dealt exclusively in Spanish books, while Albi Rosenthal, a refugee from Hitler, specialized in Spanish and Portuguese literature and Judaica. Wili Brown, who ran the import department of the long-established family bookseller Parker's on the corner of Broad Street and Turl Street, had arrived in Oxford in 1939 after his family had been murdered in concentration camps.[15] Around the same time and with the patronage of Sir Stanley Unwin, the publisher Phaidon opened premises opposite St Hilda's after leaving Vienna in search of safety.[16]

Prominent on the High Street were types of shop that have all but disappeared. Today's KFC was a furriers, and there were establishments such as Ellen Bradford's, a ladies' hatter, costumier, and milliner purveying 'Afternoon Gowns, Evening Gowns, Coats & Costumes [and] Knitwear' in The Arcade on Cornmarket.[17] There were also department stores, queen of the Oxford scene being Elliston & Cavell (PLATE 3) at 4–12 Magdalen Street:

> One of the largest and best appointed Suites of Show-rooms in the Provinces ... Everything for Ladies' and Children's Wear. Boys' and Girls' Complete School Outfitters. Ready to Wear day and Evening Gowns. Hairdressing and Beauty Salons. Men's Wear. Lunch and Tea Rooms, Rest Rooms, Circulating Library.[18]

Elliston & Cavell's tea rooms were popular with undergraduates and a 'good place for meeting girls' according to Kingsley Amis, a wartime student at St John's.[19] Tea shops and cafés abounded, a feature of life for town and gown alike. There was Cooper & Boffin's Magdalen Street Café opposite the Martyrs' Memorial, the Snack Bar opposite the New Theatre, and the Gloucester Green Café by the bus station. Fuller's, home of the legendary walnut cake, traded at 24 Cornmarket (until recently the city centre's Burger King). The Golden Kettle was at 41 High Street, Lyon's Teashop at 4 Cornmarket, and the Ritz Café on George Street.[20] The ever-popular Cadena, part of an upmarket coffeehouse chain, had premises at 43–47 Cornmarket, from which the aroma of coffee and baked goods permeated the street. Upstairs tables were arranged around a circular well, and a palm court orchestra entertained customers at morning coffee and afternoon tea.[21] The St George Café and Restaurant – 'The George' – was on the corner of Cornmarket and George Street, frequented in John Betjeman's day by the 'aesthetes', whom he dubbed the 'Georgeoisie'.

The delights of Oxford's pubs and hotel watering holes, such as the Randolph's 'modern American bar', were officially out of bounds to students, though this didn't prevent them from going, as readers of Philip Larkin's novel *Jill*, an atmospheric evocation of wartime Oxford, might recall.[22] Larkin favoured the Lord Napier on Observatory Street, while his wartime St John's contemporary Bruce Montgomery, then writing the first of his Oxford detective novels (*The Case of the Gilded Fly*) with a J nib and silver pen holder, was a permanent fixture at the Randolph bar, a place 'for the socially superior or ambitious'.[23] John Harper-Nelson and his Trinity set spent a lot of time at the Turf Tavern, then confined to its tiny front bar from which, as he found out to his cost when apprehended by a proctor (one of two senior academics elected to oversee University discipline and other matters), there was no escape.[24] The Lamb and Flag on St Giles was a major stop-off, known as the 'Flam'; the Welsh Pony, facing onto George Street and the bus station (today's Eurobar), was popular because it served until midnight; and the Gloucester Arms, today's White Rabbit on Friar's Entry, was popular with theatre types. Amis drank mostly in pubs 'despite the best efforts of the proctors', as well as in college rooms.[25] On the senior side of the house, C.S. Lewis, J.R.R. Tolkien and other 'Inklings' ranged far and wide, favoured haunts including the Eagle and Child, the King's Arms, the White Horse and the tap room of the Mitre Hotel.[26]

Hotels occupied a large part of the city centre, especially on the main shopping drag extending from the top of the High Street, down

Cornmarket and onto Magdalen Street. Mrs C.J. Vert ran the afore-mentioned Mitre (the upper floors now a warren of Lincoln student rooms), a 'well-known Hotel of 600 years standing … situated in the centre of the finest street in Europe, close to the Colleges, and within an easy distance of the river'.[27] Round the corner on Cornmarket, the Clarendon Hotel – 'Under Royal Patronage' as it was keen to point out in its advertisements – stood on the site of today's Clarendon Centre. Bought by Woolworth's in 1939 and scheduled for demolition to make way for a new flagship shop, war stayed the wrecking ball, and instead it became a club for American military personnel. Opposite the Clarendon was the old Golden Cross coaching inn (today's Pizza Express), the 'Regency calm' of its courtyard facing onto Cornmarket.[28] The Royal Oxford Hotel had only just opened on Park End Street, and the Oxenford, an 'old, established, first-class hotel', occupied the Magdalen Street (13–17) frontage between Elliston & Cavell's department store and the Randolph.

Under construction

While a reader familiar with the city would recognize much if trans-ported back in time, easily navigating their way around its long-established thoroughfares, wartime Oxford would take their breath away, and not only because of the blackout, the sand-bagged ARP posts and the profusion of uniformed men and women on the streets. For one thing, many of today's well-known buildings had yet to be built. There was no Nuffield, St Antony's, St Catherine's, Wolfson or St Cross Building. Wellington Square and Little Clarendon Street had yet to be transformed by the University's bunker-like central offices and Somerville's unprepossessing Margaret Fry and Elizabeth Nuffield House.[29] Pembroke's North Quad was still Beef Lane, a higgledy-piggledy street of seventeenth- and eighteenth-century houses.[30] The churchyard of St Peter-le-Bailey was yet to be transformed into Bonn Square, the cities not twinning until 1947 in an attempt to restore Anglo-German relations battered by war.[31]

Much of the inbuilding that has marked Oxford's physical and architectural history was still to come, meaning more space around now-crowded features. Comprising just the original Basil Champneys range and a lodge building by the gate, Mansfield College's 'tastefully laid-out grounds' commanded 'beautiful views of some of Oxford's older colleges', as the 1938 edition of *Alden's Guide to Oxford* put it. Across a wide expanse of lawn where today's John Marsh building and porters' lodge stand, one could see Savile House, New College bell tower, and Wadham to the south-west.[32] College barges were yet to give way to the uniform row of boathouses on the Isis, and there was a cattle market on the Oxpens Road, recently removed from Gloucester Green to make way for the bus station, opened in 1935.[33] From here the red, maroon and pale-green liveried vehicles of the City of Oxford and District Motor Bus Services whisked commuters around the city and to outlying towns and villages, and took tourists and ramblers on day trips.[34]

Further confounding the modern-day visitor teleported back in time, the city contained buildings and features that no longer exist.[35] A second railway station operated on Rewley Road on the site of today's Said Business School, from which 'Varsity Line' trains connected Oxford and Cambridge by way of Bletchley.[36] Worcester Street car park was a canal basin and wharf, stacked with coal and site of a fine Georgian warehouse. Part of the vanished industrial Thames, Basson's Baltic Wharf received boatloads of timber from the London docks, while narrow boats carried coal to the gasworks on the opposite bank.[37] A purpose-built Masonic lodge functioned behind the shop fronts opposite the Examination Schools on High Street, and the Indian Institute on the corner of Holywell and Broad Street still fulfilled its original purpose, training men to administer the Raj and displaying eastern artefacts in a galleried museum (shut for the duration in 1939). The Jam Factory on today's St Frideswide's Square really was a jam (and marmalade!) factory, purpose-built for Frank Cooper and making sugarless preserves, horseradish cream, mint jelly and the world-famous Oxford marmalade, soon to cease production because of the wartime dearth of oranges.[38] Though the city's big-game museum had shut in 1923, until as late as 1936 Oxford boasted a zoo at Kidlington, served by special buses from the city centre.[39]

On the Plain, the main portal to the city for generations of travellers arriving by road from London, stood a memorial to the Boer War dead of the Oxfordshire and Buckinghamshire Light Infantry (OBLI), a rifle-bearing soldier looking west to the Victoria Fountain and Magdalen Bridge from a patch of old churchyard.[40] The sprawling residential district of St Ebbe's still stood, with shops selling oil lamps, wicks and agricultural implements. Bounded by Queen Street, St Aldate's, the castle and the Thames, its narrow streets of terraced houses promoted a sense of community, served by corner shops, pubs and small businesses. Wandering here, the main protagonist in Larkin's *Jill* encounters an 'old, pre-industrial part of the town, where canal transport offices were, coal merchants and corn and hay dealers'.[41] Designated a 'clearance area' just before the war, in its aftermath it would be lost with the coming of the concrete, its communities scattered to distant housing estates, their homes replaced by the Westgate Centre and drab developments around Speedwell Street and the Oxpens Road.[42]

Abutting St Ebbe's was St Thomas's, another inner-city residential district soon to be bulldozed. Describing it in the late 1940s, Dorothy Erskine Muir wrote that visitors from bigger cities would 'be fascinated by the occasional passage of a cart laden with bales of hay, the sight of a corn chandler's shop, or an old-fashioned saddlers'.

> You will notice the country-people who come in to shop on market days and you can find a corner of Oxford which is a centre of rural life still. Here you find cows, pigs, poultry, all being bargained for, just as in any country place. You will find stalls with crockery, clothes, dress material, with loud-voiced men offering bargains. And you will find, round the market area, little old streets full of picturesqueness.[43]

Awareness of and sensitivity to this still-present 'picturesqueness' was understandable, given how rapidly Oxford was changing. 'Until almost within living memory', wrote Edmund Greening Lamborn, headmaster of East Oxford Council Boys' School, in 1932, 'Oxford remained in appearance a medieval city'.[44] For sure, its built environment had changed markedly in the nineteenth century, Victorian landmarks such as the University Museum and the Oxford Union joined by brand new colleges (Keble, Lady Margaret Hall, Manchester, Mansfield, St Hilda's, Somerville etc.). Also in this period, older colleges had built extensive new ranges (Christ Church's meadow building and New College's

Holywell range, for example), and there had been large-scale suburban construction in North Oxford. But now things were changing at a faster rate than ever before, the interwar years witnessing a remarkable burst of city-centre development. In addition, there now came unprecedented outward expansion and encroachment on the surrounding countryside, as modern industry arrived in the shape of car manufacturing, Oxford accounting for a quarter of Britain's output by 1935.[45]

As a result, many of today's landmark buildings were new or under construction in the decade preceding the war. These included Edwin Lutyens's Campion Hall, opened by the Duke of Alba in 1936, and Sir Herbert Baker's Rhodes House (1928). Sir Giles Gilbert Scott had recently completed Magdalen's Longwall Quadrangle and converted Magdalen College School hall into a library (1928–31). In 1933–34 Somerville had extended its precincts, acquiring and promptly demolishing houses on Woodstock Road and erecting the frontage we see today as it developed the new East Quadrangle.[46] This was opened by the University's chancellor, Lord Halifax, in 1934, a new chapel dedicated the following year. In 1937 the first instalment of what would become St Anne's College, containing the library and lecture rooms, was opened at 56 Woodstock Road, and the following year Lord Nuffield's liberal generosity saw a new block of fifteen sets of rooms open at the east end of Worcester's garden.[47] Balliol had recently purchased Holywell Manor, until 1929 the Oxford Female Penitentiary, completing a new quadrangle for student accommodation just before the outbreak of war.[48] Christ Church had finished its First World War Memorial Gardens at the start of the decade, replacing a stable yard and significantly changing the area's spatial dynamics by opening a new public entrance to Christ Church Meadow. T.G. Jackson's North Quad at Hertford College was completed in 1931, and Gilbert Scott's modernist Deneke Building and college hall, and Byzantine-Romanesque-style chapel, were added to Lady Margaret Hall during this particularly busy decade of construction.

Other 1930s' additions to central Oxford's university and college portfolio included Merton's Rose Lane buildings opposite the Botanic Garden, the library of St Hugh's and the St Catherine's Society building by Hubert Worthington on St Aldate's (now home to the Faculty of Music). Lincoln House, on the corner of Turl Street and Market Street, arose on the site of Lincoln College's stables in 1939. For the Ashmolean Museum, the 1930s saw considerable expansion with the construction of the West Lecture Room, the Haverfield Stack, the Sayce Room and the Weldon Gallery, and major extensions in the form of the four-storey Griffiths Institute and the Drapers' Wing.[49] A front elevation extension (1939–40) was planned as an eleven-bay affair, which would have knocked down the Georgian townhouses on Beaumont Street along to its junction with St John Street. They were saved by the outbreak of war, and only four bays were constructed.[50]

The interwar city-centre construction boom was most visible in what had been formally designated the 'Science Area' in 1934. As the study of science grew in the early decades of the century, several substantial facilities – such as outhouses and sheds – had been constructed haphazardly along South Parks Road, gradually encroaching on the University Parks, alongside purpose-built buildings such as the Electrical Lab (1910), the engineering building (1914) and the Dunn School of Pathology (1927).[51] Now 15 acres of the Parks together with the Keble Road triangle were earmarked for further development: the triangle's base formed by Keble Road, its tapering sides by Banbury and Parks roads.

New extensions and buildings blossomed. The original Science Library was extended to form the Radcliffe Science Library on the corner of Parks and South Parks roads, opened by the Princess Royal in 1934. The Dyson Perrins Chemistry Laboratory (1922) was extended for medical students in 1934 (and again in 1940–41). The Department of Engineering building at the Keble triangle's northern apex was extended in 1927 and 1931. The Biochemistry Laboratory went up between 1924 and 1927 and was extended in 1936–37, and a new Clarendon Laboratory (known now as the Lindemann Building) was opened in 1939, the old site taken over by the Department of Geology and Minerology.[52]

Other buildings were in the process of construction when war began, cranes and scaffolding integral aspects of the cityscape. New College library, a memorial to the college's First World War dead between the Bell Tower and Holywell, neared its belated completion.[53] Regent's Park College was a work in progress on Pusey Street. By far the largest build was the New Bodleian, which was to play an important role in the University's war effort. The decision to build, taken in 1931, had been driven by the pressing need for space as the library's collections grew at a rate of 22,000 standard-sized volumes a year.[54] Though an underground book repository had been excavated beneath Radcliffe Square before the First World War, more books and more readers created the need for more space. The planned new building would be able to accommodate 5 million volumes and provide workspace for library departments as well as reading rooms.[55]

Houses on Broad Street and Parks Road were demolished to make way for a capacious steel-framed structure. Its square core featured eleven storeys of book stacks, three below ground covering the whole of the 1 acre site, the top two set back so as to be scarcely visible from the street. The six levels between were encased by three storeys of outer rooms separated from the stacks by corridors. A tunnel running beneath Broad Street, with a pedestrian walkway and a conveyor belt, connected old Bodleian with new. Queen Mary had laid the foundation stone in June 1937, though the royal opening planned for June 1940 was postponed because of the war.

While all these buildings were recent arrivals or works in progress when war came, others were delayed by its impact on the construction industry. Worthington's smart 10 Merton Street, known to later generations as the Faculty of Philosophy, was designed before the conflict, though not completed until the 1950s.[56] Nuffield College, founded in 1937, had yet to transform the New Road canal basin, work severely delayed by war and the priority given to housebuilding thereafter, the foundation stone unlaid until 1949. Delayed too was Magdalen's new boathouse, work commenced in October 1939 not completed until 1946.[57] The same was true of Worcester's boat house.[58] Construction of the new Imperial Forestry Institute, allocated a prime site in South Parks Road in 1934, was similarly put off until after the war, eventually opened by Princess Margaret in 1951.[59]

City buildings, and University reaction to development

Like the University, the city experienced a flush of development in the interwar years. There was the usual piecemeal construction and renovation; a new block of flats here (Belsyre Court on the corner of

Observatory Street and Woodstock Road, 1936); a rebuild there (the Nags Head pub on Hythe Bridge Street beside the canal, 1938); and a new facade somewhere else (the Scala cinema on Walton Street, 1939).[60] The imposing late-Victorian Town Hall had recently been extended north towards Carfax to front onto the High Street, and further down St Aldate's a new police headquarters opened in 1938. Morris Garages showrooms and garages opened in an impressive new building on St Aldate's in 1932 (today's Crown Court). Between 1931 and 1936 new wards, a paying patients' block, a nurses' home, a dispensary, a maternity home, and dark rooms were added to the Radcliffe Infirmary. The Wingfield orthopaedic hospital was rebuilt, and a new isolation hospital opened at the Slade (1939).

The Oxford Playhouse and the New Theatre had just gone up, Edward Maufe's 1938 effort on Beaumont Street wearing its interwar facade more lightly than the Milburn Brothers' bluff erection on George Street (1933). The New Theatre, a plush 1,800-seat art deco auditorium, was one of several markers of Oxford's transformation 'from small market town dependent on the university to prosperous industrial city'.[61] Also on George Street, the Ritz Cinema opened its doors in 1936 following the demolition of the Labour Exchange (the Regal opening in Cowley the following year).[62]

Yet change in the centre was nothing compared to the city's breathtaking outward growth, industrialization transforming the university town as it enveloped satellite villages and sprouted housing estates and factory works.[63] At the time of the First World War, Oxford had been 'a pre-industrial town'. In the 1920s, 'large-scale industry began from scratch', and what was essentially an entirely new town grew up alongside old Oxford.[64] The city's population exploded, driven by the expansion of industry brought by the Cowley motor works owned by William Morris (raised to the peerage as Baron Nuffield in 1934, made a viscount in 1938) and Pressed Steel, which made car bodies. The motor industry attracted immigrants from around the country, particularly South Wales.[65] Between 1921 and 1931 Oxford's population grew by 20 per cent, partly because the city's boundary was extended in 1929 to take in the civil parishes of Headington, Marston, Iffley, Water Eaton, Cutteslowe and Wolvercote. Over the same period the population of the Cowley and Iffley district grew by 122 per cent, Headington by 79 per cent.[66] Population growth marched in time with factory expansion; from 40 acres in 1926, by the 1930s the Cowley works covered 80, and the millionth Morris rolled off the production line in 1939.

The speed as much as the scale of this change needs emphasis. By the eve of the Second World War, the population living east of the Cherwell had outstripped that of the old city to the west.[67] 'New town' was getting bigger than 'old town', and selling cars, rather than the activities of the University, had become the chief influence on Oxford's economic life, a reality that dons struggled to adjust to.[68] Forming an unlikely trio, Oxford, Coventry and Luton were now the most prosperous towns in the land. 'Oxford – The Place Where Morris Cars Are Made' declared a sign at the railway station. To which, wrote Christ Church don A.L. Rowse, the University drily responded by describing itself as 'the Latin quarter of Morris Cowley'.[69]

Unsurprisingly, rapid interwar development in the city centre and the suburbs raised hackles. In the case of the former, it was chiefly the style of the new buildings that was faulted. 'The modern additions to Oxford's architectural riches', wrote Christopher Hobhouse in 1939, 'constitute a tale that is quickly told, and the quicker the better' (Hobhouse died in action the following year).[70] In the *Architectural Review*, J.M. Richards said that the total effect of the new science area was 'more reminiscent of a modern trading estate than an ancient centre of learning'.[71] A 'particularly unfortunate characteristic of nearly all Oxford architecture of this period', wrote Howard Colvin waspishly,

> was the use, even for the most formal buildings, of rubble walling, apparently under the mistaken impression that Oxford colleges had some affinity with Cotswold barns and farm-houses, whereas in fact they had in the past invariably been built of dressed ashlar.[72]

In designing Rhodes House, Baker had awkwardly married 'a miniature pantheon to a Cotswold manor-house', and Gilbert Scott 'inexplicably followed suit in his New Bodleian Library (1937–40), a major public building in the heart of the city facing Hawksmoor's Clarendon Building and Wren's Sheldonian Theatre (shut just before the war for repairs because of the ravages of the deathwatch beetle).[73] This, according to Colvin, lent the New Bodleian 'the appearance of 'a dinner jacket made of Harris Tweed'.[74] Rowse wasn't a fan either, writing that the dominant feature of twentieth-century Oxford was the expansion of science, its departments 'eating up the Parks' in the process.[75] He deplored the infilling of the city: 'The tasteless Worthington did a lot to deface Oxford in the ruinous thirties – one can recognize his handiwork anywhere; Giles Scott and Herbert Baker did no better.'[76]

As for reactions to the city's suburban and industrial growth, it was the sense of encroachment on ancient university precincts that jarred. Maurice Bowra, warden of Wadham at the time of the war, described how the city's character had changed.

> It had for centuries been a mixture of university town and market town, and though since about 1860 it had been growing, not always with elegance, it was still more or less homogenous. But now it was transformed through the activities of William Morris … [and] the results were lamentable.[77]

The large new manufacturing town at Cowley had few amenities, Bowra continued, so 'it became a parasite of Oxford, which was ill-equipped to sustain it and lost much of its spacious tranquillity in catering for a large daily invasion.'[78]

Opponents and jeremiads spliced concerns about industrialization and suburbanization with alarm at elements of modernity and change to 'the way things were'. Often, there was a liberal dash of snobbery too. In his 1938 compendium *An Oxford University Chest*, John Betjeman described the city as a tripartite entity, its three components jostling one another. There was 'University', obvious enough, and 'Christminster', the old market town of *Jude the Obscure* – the St Ebbe's and St Thomas's-type areas of narrow streets, shops and pubs. And now there was 'Motopolis', the new industrial zone centred on the Cowley works. East Oxford, Betjeman lamented, was now 'as big and important a town as this once medieval city', advancing 'right up to Magdalen Bridge, bulked there by the meadows of the Cherwell'.[79] The internal combustion engine, he said, foreshadowing the war, had taken over the roads and 'booms overhead with its cargo of bombs. That its most successful manifestation in England should be at Oxford, of all places, passes belief.'[80]

The college buildings, wrote Betjeman, were now endangered by motor traffic:

> main streets are as congested as the Strand; chain-stores have taken the place of small shop-keepers; small gas-lamps have given place to the great lamp-standards; buses have supplanted horse trams ... the farmers and labourers have disappeared; views are interrupted by motor-cars; open space occupied by car-parks; the commercial consistency of shop-front and signs of the last century has been ousted by the competitive garishness in imitation marble, electric lights and lettering of big London-controlled enterprises. Oxford is no longer a provincial town. It is a replica of London.[81]

Writing in 1942, Arthur Mee said that the city had 'unhappily allowed itself to be robbed of much of its beauty in recent years. In that it has suffered with all England, though in such a city the loss is grievous beyond words.'[82] Too little attention had been paid to town planning, wrote Oxford historian Ruth Fasnacht shortly after the war, and 'the face of Oxford was changed, almost out of recognition'. There was the spread of red brick, but also, 'in the heart of the ancient City, while University and College buildings remained sacrosanct, scarcely another building was not "modernized" or demolished to make way for something considered more likely to appeal to the majority of the new working-class citizens.'[83] This was a common way of viewing things, among those who wrote about them at least. Dorothy Erskine Muir, also writing just after the war, sounded the familiar rhapsody-cum-threnody, contrasting Oxford's beauty and venerability with the ugly and the new, honey-coloured stone and tranquil quads juxtaposed with road traffic and the gas works.[84]

Oxford on the eve of war, then, was subject to anxieties about changes which were beginning to disturb the hitherto sequestered life of both dons and students, the traffic congesting Carfax, the new 'super cinema' at Gloucester Green, and Woolworths and Marks & Spencer chain stores symptoms of deeper social and economic transformation.[85] This sense of things changing would soon be compounded by war. But before we consider its approach as the international situation darkened in the 1930s, it is to the character of the University of Oxford that we now turn.

TWO

OF UNIVERSITY AND COLLEGES

In the eyes of many people, Oxford was associated with aristocracy and the Establishment, and not viewed as a destination for 'ordinary' people. Nevertheless, it held a place in the affections of many who never went near the place, perhaps because of an interest in the Boat Race or because of the city's reputation as an architectural treasure trove. It was generally well regarded, and had become part of a warped national mindscape in which University College Oxford could be viewed as 'metropolitan' while University College London could be regarded as 'provincial'.[1]

The city was widely regarded as a national asset, the words of poets and famous visitors routinely employed to promulgate this view. The 1938–39 edition of *Oxford and District* in Ward Lock's 'Red Guide' series opened with Thomas Palmer's late-sixteenth-century ode to the 'Most famous Universitie / And seate of high renowne'. Below these lines, the introduction opened with Keats: 'This Oxford, I have no doubt, is the finest city in the world – it is full of old Gothic buildings – spires – towers – quadrangles – cloisters – groves, etc., and is surrounded by more clear streams than I ever saw together.'[2] Before even beginning their walking tours or reading the potted histories of the college and University buildings they might visit, readers were left in no doubt as to the city's august status.

Arthur Mee, leaving school aged 14 and one of ten children fathered by a railway fireman, was an Oxford outsider but still an Oxford enthusiast. Penning the *Oxfordshire* volume of the famous 'King's

England' series of county guides in 1942, he wrote of the 'Citadel of our English Heritage ... the lovely city which so many of us believe to be the most beautiful, the most impressive, and the most dignified of all our treasure-towns'.[3] Describing Oxford's 'remarkable variety of institutions famous through the world', he continued:

> not only the colleges, with riches untold, beautiful chapels, great quadrangles, libraries, sculptures, and natural glories in lawns and walks and avenues almost beyond compare, but a host of places of interest to travellers from every land, for where are museums like the Ashmolean, libraries like the Bodleian, schools, observatories, theatres, laboratories, halls, such as are everywhere in this city of learning with hardly a peer in the world?[4]

Ordinary people also knew about Oxford – more so than Cambridge – because of the output of its university press. In the 1930s Oxford University Press (OUP) was the world's largest in terms of size, range of publications and worldwide scope, publishing 200 titles a year.[5] Its books found their way into countless homes as well as the churches and schools through which millions of people passed. It produced school textbooks, English-language primers, dictionaries, atlases, prayer books, Bibles, sheet music, even books of carols, the University's name and coat of arms emblazoned on dust jacket and spines. It was also a major publisher of fiction, the classics and children's literature, including the popular *Biggles* series.

Oxford was afforded additional exposure through its association with various everyday things. The Morris Oxford family saloon had entered production in 1913 and was still rolling off the production line in the 1930s; wide-legged trousers known as 'Oxford bags' were a familiar item of clothing; and the stationery company Helix's 'Oxford Mathematical Instruments' set for students had first appeared in their tins, showing a picture of Balliol's chapel and old library, in 1935. There was even an 'Oxford accent'.[6]

In contrast to this national awareness of Oxford, few people actually went there to study. Only a fraction of the population attended university at the time of the Second World War: when it began, there were only 50,000 students in Britain's twenty universities.[7] Roughly a quarter of them studied in London, a quarter at Oxbridge, a quarter in Scotland, and a quarter at the redbricks.[8] There had been teaching in Oxford since the eleventh century, the earliest colleges founded in the thirteenth. The colleges were the focal points of students' and dons' lives, 'self-contained republics enjoying the independence offered by their own endowments and eccentricities', according to one historian.[9] There were around thirty autonomous colleges and permanent private halls, accommodated by a university which provided libraries, laboratories, academic departments, courses, examinations, and the degrees with which those who passed them graduated.[10] All of the colleges were single sex — not just in terms of their students and their dons, but also the scouts, porters, and waiting and kitchen staff. There were some students at the University who were not members of colleges, women coming under the aegis of the Society of Home-Students (St Anne's Society from 1942, St Anne's College from 1952), men attached to the St Catherine's Society (from which St Catherine's College traces its origin).[11]

Within college walls

The year war broke out Oxford boasted 5,023 students, 90 per cent of them undergraduates (in 2021 there were 24,000, over half of them postgraduates).[12] The *smallness* of the University and its tight-knit college communities would strike a modern-day visitor, even one accustomed to quads and gowns. A college might have only a hundred or so students and a dozen fellows; in 1936 St Peter's had a master, three resident tutors and ninety students.[13] In 1938 Wadham had 107 undergraduates and a dozen on other courses, and eight teaching fellows.[14] Manchester, a theological establishment, had a mere four students at the outbreak of war and was accommodating a few academic refugees from Europe. In 1939 Queen's had twenty-eight fellows and a provost and 160 students in residence.[15] Oriel in 1939 had seventeen fellows.[16] The average governing body (a college's central authority) numbered fourteen.[17] Even the 'big' colleges were small by today's standards: Balliol had 265 students in the 1930s, while New College had 233 resident students and twenty-seven fellows, ten of whom did not teach undergraduates.[18] This smallness, of undergraduate year groups and SCRs with very slow membership turnover, bred a closeness, a claustrophobia even, compounded by the intimacy of college life and its single-sexness. The student body was British, particularly English, and Americans and continental Europeans were overwhelmingly absent from the SCR.[19]

Separation between members of the University and those beyond was epitomized by college architecture. 'Oxford does not set out to please', wrote Margaret Roberts (later Thatcher), who arrived at Somerville in 1943: 'Freshmen arrive there for the Michaelmas term in the misty gloom of October. Monumental buildings impress initially by their size rather than their exquisite architecture. Everything is cold and strangely forbidding. Or so it seemed to me.'[20] Typically, the colleges, each an autonomous institution on a walled and enclosed site, were entered via the porters' lodge only, unless a college had a secondary entrance, to which only fellows had keys.[21] Lodges were occupied by sometimes formidable, uniformed, and often ex-military men. A.S. Faiz, a Cypriot, arrived at Worcester College in Michaelmas 1943 to be met at the lodge by the daunting figure of Bryant, a 'bulky, six-foot-two, bearded' ex-Coldstream Guards regimental sergeant major.[22] Other staff, for example those inhabiting bursars' offices, were often ex-military too, and domestic servants (the word commonly used at the time) as well as fellows would commonly have served in the forces during the First World War.

Smallness and separateness were augmented by the very limited association that students and even dons had with people who were not associated with the University and the colleges. Surveying dons in the early 1950s, Oxford research fellow Peter Collison asked about relations with the town. Respondents registered little interest in it: 'So far as they were concerned the town was as remote as Timbuktu.'[23] Accentuating separatism and difference, until 1950 the University elected its own Members of Parliament, independent of the general franchise, the electorate formed of Oxford graduates who paid to be on a register. This distance did not apply to all University figures, of course, and senior academics formed a fifth of the membership of Oxford City Council, and some, such as Lancelot Phelps, provost of Oriel until 1930, played a major role in local government.

The sense of separation and difference extended, for many of Oxford's predominantly male personnel (which included a large number of bachelor dons), to women, of their own 'class' and of those considered to be of lower social status. Douglas Ross, a student at Pembroke during the war, writes that there was very little contact with women, 'and town girls were not so much infra dig as not thought of at all'.[24] At the time of the war,

> Oxford male undergraduates, in or out of residence, were bound by a set of rules which, in general outline, had been laid down many centuries before. Out on the street, they were judged to be different from other adolescents. As scholars and gentlemen, they had to be more carefully policed in order that they did not demean themselves or dishonour their parents.[25]

The only women Hugh Trevor-Roper mixed with were landladies, the mothers of friends, and the daughters of older dons.[26] 'Women were lacking from our lives', wrote Nigel Nicolson (Balliol 1935–38): 'Of course we knew that they were around, but somewhere in the outer suburbs, convents loosely linked to our great monastery, but unvisited, and from which no visitors came.'[27] Bowra summed up the situation bluntly; women 'were regarded with grave suspicion and allowed into colleges on rather the same terms as dogs and perambulators'.[28]

John Mortimer contends that at the time of the war the fashion was to be 'queer', and he strove to ensure that his friends did not learn of his 'sporadic adventures with WAAFs and girls from St Hilda's, [and] my grandly-titled "engagement" to a student of book illustration at the Slade', the London school of art evacuated to Oxford on the outbreak of war.[29] Harper-Nelson recalled that though 'our sexual lives were almost entirely empirical and mostly non-existent', hope still burned eternal, and 'most of us went to a little herbalist's shop in New Inn Hall street and bought a packet of French letters'.[30]

For female students, though they might be perfectly at home in their own colleges, it was easy to feel that while the University accepted women, it was not a *mixed* institution. Even though women had been allowed to graduate with University degrees from 1920, in 1927 Congregation (the University's 'parliament' of senior members) had voted to retain a limit on the number of female students, set at 840, and Oxford remained an overwhelmingly masculine environment.[31] Nina Bawden, at Somerville during the war, recalls that while one of her tutors flirted with her, another tried to persuade her that 'darning his socks was a more suitable occupation for a young girl than learning statistics'.[32]

'Characters', in the close confines of Oxford and its collegiate mini-states, were often larger than life. Some were recalled with affection, others as tyrants. A figure such as Bowra, dean and then warden of Wadham in our period, could set the tone of a college, a landmark on the University scene, a national figure even. William Stallybrass was vice principal at Brasenose from 1914 until 1936 and principal thereafter.

> His rooms in Old Quad, IV, 4, became the engine room of Brasenose, fuelled by alcohol and fired by a powerful sense of collegiate pride. Generations of undergraduates came somehow to accept that their stern mentor of the morning was actually their drinking partner of the night before.[33]

Heads of houses exercised a great deal of control over the appointment of fellows and the admission of undergraduates. Across the board, Oxford dictated its own terms, and was something of a closed shop.

It was still common for dons to view themselves not as researchers but as teachers, and to argue that the value of Oxford was in providing a generalist education equipping people for life and leadership, rather than turning out academic specialists. The fact that Penry Williams could write that 'even before the Second World War some dons in the humanities were engaged in writing and research' says it all.[34] Meeting his moral tutor Lord David Cecil, New College student Roger du Boulay was asked what he was there for. 'To work for a degree, I suppose', was his reply. 'Work!', shouted Cecil. '*Work*? If all you want to do is work, you might just as well go to one of those dreadful places like Manchester or London! No – you're here to get educated. Go and enjoy yourself.'[35] Some might even question whether it was the dons' job to educate, a Balliol adage asserting that students would educate each other.[36]

Academic life, Jose Harris writes, was dominated by the pre-eminence of the humanities, the power of the colleges, undergraduates as opposed to postgraduates, and a special relationship with the nation's elites.[37]

The major faculties were Theology, Law, Medicine, Literae Humaniores ('Lit. Hum.'), Modern History, English Language and Literature, Medieval and Modern European Languages and Literature, Oriental Languages and Literature, and Physical Sciences, including Mathematics, Biological Sciences and Social Studies.[38] By the late 1930s some men had moved away from Lit. Hum., History and Theology towards English, Modern Languages, and the recently-introduced Politics, Philosophy and Economics (PPE) degree ('Modern Greats'), women moving away from English and Modern Languages towards PPE too. But change was slow. At New College most undergraduates read Lit. Hum., Law or History until after the war, and the college had no English fellow until 1939 and no modern linguist until after 1945.[39] Oxford's slow engagement with new fields of scholarly endeavour was signalled by the creation in 1930 of the School of Geography, and the elevation of agriculture and forestry to honour school status in 1937 and 1945 respectively.[40]

Though defined by its association with the humanities, Oxford was also a university of science. In 1938, 14.6 per cent of honours degrees were awarded in science subjects, science's improving fortunes indicated by the expansion of the Science Area.[41] It had the country's biggest Chemistry department and a noted Physics department. Its reputation for science was on the rise, due in no small part to the ongoing immigration of refugees from the scourge of fascism. In the non-humanities subjects, Maths was second to Chemistry (the Mathematical Institute, without premises of its own, occupying rooms in the Radcliffe Science Library).

The University had a very public-school character, even though non-public-school students formed a significant minority: 62 per cent of Oxford's male undergraduates came from independent (i.e. public) schools, 13 per cent from direct-grant (i.e. grammar) schools, and 19 per cent from maintained (i.e. state) schools.[42] Public-school-style slang was prevalent, and address by surname the norm (the prefix 'Miss' in the women's colleges). Bullying – of non-games-playing and unassertive students, for example – was not uncommon.[43] Toffs and toffs manqué were much in evidence. Undergraduate clothes reflected those of the well-to-do and, according to Harper-Nelson, 'were almost a uniform': grey flannel trousers, shirt and tie, pullover, tweed sports jacket, brown or black lace-up shoes.[44] In winter, 6-foot-long college scarves were popular, perhaps with an overcoat draped across the shoulders. For women, afternoon dresses and gowns featured heavily, and 'slacks', while sometimes worn, were yet to find general acceptance. There were then the extraneous sartorial badges of status and identity – evening wear (white tie for some), blazers, cricket whites, and a variety of other types of sportswear.

Many Oxonians exhibited a sense of entitlement as privileged individuals, and a proprietorial attitude towards the city; University people cut about as if they owned the place, a gilded playground for undergraduates and dons in which 'townspeople' were bystanders or servants.[45] Books written at the time – fact or fiction – positively drip with this reality and this conceit, which was underpinned by the very real class distinctions prevalent in British society at the time.[46] Among the more well-to-do undergraduates, Hobhouse wrote in 1939,

> the drinking is still heavy, the debts still mount, and the snobbery of the minor gentry grows rank ... Anybody who visits Oxford on a Saturday night will find himself in a bedlam of ill manners and conceit. Drunken louts throw food about the restaurants and make shindies in the cinemas.[47]

The insularity of the college was increased, not lessened, by the position of its senior members, for whom the college was the focus of a career that could last a lifetime. Brian Harrison likens SCRs to officers' messes, clubs within a club.[48] Of 198 male tutorial fellows in 1937, a fifth had been undergraduates at their current college, and five-sixths had taken their degrees at Oxford. Only rarely did outside events impinge on governing "body discussions, and only then if they were *big* events, such as world wars, coronations or the General Strike.[49] It was a cloistered environment in which, as Tom Harrisson wrote in 1933, '[a]ll men and women become soothed and seduced by the people and buildings and light ... [and] are gradually absorbed into the quietness of centuries'.[50]

For students and dons, Oxford first of all meant college, not university. Though the creation in 1919 of the University Grants Committee (UGC) as a channel for government support for higher education had rung some changes, it was still the case that most colleges had substantial endowments compared to the University, which lacked central finance.[51]

More than this, the University had little corporate identity. Very few University teachers were not college fellows, and most lectures occurred in the college of the tutor delivering them. The college was the centre of a student's life for three or four years and organized most teaching. As Harper-Nelson put it, 'your tutor was the centre of your academic life' and life 'revolved to a great extent round the weekly tutorial.'[52] His tutor happened to be at a different college, meaning that the dons of Trinity were vague and distant figures, most commonly encountered processing into hall as the students stood, waiting for them to mount the dais and take their places at high table before Latin grace called the assembled to their plates.

It wasn't just the dons who upheld college independence and identity; as late as 1939 college junior common rooms (JCRs) had rejected the creation of a central student representative council. 'I had little feeling of University', said K.C. Bowen, who went up in 1937. 'I was at Balliol, not Oxford – there were colleges, all different, with different ways of life and different excellences.'[53] Such was the pervasiveness of the college that in all arts disciplines, the University's faculties – and the University itself –

> were remote and shadowy entities, encountered by many students only on the final day of reckoning in the Examination Schools. Material resources and the day-to-day direction of studies were concentrated in the hands not of professors and departments but of colleges and college fellows.[54]

Upon becoming vice chancellor in 1947, Stallybrass proclaimed that he was an 'unrepentant believer in the college system … Traditions and memories are bound up within the College walls, not in the Laboratories, the Bodleian or the Examination Schools.'[55]

The college was both guardian and incubator of a sense of belonging intended to last a lifetime. It acted *in loco parentis*; dons entertained and offered pastoral care to their students, and took an interest in their post-university careers, helping them if they could. The role of dons in placing students in jobs, writes the historian of the University Careers Service, 'was synonymous with the management of patronage; a don had certain contacts and knew of certain jobs (usually scholastic), and he determined that certain men would be placed in those jobs'.[56] College

OF UNIVERSITY AND COLLEGES   29

tutors' links with business grew to match the more traditional ones such as government service, education and the church. This was an extension not only of patronage, but of the pastoral role performed by colleges and their fellows. The University Appointments Committee (today's Careers Service) was the first agency established by a British university to help graduates find employment, its remit not to offer advice and help students develop employment skills – as a careers service would today – but to actually *place* them in jobs. The Committee's role was effectively that of an employment agency, maintaining a web of contacts and routinely approached by employers looking for recruits; in many cases, jobs came looking for Oxford graduates as opposed to the other way around.[57]

Rules, for the breaking of

Colleges, backed by University regulations and enforcement officers such as proctors, bulldogs (members of the University's private police force) and college deans, policed students' behaviour and morals, with vigour or indifference depending on the personalities and circumstances involved. There were plenty of rules and regulations, from those governing examinations to the rules of the road: undergraduate motorists had to register with the University authorities and display a green light on the front of their vehicles (a practice not discontinued until 1967). This allowed proctors to detect student vehicles, when, for example, patrolling the pubs for illicit drinkers.[58] Pubs were out of bounds, colleges providing drink for students. The city brewer Morrells had started to target the student and college market in the 1930s. Jimmy Morrell, Oxford graduate and former faculty member, responded to an approach in 1938 to supply the University boat crew with free beer during their month-long training ahead of that year's Boat Race. By that time, Morrells was producing Buttery Ale, the strong College Ale (as supplied to the rowers) and Proctor Ale, all much more expensive than ordinary beer and aimed at the University market.[59] The last college brewhouse, at Queen's, closed in 1939, but colleges supplied alcoholic drinks and often procured and labelled their own brews, such as Trinity's 'College Old' ale. JCRs maintained cellars which, even if not on as grand a scale as those of the SCRs, could be impressive.[60]

Drinking in college was very much the 'official policy', though drinking out was common and getting 'progged' by proctors and bulldogs prowling the pubs was a hazard that had to be accepted. In *Oxford: As It Was and As It Is To-day*, published in September 1939 and offering a rich overview of university life at the time, Hobhouse wrote that

> In theory, no undergraduate is allowed upon licensed premises; but it is possible to spend three years in residence, and fully a tithe of that time on licensed premises, without being made aware of the existence of this rule.[61]

While it might have been possible for him, memoirs testify that it wasn't possible for everyone, and run-ins with University authorities were common. As Betjeman put it, though proctors had no power within college walls, 'they find plenty to occupy them in the streets. You may see one or other of the proctors walking about the Oxford streets of an evening during term-time attended by one or more University police, who are men chosen for their athletic prowess', the former in white tie and academic dress, the latter in bowler hats.[62]

Curfews were strict and if broken risked a set-to with the proctors and bulldogs and the need to break back into college, which would be locked down at night, all students supposed to be inside. A 1936 cartoon in the student newspaper *Isis* showed Father Christmas apprehended as he scales a college wall. 'Your name and college, please', a proctor asks of the startled figure, frozen in a beam of lamplight.[63] Some enterprising students carried cloth caps, hoping to pass as local people if in the proximity of a proctor.[64] While not being caught out of college was one consideration, not being caught *not in* was another, as one didn't want to incur decanal censure for breach of curfew. A common ruse was for an overnight absentee to prevail upon a friend to ruffle their bed clothes and urinate in the chamber pot, making it look as if the individual had risen early when the scout (a college employee responsible for cleaning, tidying and generally looking after students and their rooms), who in theory at least should report missing students, called with the morning jug of hot water.[65]

Some colleges were particularly tough to break back into, others relatively easy. Magdalen was simple because spikes intended to keep people out actually helped them climb in. Trinity involved climbing in via the St John's bike sheds in Parks Road. Queen's was reputed to be the most impregnable.[66] Worcester wasn't too difficult, but the route was exposed and the likelihood of detection high. Oliver Philpot, one of the escapees from the famous 'wooden horse' breakout from Stalag Luft III prisoner of war camp at Sagan in Lower Silesia, found that the last stage of his 'home run' – boarding a neutral Swedish ship – 'was extraordinarily similar to climbing after midnight round the railings which jut out into the lake of Worcester College'.[67]

Some proctors and 'bullers' pursued this game of cat and mouse with vindictive pleasure, but perhaps the norm by this time was to play along and turn a Nelsonian blind eye towards minor infringements (as happened to Harper-Nelson, who was caught in a pub by his own tutor). Nevertheless, it was a hazard to be avoided if possible. Larkin was caught trying to escape a pub through the side door, while his more enterprising drinking companion that evening, Montgomery, hid in the kitchen and waited for the coast to clear.[68] It was sometimes possible to avoid the proctors by crawling pubs a step behind them.

When it came to clambering back into college, while there were some minatory dons, others weren't overly enthusiastic about enforcing the rules. Australian Kenneth Wheare, dean at University College, took a relaxed attitude. The spiked iron fence by his house on Kybald Street was a popular access point after closing time. 'Therefore, to prevent damage to his garden, he discreetly opened a small gate nearby to let people in', and would 'turn on his bedroom light if he heard the muttered curses of a student who'd caught his clothing on the spikes, allowing him to extricate himself.[69] In the late 1940s Christ Church don J.I.M. Stewart was 'still collecting an irregular sort of gate-money as a consequence of the survival of this antique practice'. One of his windows gave on to a 'garden of easy access', so he would leave a window open, 'and through it would jack-knife young men whose small change tumbled from their pockets in the process'.[70] 'Gate fines' were still in place at colleges like St Edmund Hall during the war.[71]

Attendance at Sunday chapel was expected.[72] More regular chapel attendance remained compulsory in Pembroke for Church of England adherents into the 1930s, though had been abolished in Brasenose and

Wadham by the time of the war. The wearing of gowns after dinner, even if going to the cinema, was a requirement, though in Harper-Nelson's experience this rule 'was almost totally ignored'.[73] But during the day gowns were certainly required for lecturers, tutorials and access to libraries, and for dinner in hall. At Trinity, Cadman, the head scout, would check students' attire as they entered hall, 'the judge and arbiter of correct dress for meals' and a man who 'had no compunction about refusing admission to anyone he thought was improperly dressed'.[74] It became normal during the war for St Hilda's students to wear 'slacks' to keep warm, though they could not be worn with gowns, which had to be donned outside of college at night. Formal dinners still saw members of the SCR in evening gowns, though students were allowed to wear afternoon dresses.[75]

There were restrictions on visitors, particularly those of the opposite sex. At St Hilda's, male visitors were only permitted on Saturday and Sunday afternoons. At 6 o'clock sharp, college maids would walk the corridors banging gongs, rousing them to depart. During the war, brothers were allowed into breakfast on Sundays if they were in the forces and on leave. According to college historian Margaret Rayner, 'Predictably there were doubts about the number of brothers some undergraduates had.'[76] At best, writes Laurence Brockliss, 'a male undergraduate could visit a female student in her college at set times on Sundays when at St Hugh's the bed was ceremoniously wheeled out into the corridor'.[77]

But such regulations could not stem the tide of human affection. James Thompson, an undergraduate when war broke out, though soon to be flung around the world by the Royal Marines, described the situation:

> Each Saturday afternoon I met Dorothy off the London train, alive in the vigour of Oxford talk and Oxford dreams. We walked down the High, hands touching, in the sunshine of Summer Term. And our youth went over Magdalen Bridge, and all life ahead under a wide clear sky, love and happiness destroying all shadows.
>
> One vivid image of Dorothy, in a summer frock, knees up to her chin, sitting on the deep window-sill of my room in Lincoln College. Quizzically, whimsically, looking down on the Turl, listening to the tireless bells. 'This is a lovely place, Alan ... I love Oxford. I love this room. I wonder if you know how lovely it is, being here, after a week in London'.

Dorothy would smile, eyes following the changing figures in the Turl; then she would wait for her cucumber sandwiches, her strawberries and cream, her iced cider.

At seven o'clock, her hair hurriedly combed, the fresh lipstick moist on her lips, she would step over the great oaken lintel of that ancient door. Seven o'clock, the deadline, the hour of the Oxford Cinderellas; for it was a rule in Oxford that all ladies must be out of College by seven o'clock. And so five minutes previously, the narrow beds are vacated and the Colleges return to a temporary semblance of monasticism, the rooms silent, the bright, moth dresses now decorating the cafes, the restaurants, the expensive, rambling hotels.[78]

While rules were there to be broken and attitudes were changing, the rules were still the rules; in 1937 a Somerville undergraduate was sent down (dismissed from the University) for having spent the night with her boyfriend, and John Mortimer's departure from Brasenose in 1942 confirmed the fact that 'inappropriate' behaviour could land one in hot water.[79]

Living the life

While some colleges boasted impressive student rooms and sets (bedroom *plus* a living room and perhaps an anteroom, sometimes shared), most students didn't get to live in them. Standard rooms might be 'bleak and unprepossessing by latter-day standards ... The furniture was likely to be battered ... and the exclusively coal fires dusty and smoky.'[80] Arriving for the start of the academic year 1940 (Michaelmas Term, the other two being Hilary and Trinity), Harper-Nelson was shown to his room by the Staircase 11 scout North (*not* 'Mr North', he insisted). The door – with its 'oak' latched back – gave on to a 'sombre sitting room'.[81] There he beheld threadbare carpet, brown furniture, brownish wallpaper, and brownish curtains backed by blackout curtains. Two small windows looked out onto Chapel Quad. The bedroom sported a faded rug beside an iron bedstead, a brown wardrobe, and a washstand holding a china basin in which stood a ewer of water. There was a brown bentwood chair, a bedside cupboard bearing a 'china po' (a chamber pot). Under the washstand there was a large enamel slop bucket.[82]

'En suite' facilities were rare; shared lavatories and communal baths were the thing, the latter usually at some distance from one's room.

It took Nigel Nicolson a week to discover Balliol's ablutions– 'steamy catacombs where no bathrooms should be'.[83] It was the same over the wall at Trinity. Giving Harper-Nelson the lowdown upon his arrival, North explained that 'the bathroom and lavatories are out the back down the stairs through the arch past the Hall and keep going till you get to the bath-house. It's a tidy walk on a cold morning. Have you got a torch?'[84]

Undergraduates enjoyed privileges. They could open accounts in shops without identification by leaving their name and college. They did not perform domestic chores; laundries were cheap and scouts sent washing out and checked it back in.[85] K.C. Bowen wrote that scouts 'were among the most important people in the College, philosophers and friends who addressed us as "Sir", told us off when stupidity overrode intelligence, sold useful things like gowns and teapots, and kept our rooms tidy and serviced'.[86] Dinner was normally taken in hall, and lunch might be bread and cheese and beer from the buttery. Scouts could be 'prevailed upon for money to "look after" their "gentlemen"', and this might include serving lunch and breakfast to students in their rooms.[87] Routinely, they would make beds, pour tea, light fires, empty chamber pots, and bring hot water for shaving each morning.[88]

The JCR – 'a grubbier version of a gentleman's club' – was the centre of social activity, and a place where tea was served each day. Sport w§as strongly encouraged – 'effectively part of the syllabus' – partly in the hope that it would curtail the activities that people like James and Dorothy might otherwise be interested in.[89] The nineteenth-century emphasis on team sports making healthy bodies and healthy minds while turning out men capable of running an empire had passed to Oxbridge from the public schools, and thus undergraduate afternoons, ideally, were to be spent on the playing fields or the river. University and college servants' sports clubs thrived until the war, and punting was ever popular in Trinity Term.[90] Debating societies, dining societies, political clubs and reading groups were important features of student life, some colleges offering reading retreats abroad, the swankier maintaining alpine chalets for the purpose.[91] St Edmund Hall, as a typical example, reported annually in the college magazine on the activities of the following: the Debating Society, Essay Society, John Oldham

Society, Musical Society, The Makers, the Liddon Society, the Diogenes Club, the Methuen Society, the Moot Club, the Conservative Discussion Group, the Labour Club Group and the William Morris Society. The college also had clubs for rowing, football, rugby, hockey, athletics, tennis, swimming and squash.[92] Relaxation, both for dons and their students, was often to be found (according to Rowse) 'in argument and discussion in one's own college rooms of an evening or on long walks in the country which then lay within easy distance of the University'.[93]

Pastoral pursuits, even a lingering Ruskinesque inclination towards 'public service' manual labour, featured in the lives of some dons and students. Edmund Blunden, poet and Merton English fellow, took an active part in country life, helping bring in the annual harvest on a New College tenant farm near Stanton St John.[94] Trevor-Roper was not alone in being a frequent and passionate foxhunter, and some of the colleges kept beagle packs. Writing of college life in the 1930s, Australian Carleton Kemp Allen, Professor of Jurisprudence and warden of Rhodes House, said that even those undergraduates who did not partake of sport could find the time for exercise:

> Failing anything else, one can always walk: and it is unnecessary to remind anybody who has ever read Matthew Arnold that the Oxfordshire country is worth exploring. Much is said of the ravages of the motor-car and the charabanc, but in reality, as soon as the wayfarer leaves the more populous highways, the greater part of the English countryside is still unspoiled, and there are villages within ten miles of Oxford where one might suppose that the internal combustion engine had never been heard of. Indeed, for the country walker, the ubiquitous omnibus is a blessing rather than a curse, for it will save him the time and tedium of journeying through the ever-spreading outskirts of Oxford, and within half an hour it will deposit him at some point where he can enter at once into an Arcadian world.[95]

The college, along with the wider cityscape and its bucolic surrounds, became a place of profound significance for students, both at the time and as they grew older. It encouraged people to think of themselves as 'Magdalen men' or 'Somerville women', fostered intercollegiate rivalry, and strove to retain a place in the hearts of graduates, through old members' events such as gaudies and the publication and distribution of college records (an annual round-up of happenings from across the college, academic and sporting reports, obituaries and news of old members). Colleges venerated their war dead and distinguished fellows and heads of house in memorials and portraiture; they bore their own crests, toasts, graces and colours, and nurtured their own traditions, marking special days and feasting at founders' dinners.

Thus the college system created psychological communities, eliciting bequests from old members, from silver tableware to significant endowments. 'I do not suppose any adolescent susceptible to man-made beauty', wrote J. Lees-Milne, 'can spend a large part of three years at Oxford without being profoundly moved by those grey stones.'[96] For most, 'College life is an unforgettable adventure, every incident of which stands out in vivid colours thirty years afterwards.'[97] At the time of the war the college was 'far more than a set of buildings: it was a group of people scattered throughout the world'.[98] The college community 'extended far beyond Oxford, for membership of the college was conceived of as a lifelong affair'.[99] The poet Keith Douglas, reading English at Merton early in the war and dying in Normandy on D-Day+3, wrote that 'For them it is not a city but an existence; / outside which everything is pretence.'[100] 'I could hardly bear to be more than a mile or two from Carfax', wrote Ann Thwaite of her time at St Hilda's: 'I never went to Blenheim or even Boar's Hill.'[101] Throughout his life, recalled Nigel Nicolson of his father, 'the name of Oxford, even on a pot of marmalade, quickened his pulses'.[102]

Not everyone adored Oxford, of course; it might be less 'magical' to those who were to the manor born and from a top public school, little more than a rite of passage on a privileged journey through life. But for many youths passing through, it was a place of wonder. 'One would scarcely be human to live within its precincts for a while without feeling deeply its magical charm', wrote Betjeman.[103] The brief period spent there could form a stand-out chapter in life, for some a pinnacle never to be equalled.[104] It was, in Waugh's words, 'an enclosed and enchanted garden'. As Selina Hastings writes, it was

> still a city of grey and gold, from its spiked pinnacle medievalism to the plain ashlar beauty of the eighteenth century. The ancient colleges with their cloisters, lawns and quadrangles were networked with narrow streets and passages, beyond which lay woods and water

meadows, a slow-moving river and the lush pastoral beauty of the Thames valley. Cattle were still driven through the streets to market, and at certain times of day nothing was heard except the sound of church bells.[105]

Elitism and reputation

While 'sets' were a well-known feature of university life, they were not unique to the ancient universities, and many people weren't in them. As the novelist Anthony Powell remarked, when we think about the 'Brideshead generation' 'we're talking about a tiny minority whose impact on most undergraduates was practically nil'.[106] Pursuits such as sport, Christianity and working hard for future careers were more important for many students, even if Oxford's imprint on popular memory was largely dictated by the 'aesthetes', because they wrote the books and gave the interviews. But Oxford was not, Powell insisted, 'one long round of Evelyn Waugh and Maurice Bowra'.[107]

Nevertheless, mid-twentieth-century Oxford was an island of the privileged, Collison contending that it retained a Brideshead-style exclusivity until the 1960s. If we move beyond Powell's more literal interpretation of Bridesheadian Oxford, it's difficult not to see it as a major incubator and manufacturer of a ruling elite. Yes, there were working-class men and women, but most of their like would probably have agreed with Welsh publican's son Emlyn Williams that getting in was the 'social equivalent of scaling Everest'.[108] Denis Healey was initially so uncomfortable with the super-confident public-school men that he sought to make friends among students from America, the Commonwealth and Scotland, to whom class was, he thought, 'irrelevant'.[109] The gulf between stonemason Jude in Thomas Hardy's novel and the young Oxford gentlemen who looked at him as if he wasn't there had narrowed since the 1890s but was still very much in evidence. The culture of the place meant that many of those who weren't upper crust aped those who were, and Oxford covered a multitude of past 'sins', of birth, heritage and education.

The social cachet of an Oxford degree was immense, a passport to opportunity in an unequal world, one in which meritocracy was valued but in which hierarchies of class, and who you knew and what school or university you'd been to, mattered enormously too. By the 1930s Oxford's connections to the elite were long established, and it was an unsurpassed recruiting ground for top jobs. Oxford graduates occupied senior ranks of government, Parliament, the civil services (home, foreign and colonial), the professions, the secret intelligence services, the church and, increasingly, business and industry.[110] They were prominent in scholarly communities on the frontiers of knowledge and incestuous circles of authors and creative people influential in broadcasting, literature and the arts. Disputes at the University made the news. The Oxford of 'Our Age', the period from the end of the First World War to the early 1950s that Bowra considered a single generation, was very influential.[111]

Even people from the professions, perhaps possessing Oxbridge degrees themselves, might still view themselves as 'outsiders' in a city where the University was a clique of cliques. Charles Williams, the Inklings' third pillar, hated Oxford when he was evacuated there in 1939 by his employer Oxford University Press, finding himself 'in a society where cliques really did play a large part'.[112] It was not an uncommon feeling. Madge Martin moved to Oxford in 1938 when her husband became vicar of St Michael's at the North Gate on Cornmarket, also responsible for All Saints on Turl Street (now Lincoln's library) and acting rural dean of Oxford. Though enjoying a leisured life, living at 1 Wellington Place off St Giles, and well connected courtesy of her husband's position, she was desperately conscious of not being part of the University set. Though it was 'lovely', Oxford was 'so very depressing at times', she wrote. 'Perhaps it's the people who live in it', she added with penetrating simplicity.[113]

A sense of separation existed even for those with a close family connection. To Edith Tolkien, 'the University seemed an almost impenetrable fortress, a phalanx of imposing buildings where important-looking men passed to and fro in gowns, and where Ronald [her husband] disappeared to work each day.'[114] Examining A.J.P. Taylor's wife Margaret's wartime infatuation with a student, Adam Sisman describes Oxford as a lonely place made more dreary by war: 'The university was still organized as if all the dons were bachelors ... Alan often dined in college, where women were not admitted.'[115]

OF UNIVERSITY AND COLLEGES   39

Just as 1930s' Oxford looked different in some ways from the city of today, the role played by universities in national life had a different character too.[116] To paraphrase Leslie Mitchell, the ancient universities pronounced with authority; vice chancellors were often national figures; and academics spoke on lofty subjects such as the meaning of civilization, assured of a hearing.[117] In a world with far fewer universities, fewer sources of power and information, and with smaller and consequently tighter networks of patronage, knowledge exchange and influence, Oxford's prominence stood out in sharp relief. It was for good reason that *The Times* was sometimes called the 'All Souls Parish Magazine', and that Noel Annan could write of 'the Christ Church Mafia under its *capo*, that quintessential Establishment figure, J.C. Masterman ... promoting its outstanding undergraduates' and injecting them into the sinews of national power.[118]

Oxford was significant because its conversations were of national importance, often embracing outsiders from the upper echelons of government, the civil service, the church and the professions. Passing through Oxford, attending dinners and events, sometimes trawling for talent, many of those people had studied there themselves.[119] The Oxford Union trained parliamentarians, and parliamentarians and other luminaries visited the Union. As the University historian Brian Harrison puts it, 'there the elite made new recruits and the recruits learned from the elite'.[120] The memoirs of later political luminaries up at Oxford in the 1930s and 1940s – Healey, Heath, Jenkins, Thatcher – all contain chapters on their time at Oxford, shaped by the refracted national politics of the day as they cut about the Union, the Labour Club or the Conservative Association.[121]

Politicians deliberately reached out to Oxford's student body. In 1936 the student magazine *Isis* carried a letter from Labour Party leaders urging readers to join the Fabian Research Bureau founded by G.D.H. Cole, doyen of the University's left, and this 'channelled Oxford towards moulding Labour Party policy in London'. Eventually merged with the Fabian Society, the Bureau provided 'policy making backing for the Attlee government' that assumed power in 1945.[122] Hugh Dalton, sometime chairman of the Labour Party and cabinet minister under both Churchill and Attlee, was a 'frequent visitor and talent spotter for the party'.[123]

Oxford's political preoccupations were nourished by ready access to the political elite – a tight network whose members met one another by chance quite as often as the characters in Anthony Powell's novels. But many such meetings were engineered, and happened in Oxford.[124] High table, innumerable little drinks parties and lunches, club and society meetings and dinners – there were manifold links between Oxford students, dons and the world beyond. Heads of houses and senior University figures such as chancellors, vice chancellors and registrars were among the great and good (more so than was the case in Cambridge).

Oxford's international reputation was similarly pronounced. On the evening of Thursday 9 February 1933 the debating society of the Oxford Union carried the motion 'That this House will under no circumstances fight for its King and Country' by 275 votes to 153. News of the decision reverberated around the globe, given unusual reach by Randolph Churchill's ill-advised attempt to have the vote expunged.[125] Mussolini pointed to it as proof of English effeteness, while Churchill senior believed that it had imperilled the security of the British Empire and emboldened Hitler in his plans for European domination. On the other side of the Atlantic, American anti-war campaigners welcomed the vote, which came to be known as the 'Oxford oath' or 'Oxford pledge'. The British embassies in Madrid and Santiago telegrammed the Foreign Office, alarmed by unflattering coverage of the debate in the Spanish and Chilean press, and the consequent damage to Britain's reputation.[126]

The weight attached to the opinion of a small group of callow undergraduates reflected Oxford's status as a place of far-reaching influence. The fame of a university older than Parliament, the common law and the Church of England – nearly as old as the monarchy – had earned both the University and the city a celebrity status, something that Britons, and not just Oxford types, were liable, if they cared at all, either to crow about or to decry as symptomatic of a class-ridden society.

Oxford was viewed as a landmark national institution, a cradle of Western civilization no less. This was explicitly played up in wartime propaganda, the 1941 British Council film *Oxford* making the point very clearly. In it, the well-known Movietone announcer Leslie Mitchell (no relation to Bowra's biographer) declaimed:

For more than seven hundred years Oxford has existed as a centre of learning and culture. But it is not only a city of the past, loving and caring for its great traditions; it is also a city of the present and the future. Its streets are thronged with the young men and women who one day will provide Britain's scholars, scientists, and statesmen. In the university, students from far off parts of the Empire, rich men's sons and scholarship winners from Britain's industrial areas share alike the knowledge and culture offered by the university.[127]

Internationally, it was perceived as a breeding ground of the British ruling class, and it had 'acquired a cachet among the academic community bestowed on none but a handful of European and North American universities'.[128] As Oliver Hardy put it in the 1939 Laurel and Hardy film *A Chump at Oxford*, it provided 'the finest education money can buy'. It also retained an association with notions of breeding, social hierarchy and *noblesse oblige*. As late as 1938 Ward Lock's Oxford *Guide Book* promulgated vague but familiar patrician notions in its section on 'The Influence of Oxford'. Based on 'clean sport' and 'playing the game', it welcomed the 'annual supply of the best type of Englishmen from Oxford'. Reflecting the worry that abounded at the time given the international situation, it concluded that this represented 'an asset the value of which cannot be overestimated and which may prove priceless in the not distant future'.[129]

Whatever may or may not have been 'special' about Oxford and its graduates in the 1930s, nothing could insulate it from the tide of events then washing across Europe as the dictators challenged the established international order and Britain and its allies struggled to find a response. Given added momentum by the Munich crisis of 1938, preparations included practical measures for civil defence and, as in the First World War, plans for a state takeover of the real estate and intellectual and scientific resources of the universities. The politics of the 1930s and the drumbeat of approaching war form the subject of the following chapter.

THREE

RISING FASCISM, APPROACHING WAR

The First World War cast shadows across the country. In Oxford, colleges mourned their dead and erected memorials, and undergraduates sensed the presence of a 'lost generation'. Army life and trench warfare coloured the outlook of dons who had seen active service. Partly because of the unpleasantness of this collective experience and national memory, wrote William Hayter, 'a forlorn attempt was made to revert to a pre-1914 life-style ... Oxford in the twenties was apolitical, the time of the Oxford aesthetes.'[1] But come the 1930s, it was no longer the done thing to be apolitical. The significance of communism and fascism on the international scene, wars and invasions, and debates about collective security, disarmament and rearmament, meant that politics suffused discussions as never before. No one could ignore what was going on in the world, even if they didn't want to talk about it.[2] 'We were perhaps the most political generation in Oxford's history', wrote Denis Healey.[3] Students and townspeople left Oxford to join the international brigade fighting Franco in the Spanish Civil War (1936–39), and in the opposite direction came refugees from fascism seeking sanctuary in the city. As the decade matured, the 'unthinkable' prospect of another war with Germany hove into view. The choices of the time were stark; as Healey wrote, 'no later generation has enjoyed the same political certainty'.[4]

As the spies nurtured by the Apostles gestated in Cambridge, Communists flourished in Oxford too, becoming very influential in the University's Labour Club, the Union leaning to the left as well.[5] Peace, pacifism, disarmament and the Soviet Union were subjects of debate. It wasn't only international affairs that heightened the political temperature in interwar Oxford: domestic matters played a part too. Students joined hunger marchers progressing towards London from northern towns in 1932 and 1934. 'Oxford Students Aid Hunger March', declared the *New York Times*: 'Several hundred carry red flags and sing the 'Internationale'. DEBUTANTES OFFER FOOD. Automobiles are lent to assist infirm.'[6] Oxford's growing working-class population also affected things. Those keen on unionization and the politics of the Labour Party or perhaps the Communists looked askance at older 'labouring classes' in Oxford, with their conservative politics and apathy towards trade unions.[7] The influential Communist activist Abe Lazarus was sent to the city, busmen went on strike, and there were numerous walk-outs at Pressed Steel.[8] A mass meeting of thousands of people gathered at the Town Hall in April 1935 to protest conditions in the new housing estates, and the following month thousands more gathered at Cutteslowe, intent on tearing down the wall erected by a private developer to stop residents of a neighbouring council estate using its roads.

But it was the international situation that really caught the eye in Oxford. The war in Spain was big news for left-leaning and liberal townspeople and students alike, and Oxford became a hub for activists for the Spanish republic.[9] 'SUPPORT SPANISH DEMOCRACY' read graffiti on the wall of Jesus College chapel.[10] Spain 'was so real that it hurt', wrote Balliol student Denis Healey, arousing passions for his generation as Vietnam would for a later one.[11] Oxfordshire had its own 'Aid Spain' organization, and the Oxford University Peace Council sent food parcels. Hundreds of Basques found homes in the county following the bombing of Guernica (April 1937) and the arrival at Southampton of nearly 4,000 child refugees. Groups of them ended up in Thame, Witney, Shipton-under-Wychwood and at Buscot Park near Faringdon. Some of them were invited to tea at Balliol by its master, A.D. 'Sandie' Lindsay, and colleges responded to an appeal to adopt refugees, the Corpus Christi College JCR wickedly agreeing so long as they were over 15, buxom and female.[12]

Other students responded more compassionately. Cora Blyth, studying modern languages at St Hilda's, started visiting the colony of 265 children at Aston near Witney to improve her Spanish.[13] She bussed

44 OXFORD'S WAR

out every Sunday with a small group, including the administrator of the University Museum, who took along a gramophone and a case of Spanish records. There she met her future husband, Republican refugee Luis Portillo (parents of Michael Portillo).[14] Fundraising and cultural events supported the cause, Healey arranging for the preparatory sketches of Picasso's painting *Guernica* to be exhibited at Oriel.[15] At a factory on the Botley Road, Harley-Davidson motorbikes were fitted with stretchers for the evacuation of battlefield wounded, shipped to Spain as 'potatoes' on a blockade-running ship. People like Richard Symonds of the Oxford Pacifists Association visited Spain and wrote articles for the national press and local publications like *Oxford Forward*, a radical magazine produced at St Michael's Hall in Shoe Lane (behind today's Clarendon Centre). Edward Heath travelled to Barcelona in 1938 at the invitation of the Republican government in his capacity as chairman of the Federation of University Conservative Associations.[16] A dance at the Randolph in May 1939 raised funds for the Basque child colony at Shipton-under-Wychwood.[17]

The 1930s brought intense scrutiny of British foreign policy: the pros and cons of appeasement were debated at the Union, in student societies and political clubs, and across high table. Oxford became 'nervously political' and noticeably more radical.[18] This was partly caused by the changing composition of the undergraduate body as more working-class students joined its ranks, and by contact with the increasingly politicized industrial population.[19] Some dons travelled in Europe and beyond and met Continental scientists and scholars, well aware of the troubled political climate.[20] Frederick Lindemann toured the continent as soon as Hitler came to power, enticing academic opponents and victims to come to Oxford's laboratories. Bowra spent a lengthy sabbatical in Germany in 1932 and travelled twice to see a love interest, the historian Ernst Kantorowicz, in 1934–5. He visited again in 1938, his experiences stimulating a desire to assist those fallen foul of Nazi oppression.[21] Merton research fellow Hugh Trevor-Roper visited Germany in 1935, observing at first hand the loathsome bullying of persecuted communities and learning the language, an ability that would be put to good use during the war. James Brierly, Chichele Professor of International Law and Diplomacy at All Souls, became an expert on

RISING FASCISM, APPROACHING WAR 45

the Nazi party's rise. He campaigned against its unlawful acts once it attained power, and championed the cause of refugees, even securing the release of young Austrians and Germans from imprisonment and sponsoring their migration to Britain.[22]

Nathaniel 'Nat' Micklem, principal of Mansfield, visited Germany in the late 1930s as he developed his thinking on national socialism and Christianity, one of the few Christian leaders attempting to understand how Hitler was affecting Europe. His trips enabled him to witness the persecution of the church.[23] He attended an illegal ordination ceremony and other activities of the Confessing Church, formed in opposition to the official German Protestant Church, which had come under Nazi influence. He reported his experiences to Archbishop of Canterbury Cosmo Lang, among others. Micklem warned that the Nazi regime was 'the negation of God erected into a system of government', and that it preached 'illimitable anti-Semitism'. In 1938 he sent his chaplain, John Marsh, on a covert mission to Berlin to deliver a letter to members of the Confessing Church, which along with various secret papers was 'stitched into J.M.'s surgical corset by his wife Gladys'.[24]

Oxford did its bit in the struggle against fascism, supporting Spanish republicanism, opposing Mussolini's invasion of Abyssinia (1935–36) and championing the League of Nations.[25] The 1933 'King and Country' debate at the Union induced 'apoplexy in Cheltenham and Bournemouth', wrote Hobhouse, 'and whoops of joy in Berlin and Rome'.[26] There was plenty of media attention; 'Roosevelt watched it, Mussolini watched it, especially Hitler watched it', claimed *Picture Post*. 'Disloyalty at Oxford: Gesture Towards the Reds' was the *Telegraph*'s headline. The *Daily Express* also managed to avoid sitting on the fence:

> There is no question but that the woozy-minded Communists, the practical jokers, and the sexual indeterminates of Oxford have scored a great success in the publicity that has followed this victory ... Even the plea of immaturity, or the irresistible passion of the undergraduate for posing, cannot excuse such contemptible and indecent action as the passing of that resolution.[27]

Yet indications of pacifism in Oxford's student body did not equate to an unwillingness to fight against fascism or a lack of patriotism, and the debate had really been about those who believed in 'England, right or wrong', and those who rejected the idea. It was a vote against the shrill patriotism of the popular press of 1914, against the language of *dulce et decorum est pro patria mori*, against the persecution of conscientious objectors: in sum against the stance of an earlier generation which spoke an older language about honour, duty and empire.[28]

Although the motion was carried, many voted against it: Oxford, like any other place, accommodated a spectrum of political views. Not everyone was critical of the dictators, welcoming towards refugees or dismissive of prime minister Neville Chamberlain's foreign policy. Oxford provided platforms for views across the spectrum. Churchill, then in his 'wilderness' period out of government, addressed Conservative undergraduates at the Union in 1936 on the subject of rearmament, for which he was campaigning.[29] Following the meeting, he went back to his friend Lindemann's rooms in Christ Church with a group of Tory students including Heath, leaving for bed at Blenheim in the early hours of the morning.

Arguments about the challenge posed by the dictators and Britain's response reverberated across the city, not just in the parliamentary preschool of the Union debating chamber. The University's Labour and Conservative parties were very active: of 4,500 undergraduates in June 1938, over a third were members of the Labour Club. Its activities overlapped with those of the vocal Oxford branch of the Communist Party of Great Britain. The People's Bookshop at 36 Hythe Bridge Street acted as agent for the party and distributor of the *Daily Worker*, and was the local headquarters of the Left Book Club, a nationally influential publishing house established in 1936. Different political opinions, and the strength and ambition of the Oxford student 'voice', were captured in the 1934 book *Young Oxford and War*. In it, students Richard Freeman, Michael Foot, Frank Hardie and Keith Steel-Maitland set out different political opinions representative of those held among the student body.[30]

Though fascism had far less impact in Oxford than communism, the city did not escape the attentions of the Blackshirts, and British Union of Fascists events in 1933 and 1936 led to violence.[31] On the latter occasion, Oswald Mosley 'descended on Oxford with a small army of uniformed fascist stewards. They were spoiling for a fight, as were the Oxford busmen, a very left-wing element active at the time.'[32]

Mosley stood alone on the platform in the Carfax Assembly Rooms on Cornmarket, repeatedly interrupted by shouts of 'Red Front'. Attended by uniformed guards and taunting opponents after the Horst Wessel song, the anthem of the Nazi party, had been played as a warm-up, Mosley was looking for trouble, which came when he ordered his men to eject a heckler.

Christ Church don Frank Pakenham was injured in the ensuing fracas, the experience speeding his journey from the Conservatives to the left and determining him to play a part in breaking the fascists in Oxford. 'Oxford is not likely to be impressed', he said, 'by the mechanical bleating of this gimcrack fencing master, so facetious about working-class accents, so deaf to the sound of his own.'[33] Protesters were set upon by truncheon-wielding Blackshirt 'stewards', but they did not have it all their own way, recorded Trevor-Roper: 'Great damage to the Blackshirts was done by one of the dons of Christ Church [Pakenham], who, being struck over the head by a Blackshirt with a steel chain, was roused to a berserk fury.'[34]

Anti-fascist momentum grew as the decade progressed, the 1938 May Day march from the Plain to St Giles a mass demonstration of support for the victims of right-wing extremism. Oxford's students gravitated from an anti-war position to an anti-fascist one by the time of the Munich Agreement of September 1938, when Chamberlain declared that he had secured 'peace in our time' by agreeing to Germany's absorption of the Sudeten territory of Czechoslovakia. This hugely controversial act of 'appeasement' led opponents in Oxford to ally with Tory critics of the government, such as Heath. Together, they swung the Union strongly against Chamberlain's foreign policy, a debate attended by 800 students rejecting a motion in support of the agreement by 320 to 266.

Munich and what would become known as appeasement was the central issue in an extraordinary parliamentary by-election triggered by the death of the sitting Tory MP.[35] On 24 September a crowded anti-Conservative meeting at the Town Hall, led by the Labour candidate for the vacant parliamentary seat, Patrick Gordon Walker (a Christ Church don), and Councillor Richard Crossman (a New College one), affirmed support for collective security and condemned Britain's 'betrayal' of Czechoslovakia.[36] There were street protests the following day, punctuated by cries of 'Down with Chamberlain' and 'We want peace!'[37] Campaigning for the October by-election publicly ranged don against don and was closely watched across the nation. Against his and the national Labour Party's wishes, Gordon Walker withdrew, leaving Balliol's master to take on the Conservative candidate, Quintin Hogg.[38] Lindsay stood as an independent 'Popular Front' candidate, on the platform that 'a vote for Hogg is a vote for Hitler'.[39] Ten heads of houses and two professors supported the pro-Munich Hogg, while six heads of houses and three professors sided with the anti-Munich Lindsay.[40] While Lindsay was defeated, he almost halved the Conservative majority.

The by-election had coincided with the election of a new warden at Wadham, the position won by college dean Maurice Bowra, despite his relative youth. Moving into the Warden's Lodgings, he set about making changes, establishing a library and buying new furniture from shopkeepers who, because of the international situation, were so nervous that they were easily bartered down. 'Though I enjoyed all this', wrote Bowra, 'I had a carking fear that in a year or two the college might be destroyed from the air and that I myself might be, as Ernst [Kantorowicz] gloomily prognosticated, the last Warden of Wadham.'[41]

The threat of war, and the aerial bombardment that it was believed would accompany it, now hung like a pall. A full year before the outbreak, Madge Martin was waking from sleepless nights 'feeling awful ... worrying and worrying about the probability of war. It is too dreadful.'[42] The day after writing this, 29 September, Madge and her husband went to the Playhouse on Woodstock Road. Just decommissioned as a theatre due to the construction of the new Playhouse on Beaumont Street (its opening night occurring on 20 October), the building now served as a gas-mask distribution centre.[43] 'It really depressed me more than anything', Madge wrote, 'to see the patient ordinary crowd of men, women, and children waiting to be fitted on with these hideous monstrosities.'[44] As well as doling out 100,000 masks, the council opened gas decontamination centres.

In her 'Principal's Letter' for the 1938–39 edition of the *St Hugh's Chronicle*, Barbara Gwyer wrote that Michaelmas 1938 had been remarkable for the parliamentary election, and the extraordinary amount of energy devoted by members of the University to the many forms of relief now occupying the minds of English people. The persecution of men and women unpopular for reasons of race, politics, or religion under the present regime in Germany has been brought home to us for some years past by the arrival here of distinguished [refugee] scholars.[45]

International Student Services, she continued,

> is still the centre of work for the benefit of younger students cut off in mid-career from all hope of completing their courses or training for adult life in other ways. The Oxford Association of the British Federation of University Women is actively arranging for hospitality needed by women graduates; while orphaned children and others fleeing from danger are finding help through the work of a committee under the chairmanship of Dr Henry Gillett, Mayor of Oxford [founder of the Spanish Relief Fund].[46]

In January 1939, as Barcelona fell to Franco and the Republicans foundered, one of the largest student protests ever seen in Oxford took place, hundreds marching with banners demanding 'Arms for Spain' and 'Food for Spain'.[47] A joint city–University delegation took a petition to 10 Downing Street, delivering messages from Pakenham, Lindsay, the scientist Howard Florey, and the feminist and anti-fascist writer Charlotte Haldane. The increasingly oppressive political backdrop could not but affect the lives of students. Somerville's Iris Murdoch energetically engaged in Communist Party activities, proclaiming the wonders of the Soviet Union. Frank Thompson of New College, brother of the historian E.P. Thompson, wrote and acted in a play titled *It Can Happen Here*. Performed for the University Labour Club at St Michael's Hall on 6 March 1939, it imagined Britain as a fascist police state, portraying intense SCR arguments and the establishment of a concentration camp in Christ Church Meadow.[48]

On 27 April 1939, with war perilously close, the Union debated the motion 'In view of this country's new commitments [to guarantee Poland's integrity] and the gravity of the general situation in Europe this House welcomes conscription'.[49] A record crowd squeezed into the red brick Victorian debating chamber tucked behind Cornmarket. 'Every available space was occupied in the gallery, on the floor, the window sills, and even the President's rostrum. Many had to be turned away.'[50] Under the headline 'Oxford Union Give Decisive Vote for Conscription', the *Daily Mail* declared that the Union, which 'startled the world six years ago by voting that they would not fight for King and Country, reversed that decision last night. By 423 votes to 326.'[51]

Corporately, the University had opportunities to assert its position, in May 1937, for example, declining the invitation to send representatives to the University of Göttingen's bicentenary.[52] But perhaps its most notable collective reaction to the rise of political extremism occurred at the intellectual level. In summer 1939 Oxford University Press launched the 'Pamphlets on World Affairs' series with the publication of Alfred Zimmern's *The Prospects of Civilization*. Thirteen titles were in print before war began, the purpose of the series to address the international situation and to contest the world-view of the dictators (see PLATE 26). Reviewing the early titles for the *Review of Politics*, Willis Nutting, lecturer at the University of Notre Dame and former Rhodes Scholar, described them as 'an eleventh hour attempt on the part of British scholars to answer the charges that Hitler has been hurling at the makers of the Versailles treaty, and to criticize Hitler's own program and himself'.[53]

The First World War had proved a setback for the University's engagement with Europe, severing a burgeoning Anglo-German connection while reinforcing those with the Empire and America.[54] The crisis of fascism saw the European strand revive with the arrival of fleeing scholars, artists and intellectuals and the perceived need to make Europe's problems the subject of academic study. The 'catastrophe of interwar extremism', writes John Darwin, led to the 'most important revival of continental academic influence in Oxford between the wars'.[55] The passage of the Nazi regime's law for the 'Restoration of the Professional Civil Service' in 1933 resulted in the dismissal of over 1,000 Jewish and 'non-Aryan' academics from university posts. It led some to migrate before they were sacked, Albert Einstein among them. This turned out to be 'Hitler's gift', as top scholars and scientists left Austrian and German universities, Oxford, Cambridge and London the main British beneficiaries.[56] Britain, writes Anthony Grenville, 'was unique in its response' to the emergency afflicting people of Jewish and non-Aryan heritage in Europe, and Oxford was very much a part of this.[57]

One of those to take advantage of misfortune was Lindemann, who saw the accession of Hitler as an opportunity. He'd long wanted to make Oxford a world centre of low-temperature physics and now targeted a group of Jewish scientists under the leadership of Kurt Mendelssohn, an acknowledged leader in the field. Trawling Germany for talent and able to offer financial support courtesy of Imperial Chemical Industries (ICI), he was able to bring the scientists he wanted to Oxford.[58] Mendelssohn arrived in April 1933, followed by his assistants Franz Simon and Nicholas Kurti and doctoral students Heinz and Fritz London. By the end of the year, spectroscopist Heinrich Kuhn and theoretical physicist Erwin Schrödinger had arrived too (neither Jewish, though Kuhn had lost his post for being non-Aryan, and Schrödinger, an Austrian Catholic, wanted out). The latter had no sooner arrived and been given a Magdalen research fellowship than he was awarded the Nobel Prize.[59] A separate strand of activity pursued by Lindemann, which was also to have repercussions of national importance, concerned air defence and the intense debates that surrounded it. He became an expert on the subject, standing unsuccessfully on the basis of this expertise for one of the University's parliamentary seats in 1936. He fought to convince government that science could help protect British cities from the threat of air attack, the great fear of the age. He became a member of the Air Ministry's Air Defence Committee in 1935 and, from 1938, along with Churchill, of the Committee for the Scientific Survey of Air Defence, also known as the Tizard Committee after its chairman.[60]

The University participated in numerous schemes providing sanctuary for refugee scholars. Somerville welcomed the Egyptologists Käthe Bosse and Elise Jenny Baumgartel, the Hittite scholar Leonie Zuntz (who took her own life in Norham Gardens in 1942) and Lotte Labowsky (who ran the library when Miss Evans took on a war role in Whitehall).[61] Mansfield hosted Hans Kramm, a pastor, Herbert Hirschwald, a Prussian supreme court judge, and Dr Gunther Zuntz, a classicist.[62] Deprived of his chair at Freiberg, the eminent German classicist Eduard Fraenkel was invited to Christ Church in 1934.[63] The following year, with the encouragement of the likes of Bowra, he applied for and won the recently vacated Corpus Christi professorship of Latin, his appointment opposed by John Buchan (Lord Tweedsmuir) and others who wanted to protect positions for British nationals.[64]

European refugees became a feature in Oxford, leaving an indelible mark on the University's research. Germany, wrote Rowse, 'paid a heavy price for her insane barbarism towards the Jews and others; Oxford profited by the brilliant men of science saved from the Nazi regression to type'.[65] By February 1939 twenty-seven of the 128 academic refugees officially in Britain were in Oxford, though this figure doesn't give the full picture. Brockliss calculates that there were at least fifty refugee academics being supported in Oxford by the outbreak of war, and in addition there were non-academics too, including artists.[66] The *Jewish Chronicle* put the number of Austrian and German Jews in Oxford in summer 1939 at 300.[67] By February 1940 the local Refugee Committee counted 700.[68] There were so many German students and academics in Oxford that the vicar of the University Church conducted services in German.[69]

Some European scholars and their families found their way to Oxford with the aid of the Society for the Protection of Science and Learning (SPSL). It was founded in 1933 as the Academic Assistance Council (changing its name in 1936) by William Beveridge, then director of the London School of Economics (LSE), following a visit to Austria during which he learned of German academics losing their jobs on political grounds.[70] Lindsay was a leading figure in the work of the Council, and Balliol alone created ten positions for displaced German and Austrian scholars. Oxford colleges worked with the SPSL and its 'devoted secretary', Esther Simpson.[71] By the end of 1938, the Society had 'already brought hope to 550 displaced members of University Faculties and research departments'.[72]

Gilbert Murray, Regius Professor of Greek and chair of the League of Nation's International Committee on Intellectual Cooperation, was involved with its work, and vice chancellor and president of Magdalen George Gordon led a University-wide assistance programme under the Oxford Committee for Refugee Scholars, established in February 1939, which was principally driven by female figures in the city and University, such as Helen Darbishire, principal of Somerville.[73] The

University also provided funds, and OUP extended financial assistance to several world-class academics driven out by the Nazis, Rockefeller money enabling it to employ around twenty refugees scholars throughout the war.[74] Support also came from the Oxford Society of Friends (the Quakers), which maintained a hostel for refugees in Linton Road.

For some refugees arriving in Oxford, it was the second time they had migrated in order to escape persecution; renaissance historian Nicolai Rubinstein for instance, having moved from Berlin to Florence before arriving in Britain in 1939.[75] Networks formed among refugees, such as the local Jewish committee, were important in helping people settle into a new life. British support organizations and colleges were central to the process too, as were links with individuals who took refugees working in similar academic or artistic fields under their wing. Rubinstein's entry into Oxford society was smoothed by Buchan and the Regius Professor of History, Maurice Powicke. Many of these people had been tenured academics in Austria or Germany, or well-established, even renowned, artists. They did not walk straight into an equivalency of status, security and income, and often struggled to establish themselves and 'start over'. Short-term fellowships, money from special funds, piecework to make ends meet and less well appointed living quarters than those they were accustomed to were prominent aspects of their experience.

Inevitably, refugees faced a cool reception from some individuals, if not quite open hostility. They were both incomers and foreigners in a rather provincial environment dominated by tight-knit scholarly and collegiate communities. There were antisemitic undertones and prejudice against non-Christians, and a sense that academic jobs, when they became available, should preferably go to Britons. Even Einstein's appointment at Christ Church in the early 1930s had been vigorously contested from within. The situation was further complicated when Austrian and German nationals were designated 'enemy aliens' shortly after the war began. Refugees also encountered set British ways of doing things, such as teaching music composition, that did not readily embrace continental practices.[76] The more renowned refugees were used to a 'much larger, more cosmopolitan stage – Berlin, Florence, Paris' and Oxford 'could never have attracted the stellar line-up of some of the greatest names in scholarship' without the push of political extremism.[77]

54 OXFORD'S WAR

Émigrés brought with them new ways of printing and new reproduction methods, and developments in academic fields such as art history and music. The 'enforced internationalism' of the 1930s and 1940s was to change the University's character forever.

Preparations for war

The 1914–18 war provided a blueprint as to how universities could contribute to a national war effort. Students had been called up in huge numbers, University and college buildings had been requisitioned by military and government departments, and university science had played an important role in arms production. Afterwards, there were discussions across the higher education sector regarding the employment of students in the event of another war. The 1922 Graham Greene Report considered the problems involved in preventing the military from 'misemploying men of high education and scientific attainment'. By 1937 a scheme had been produced for the recruitment of members of Oxford, Cambridge and London universities under the age of 25 through selection boards established at the universities, rather than through the usual channels.[78]

Thought was also given to the most efficient use of academic staff: those over 25 would be designated as belonging to a reserved occupation, and in early 1939 the Ministry of Labour invited all British academics who were prepared to enter government service if war came to place their names on a register.[79] At the same time, the ministry canvassed universities about the staffing levels they would need to maintain in order to continue to function, so as to ensure that the armed forces and government departments did not overgraze the range.[80] This was all part of a vast preparation for war within Whitehall, the Munich crisis turning paper plans into people as the expansion of existing ministries, and the creation of new ones, was envisaged. Of the latter, the Ministry of Food was to grow from 300 to 30,000 people dispersed in local offices across the land, and the Ministry of Supply became a mega-department of 60,000, directly employing a quarter of a million industrial workers.[81] The Ministry of Labour's Central Bureau, which maintained the 'Central Registry' of professional people likely to be useful during the war, was owned by the formidable senior civil servant Beryl Millicent le Poer Power, and contained 80,000 names by the start of the war. Though in the event it could not prevent 'private enterprise' as ministries competing for talent tried to make their own direct arrangements, the register helped regulate the flow and maintain a balance so as to ensure that one government department did not unfairly hoover up all the talent, and that universities retained sufficient staff to function.

Lord Privy Seal Sir John Anderson was instructed to address the issues that war would pose for universities, part of a wider remit for civil defence and evacuation handed him by Chamberlain. He was a fortunate choice for this role, having conducted postgraduate research on the chemistry of uranium and therefore cognizant of the intricacies of advanced scholarly and scientific activity. The national Committee of Vice-Chancellors and Principals was keen to emphasize the value of their institutions if war came. They could 'make a vital and specific contribution to the war-time needs of the country and they are prepared to undertake that duty', they told the government. But a balance had to be struck. In late 1938 university authorities across the country were asked to consider how things might best be handled – and how the state might use universities to support a national war effort. The Committee of Vice-Chancellors and Principals submitted a memorandum outlining the services universities could render in science, technology, medicine and agriculture, all the while stressing the importance of continuing to teach arts subjects rather than focusing overwhelmingly on science.

The memorandum formed the agenda for a meeting between Anderson and the vice chancellors on 30 January 1939, at which the main lines of policy for the opening stages of war were agreed.[82] It was decided that all medical students and final-year and postgraduate students in certain scientific and engineering subjects would be given reserved status and thus not be called up. The meeting also agreed on the evacuation of the constituent colleges of London University, and that wherever possible university courses would be maintained in arts subjects.[83]

If war came, many government departments would have requisitioning powers, and Anderson was keen to coordinate arrangements through the Office of Works (which in 1942 was taken over by a full-blown

Ministry of Works and Buildings, known from 1943 as the Ministry of Works – the term used henceforth to avoid confusion). This was in order to prevent an unseemly free-for-all as ministries and the armed services raced to acquire the real estate with which to accommodate their expanding organizations and cope with the anticipated migration of government activities from London. Vice Chancellor Gordon conducted the contingency planning regarding Oxford's role in a forceful demonstration of leadership.[84] Following negotiations with various government departments for the use of buildings and the conversion of science departments for government work, his prescient plans were approved by Hebdomadal Council (the University's senior executive body) early in 1939.[85] At a heads-of-house meeting on 9 February, Gordon described the function of the University in a national emergency. College heads agreed to entrust negotiations on the use of buildings to a central committee appointed by the Council, a significant concession given college autonomy and the University's inability to dictate. They also agreed to the University's proposal for the pooling of payments received for the 'renting' of requisitioned buildings. The monies would be paid into a fund that would be distributed by the University on an equitable basis among the colleges.[86] Oxford's response to requisition demands would therefore be coordinated by the registrar and a committee of bursars dealing with the government's main requisitioning authority, the Ministry of Works.

Thus forewarned, libraries, laboratories and colleges could begin local planning for the disruption that would follow a declaration of war. Balliol's governing body had discussed Air Raid Precautions (ARP) as early as November 1937 and investigated storing college treasures securely the following May.[87] The near crisis at the time of Munich in September 1938 was a catalyst for action across Oxford. 'Everything here is in a frightful mess, what with wars and rumours of wars', wrote Trevor-Roper to his brother. 'Merton has been active all day preparing a gas-proof, sandbag-lined refuge in the Stores; and I have been to the Town Hall to sign on for the volunteer clerical canteen.'[88] The fellows of St John's examined the insurance provisions covering the college's precious possessions, including silver, old books and rare manuscripts, in the event of bomb damage. The House Committee of Manchester

College discussed ARP and approved the purchase of fire buckets and sandbags. The Ashmolean adopted ARP measures shortly after Munich and closed for a week at the end of August 1938 to make plans. The museum's Board of Visitors resolved to remove the most important parts of the collections from Oxford for safekeeping in the countryside, and the following March the Keeper of Fine Art, Dr Karl Parker, visited Chastleton House near Moreton-in-Marsh to see if it would be suitable for the storage of its treasures.[89]

The steward and senior porter at Jesus College were appointed air raid wardens, and in June 1939 the college made arrangements for blackout and built a reinforced strongroom in the butler's kitchen to accommodate college treasures.[90] Corpus Christi College appointed its first SCR air raid wardens in March 1938, and Oriel formed an ARP committee the following January.[91] Principal Gwyer of St Hugh's told old members in the 1938–39 *Chronicle* that the college was in close touch with University authorities on matters relating to security, and that ARP wardens had been appointed from among the members of the SCR.[92]

The Bodleian's preparations were in hand many months before the outbreak, led by Frank Dubber, who in February 1938 was appointed superintendent of Bodley's book service.[93] His main task was to supervise a mass movement of books as the library prepared to reorder its holdings and occupy the enormous new facility then under construction, the New Bodleian (see PLATE 21). The plan was to decant crowded collections currently stored in the Schools Quadrangle, the basements of the Old Ashmolean museum (the Museum of the History of Science since 1935), the Sheldonian Theatre and the Examination Schools. But Dubber and his bosses were mindful of the fact that if war came they would probably be called upon to perform an important local and national service by providing bomb-proof accommodation for books, manuscripts and valuable objects and collections from institutions in Oxford, London and elsewhere. To that end, the library 'circularized Oxford colleges, offering to make the new library's basement available for the deposit of their treasures', stirred to action by the Munich crisis.[94]

The library had performed this role before. Due to the threat of Zeppelin raids in the previous war, its most precious manuscripts had been stored in a sandbagged redoubt constructed in the south-west

58 OXFORD'S WAR

corner of the then-new underground bookstore between the Radcliffe Camera and the Old Bodleian. The curators decided to adopt the same approach now, but on a larger scale and using the underground floors of the new library. In March 1938 a redoubt was formed using 200 sandbags, and 146 of the Bodleian's most precious treasures went underground. It wasn't long before external institutions were requesting sanctuary for their valuables. In September 1938 Sir Charles Travis Clay, librarian to the House of Lords, wrote to Bodley's Librarian, Edmund Craster, asking about storage, and later that month four tin boxes were sent to Oxford by the Ministry of Works. They contained documents previously displayed in the library of the Lords, including the death warrant of Charles I, the Petition of Right, the Great Reform Act, and records from the Tower of London like the remaining Naseby letters. In April 1939 a second redoubt of 500 sandbags divided into three compartments was installed to accommodate more material, including a first edition of Edward Fitzgerald's *Rubaiyat of Omar Khayyam*. The sandbags were supplied by E.I. Hedderly, a rope and twine merchant and tarpaulin rick-cloth (waterproof sheets to protect hayricks) maker in St Ebbe's. It was discovered, however, that the sandbags became damp, damaging the books, so new ones were sourced from Minty on the High Street.

As the University made plans for war, so too did the city. It was agreed that the Great Hall of Rhodes House would replace the Town Hall should the latter be damaged or destroyed. Civil defence became a major preoccupation because of the prevailing belief that 'the bomber would always get through', meaning that if war came large civilian casualties from bomb blast and possibly even poison gas would occur, and buildings would be destroyed or damaged. In April 1939 Charles Fox, chief constable of Oxford City Police, was appointed ARP controller and the city divided into eleven areas, subdivided into 210 sectors supported by seventy wardens' posts and an initial establishment of 1,337 volunteer ARP wardens.[95] The city's ARP system was coordinated from the basement of the Town Hall, where reports from the wardens' posts were plotted on a wallchart (later moved to Alexandra Courts in Summertown because of the threat to the city centre). Oxford businesses formed a Fire-Fighters' and Watchers' Corps.

Manpower for rescue parties was identified from among the city's construction companies, and city council employees trained for service on decontamination squads should the Germans use gas. Special constables were detailed to man air raid sirens around the city, and reflective surfaces on traffic islands were to be blacked out in places such as St Giles. Plans were also made to accommodate people after Oxford had been designated a reception area for evacuees from London and the south-east. The Majestic Cinema in Botley was taken over as a reception centre, and a census undertaken to establish the city's evacuee capacity. In the process, 26,000 homes were inspected, and Oxford's evacuee capacity was set at 31,000 people.[96]

Emergency medical facilities were also prepared, catering for Oxfordshire's population and the expected evacuees. The Ministry of Health delegated responsibility for emergency hospitals to the Oxford and District Joint Hospitals Board. Somerville College was earmarked as an annexe of the 421-bed Radcliffe Infirmary; used as a hospital in the previous war featuring hutted accommodation, its drainage and water supply infrastructure remained in place. Nuneham Park was also available for hospital purposes, offered up by its owner, and the Emergency Medical Services planned a hospital for the treatment of air raid casualties (what became the Churchill Hospital).[97]

The last summer

The world held its breath, wondering what Hitler would do next. July 1939 brought blackout rehearsals, inspections of ARP equipment and a parade of civil defence workers. On 5 August the University Registrar, Dr Douglas Veale, told college bursars that he had corresponded with the Ministry of Works regarding the blacking out of colleges requisitioned for 'national purposes' if war came.[98] The ministry decreed that each college should provide all necessary ARP services, including air raid shelters, fire-fighting equipment and dark window blinds in accordance with government policy, whether or not they were to be taken over. 'The war might come on you suddenly before the occupants of the College have left', Veale warned, and college and University authorities would be liable for criticism if they had not prepared adequately when the bombs began to fall.

In August a party of twenty Government Code and Cypher School (GCCS) employees moved discreetly into Mansfield College to be close to OUP, where stationery necessary for the work of codebreaking and code-making was to be printed in conditions of strict secrecy. At the same time, a larger GCCS party moved to Bletchley Park. Similarly shrouded in secrecy, Morris Radiators in North Oxford began work on the production of an experimental radiator for the Spitfire, a new fighter aircraft entering service with front-line RAF squadrons around the country.

Bowra thought he was living through 'the last months of an *ancien régime*' in the summer weeks of 1939, convinced that if war came 'there would be only increasingly pale imitations of what had once existed' by the end of it.[99] Undergraduates, affected by their own generational impulses, could not help but be aware of the astonishing times through which they were living. Tom Fletcher of Ruskin College, who lodged on Magpie Lane between High Street and Merton Street, organized a dozen student-actors into a theatre group called the Magpie Players (including Iris Murdoch), 'reminiscent of J.B. Priestley's *Good Companions*'. In the depths of the long vacation they toured the countryside around Oxford performing set-piece ballads, songs, and dramatic and comic interludes.[100] Proceeds would be donated to the University appeal fund for Jewish refugees, casualties of the Sino-Japanese war and the Spanish Civil War, and the Lord Baldwin Fund for Refugees.[101]

Murdoch chronicled the company's progress around the Cotswolds as the tour kicked off on 16 August with a performance for Basque children at Aston Bampton.[102] The 'papers seem scared', she wrote on the announcement of the Nazi–Soviet Pact of 23 August: 'And I suppose a grave crisis is on but I can't seem to feel any emotion about it whatsoever. This is such a strange, new, different existence I'm leading & so entirely cut-off from the world.'[103] That day, the company performed at Filkins village hall, interrupted by a speech on the wireless by the foreign secretary (and Chancellor of the University), Lord Halifax. They went on to perform at a theatre in the grounds of Buscot Park and at

Northleach, in a hall stacked with gas masks on a pretty market square festooned with army recruitment posters.

The 27th of August found the company at Water Eaton Manor near Kidlington, home of Professor Alexander Carr-Saunders, director of the LSE (having succeeded Beveridge when he took up the mastership at University College in 1937). After the performance at this charming seventeenth-century manor, wrote Murdoch, 'Hugh & I wandered down to the Cherwell which flows thro' the meadows below the house, & sat and watched the moon rise. A group of white swans sailed silently past. It was a most magical evening.'[104] They stayed overnight at Yarnton and then moved on to Shipton-under-Wychwood, progressing on 29 August to Tusmore Park, home of Lady Bicester, all silver tankard opulence and a pavilion theatre in the grounds. 'I wonder if this is the end of everything at last?', Murdoch wrote. 'Anyhow, if it is, I am having a very grand finale.' The tour, one of the company wrote later, was 'an amusing way to spend a summer … [which] came to represent a sort of fairy-tale close to the care-free prewar period, detached even from the reality of our own lives at the time' – a reality that would very soon feature the violent death of student friends.[105]

Bowra returned from an overseas trip in late August and set about preparing Wadham for war. 'There was much to be done, and we were all kept busy, devising air raid shelters, preparing to receive medical students from London, taking the stained glass out of the chapel and sending it away for safety.'[106] The First World War was still fresh in the minds of many people – one only had to be in one's late thirties to have experienced it as a combatant – and they wondered what would happen if war came again. 'Last time Oxford had survived', wrote Bowra,

> not merely physically but in its institutions. This time it was possible that its buildings, erected with pious and loving care over seven centuries, might be destroyed, but even if they were not, its institutions could hardly survive another challenge on so enormous a scale.[107]

'Decided to pack', wrote Keeper of the Ashmolean Dr Edward Leeds in his diary on 25 August. He informed the University that the museum would close for the foreseeable future, and got out the cotton wool, boxes and string that he'd procured for this very moment. The first consignment of treasures was soon dispatched to Chastleton, accompanied by the museum's stoker as caretaker.[108] 'All the world has its eyes on Poland and Hitler', wrote Madge Martin on 26 August. 'My legs grew weak and the mouth dry at the signs of ARP activity, dimming of lights for traffic etc. I can't help feeling awfully scared and miserable.'[109] It was a 'night-mare life', she wrote, 'waiting for news from the wireless, everybody *waiting* for the final word.'[110]

On the same day, C.S. Lewis and Reading University academic and fellow Inkling Hugo Dyson began a river tour aboard Warnie's cabin cruiser, *Bosphorus*, setting off from Salter's Boatyard (located then at today's Head of the River pub). Having rejoined the army, Warnie couldn't make the trip, and so the Lewis family doctor and honorary Inkling, Robert Harvard, was enlisted as navigator. The party met at Folly Bridge, spirits high despite news of the Nazi–Soviet Pact, the men looking forward to a break from politics and the daily routine.[111] They stopped at the Trout that evening, debating the Renaissance, and then progressed through darkness to the Rose Revived at Newbridge. The following morning, Sunday, the voyage continued. They moored at Tadpole Bridge and walked to church at Buckland. Moving on, over the ensuing days they visited Radcote, Lechlade and Inglesham. On Friday 1 September, approaching Oxford on the return journey, they learned at midday that Germany had invaded Poland. 'The news broke on us, I think, at Godstow', wrote Harvard, 'and the return to Oxford was in an unnatural silence.'[112] The friends agreed to meet that night at the Clarendon Hotel to take stock of the situation. Attempting to lift their spirits, Lewis said: 'Well, at any rate we now have far less chance of dying of cancer.'[113]

On that same day, 1 September, the city's first trial run of full blackout regulations occurred, and OUP evacuated its London premises, moving lock, stock and barrel to Oxford, a 'Maginot Line' of files, manuscripts and proof copies sent to Southfield House on Hill Top Road, Headington.[114] Learning of the invasion, Trevor-Roper drove back from Northumberland without headlights, a policeman having told him to switch them off because of the blackout. Arriving in Oxford he found Merton preparing to receive refugees, and walked round to Christ Church to see Pakenham, whom he found reclining on a camp bed, expecting to join the army and preparing 'for the rigours to come'.[115]

On that decisive day the War Office telegrammed the University: 'Convene Joint Recruiting Board and proceed to function'. This was the signal to activate the Board under Lindsay's chairmanship that would interview student volunteers in the Clarendon Building.[116] The following day the bursar of Exeter College published a notice asking for volunteers to help dig trenches in the Fellows' Garden.[117] The first Jesus fellows were given permission to leave Oxford to serve with the Officers' Training Corps, and preparations were made to store the college's valuables, the pictures packed for storage in the cellar of Ripon Hall on Boars Hill.[118] On holiday in Savoy when German troops crossed the Polish border, A.J.P. Taylor and his family decided to make a dash for home, French troops mobilizing as they tore across France.[119]

People rushed to buy the *Oxford Mail* from street sellers shouting out the news. Britain was at war, and that day's special edition contained a warning to Oxford's residents about the threat of air raids.[120] 'The worst has now been declared', wrote Madge Martin.

> Since we have had no reply to Britain's final offer, we are now at *war with Germany*. It is all too horrible to contemplate and we dare not think of the horrors to come ... We expected it, but one always hopes till the end.[121]

The announcement came over the wireless at 11.15 a.m. At the Pear Tree pub in Hook Norton a huddle of locals crowded around landlady Mrs Heritage's radio.[122] It being a Sunday morning, many people were at church as opposed to the pub, including Mansfield's nonconformist flock, assembled for its first service in the University Church, the college having already been annexed by the Admiralty. Madge Martin left her house in Wellington Place and walked the short distance to St Michael's on Cornmarket, where her husband Robert was in the middle of morning prayer. She slipped him a note saying that war had begun. 'Gas attacks were expected at once', Reverend Martin wrote, but fortunately his parishioners had for months been carrying their gasmasks wherever they went. Though a few left immediately, most heeded the plea of the preacher, Bishop Edmund Sara of Jamaica, and remained for Holy Communion.[123] Bishop of Oxford Kenneth Kirk distributed a message across the diocese: 'As a Christian nation we are pledged to do our utmost to check this constant aggression upon the freedom of others, even though it involves us all in all the agony of war.'[124]

Edmund Blunden was at his flat in North Oxford with St Catherine's student Laurence Brander when they heard the radio announcement.[125] 'We walked to Port Meadow, anywhere, and back past Binsey and Godstow. The aspens shone, the river was illuminated with white columns of clouds and sapphire sky-reflections.'[126] Before returning to the flat they stopped at the Dewdrop Inn in Summertown, where 'we drank in the bitterness to come'.[127] Arriving at Dieppe as war was declared, A.J.P. Taylor and his family abandoned the car in their panic to cross the Channel.[128]

It had begun. The talking and politicking were over. At that moment, this city, of factory chimneys as well as dreaming spires, was just like any other in Britain, stoically facing the prospect of war, though with none of the enthusiasm of 1914.

FOUR

CONSCRIPTION
AND REQUISITIONING

The impact of war was immediate. Some 2,000 evacuees arrived in Oxford by rail on the day it started. St Hilda's first contingent of sixty mothers and children arrived the following day, and over 8,000 evacuees had entered the city by the end of the first week.[1] 'The town is bristling with war activities, and soldiers marching off', wrote Madge Martin.[2] A battalion of the Oxfordshire and Buckinghamshire Light Infantry (OBLI) left for France as part of the British Expeditionary Force (BEF), and other units heading there passed through the county, including the ninety-five Durham Light Infantry men briefly billeted at Hook Norton Brewery.[3] Headington Hill Hall, home of the Morrell family, was requisitioned, all its contents hastily sold off to make way for military tenants.[4] Cinemas closed their doors for a week and the University's joint recruiting board got down to business in the Clarendon Building. The production of cars at Cowley ceased immediately and more than half of Morris Motors 5,000-strong workforce left. Gloomily, C.S. Lewis moved all the books from his rooms in Magdalen's New Building and stashed them in the basement with his brother's help, the college preparing for requisition.[5] Michaelmas Term 1939 saw 1,000 fewer male undergraduates come into residence than in the previous year, a 30 per cent drop. Of 193 students on the books for that academic year at Oriel, 115 now volunteered for military service, 52 prevented from doing so because of their nationality or because their degree subjects classified them as belonging to reserved occupations (medicine and science, and also theology).[6]

Returning second, third and fourth years found things very different as the first wartime term commenced. London University medical students were in Keble and Wadham. All the men of St Peter's were sent to lodge in other colleges because their own had been occupied by the women of Westfield College, University of London (requisitioned for the training of Women's Royal Navy Service (WRNS) personnel). The women of St Hugh's were spread across satellite houses on Banbury and Woodstock roads and in other colleges, including Balliol's Holywell Manor site, their own in the process of being converted into a hospital for servicemen with major head wounds. Returning to Balliol and assigned rooms in Holywell Manor, Roy Jenkins found himself in the Front Quad of Trinity instead.[7] In addition to disruptive migrations and occupations, university life was soon to feature shortened 'war degree' courses, drilling and air raid and fire-watching duties. At the end of that lay the prospect of the army, navy or air force, overseas service and extreme danger.

Across the city, preparations already underway were given extra urgency now war had commenced. Homes and business premises were adjusted to withstand bomb blast, air raid shelters were fashioned under stairs and tables, and Anderson shelters were bolted together and dug into gardens. Huts containing makeshift offices and ARP wardens' posts appeared around the city. People joined civil defence outfits, the military and voluntary organizations supporting the war effort in myriad different ways.

The first air raid warning came at 7.40 a.m. on 6 September.[8] 'I moved the more precious of my exhibits into safe quarters, though nothing is really "safe" against a direct hit', wrote Dr Robert Gunther, curator of the Museum of the History of Science on Broad Street. The Exam Schools building was taken over as a military hospital, its writing schools soon painted 'institutional' green and cream. Its requisition necessitated the 'immediate and hurried evacuation of the 200,000 volumes that were kept in its cellars', wrote Craster, to be 'dumped' in the basement of the unfinished New Bodleian.[9] University exams – moderations, preliminaries and finals – could no longer be held in their purpose-built home, that 'large, lugubrious building with its great Jackson-Jacobean windows overshadowing

CONSCRIPTION AND REQUISITIONING 67

the lower High Street'. It had 'ceased to fulfil its gloomy function for the "duration"', wrote Rowse, given over to 'a nobler and more pressing purpose'.[10]

Oxford's war industry

The outbreak of war saw an immediate redirection of Oxford's industrial base towards war production. In contemplating the extent of the takeover of Oxford, be it sports grounds converted into allotments or colleges occupied by army officers, a view of the city's industry is essential. Oxford was not a major centre of British war production, but it *was* an important one. The cumulative output of its factories and workshops was impressive, manufacturing items of equipment and military vehicles and aircraft, modifying vehicles to meet specialist requirements, and salvaging and repairing crashed and shot-down aircraft. On the outbreak of war Morris Motors was producing a quarter of the nation's cars, about 105,000 a year, and employing 3,700 people at the Cowley works with over a thousand more at Morris Radiators. Part owned by Lord Nuffield, the Pressed Steel works in Cowley, which manufactured car bodies, employed a further 5,000. In the first year of war factory production came to a standstill, and local unemployment soared to record levels.

Salvation came through war work. The Air Ministry designated Cowley a depot for aircraft repairs, and the production capacity of the Nuffield factories and Pressed Steel was harnessed to the war effort.[11] Morris won a contract to build de Havilland Tiger Moths, the RAF's primary training aircraft, and over 3,000 would be manufactured at Cowley. This kind of contract war work brought spin-offs elsewhere in the county, Dent's glove factory in Charlbury, for example, becoming the main repair shop for recovered fabric components such as Tiger Moth wings, de Havilland using its Witney premises to participate in the work of the national Civilian Repair Organization (CRO).[12] Some Oxfordshire war production work was also stimulated by incapacitation elsewhere, the concealed factory manufacturing Bofors gun barrels at Tubney Wood, for example, established after production in Coventry was halted by enemy action.[13]

The CRO was a major, Oxford-centred element of the battle to keep the RAF supplied with sufficient aircraft to mount its defence of British airspace and, later, to take the fight to German-controlled airspace. Cowley became both the administrative headquarters and a major operational base for the CRO, which across the country was repairing 160 aircraft a week by July 1940, sustaining this figure during the crucial months of the Battle of Britain.[14] The organization's job was to coordinate repairs conducted by scores of civilian firms, initially under the direction of Lord Nuffield, who distributed salvage jobs to companies across the land.[15] This represented a major contribution to the nation's defence; during the Battle of Britain, only 65 per cent of aircraft issued to squadrons were new, the other 35 per cent having been reconditioned by the CRO.[16]

The operational side of this work was the preserve of Air Ministry organizations called civil repair units. No. 1 Civilian Repair Unit (CRU), formed at Cowley in September 1939, received its first consignment of damaged Spitfires and Hurricanes in November, its work also involving City Motors on the Botley Road. The damaged airframes were collected from around the country by No. 5 Maintenance Unit and tested in flights around Oxfordshire before being sent on to operational squadrons. Cowley was also home to No. 50 Maintenance Unit, one of the country's two Metal Produce and Recovery depots tasked with salvaging and cannibalizing aircraft too badly damaged to be patched up. It handled 12,000 aircraft during the war. No. 1 Metal Produce and Recovery Depot, to which crippled British and German aircraft were taken, covered 100 acres of farmland between Cowley and Horspath. It employed 1,500 people, its eight miles of highway bearing names such as Battle Road, Hurricane Road, Spitfire Road and Sunderland Road (the last name in honour of the Short Sunderland flying boat in service with the RAF and navy).[17] The depot was the inspiration for Paul Nash's well-known 1941 painting *Totes Meer* (Dead Sea), depicting its static 'dead sea' of wrecked aircraft (PLATE 13). By 1946, Morris and Pressed Steel were employing 12,000 people between them, registering 17,000 employees at their wartime peak.

The Cowley works and other Oxford industrial premises also contributed to the war effort through the production of military

CONSCRIPTION AND REQUISITIONING 69

vehicles, weapons and equipment. They made torpedoes, wireless sets, searchlights, sea mines, tail units for Horsa gliders, tripods for machine guns and power plants for Beaufort and Lancaster bombers. Their premises housed stocks of depth charges, brought by rail from vulnerable towns such as Portsmouth, and in 1942 the buildings at Cowley were reinforced and refitted for the manufacture of Crusader tanks.[18]

The activities of the city's war industry did not end there. Pressed Steel produced over 230,000 tons of steel and 27,000 tons of light alloys. It also churned out sundry items of equipment: nearly 2 million jerricans, 3.5 million steel helmets, 1.75 million landmines, and over 1 million frames for babies' gas masks. The Ministry of Supply built a large cartridge-case factory at the northern end of the Cowley site in 1941, employing 900 people at peak production. Morris Radiators in North Oxford made a new exhaust system for the Rolls-Royce Merlin engine, along with radiators for Beaufighters, Lancasters, Mosquitos and Spitfires. It manufactured 250,000 helmets, 500,000 mess tins, thousands of field cookers, and over a million boxes for 25-pounder artillery shells. The factory doubled in size and the workforce trebled to 3,000. Oxford, therefore, was a significant centre of general war production, and of support for the operations of the RAF during a crucial phase of the conflict. As will be explained, this was to have a direct impact on the requisitioning of buildings, one of the most significant impacts of the war on the University and the colleges.

Undergraduate recruitment, war degrees and cadet courses

Before the academic year 1939–40 commenced, Vice Chancellor Gordon asked students who were expecting to resume or begin their studies to notify their colleges as to 'whether they had already taken some form of National Service or whether for the time being at any rate they are at liberty to come into residence next Term, and desire to do so'.[19] When war began, men aged 20 and 21 were conscripted, though call-up papers could take time to be sent out, so it was still possible for men in this age group, along with the 18- and 19-year-olds, to volunteer.

The joint recruiting board established by the War Office at Oxford and administered by the Ministry of Labour consisted of representatives of the armed forces, the science departments and the ministry, Lindsay in the chair. Particulars of those covered by reserved occupations were sent to the ministry, while others were interviewed to see if they were suitable for officer training or whether they should be called up in the normal way. The board could recommend a particular type of employment in the armed forces that might best suit a candidate's accomplishments and skills.[20] 'Generally speaking, they were either recommended for training at an ... OCTU [Officer Cadet Training Unit] or, in the case of scientific or medical students, instructed to continue with their studies.'[21] Students presenting themselves to volunteer assembled in the Sheldonian, where they filled out form 'C' while waiting to be called in to interview.[22]

Addressing the University community on 7 September, Gordon declared that

> The principal activity of the University at the present time is the interviewing of the large number of undergraduates and resident graduates under 25 who have offered themselves for National Service through the agency of the Joint Recruiting Board now sitting in Oxford ... It does not deal with Freshmen.
>
> All undergraduates who undertake any form of National Service may be assured that that service will be recognized when arrangements come to be made for the continuation of their academic careers.
>
> There will remain over and above the reserved classes of medical and science students, a substantial number of undergraduates as well as of Freshmen not yet matriculated who are not at present needed for National Service. A certain number of University and College buildings have been taken over for hospital and other purposes, but the University and Colleges will do their best to enable normal academic life, so far as this is possible, to be maintained.[23]

Of a potential group of 3,000 volunteers, 2,362 came forward.[24] Of those who did not, some simply did not want to do so, or do so at that time, happy perhaps to allow the wheels of bureaucracy to turn and their call-up papers to arrive. Some students were conscientious objectors and refused to serve.[25] There were then those declared medically unfit or invalided out of the forces, able therefore to undertake full three- or four-year degrees courses, Philip Larkin among them. 'With our artificial legs, our glass eyes, our deflated lungs, our asthma, our heart diseases', wrote John Wain of St John's (a future Professor of Poetry), 'we limped about, discussing Shakespeare and Milton amid the skirling of huge lorries running in four-wheel drive'.[26]

There were various ways of going about things: with war declared during the long vacation, Denis Healey volunteered immediately and assumed he'd soon be called up, and that his final year reading Classics at Balliol would simply have to wait. He didn't return to Oxford when term began a month later, but the call didn't come. Eventually advised to go back to college, by the time he got there he'd missed most of the term and someone else had taken his job as JCR president (he'd succeeded Heath). Many other men were in the same boat. With little confidence that they would survive the war, 'we were not very concerned with our examinations. The year of the phoney war was accompanied by a year of phoney academia.'[27] Healey was to play out his final year nonetheless, before the army finally claimed him. He sat down to the first of twenty-four gruelling Greats papers 'on that hot summer day when German motor cycles roared into Abbeville, just across the Channel'.[28]

The University Officers' Training Corps (UOTC) under Colonel Cyril Wilkinson was based in Manor Road.[29] Wilkinson happened to be English fellow, librarian and dean at Worcester College. A former officer in the Coldstream Guards, he was also Defence Commander for Oxford city.[30] The UOTC initially held voluntary courses of instruction, advising its recruits thus: 'Canvas clothes will be provided; uniforms may or may not be available; gentlemen should bring with them some old clothes.' There were two divisions, each parading on three afternoons and one morning a week. The plan was that when called up 'at 20 these men will go to an Other Ranks Training Unit exactly the same way as members of Home Defence Battalions or those who have belonged neither to an OTC or Home Defence Battalion.'[31] Douglas Ross's first UOTC muster in the Town Hall was divided into those going for the Royal Artillery ('the Gunners'), the Royal Corps of Signals ('Signallers') and the infantry, with some heading for the tank corps or the cavalry. Several times a week he would go to the UOTC's 'dismal collection of huts' on Manor Road, with its tank and mock turret.[32] Eversley Belfield joined the UOTC's Royal Artillery division 'largely to avoid being called up into the infantry'.[33] Other Pembroke men joined the Gunners too, as they had horses, which cadets were allowed to exercise. Belfield would like to have joined the University Air Squadron, but it was, he'd been led to believe, 'an elite organisation and one seemed to need a private income … [I]ts casualties were extremely high, few surviving; the same was true of the Fleet Air Arm which some Pembroke men volunteered to join.'[34]

The RAF had a particular appeal to many students because it was associated with notions of 'clean' combat and chivalry. Australian-born Richard Hillary, a student at Trinity and member of the University Air Squadron, described the appeal of flying to a pacifist fellow student, David Rutter. 'I have none of your sentiments about killing, much as I admire them', Hillary said.

> In a fighter plane, I believe, we have found a way to return to war as it ought to be, war which is individual combat between two people, in which one either kills or is killed. It's exciting, it's individual, and its disinterested. I shan't be sitting behind a long-range gun working out how to kill people sixty miles away. I shan't get maimed: either I shall get killed or I shall get a few pleasant putty medals and enjoy being stared at in night clubs.[35]

Men like John Harper-Nelson got on with enjoying university life while they could, aware that military service awaited them. When the call-up age was reduced to 18 in March 1941, it became necessary for him to obtain an exemption in order to continue his studies. As was the procedure, this was granted on condition that he enrol in one of the armed services' officer training organizations. He opted for the army, membership of the UOTC meaning that, on being called up proper, he only needed to do an abbreviated recruits' course before going to an OCTU. Harper-Nelson now began regular training exercises in Christ Church meadow, members of the University Officers' Training Corps automatically becoming Home Guardsmen.

> Yells from the RSM [Regimental Sergeant Major] echoed over the meadows ['Mister Lord Fitzmaurice Sir!'] as we marched or counter-marched up and down the Broad Walk, or charged with fixed bayonets at the straw filled dummies lined up on the grass outside Merton. 'Come on, Sir, show a bit of aggression, we don't want them to die laughing'.[36]

The trainee warriors took turns leading 'sections in mock attacks across the meadows, trying to avoid the cowpats as we tumbled to the ground and pretended to engage some distant enemy'.[37] The men would hurl themselves down at shouts of 'Under fire!', 'crawling past cowpats that were becoming depressingly familiar – down, crawl, observe, fire'.[38]

For all too many of these young men, their time in university training organizations would lead to the regular forces and untimely death. Tom Roberts went to Hertford to read engineering in Michaelmas 1939. A keen photographer, he took snaps of the Bridge of Sighs and the sleek lines of the New Bodleian from his bedroom window, his camera accompanying him on picnics and punting expeditions.[39] Turning 19 the following term, he joined the Royal Engineers, dying in France shortly after the Normandy landings. Foreign Secretary Anthony Eden's eldest, Simon, went up to Christ Church in 1942, joined the RAF in 1943, and was killed in Burma (present-day Myanmar) in 1945.

Adjusting to the need for shortened periods of undergraduate residence, the University issued a 'War Decrees' amendment to the 'Exam Decrees and Regulations'.[40]

> The underlying principles, agreed in outline in Michaelmas term 1939, were simple enough. Undergraduates who faced the call-up were to be examined on the basis of a shortened curriculum, and provided they satisfied the examiners would obtain a special certificate. This, together with a period of military service in lieu of residence, would qualify the holder for a war degree. A war degree, however, was not to be confused with a peacetime honours degree. At the end of the war the holders of a war degree would be entitled to return to Oxford and to convert it into a full honours degree. Faculty boards rapidly instituted shortened honours courses based on 'sections' – one-term of courses examined at the end of each term. In each section it was possible to obtain either a pass or a distinction. The shortened course consisted of three sections, and students were allowed to count the first public examination ('prelims') as one section.[41]

After passing all three sections students would qualify for the special certificate that, after service in the military, qualified them for a war degree. The arrangement meant that hundreds, perhaps thousands, of students would want to return when they were demobilized for further study in order to convert their war degree into an honours degree.

Exempt from military service himself because of defective eyesight, Philip Larkin wrote that although the call-up age was 20 when he matriculated in 1940,

> everyone knew that before long the nineteens and the eighteens would take their turn. In the meantime, undergraduates liable for service could expect three or four terms at most: if they wished then to become officers, they drilled with the un-uniformed Officers' Training Corps half a day a week (later they got uniforms and drilled a day and a half a week).[42]

It all represented a seismic change to Oxford life. While admiring the way students adapted, dons such as Rowse lamented the impact:

> You cannot take away the top layer of undergraduates, the third-year men, and the most active junior dons, without dealing a great blow to the University. Those who remain do their best to carry on, though University life has lost much of its spaciousness, the leisureliness which enabled young men to develop their minds in the best of all possible ways in the most formative years of their life.[43]

The number of male students declined sharply while the number of women remained constant. Undergraduates in residence in the academic year 1938–39 had numbered 3,750 men and 850 women. At the beginning of Michaelmas Term 1939, 2,761 men and 750 women came into residence.[44] In 1942 the figures were 1,799 men and 816 women.[45] But despite these year-on-year reductions, unlike 1914 there was no sudden emptying of the University through mass military enlistment. This was partly because the need to flood the services with conscripts was not as great as it had been in 1914, and partly because of the conscription laws and exemption provisions.

In December 1941 conscription was extended to women. The terms of their service at first allowed them to spend up to two years at university, with a further year of study leading to 'professions or callings of national importance'.[46] This meant that initially most women were able to continue reading for a full honours degree. But in March 1943 the regulations were tightened to restrict entry to women who could complete at least six terms by the age of 20, thus preventing those over 19 from entering, while most of those under 19 would now be unable to complete a full degree course. The result was that from

Trinity Term 1943 most women switched to sections or parts of the shortened honours curriculum.

From December 1942, entry to university was further restricted to those under 18 at the time of matriculation. This would have drastically reduced the number of male undergraduates but for the fact that the University agreed to introduce short six-month courses, free of normal entry requirements, for service cadets (army cadets confined to science courses, navy and air force cadets allowed a free choice). These courses combined military training with part-time study, very different to the degree courses.[47] Nevertheless, the cadets lived in college and adhered to academic rather than military regulations.[48] The courses were arranged by the military and were intended to provide basic training for technical work, such as signalling.[49]

Cadets were chosen while still at school and came to the University already enlisted, becoming members of the Naval Division, the UOTC or the University Air Squadron.[50] The admission process was wholly centralized; for the RAF the entrance exam was a sheet of thirty questions to be answered at home and posted to 'The Director of Studies, RAF cadets, Wadham College'. The cadets were then informed of their assignment to a college by letter from the Air Ministry.[51] Because of these arrangements, Oxford became 'a part-time training ground for officer cadets'.[52] One of them was Ken Coombe, who arrived at Worcester in Michaelmas 1943. He had been accepted by the Air Ministry as a volunteer 'for flying training consequent on an academic year at Oxford under the wartime "short university course scheme" for aircrew with suitable school leaving qualifications'.[53]

> Not only did all RAF service undergraduates have to read a normal discipline [he chose Modern History], but they also became auto-matically members of the University Air Squadron, and underwent, suffered, endured or otherwise subsumed a course and examination covering theory of flight, meteorology, mathematics, armament, signals and so on, to say nothing of 'square bashing' and physical training.[54]

Training took up two days a week, and every morning began with a run to the Air Squadron's premises on Manor Road for half an hour's physical training, before running back to college for breakfast.

The arrival of short course cadets was not to the liking of some senior members. An egregious case involved Sir John Townshend, Wykeham Professor of Physics and head of the Electrical Laboratory (which along with the Clarendon Laboratory made up Oxford's physics provision), an outmoded figure who had taken up his professorship in 1900. His reluctance to teach cadets and obstructiveness on the matter led to a formal complaint to the vice chancellor. This prompted a full-blown enquiry and the appointment by Hebdomadal Council of an investigative and adjudicatory Visitorial Board. The Board, comprising the vice chancellor, five heads of house and the proctors, conducted seven meetings over the course of summer 1941 and received witness statements. Concluding its investigation, the board pronounced 'sentence of deprivation of Professorship', and Townshend resigned before he was sacked.[55]

The novel situation, in which students entered the University on short military courses alongside those admitted 'normally' for degrees, meant that the background of Oxford students shifted perceptibly, becoming more diverse. Men such as the future actor Richard Burton, a miner's son from the Rhondda, entered the lists in greater number than ever before. Cadet-course students formed a distinct element of wartime Oxford's academic population. 'The place of these army students in the College was slightly uncertain', one of them remarked. 'Though *in* the College, we were not quite *of* it.' Nevertheless, 'they signed the Admissions Register, played an active part in College life, and some of them remembered being made very welcome by the "ordinary" undergraduates.'[56]

Dons and university teaching

Universities contributed to the war effort by supplying academic staff for government service, as well as providing real estate and student recruits. By 1944 over 30 per cent of full-time postholders in British universities were absent from their posts, the expansion of the higher grades of the civil service necessitated by war absorbing them into the machinery of state.[57]

As well as preparing for the requisition of buildings and the recruitment of students, the University had made moves before the outbreak

CONSCRIPTION AND REQUISITIONING 77

to ascertain what academic staff might do if war came. In April 1939 the vice chancellor had asked any senior members who had been approached about government work in the event of war to inform him.[58] The replies offer insights into the type of war work performed by dons. J.H. Whitfield, university lecturer in Italian, was going into censorship, as were several others. G.F. Hudson of All Souls said he was going to work for Chatham House (the common name for the Royal Institute of International Affairs). C.H. Roberts of St John's had been approached by Commander Alastair Denniston of Room 47 at the Foreign Office (the cover name for the Government Code and Cipher School). Others had been in touch with him as well, Denniston being an inveterate gatherer of talent. T.F. Highman of Trinity mentioned Denniston (who would become Bletchley's boss) and Room 47; the LMH classicist Amy Dale said she was going into 'deciphering', and was taking a training course in June; and R.R. Trotman of the Bodleian had signed up for Foreign Office 'deciphering' too.[59]

An irritation encountered by Beryl Power, in charge of of the central register, was that regardless of its existence and agreed protocol ministries and agencies such as GCCS often tried to take the 'private enterprise' route to get the people they wanted rather than stand in line and get what they were given. Denniston had planned meticulously for acquiring GCCS staff, as early as June 1938 contacting the Women's Employment Federation to reach out to universities to identify suitable people, who were then invited to get in touch with Miss Moore in Room 47 (and making a fell swoop when war was declared and the green light went on). Scientific outfits had also been busy tapping up potential recruits. E. Bolton King of the Clarendon Laboratory was going to construct special apparatus for the Air Ministry, and E. Walker of the Biochemistry Department had agreed to serve in a chemical-warfare organization. Richard Southwell, director of the Engineering Laboratory, had accepted 'an invitation from Sir John Anderson to join a new Civil Defence Research Committee'. He expected also to be called to assist the Air Ministry, and, as chair of the Engineering Sciences subcommittee of the Royal Society committee advising the Ministry of Labour on the Central Register of British academics, a good deal of his time would be absorbed advising on the 'best man for some particular war-time need'.[60]

Other dons were going into the regular forces or the reserves. R.W.G. Holdsworth of University College had joined the University Air Squadron with a view to qualifying for the RAF Volunteer Reserve. Hugh Gow Booth of the School of Rural Economy was a reserve officer cadet attached to the Irish Fusiliers. Reverend T.M. Layng of Balliol told the vice chancellor that 'on mobilization I proceed immediately to join the Regular Army as a Chaplain'.[61] Kenneth Mason, head of the School of Geography, had been notified by the India Office that he had been released from the reserve for India, and had placed his services at the disposal of the War Office, MI4 being a likely employer. The master of St Benet's Hall, P.J. McCann, was going to be an ARP warden, and the retired university lecturer-surgeon Arthur Dodds-Parker had been invited by the local ARP to work as a medical officer at a first aid post in Oxford.

Other dons replying to the vice chancellor's request included Maurice Bowra, who said that he would be working in the Foreign Office's propaganda department (as we will see, he wouldn't, and he was probably referring to Chatham House). Sir Ernest Swinton replied that 'in case of war I am to go to the Committee of Imperial Defence'. With splendid pomposity, his All Souls colleague Lionel Curtis wrote: 'I am in the position of a number of other resident fellows who have already accepted highly confidential war jobs, so you can write me off as far as this circular goes.' Edward Thompson of Oriel had been doing work for the India Office, broadcasting monthly to the subcontinent on a programme called 'Matters of Moment'. If war came, he wanted to leave Oxford and get closer to the action (by which he probably meant London, not a battlefield). He had experience as a public speaker, had contributed to Korda films, and would happily take on any propaganda-style work.

Through this survey, the University had a vague sense of how war would impact staff numbers. Pragmatism was essential, and University requirements had to be considered alongside those of the war effort. On 19 September 1939 Vice-Chancellor Gordon addressed the dons.

> Many Senior Members who have filled up Ministry of Labour (central register) cards, and have not yet been called upon, are asking what they should do in the present circumstances. It has already been explained that the Ministry's Central Register, in which their names and qualifications are noted, is intended as a pool from which to draw.[62]

Until approached, there was nothing that the individual or the University could or should do.

> I would suggest to Senior Members that the situation calls for patience, and that the moment is hardly opportune for pressing one's services on Government Departments which already have organized access to the kind of assistance they need. There is an additional reason for restraint. It was made clear by the Government, when this emergency was being prepared for, that they wished the Universities to go on in the event of war. The University of Oxford, with whatever dwindling of its activities, will continue to function.[63]

Despite this gentle instruction and the pledge not to drain the universities, by November 1940 it was estimated that 132 senior members were absent on war service, of whom 60 were in the armed forces and 72 employed as temporary civil servants.[64] This represented over a quarter of the University's academic staff. To avoid a breakdown in tuition, faculties were asked to fix a minimum teaching strength in each subject, and the Ministry of Labour agreed to consult the University before civil service posts were offered to academic staff. The situation encouraged some 'federal' solutions that were to be of long-lasting benefit, such as pooling of tutorial resources. While the tutor drought caused difficulties for all arts subjects, it also encouraged intercollegiate teaching and a reassessment of the tutorial system, resulting in a University-wide senior tutors' committee'.[65]

Nevertheless, grave concerns were aroused regarding the University's capacity to continue to function, with buildings requisitioned and staff departing.[66] A newspaper article in summer 1940 entitled 'War-Time Oxford: Prospects for Next Term' attempted to reassure parents and schoolmasters who were asking 'Is there going to be a next term?'[67] The year's final edition of the *Oxford Magazine* (an in-house publication for senior members) said that the 'question of whether the University will reopen in October can only be determined by the course of the war in the next few months'.[68] There was a nationwide fear that arts faculties might collapse, in the face of which humanities scholars, while acknowledging the special place of science in wartime, argued that the arts played a vital part in higher education's contribution to life, society and civilization.[69] 'In the future there would be a need, perhaps greater than ever before, for trained minds, historical perspectives, understanding other nations and for fully educated teachers.'[70]

Education Secretary R.A. Butler was concerned, and 'wondered whether the virtual decapitation of universities under the arrangements being made by the Ministry of Labour were justified'.[71] Related to this was the prospect of reductions in state aid given the national emergency. Butler thought that the government had 'abandoned the universities' by leaving them to the University Grants Commission (UGC), which advised government on financial distributions to universities. It was, Butler said, unconnected to any government department except the Treasury, which 'took a skeleton-like view of universities'.[72] But the UGC was not a Treasury lapdog: when Treasury official F.N. Tribe indicated that cuts to universities might be on the cards because of the war, instancing the dramatic economies being made in grant support for museums, the arts and music, the UGC's Mr Beresford protested. Replying, he wrote that from his past experience of years working for the Treasury

> I well realized My Lords' [of the Treasury's] propensity for trampling on the weak, but that the Universities stood for Civilization with a capital C and appealed to him [Tribe] as an Oxford man. I think this somewhat immoral shaft went home.[73]

University leaders took every opportunity to proclaim the value of their institutions. Replying to a fraternal message of support from Harvard and Yale in 1941, the vice chancellors of Oxford and Cambridge said that the role of British universities in wartime was 'to maintain the continuity of scholarship and to keep, even in these days, the standards of knowledge unimpaired and the source of truth unsoiled'.[74] A platitudinous statement, but one representing a fundamental verity exposed by a war against foes seeking to expunge cultures and rewrite history. With the battle against fascism joined, the universities 'saw themselves as custodians of civilised values', and this was one of the key arguments presented to the Treasury for sustaining the level of grant support: universities needed it to help them function in war and help the country recover when peace returned.[75]

One way in which the University was able to demonstrate its utility was by conferring honorary degrees on eminent people from threatened or conquered nations. Oxford honorary degrees were increasingly deployed for diplomatic purposes.[76] Early in the conflict Edvard Beneš, leader of the Czech government in exile, was awarded a degree (and spoke at the Union), and Queen Wilhelmina of the Netherlands and King Haakon of Norway were similarly honoured. In 1941, courting an important neutral ally, a degree was conferred on Portuguese prime minister António Salazar, greeted by a welter of positive publicity in a region of strategic moment. A cock-a-hoop British diplomat remarked that the award and its reception in Portugal was 'first-class propaganda for our cause'.[77]

The conferment of honorary degrees was a two-way process, for when a conferee accepted an award, even *in absentia*, the ceremony allowed him or her to make a statement in reply. This is what President Roosevelt did in June 1941 when, amid great ceremony, he received an honorary Oxford degree at Harvard. Delivered on his behalf by Major General Edwin M. Watson, Secretary to the President, his speech read:

> All the world can be enriched by a new symbol which supports truth and the search for truth. In days like these, therefore, we rejoice that this Special Convocation, in breaking all historic precedent, does so in the great cause of preserving the free learning and the civil liberties which have grown stone upon stone in *our* lands throughout the centuries. That is why I am proud to be permitted to have a part.
>
> It is right that this unfettered search for truth 'is universal and knows no restriction of place or race or creed'.[78]

Requisition

One often reads that Hitler fancied Oxford as his capital once Britain had been conquered, nearby Blenheim Palace earmarked as his country residence. Less often remarked is the fact that Oxford, along with other towns and cities, became an extension of Churchill's wartime capital as elements of the state migrated from London. The prime minister himself used the stately home at Ditchley Park, a couple of miles north of Blenheim, as a weekend headquarters when the Luftwaffe threat to the official prime ministerial country residence, Chequers in Buckinghamshire, was considered too great.[79]

Because of its proximity to London, its good transport and tele-communication links, and its high volume of real estate suitable for official purposes, Oxford was well placed to accommodate part of London's overspill. Military and civilian government agencies decamped from grey London ministries and opened for business among the quads, as did hospitals, training establishments, clandestine military outfits, and the gentle propagandists of the British Council and would-be seers of Chatham House, who fed the Foreign Office with up-to-date assessments of areas of interest around the world. A 1943 cartoon showed two bowler-hatted civil servants walking across Corpus Christi College's front quad. 'Balliol may be a bit earlier', one was saying, 'but this is one of the oldest Ministries in the University.'[80]

Under the machinery established before the war, the University Registry, in the form of Douglas Veale, would act as the broker fielding government requisition requests from the Ministry of Works and connecting them to appropriate University and college buildings.

Committee N would then deal with all matters of compensation and recovery of losses attributable to requisitioning. Its chair, St John's bursar Ronald Hart-Synnot, explained the set up:

> Hebdomadal Council has deputed to a committee consisting of six Estate Bursars, the Registrar, the Secretary of the University Chest and the Steward of Christ Church, the task of negotiating claims for compensation [under the Compensation (Defence) Act 1939], where College premises have been commandeered.[81]

The committee employed Messrs Whinney Smith & Whinney of Frederick's Place, Old Jewry, London to enquire of colleges as to actual losses, claims to be based on floor space. To help manage the collective University and college response, Noel Dean of the Cambridge University Estate Management Branch was commissioned to report on the rental value of Oxford facilities requisitioned by the government.[82] He performed the same role for Cambridge, the two universities cooperating 'systematically in all requisitioning matters'.[83]

As we have seen, heads of houses had already agreed that rents received from government for buildings requisitioned were to be paid into a hardship pool. The logic was that no college would have a choice as to the war purpose to which it was put; some might have profitable tenants, some might not. Some might have occupants likely to treat their surroundings kindly, others might be full of young soldiers less inclined to do so. Similarly, some colleges designated 'reception' colleges reserved for undergraduates might be full of fee-paying students, others not. It would be unfair, the registrar explained, if the amount of compensation received by a college should depend on the chance use to which it was put. The pool was intended to remove this unfairness, colleges paying 75 per cent of income from the use of buildings into a common pot, proceeds shared out in proportion to the number of students each college had had in residence in 1938–39.[84] The remaining 25 per cent would be reserved to meet cases of inequity. The University would also pay into the pool from its rental proceeds.[85]

Five colleges were permanently earmarked under the government scheme as *reception* colleges for the overflow of students from *appropriated* colleges – the ones reserved for occupation by civil servants or the military. The reception colleges were Exeter, 'the old part' of New College, Trinity, Jesus and Hertford.[86] These were selected because they were concentrated in what the University considered to be the city centre – essentially, Broad Street and its environs.[87] One can see the geographical logic, as these colleges are clustered towards the eastern end of Broad Street, including 'the old part' of New College, with access under the Bridge of Sighs and downNew College Lane.

The appropriated colleges, requisitioned in whole or in part for government use, were Balliol, Brasenose, Queen's, Magdalen, Pembroke, Somerville, Merton, Lincoln, Mansfield, St Hugh's, Oriel, All Souls and St John's. Some of these colleges would be 'able to house some if not all of their own resident members'. But for most of them, some at least of the students usually accommodated in college rooms would have to live out: some in lodgings, the majority in reception colleges. The aim was to keep students from an appropriated college sent to a reception college together, hopefully in the same block of rooms. Students in a reception college would pay to it, through their own colleges, a flat rate of 12 shillings a day, 9 shillings being the allowance for food, service, heat, light 'and such', 3 shillings covering rates, rent, insurance and upkeep. There was a general understanding that, where possible, fellows would be left undisturbed in their rooms, and SCRs left untouched. When the rector of Lincoln College heard an 'intimation' that the army would requisition the SCR, he protested to Veale: 'The College has never consented, or even contemplated, such a monstrous proposition, and I am certain that it would resist it tooth and nail.'[88] Forming a sort of reserve, Christ Church, Corpus Christi, St Edmund Hall, University College and Worcester were 'liable to be requisitioned for Government purposes' but, as things stood in September 1939, were 'likely to remain unappropriated at present', it being important for the University to factor in the possibility of sudden requests for premises.[89]

And so it began. Half of Queen's was taken over by the Ministry of Home Security. New College's Founder's Library was occupied by Admiralty staff, air raid shelters were opened in the cellars of the New Buildings, the passage under the hall became a first aid station, the Holywell porters' lodge became Air Raid Wardens Post A17, and there was an observation post on the Muniment Tower.[90] The Naval Intelligence Division took over the School of Geography and Manchester College, and Lincoln College accommodated army short courses for the first two years of war (resultant damage leading to complaints) and then nurses working in the Exam Schools hospital.[91] Elements of the Food Defence Plans Department moved into St John's at the start of the war.[92] Among other things, the college housed the Ministry of Food's controllers of fish and potatoes, 'making this ancient seat of higher learning', as Hennessy puts it, 'the biggest fish and chip shop the world has ever seen'.[93] A prominent London fish merchant was director of Fish Supplies, the chairman of the Potato Marketing Board in charge of the essential tuber. An inventory of St John's requisitioned spaces gives a sense of things (PLATE 4). Pinkerton Passage (by the President's Lodgings) was used by the Ministry of Works as an ARP shelter and for access to the hall and buttery staircase, where it occupied seven sets. On staircases 12, 13, 14 and 15 it accounted for twenty-one sets, eleven lavatories, eight baths, the Upper Lecture Room, the North Porch and gate, and the North Lecture Room. On staircase 16 the ministry took two sets, the Food Control Department another two as well as the common rooms, leaving the college with two sets. On staircases 17, 18, and 19 the ministry occupied twenty-four sets.[94]

Christ Church took in ninety Brasenose students, accommodated in the Meadow Building, while twenty-five men from Pembroke lodged in the Old Library and Tom Quad.[95] Some University College buildings were requisitioned by a government department, but the two main quadrangles continued to house undergraduates, including men of Merton and Keble.[96] Corpus Christi found rooms for Chatham House, made the Annexe available to Oriel, and accommodated the undergraduates of St Peter's in the main college buildings.[97] Reception colleges appeared less affected than others because they continued to fulfil their basic function – the accommodation and education of students – rather than being taken over by alien ministries. On closer inspection, their role as dormitories for a range of exiled undergraduates from other colleges, along with students on short cadet courses and civilian evacuees, meant significant change from the norm.

Numbers were maintained at Jesus because it was a reception college, accommodating students from other colleges as well as short course cadets, state bursary students training for scientific research, and other special war course students. 'At first', writes Trinity's historian, 'war's impact on College life seemed small, for Trinity remained full of undergraduates, their days busy with tutorials, meetings, and regular bursts of physical activity.'[98] By the end of 1944 it was the fourth largest college, 'and had more of its own members in residence than any other college except New College'.[99] It was accommodating Balliol students in the Jackson Building as its neighbour was given over to Chatham House and the entertainment of visiting troops.[100]

While some colleges were requisitioned very early in the war – even before it started – others experienced a period of limbo, obliged to evacuate large parts of their real estate *in case* they were needed. This was Oriel's fate. In Hilary 1940 it had 132 students on the books, but only 22 of them were in college; 43 were at Hertford, the rest in lodgings.[101] Since the war had begun, the college had 'taken on an increasingly disused aspect', the greater part of it empty, waiting.[102] Magdalen experienced

86 OXFORD'S WAR

similar uncertainty at the start of the war, as Lewis's emptying of his rooms indicates; 120 of its rooms were requisitioned but not needed immediately, the Ministry of Works granting permission for 80 of them to be occupied by students coming up for Michaelmas Term 1939.[103]

The issue of underoccupancy and not knowing what was happening affected other colleges too. Worcester's junior bursar, R.L.P. Milburn, wrote that 'after the medical students had been ejected from the College in June 1940 to make way for the French military mission which never materialized [see next chapter], we were left with a number of empty rooms which were filled in time by officers attending the Army Administrative Staff Course.' But in December 1941 the Army Staff School was suddenly moved to Brasenose, leaving Worcester with thirty-eight vacant sets of rooms come Hilary. All Souls and Brasenose prepared to receive the Royal Courts of Justice, but they didn't come. St Edmund Hall awaited the women of Westfield College London, but they went elsewhere ('Fortunately it was found possible to deflect from the Hall the feminine invasion prepared for it', wrote the editor of the college magazine).[104]

Eventually, 'tenants' appeared. Oriel was one of the colleges not taken over by a single entity but servicing a variety of organizations and groups, some only fleetingly. It accommodated the Prison Commissioners, Royal Army Medical Corps (RAMC) officers, and resting Auxiliary Fire Service personnel and civilians from blitzed-out Bristol and London. It also became, along with Pembroke, the home of the officer training school for the newly created British Army Intelligence Corps. Middle and St Mary Hall quads were occupied by the Ministry of Aircraft Production and the British Council.[105] The latter organization had been set up in 1934 to bolster British influence around the world as a direct counter to fascism and communism. Working from Oriel's Rhodes Building, John Betjeman was principal of its Books and Periodicals section, presiding over around 200 mainly female employees.[106] Like other colleges, the nature of the requisition changed at Oriel; in September 1943 the War Office took over more space. While permitting the college to regain use of some rooms on staircase 11 and Lecture Room 4, it now took over the basement under staircase 15 in St Mary's Quad, a room used as a cycle shed, two other rooms, a lavatory and a coal shed in the annex by the lecture rooms, and Lecture Room 1. It also occupied five lavatories and the pantry under the archway of the Rhodes Building, and storage space on staircase 11.[107]

Magdalen, meanwhile, was adopted in February 1941 as the administrative headquarters of the RAF salvage outfit established at the Cowley works, No. 43 Group Maintenance Command, which came to occupy much of Longwall and St Swithun's quads. This occurred because, with the fall of France and the prospect of the Luftwaffe targeting Cowley, alternative accommodation was required. Like so much of the office-based military work done in Oxford during the war, the arrival of the RAF meant large numbers of female personnel entering a space that for centuries had been exclusively male. Dons, Lewis among them, took a dim view of WAAFs parading in front of New Building (they would have been aghast to learn of the WAAF who nearly set the college alight while burning secret papers).[108]

Merton also supported the vital work of the RAF's Civilian Repair Organization at Cowley by accommodating headquarters staff and Ministry of War Transport employees. As well as the JCR and a lecture room, as late as February 1945 the CRO was occupying fifty-seven sets of rooms (the college seventy-two).[109] The ministries of War Transport and Works took over Grove on the corner of Grove Walk and Deadman's Walk, St Alban's Quad, Front Quad, and, in Fellows' Quad, staircases 1, 2 and 3 save for the rooms of the Classics don H.W. Garrod.[110] The Home Guard were allowed access in emergencies to a catering facility comprising a kitchen and dining room.[111]

The University stood ready to respond to requests from government and the military as and when they were received. For example, on 21 November 1941 an emergency meeting of reception college bursars was held in the Delegates' Room in the Clarendon Building to consider an RAF request for accommodation for 120 officers. The RAF would provide batmen to look after their rooms and serve their meals, and would provide cooks to help in the kitchens, who would also be permitted to help in general college work. Each officer would have a £3 7s fee attached, would be under college discipline, and would take their meals with the undergraduates.[112]

The takeover of college and University buildings by government and military authorities was a central aspect of Oxford's war experience. The following chapter takes a closer look at what occupation meant for the people who customarily inhabited those buildings, and the variety of uses to which they were put as Oxford supported the national war effort.

FIVE

LIVING UNDER REQUISITION

At Queen's the outbreak of war found the few college servants not with the Territorial Army or on civil defence duties turning 'with a will to constructing shelters'.[1] They excavated near the stableyard in the Fellows' Garden, turning up old beer jars and the bones of a finely tusked wild boar, and built a steel shelter surrounded by hundreds of sandbags in the Provost's Garden. The manuscripts and archives were placed in a cellar and bedlinen was dyed black to provide covering for all the windows, the college seamstress and carpenter working overtime. Provost Robert 'Robin' Hodgkin, entering Back Quad one day, thought that bombs had started falling given the sound of mattresses and pillows being thrown from upper storey windows as junior fellows prepared space for the anticipated arrival of evacuees. 'We expected three things to happen', he wrote. 'First, the arrival of evacuee babies; then that of evacuated [government] officials and then German bombs.'[2] Simultaneous preparations were made for the continuation of academic business in a confined space as the college surrendered the east side of the Front Quad, the whole of Back Quad and the dining hall to the Ministry of Works. Soon, the hall's long tables were piled with papers and its walls lined with shelving as it became a large open-plan office for civil servants.

Junior and senior members now took their meals in the Taberdars' Room, communal feeding also made necessary by the loss of scouts and college servants. A new system of battels was initiated (the flat 12 shillings a day student rate) and a new JCR created in the Writing Room.

Arrangements were made to accommodate twenty-five undergraduates at Headington Hill Hall. Like other colleges, Queen's then had to deal with uncertainty as it awaited its occupiers. 'The endless worries occasioned by the authorities' delays and changes of plan, and the burden of adapting the College to its new use, descended on the Domestic Bursar, Major Gore.'[3] The arrangement with Headington Hill Hall was gazumped when it was requisitioned by the army. New College came to the rescue, taking in the overspill of two dozen Queensmen.

Ten days after war broke out, Principal Stallybrass received the order of requisition notifying him that Brasenose had been taken over, with a view to it being used by the Royal Courts of Justice. All ninety 'living in' students trooped off to Christ Church, followed by Brasenose scouts to look after them along with furniture, bedding, 1,450 items of cutlery, and ninety-five chamber pots.[4] And that was that. No Brasenose for Brasenose students for the next five years. John Mortimer went up from Harrow in 1940, but beyond a bizarre lunchtime admissions interview, conducted by a don 'reading a recipe from the book propped up on a stand in front of him whilst he feasted', he was an exile from his own college. 'I never saw the bald gastronome or, indeed, very much of Brasenose College again.'[5]

Brasenose's buildings were adjusted for war, cellars strengthened and equipped for emergency use, windows boarded up, and sandbags deployed and placed on the Old Tower and in its vicinity. Staff and servants on the Reserve and City Fire Brigade departed.[6] Ancient glass was removed from hall and the pictures taken down, stored with the college silver under the bursar's office in a cellar rendered gas-proof. Cellars under the porters' lodge were strengthened to provide air raid shelter for 300 people, equipped with tools, firefighting gear, water and closets.[7] Supplies of sand and water were placed on each staircase alongside stirrup pumps. Gas masks, steel helmets and decontamination suits were provided, and a motor pump procured and housed in the south-east corner of the tiny quad known as the Deer Park, where a 5,000-gallon water tank was also erected. Dish cloths were attached to windows to protect from splintered glass. The posts on Brasenose Lane were lowered to allow for the movement of firefighting vehicles and a fire picket of college servants slept in college each night until the

LIVING UNDER REQUISITION 91

military assumed the responsibility. Until July 1940, the entrance to the porters' lodge doubled up as an ARP wardens' post.[8]

In expectation of the Royal Courts (former barrister Stallybrass attempting to pull strings in order to get these choice tenants), rooms were allocated as courts and other judicial spaces.[9] But this was not to be. Instead, from October 1940 Brasenose was transformed into a mini Sandhurst-cum-Camberley, serving variously as a Liaison Officers' School, a Junior Staff School, and a Senior Officers' School.[10] There was an RAF contingent in the college from May to December 1941, the RAMC colonized several staircases, and nurses working in the Exam Schools military hospital also roomed there. The army assumed responsibility for catering from January 1941, college facilities restricted to the Pastry Kitchen, a new doorway opened into the stores. Cloisters 1 to 4 were used as military offices, and room 1.4 was adapted as a smoking room when members of the Auxiliary Territorial Service (ATS) arrived, accommodated on Staircase III. In October 1943 the Senior Officers' School was granted permission to erect a Nissen hut in the Deer Park for messing purposes.

The activities of the various training establishments that lodged in Brasenose await their historian. But it is interesting to note one snippet, drawn from the history of the US Army's 102nd Cavalry Regiment (later forming part of the 117th Cavalry Reconnaissance Squadron).[11] It had stood up as a horsed cavalry unit shortly after Pearl Harbor, reorganized as a fully mechanized one in April 1942 once it was realized that modern warfare had rendered the battlefield horse redundant. On 1 October the regiment embarked aboard a Dutch passenger liner under British Army control and sailed for Liverpool. Most of its personnel made for billets at Fairford in Gloucestershire, where the regiment received its tanks, few of the troopers ever having seen one before. Officer training was conducted by British personnel with combat experience in the Western Desert, and took place at the Royal Armoured Tactical School, located at Brasenose.

All of this activity meant that college life as it had been known at Brasenose came to a standstill. Chapel services ceased, regular worshippers advised to use Christ Church cathedral instead. A tiny Brasenose presence remained within the college precincts, including the bursar, two professorial fellows, a retired life fellow, and some domestic and administrative staff. While the college battled with the War Office over who was to pay for feeding military residents, its fellows, keen to retain the considerable benefits of SCR membership, including common table, were invited to avail themselves of neighbouring Lincoln's facilities. Lincoln had its own catering difficulties, however, as Veale explained to government authorities responsible for ascertaining which parts of which colleges had been requisitioned and were therefore liable to rates rebates. The kitchen, he explained, had been requisitioned by the War Office and then handed over to a contractor to feed military personnel. While it still fed a few fellows, it had definitely been 'taken over', he wrote.[12] So, too, had most of the college, all its students housed next door in Exeter.[13]

Mansfield experienced a similar near-total closure and migration. On 24 August 1939, explained Principal Micklem to the college's trustees, 'being away on my summer holiday, I received from the bursar a telegram indicating that the College buildings were to be "taken over" on the morrow'.[14] He hurried home, arriving at the same time as 'His Majesty's representatives'. At this early stage the college still had use of the chapel, the library and the Principal's Lodgings. A temporary JCR was fashioned in the basement of the principal's drawing room – 'half common room and half dug-out' – but the rest of the college was taken over by the Admiralty and the Government Code and Cipher School, including, after stout resistance, the commodious library.[15]

Following the practice adopted across the University, other colleges helped Mansfield out. Recently moved into its new premises on Pusey Street, fellow theological college Regent's Park offered 'instant and unlimited generosity', Mansfield staff and students given the use of its hall, common rooms and lecture rooms.[16] The students, the JCR president wrote, 'settled down to our eschatological existence in the catacombs', 'well sandbagged' and with 'an electric kettle and telephone'.[17] Small comfort it might have been, but it was an important one in their eyes, for it meant that they could preserve JCR life, and in their own college's precincts, too. In the end, the one part of the college not taken over was the chapel, because the stained-glass windows were judged too large to be adequately blacked out. It was thus available for the occasional wedding, including that of University College research

LIVING UNDER REQUISITION 93

fellow and New College economics lecturer Harold Wilson, who tied the knot with Gladys Baldwin on 1 January 1940 (five years before becoming an MP), Micklem officiating.[18] But the chapel was not to be used at night:

> So determined and awe-inspiring was the appearance of the JCR as it issued forth from evening Chapel that in the interests of the sentry, intimidated in spite of his bayonet, we have been debarred from the use of our Chapel after dark.[19]

Mansfield was one of the colleges that suffered a double requisition, as the government came back for a second bite of the cherry when it demanded the library nearly eighteen months after the initial requisition. This was intensely frustrating, as it meant that a college that had settled down after initial requisition faced further disruption. In Mansfield's case this occurred because the work conducted there on behalf of the Admiralty and Foreign Office as Bletchley's 'Section 47B' expanded. As it did so, more space was needed. The section's superintendent, Paymaster Commander Edward Hok, informed the Treasury that 'we are now requisitioning the large College Library'. With the benefit of this extra space and more duplicators and extra staff, the section would 'be able to do far more printing [of secret codebooks]' in-house.[20] Micklem protested, enlisting the support of Veale. A room at the Ashmolean was potentially available for Mansfield's use as partial recompense, and there was always the option of building huts in the grounds. Veale agreed with Micklem that the library's requisition was a 'breach of public faith' and that the Foreign Office should have foreseen the need. Micklem was unimpressed, saying that the Ashmolean room was too small, and rejecting the idea of huts. But Hok was in no mood for compromise:

> We must have this Library and the University authorities must find somewhere to store these books. They are duplicated for the most part in more than one theology library in Oxford and, if necessary, could be stored until accommodation suitable for a College library can be found.[21]

Hok understood the college's objections but insisted that 'our necessity was vital to national interests'. Work was put in place to convert the library in December 1940, and His Majesty's Stationery

94 OXFORD'S WAR

Office (HMSO) and the Treasury were approached for the additional printing machinery that would come to fill it when the books had been shipped out. The books were relocated to New College under the supervision of Bodleian staff, where they would remain for the next six years. Less contentiously, in November 1942 Mansfield's Bletchley residents also took over the scullery and kitchen.[22] The windows at the side of the long corridor in the main building were bricked up, and an air raid shelter built behind. 'If you peep into the front door', wrote Micklem, 'you would see a vast erection of sandbags stretching from floor to ceiling ... and the library can only be entered (and that by the slim) by means of the private staircase from my lavatory'.[23]

Nowhere was requisition more complete than at St Hugh's, the college's fifteen tutors and 140 undergraduates dispersed around Oxford. 'Our buildings', wrote the principal, 'with exception of the Whitehead garden, the Lawn, and 82 Woodstock Road with their two gardens have been requisitioned', the exiles moving into new quarters just in time for the start of Michaelmas 1939.[24] The bulk of the senior and junior members went to Holywell Manor, starting with its north wing. It was, wrote the principal in the 1940 *Chronicle*, 'an adapted sixteenth-century house of great charm, with wings added in the present century by Balliol College, thoroughly modernized throughout and possessed of a charmingly laid-out garden'.[25] To begin with, St Hugh's students were also billeted at New College's Savile House on Mansfield Road, and thirteen at St Hilda's. Other institutions helped out too; Lincoln hosted the Commemorative Service on St Hugh's Day, Rhodes House put on an evening party in Milner Hall, and the carol service was held in Somerville's chapel. 'St Hugh's in war time has a special flavour', wrote a 1940 matriculant. 'We hardly knew the St Hugh's buildings, apart from the Library', the one part of the main college site remaining open to students.[26]

In engineering the logistical feat of decamping from its home, Gwyer praised the registrar. Veale's

> extraordinary powers of work, combined with imperturbable patience and tact, have been of inestimable service to the University, and not less to St Hugh's, which has found in him an ideal protector and leader amid the quicksands of negotiation with a Government Department.[27]

LIVING UNDER REQUISITION 95

Despite the facilities offered by other colleges, St Hugh's needed even more space in order to cope with its eviction, taking leases on 1 Canterbury Road and 1 and 20 Holywell Street.[28]

> The last two are fine specimens of old Oxford, panelled, 'poky' in some corners, but each with a few beautiful rooms, and full of character. 1 Holywell has a charming garden, with an ancient mulberry-tree the planting of which is attributed to Charles I. These houses replace, and a little more, the rooms kindly made available for us during 1939–40 by St Hilda's.[29]

In summer 1940 Oriel and Pembroke became home to the headquarters and Officers' Training Wing of the British army's Intelligence Corps (other ranks going to Winchester). This was a brand-new unit, founded that July 'to provide for the efficient centralized administration in one corps of personnel employed on intelligence, cipher and censor duties' dispersed across the army.[30] Like the topographical intelligence organization that would soon occupy Manchester College and the School of Geography, its creation was driven by defeats and setbacks in Europe in the war so far, and deficiencies in military intelligence. The original idea was to take over the splendid buildings and grounds of Royal Holloway College near Egham in Surrey, but the Secretary of State for War vetoed this on the grounds that its requisition would interfere with the education of women (for which purpose the college had been founded). Attention then focused on Oxford. A captain in the new unit, John Russell, was a former Union president, and he was asked by the Intelligence Corps' commandant, Colonel William Jeffries, to broker an arrangement if he could.[31] Soon, Veale was in contact with Oriel and Pembroke, to say that living accommodation was required for 21 permanent training staff and 100 students, possibly doubling to 200.[32] Jeffries and his staff chose to move in to Pembroke, and Oriel became the headquarters and officer training centre. Soon Jeffries arrived in Pembroke with five officers, and the Officers' Wing opened at Oriel under Major Squire Duff-Taylor. Pembroke's beds were loaned to the new arrivals, soon joined by more army officers, and its hall, JCR and library taken over, along with a lecture room in the Old Master's Lodgings. So too were sixteen sets of undergraduate rooms in

New Quad, seventeen in the Old Master's House, two in the Tower, and five on a staircase in the Old Quadrangle. Anthony Leatherdale, a medical student, recalls that undergraduate accommodation was limited to four staircases in the front quad and two rooms in the Almshouses.[33] The library was used as a refectory, the JCR for lectures. An armed guard was positioned at the gate, and officers were billeted two or three to a set. Military personnel were 'forever coming and going', recalls Douglas Ross, 'looking solemn and carrying briefcases, portfolios, and bundles of paper'. Their 'minders' were military police, probably Field Security Police as opposed to Royal Military Police, 'squat, khaki-clad figures, beautifully green-blancoed and weighted down with Webley or Smith and Wesson revolvers'. They 'prowled round all the time and made moving around college after dark exciting'.[34]

Another intelligence directorate, MI1(x) – responsible for organization and administration – worked in Pembroke's Old Master's Lodgings. Army intelligence took over all but the first quad of Oriel, where officers were accommodated, drilling on the Broad Walk.[35] James Cobban, who had been through the Blitz in London commanding the Dulwich College Home Guard, was posted to MI1(x) in April 1941. He spent the next eighteen months 'living in a spacious set of dons' rooms' in Oriel, walking twice daily through Christ Church to the offices in Pembroke. When the Intelligence Corps finally departed in December 1943, bound for new headquarters at the stately home Wentworth Woodhouse in Yorkshire, it was replaced in Pembroke by the Oxfordshire War Agricultural Committee, part of a national initiative to stimulate increased food production.[36]

St Hilda's role was to accommodate students from other colleges when necessary but to remain a 'normal' undergraduate college as much as possible.[37] Somerville expected to be taken over as an annexe of the Radcliffe Infirmary, its students and staff decanted into the Holywell Building at New College. As it happened, the only part taken over was West, chiefly by nurses working at the Infirmary, though ground-floor rooms were occupied by the medical school's clinical section and dubbed the 'Isle of Man'.[38] The college also took in evacuated schoolchildren, and thirty displaced undergraduates were accommodated at Lady Margaret Hall.[39] In the vacations, Somerville let rooms to civil defence workers, relatives visiting patients in the military hospitals, and old college members seeking a break from dangerous areas of the country.

Mansfield Road became one of the most heavily requisitioned parts of Oxford. As well as Bletchley Park in Mansfield College, the School of Geography was requisitioned by the Admiralty's Naval Intelligence Division (NID) in spring 1940 and the expansion of the activities relocated there from London led to the takeover of Manchester College the following year. The work conducted in these two institutions, facing each other across the southern end of Mansfield Road, spilled over into huts erected on Mansfield's grounds, the Master's Field of Balliol College sports ground on Jowett Walk, where huts also sprouted, and New College's Old Library. That wasn't the end of it: they also took over rooms at the Ashmolean for draughtsmen and mapmakers and extensive facilities for map and image production in the New Bodleian. Their prolific output of secret maps, plans and bound volumes also led to an intimate relationship with OUP, the lion's share of the press's capacity taken up by the requirements of the units working in Manchester College, Mansfield College and the School of Geography. In June 1943 Naval Intelligence also took over the Holywell Music Room, with Wadham's permission. Towards the end of the war it was being used as a store for 'obsolete but secret papers'. A paper milling machine arrived with which to destroy them, but was too large to be operated within the Music Room's confines. Instead, a Wadham squash court to the building's rear was employed for the purpose.[40]

From the start of the war, Manchester College had been keen to participate, Principal Reverend Robert Nicol Cross offering the hall, JCR and lecture rooms for officer recreation, an offer not taken up though considered by the headquarters of an anti-tank regiment. Olive Jacks, wife of former principal Lawrence Jacks, suggested that the college should devote its buildings to work of 'national usefulness', and an emergency subcommittee was formed to deal with any applications which might be made for use of the buildings. In June 1940 the Arlosh Hall was opened as a rest room for members of the forces and their friends at weekends.

Two years passed before Manchester College received its marching orders. These came on 17 October 1941, when the Ministry of Works wrote to the principal explaining that 'the whole of Manchester College, Oxford, including the Arlosh Hall' was to be requisitioned. 'I have to inform you that the Government have come to the conclusion that it is essential, in the national interest, to take immediate possession of the above premises … [and] such chattels therein as may be required.'[41] Initially, 'the Chapel, Main Library, Kitchen and pantry, College Domestic Flat and the Hostel adjoining the College' were to be left in the hands of college authorities, something of a 'share' arrangement developing as scholastic business continued in parts of the premises. But as the House Committee minutes show, as requisition orders grew, college activities were increasingly squeezed into smaller spaces, and in early 1943 the rest of the college was taken over as well.[42] The books from the library were moved to the hostel (on the site of today's Siew-Sngiem clock tower and Sukum Navapan gate) and the New Bodleian. Then the domestic facilities were taken over, as well as rooms in the hostel and garages on Savile Road. Huts were erected in both quads to extend office space.

The enthusiasm prevalent at the start of the war waned as the practicalities of requisition became manifest. Correspondence, internal and with the University and Ministry of Works, addressed rates, rent, utility bills (who was responsible for what), times for lunch and dinner, and compensation for tutors using their homes as office space. As the principal wrote, 'requisitioning, like other vices, grows by what it feeds on, and the Ministry of Works commandeered both quads and the tennis court. The lawns have been submerged under a mushroom growth of white huts and sooty outpourings.'[43]

The interiors of college rooms were altered by Manchester's new occupants. The library, once emptied of books, was equipped with chart racks, filing cabinets, chart presses and drawing tables. Workmen put up blackout screens made of wooden frames and 'rubberoid' and installed telephones throughout the buildings. Given the highly secret nature of the work, all college doors were fitted with Yale locks. Sentries monitored arrivals and checked passes in the entrance hall. An air raid shelter protected by sandbag revetments was established in the refuge beneath the chapel, and the college housed water pumps in case of fire.

Tutors were moved out of their rooms: Nicol Cross and the tutor-librarian Reverend Raymond Holt took tutorials in their own homes, and Reverend Professor D.C. Simpson, Oriel Professor of the Interpretation of Holy Scripture, in his Oriel rooms. Tutor Reverend L.A. Garrard worked from a small room adjoining the requisitioned bursary, and mid-week services for the students were conducted at Holt's house.[44] An inspection by the Security Department in December 1942 objected to students walking through the corridors where, owing to an overflow of naval intelligence staff, 'a lot of work has to be done'. Colonel Sam Bassett of the Royal Marines, superintendent of the Inter-Service Topographical Department (the name of the NID branch occupying Manchester College and the School of Geography) told the principal that it was 'obviously impossible and would be silly for the girls to cover up maps, etc, when someone passes ... Two persons passed by to-day and commented on certain of the maps which were exposed.'[45] In May 1943, with the number of female staff rising, Bassett was obliged to approach Nicol Cross on the 'somewhat delicate' matter of ladies' lavatory accommodation, requesting access to the toilet by the library (eventually a new one was built in the Tate Quad).[46]

Keble's war role was determined by the requirements of the Security Service, commonly known as MI5, which had moved to Wormwood Scrubs prison in August 1939 because of the need for more office space.[47] But the Scrubs proved far from ideal, staff having to leave its upper-storey offices (which were prisoners' cells) during air raids, its precious Registry index and files at ever greater risk as the Blitz began in earnest. Hopefully, it wouldn't have to move *again*, but it would be remiss not to plan for such an eventuality. It was because of this situation, and commendable anticipation of it, that Oxford readied itself to receive government and military establishments even if precise arrangements had yet to be made. It was all about building contingency into a situation in which, often, the authorities did not know what would be needed and when, the uncertainty cascading downwards to local authorities, such as Oxford University's Registrar, juggling available space against known and unknown demands.

So it was with Keble. On 24 August 1940 a fraught Major Marcus Heywood wrote to Veale from Room 055 at the War Office, MI5's

100 OXFORD'S WAR

'secret' address.[48] He was worried because he'd heard from the Ministry of Health, who'd heard from the Ministry of Works, that the University would require Keble 'for its own purposes'.[49] 'As you know', wrote Heywood, 'we were banking on having 300 of our staff billeted at Keble' in the event of MI5 having to leave the Scrubs after all, a matter the two had discussed back in May.

> In the event of the College not now being available our whole evacuation scheme will fall to the ground, owing to our increase in numbers and the congested state of the [Oxford] area, where no alternative accommodation now exists. Though it seems most improbable that we shall have to move, it might become necessary, and detailed plans for billeting and transport must be held in readiness.[50]

Veale wrote to Sir Eric de Normann, the lead civil servant for parks and public buildings at the Ministry of Works, explaining the situation. Whatever MI5 had heard, Veale said, as far as *he* was concerned the University was holding Keble ready 'at 24 hours notice'. Whatever Heywood thought, the college was available for MI5 if the ministry willed it.[51] In his letter Veale lamented the fact that some ministries seemed unable to follow the agreed rule that all matters regarding requisitioning in Oxford be handled by his office and the Ministry of Works.[52] 'Why does not the Ministry of Health leave you to deal with questions of accommodation instead of continually butting in on your work and neglecting its own?'[53]

It was a good job that this matter was straightened out because despite Heywood's sense of things in August, come September circumstances had changed, and MI5 *did* need to move again. Bombing was getting worse, the final straw coming when an incendiary bomb hit the Registry. Annette Street, a 'snagger' whose job was to track down files, arrived at the Scrubs one morning to find the machine shop housing the Registry reduced to smouldering rubble.[54] The whole central card index and about 800 files had been damaged or destroyed. It didn't take long for the order to be given to leave the capital, staff instructed to pack and prepare to move immediately. Unbeknownst to them, Blenheim Palace had been made available as their new home. They were issued with secret instructions, to be opened only when they were out of

London, and given a Post Office box number at the War Office so that anxious relatives could contact them. Despite the hush-hush nature of the move, 'the whole operation was blown by the sight of huge lorries of filing cabinets driving through Oxford with "MI5 Blenheim Palace" scrawled on the side!'[55]

MI5 now moved 'from prison to palace' as the greater part of its activities left Hammersmith for the sanctuary of Oxfordshire.[56] Blenheim became MI5's 'country office', its director and some senior staff remaining in London in a building on St James's Street known as the 'town office'. Moving into Blenheim, the 'irony of the contrast was not lost on anyone', wrote Street, 'and I remember falling about with laughter, changing to awe at our splendid venue'. The Ministry of Works had already boarded up the pictures, and vulnerable artefacts had been removed. Men dragged filing cabinets about, set up desks and chairs and heaved typewriters up the marble stairs, and by the end of the day there appeared the semblance of an office, in which around 500 people would work. Registry occupied much of the palace's ground floor, including the Great Hall, the Long Library and some of the state rooms. There were huts in the courtyards, 'inadequately warmed by paraffin and imperfectly ventilated. Though drafts of cold air came in, fumes of paraffin and tobacco were unable to get out.'[57]

The one thing Blenheim and the adjoining town of Woodstock could not provide was accommodation, and this is where Keble came in. A relieved Heywood was able to write to Veale on 19 September, telling him that MI5

> had at last heard from the Office of Works how we stand regarding Keble. We are to have the use of the top two floors, which the Office ... assures us will take 210 billetees. We are to have the use of sufficient Common Rooms for that number, and the use of the Dining Hall.[58]

By December, Heywood's headed notepaper had changed, and he now wrote from Box 500, GPO, Oxford, with the telegraphic address 'Snuffbox, Oxford'.[59]

Thus, hundreds of young women came to roost in Keble, experiencing the delights of college life in wartime. Their number swelling well beyond 210, they were billeted two to an undergraduate set. MI5 also sent a 'lady in charge', four nurses and fourteen charwomen 'to augment the college staff'.[60] Porters relayed messages by standing in the quad and bellowing the names of intended recipients. Coal was rationed and cold and condensation were unwelcome companions for much of the year. After a spartan breakfast in the cavernous hall, the women boarded waiting buses for Woodstock, conductors booming 'Blenheim Palace for MI5' as they arrived at the Hensington Gate. Working for the War Artists' Advisory Committee's 'Recording Britain' scheme, the artist John Piper visited Blenheim in order to paint it. The palace 'rears its walls', he wrote, 'out of a sea of huts into which rivers of war workers pour daily'.[61]

Worcester provides a good example of a college that was not requisitioned and that suffered far less upheaval than some of those discussed so far. This at least is the impression one gains from articles written at the time and subsequently in the college record by both students and fellows (as well as the published college history). Nevertheless, the considerable amount of activity that *did* occur there provides a measure of just how disruptive the war was throughout the University. There were, of course, the usual preparations, such as air raid shelters underneath the hall and in Lecture Room A, and blackout.[62] There was then the war's imprint on the student population – of around sixty undergraduates living in for most of the war, half were short course cadets, half regular undergraduates. There were also a dozen medics living in college in case of air attacks on the city and ten or so St John's students, and the Worcester JCR was shared with its twinned college at the other end of Beaumont Street. The two colleges also combined to field sports teams, in this instance the St John's sports ground being used because Worcester's had 'run to grass' since the groundsman left for the army.[63] A range of military and related activities occupied space within the college. Some sets of rooms were taken over by army clerical and administrative departments (leading to the arrival of the college's sole female, a civilian clerk working in the army's Railway Transport Office which occupied the lower rooms of staircases III and IV).[64] Mrs Lys, the provost's wife, opened a depot for the Central Hospital Supply Service of the Red Cross and Order of St John on the outbreak of war, operating from the Provost's Lodgings. The depot's 200 members raised

LIVING UNDER REQUISITION 103

over £4,000 for war charities and knitted and sewed 34,637 garments.[65] There was then the war-related activity that occurred in the rooms of the dean and commandant of the UOTC, Wilkinson (when not conducted from his Manor Road HQ), together with that of Colonel E.L.W. Henslow. The former commandant of the Army School of Physical Training, he was given rooms and SCR membership when he came into residence in Oxford in 1942 at the request of the University in order 'to coordinate facilities for games during the war'.[66]

Even without requisition, its prospect impinged on Worcester. Fellow and chaplain 'Bobby' Milburn describes how at the start of the war a Home Office inspector was shown over the premises but rejected the college because the lavatory seats in the new though not quite finished Nuffield-funded accommodation block lacked hinges. Then, in June 1940, the registrar summoned Milburn to a meeting. A group of French officers had arrived in Britain for a top-level military conference. But when France capitulated, the decision was taken to intern them 'in circumstances of respectful but inflexible custody' so that they could not pass on secret information.[67] Worcester was the chosen venue. Veale told Milburn that fellows would be allowed to keep their rooms but that all other accommodation was to be assigned to the French officers, adding, 'on a note of velvety menace, that, unless I was prepared to co-operate to the full, the whole place would be taken over by the military authorities under some heading or other of the Governments emergency powers'.[68] Provost Francis Lys took this most unwelcome development resignedly, regarding it as indicative of 'the general dottiness of the times', while the martial dean, Wilkinson, appeared delighted, approaching the matter 'in the manner of a warhorse scenting the whiff of battle'. The college staff worked like beavers to get rooms ready and came up with a zoning scheme to ensure that generals were not billeted alongside lowlier lifeforms. After feverish activity and several false alarms, having been told to expect the new residents to arrive by train (reheating the toad in the hole prepared for their arrival one day to the next), the college was informed that the whole thing was off. Eventually, administration and supply officers on 'quartermaster courses' arrived, replaced with short service cadets when they departed.

Few colleges were left as relatively undisturbed as St Edmund Hall, a fact remarked upon by the editor of the college magazine in each of the wartime issues (1939–42) and the synoptic bumper 1943–48 volume (production had ceased in 1943, partly because of paper shortages but mainly because of Principal Alfred Emden's appointment as commander of the University Naval Division). The college avoided any form of requisition, and remained full of undergraduates, its membership from 1943 changing 'with bewildering frequency, as by then the majority of those in residence were 'Service Probationers' on six-month short courses.[69] Left largely to its own devices, 'the corporate activities of the Hall' were 'maintained to an extent and with a success that most colleges might envy'.[70]

Keeping tabs

As soon as requisitioning began in late summer 1939, so did the number-crunching and the careful recording of alterations and damages by bursars and heads of house. A tariff of charges was worked out whereby the Ministry of Works covered the cost of college servants in buildings requisitioned though not immediately used. (Why should a college pay for staffing quads and rooms it was not permitted to use by government edict?) The tariff covered essentials such as running the porters' lodge, ARP night-watch duties, and the airing and servicing of unoccupied rooms. The archives of the University and the colleges reveal voluminous internal correspondence (University – especially the registrar – to college bursars and heads, and the latter to the chairman of Committee N), and correspondence between the University and government officials (for example, a list of the apportionment of rates made by the Treasury Valuer in respect of University and college premises).[71] They also contain the registrar's extensive handwritten notes on the law regarding compensation, and stacks of letters about the payment of rates, the valuation and warehousing of furniture, insurance, compensation for wear and tear, and staffing.[72] Correspondence also addressed conference trade losses; what if a conference that normally went to college 'A' was now taken in by college 'B', and remained there after the war? What if conferences went to Aberystwyth or Bangor, considered safer than Oxford, never to return?[73]

The registrar, variously described as the head of the University's 'civil service' or chief of the 'cabinet office' to the vice chancellor's 'prime minister', engaged with college authorities, the one side unable simply to dictate to the other, reason and consensus essential to the functioning of a collegiate university. After Veale had made a 'mild protest' to Hart-Synnot, St John's first full-time professional estates bursar and a powerful figure in the University, about possibly committing the University to joint action on requisitioning with Cambridge, the latter assuaged his concerns.[74] He assured him he would do nothing without Committee N's approval in preparing the colleges' compensation claims. But it was his duty, he wrote grandly,

> to collect, from every source, information which may throw light on our complex problem, and so permit of a wisely drafted claim. The Bursars are competent persons who cannot be treated like a flock of sheep. For the last 20 years I have been closely connected with their pack-working, and know their ways. They like to be fully consulted and to be able to have attention for their views as individuals. That is why I scatter among them so much paper.[75]

Archives reveal a smooth and effective coordination of effort across the University. Bursars, severally and in alliance with and ably supported by Veale, worked out how much compensation they would be due. The percentage of colleges taken over by the government by rateable value of buildings was carefully calculated: at the start of the process, though liable to rise, this ranged from 11 per cent at All Souls to 105 per cent at St Hugh's. Other high scorers were Mansfield at 61 per cent (later increased as more of the college was taken over), Lincoln at 72 per cent and Brasenose at 84 per cent.

The impact of requisitioning is illustrated by Pembroke in the first year. Part-requisitioned on 7 September 1939, it was informed by the Treasury's Valuer that the college covered 909,549 cubic feet, excluding the chapel. Of this, 453,864 feet had been requisitioned. The whole site bearing a rateable value of £1,645, the requisitioned portion's rateable value therefore amounted to £700.[76] The college lost on the normal profit earned through catering because of the requisition of college rooms: the twenty-seven students living in would have been forty-one under normal circumstances, and the fifteen living out were charged less due to the loss of amenities in college.[77] Pembroke estimated its net annual loss of income attributable to requisitioning to be £1,411.[78]

Running battles between hosts and hosted were common. Early in 1941 and without permission, the CRO took over the carpenters' shop in Merton's basements as a control room 'in case of a blitz'. It was also angling for the beer cellar under the hall, which, the college protested, was used as an air raid shelter for undergraduates.[79] Harold Newboult, maths fellow and wartime bursar, told Veale that while the college had tried to be as accommodating and welcoming as possible, they faced 'repeated attempts to encroach on the unrequisitioned rooms'.[80] The principal of Manchester College took the Ministry of Works to task because college furniture stored in the gallery of the hall had been carted off to the depository of the Oxford Cooperative Society without notice.[81] He also had occasion to enquire if the college could harvest the produce of the fruit trees in the college garden, which – along with the tennis court, the vegetable garden and the garden tools – were covered by a requisition order. In reply, a civil servant informed Nicol Cross that the fruit was also part of the requisition, but that the college might seek to buy it back through the District Surveyor's Department.[82]

There was quibbling aplenty; the Ministry of Works would not meet the £124 cost of blacking out Manchester's library, it being claimed that the blackout they inherited from the college was deficient, and had had to be replaced. There was correspondence to and fro on who should pay for utilities in buildings requisitioned but which college communities were still, to a greater or lesser extent, using as well. It was all rather bewildering: 'I am glad we have now got the electricity and gas clear', wrote Herbert Gimson, assistant secretary of Manchester College, to Nicol Cross, 'but I am afraid I am still in rather a haze about the coal and coke.'[83] The Ministry agreed to pay for water, minus a sum covering college use, and furniture to the value of £501 1s would be hired at 7 per cent per annum.[84]

There was then the ubiquitous issue of 'dilapidations', colleges keeping detailed records of damages, wear and tear, and alterations made by occupying government departments that would have to be made good at the cessation of hostilities. Keble's bursar, Lieutenant Colonel Octavius Milman, complained that MI5 staff were clocking up more breakages than undergraduates. He met his match in the form of Heywood, another old sweat from the First World War, who mounted a spirited defence on behalf of 'the Service'. He pointed out that not only was 'wear and tear' covered in the fee paid to the college for accommodation, but that the women concerned were resident for far longer than undergraduates (who were in college for only twenty-four weeks per annum), the implication being that more breakages were therefore to be expected. Even so, Heywood wasn't wearing the charge levelled at the hundreds of women in question; 'it is difficult to envisage', he wrote, 'that, among other things, our staff have broken 28 large coffee pots, 740 plates [and] 104 dishes in the dining room, unless there has been a free night'.[85] Far from being their fault, Heywood ventured to suggest that the breakages were probably the responsibility of college servants, most likely occurring as items were delivered from the kitchens to MI5 staff waiting for their breakfast or after-dinner coffee.

Balliol had a singular experience of wartime usage, falling in two parts. From the start of the war, most of the college was occupied by 'the political intelligence division of the Foreign Office, a subdivision of Chatham House' (its work is explained in Chapter 10).[86] When Chatham House returned to London in 1943, the college found a new role 'extending hospitality to members of the allied armed forces'. With a Canadian army camp nearby and an American one at Cowley, in 1942 arrangements were made for part-time courses, spread over a week with attendant social events, amounting to a sort of 'Oxford experience' package. 'So successful was the venture that in [August] 1943 it was formally adopted by the University, housed at Balliol ... and extended to troops of other allied powers', running until October 1945.[87] The week-long Oxford short-leave courses, or 'Oxford University Courses for American, Canadian, and British Forces' as they were formally known, were the brainchild of (among others) Arthur Goodhart, Professor of Jurisprudence, and conducted 'under the auspices' of the Westminster Fund. The master of Balliol chaired the governing committee, and the day-to-day administration was performed by Giles Alington, from 1944 a fellow of University College. Upon arrival course members paid a week's rent to Alington, handed in their ration books, and purchased tokens for beer or cider from the buttery. They took their meals in hall and were expected to take their turn on the fire-watching rota. They were granted access to the library, advised that the gate shut at midnight and that no 'lady visitors' were permitted after 10.30 p.m., and asked not to tip the college staff. Lectures occurred in Lecture Room 22, topics regularly featured including Reverend Martin's talk on Oxford, Shakespeare (by Lord David Cecil), the characteristics of the British state, political theory and the politics and history of France and the Soviet Union. There was a weekly reception and dance at Rhodes House, a bus trip to see a play at Stratford-upon-Avon and a Friday night 'brains trust' discussion. Each cohort numbered around seventy, comprising mainly American, British and Canadian personnel (both officers and other ranks), along with the odd Pole or New Zealander. On departure, each attendee received a certificate from 'The Trustees of the Westminster Fund and the Chairman and Members of the Oxford Leave Courses', bearing the University crest.[88]

University buildings

Numerous University buildings were turned to war purposes in whole or in part, including the Ashmolean, the Examination Schools, the Indian Institute, the School of Geography, the New Bodleian, OUP, the Clarendon Laboratory, and the Dunn School of Pathology. The Slade School of Art, evacuated from London in October 1939 and merged for the duration with the Ruskin School of Drawing and Fine Art, came to lodge in the former Cast Gallery of the University Galleries at the Ashmolean.[89] Rooms in the Indian Institute were found for (buildingless) Nuffield College and for School of Oriental and African Studies-led short courses in Hindustani for officers destined for the Indian Army, also to support the work of the army Liaison Officers' School at Brasenose when it required an additional lecture room and a 'cloth model' room (cloth models being tabletop terrain 'maps' showing contours and features in relief).[90]

The Examination Schools had been earmarked since July 1939 as a military hospital, reprising the role that the spacious and accessible building had performed in the previous war. Handed over to the Officer Commanding 6th (1st Southern) General Hospital on 6 September 1939, an inventory was taken, entrusting to the military, among other things, 801 desks, 1,118 chairs, eleven thermometers, and thirteen umbrella stands.[91] As a matter of urgency, Bodley's Librarian was required to move out the mass of books stored there, as well as the bookcases, as they were a fire hazard and therefore 'dangerous if incendiary bombs should be dropped on the building'.[92] The pictures also had to go because of the risk that 'those hanging in the rooms now being used as wards may fall on the patients' heads in the case of severe vibration during air raids'.[93]

With the Examination Schools out of bounds, alternative arrangements had to be made for the major business of Finals and other pan-university examinations. The Indian Institute, Sheldonian and Taylorian were 'roped in for the emergency', though the main examination centre was the old Schools quadrangle of the Bodleian.[94] This, Rowse said, had once been 'the real heart of the University', and from 1940 onwards each Trinity Term now witnessed

> vivacious, chattering little crowds of undergraduates in gowns and white ties, and undergraduettes in caps and gowns and black ties, waiting at the doors of those old, dead buildings for their examinations to begin … [O]rdinarily in peace-time it would be the High Street that would be dominated during the weeks when 'Schools' are going on by these groups, these droves of black-gowned young men and women, all dutifully clad in *sub fusc*.[95]

Though not under a requisition order, the New Bodleian was one of the most important Oxford buildings utilized for war purposes. In spite of its controversial facade, the new structure's spaciousness – and emptiness when war broke out – rendered it ideal for a range of war-related organizations, and for the safe storage of treasures from Oxford and beyond.[96] As the war progressed, its basements were stuffed with precious items (as the next chapter describes). An enormous air raid shelter capable of holding over a thousand people was opened underground and put at the disposal of the city council. The building also housed elements of the Admiralty's Naval Intelligence Division, the regional headquarters of the Royal Observer Corps, the British Red Cross Prisoner of War Postal Book Service, and the Oxford Blood Transfusion Service. Established in July 1940, the transfusion service held 323 sessions attracting 3,000 donors over the next three years, collecting enough blood to provide for the entire needs of the Radcliffe Infirmary and Wingfield-Morris hospital, and to support the Churchill Hospital when it opened in 1942. The New Bodleian also provided a home for the University's Institute of Statistics, which had been repeatedly evicted from other premises since its foundation in 1935.

The Bodleian's contribution to the war effort also involved its stock in trade – books. It loaned volumes to NID staff in Manchester College and the School of Geography, and by decree of Congregation in May 1944 its curators were authorized to lend works of German law to General Dwight Eisenhower's Supreme Headquarters Allied Expeditionary Force, preparing for the reoccupation of Europe, on condition that they were not taken out of the country. Nearly a hundred volumes were sent. Items and expertise housed in the New Bodleian on behalf of other institutions were also utilized, including Natural History Museum geology texts. The keeper who accompanied the extensive Kew Gardens collections sent to Oxford, Dr William Turrill, was recruited to provide reports on vegetation to the Admiralty.

Also resident in the New Bodleian, the British Red Cross Prisoner of War Postal Book Service dispatched reading material to servicemen incarcerated overseas, a team of advisers chaired by the master of Balliol and including C.S. Lewis recommending titles. The department also arranged for POWs to sit exams, and an Oxford University course on English Literature was specially created by Lewis. Books were selected from stock or ordered from Blackwell's bookshop next door on Broad Street. Before dispatch from Oxford, all books were scrutinized, pencil or ink marks erased and maps removed in order to pass Axis censors when they reached their destination.

In June 1941 Ethel Herdman described the work of the department at the annual meeting of the St Hugh's Association.[97] It enabled POWs

> to continue their studies, and to prepare for their examinations whether technical, vocational, or professional. We send out the necessary books, syllabuses, and study courses where possible, and give advice when desired to do so. We build up Libraries in the Camps and are now arranging for them to take the examinations next year in the Camps ... We send out 'request' forms to the Camps and these are filled in by the prisoners and returned to us for action. London University gives us all its

study courses, and many other institutions, such as Pitman's, the College of Estate Management, and the School of Navigation (Southampton University College) have sent us courses as well. The Merchant Navy Officers' Training Board have prepared a course to cover all the needs of the Merchant Navy.[98]

Through the labours of Herdman and her staff, POWs like Sub Lieutenant R.F. Morgan, former pupil of the City of Oxford High School for Boys on George Street, received reading matter of incalculable value to their mental well-being as they endured long years of imprisonment. In Morgan's case his parcel from the Bodleian contained maths, science, French-language and mapping textbooks, delivered to him at a Vichy French internment camp in the Sahara Desert.[99] Titles on engines and electricity were sent to a POW in Stalag VIIIB near Lamsdorf in Silesia, and a volume entitled *An Introduction to Laboratory Technique* to one in an Italian camp. The department also corresponded with the inmates of a camp in Sulmona, Italy, with the unlikely name of Fonte d'Amore (fountain of love).[100]

Oxford University Press made a signal contribution to the British war effort. Its Oxford branch, established in its stately Great Clarendon Street residence, was joined by the 'London Business' when its headquarters at Amen House in Warwick Square EC4 was evacuated on the outbreak.[101] A whopping 90 per cent of OUP's capacity was absorbed by war work, almost entirely on behalf of Bletchley Park, orchestrated by its Mansfield College outpost, and the NID branches based in Manchester College and the School of Geography.[102] Working non-stop, OUP bound and printed material for NID and mounted and bound photographs. For Bletchley it printed the pads and forms used to record intercepted messages to be decoded, and printed codebooks for British forces and government departments. As well as printing special forms, pass cards and codebooks, the Press rebound publications of use for intelligence purposes, including atlases, Spanish dictionaries, Italian vocabularies and the *Liste Navale Française*.[103] OUP won the government contract to produce one-time pads for Bletchley Park, a deal that 'kept its machines running and machinemen employed'.[104] The Press printed an estimated 170 million maps for ISTD alone. Each week Margaret Godfrey, in charge of tasking OUP on behalf of NID/ISTD and wife of its director, Rear Admiral John Godfrey, compiled orders of maps, reports and intelligence handbooks. OUP was well placed to undertake this work in terms of scale and security requirements, responsibility for printing 4–5 million exam papers a year having 'taught them all they needed to know about secrecy'.[105]

Despite shortages of paper and pulp, constraints on binding and loss of staff to the armed forces, OUP performed a role of national significance and, as in 1914–18, enjoyed record profits. Precautions were enacted to protect the Press's sites in and around Oxford from attack. John Johnson, Printer to the University and an 'unacknowledged wartime hero', felt compelled to sleep on the premises in case of air raids.[106] He offered to set up an alternative printing plant in Juxon Street 'so that in the event of the University Press itself being unfortunate enough to receive damage in a raid, this plant can undertake the more important items of work until repairs have been affected'.[107] In May 1940 the decision was taken to disable vital parts of the Clarendon Press machinery in case the Germans invaded, and to hide unique fonts and technical equipment in mines, ensuring that the Nazis would never be able to produce an original Clarendon imprint.

With so much of its capacity devoted to the war, OUP became a 'veritable arm of the government'.[108] Other publication work declined, though did not cease altogether. Information and propaganda work featured the 'Oxford Pamphlets on World Affairs' series, through which the University asserted its identity 'as a national institution and an integral part of the state'.[109] Shortly after Munich, the historian G.N. Clark had proposed a series of pamphlets similar to those produced during the First World War, explaining 'why we are about to be at war again'.[110] The idea was taken up by the Press, and the first pamphlet in the series, Alfred Zimmern's *The Prospects of Civilization*, appeared in July 1939. Designed to help counter German propaganda, the series ran to over seventy titles, selling around 6 million copies worldwide. The Foreign Office ordered 70,000 copies in English of the first seven pamphlets and 100,000 each in French, German, Dutch, Spanish and Italian. Many different subjects were addressed, often stimulated by talks and lectures. Professor Brierly of All Souls (an OUP delegate) took part in a series of lectures at the Sheldonian in Michaelmas 1939, published the following January as *The Background and Issues of the War*. Another example was Sir Harry Luke's *The British Pacific Islands* pamphlet. Luke had returned to Britain in 1942 after retiring as Governor of Fiji and High Commissioner for the Western Pacific. He now penned an overview of the Empire in the region – quite a bit of it under Japanese occupation – the propaganda value lying in the benign and permanent picture of British rule that it presented.

Despite its war work OUP was also able to turn out, on second-rate paper and with reduced print runs, works of popular literature. Flora Thompson's *Lark Rise* trilogy was published between 1939 and 1943.[111] The memoir was set in Oxfordshire – 'Lark Rise', where Thompson grew up, being Juniper Hill near Bicester, while 'Candleford' represented a blend of Banbury, Bicester and Buckingham. OUP viewed *Lark Rise* as a 'healing balm to a nation suffering in wartime'.[112] For children, meanwhile, OUP published war-related books such as the illustrator Enid Marx's *Bulgy the Barrage Balloon* (1941), and had been publishing the lucrative Biggles series for some time, including wartime additions such as *Biggles Defies the Swastika* (1941, PLATE 12).[113]

The demands of requisition and the movement of institutions out of London reached far and wide. Cuddesdon, traditional home of the bishops of Oxford, was given over to the authorities of Queen Anne's Bounty (a scheme providing financial support to less well paid church livings) so that they could escape the dangers of the capital.[114] The principal of Brasenose had his garage taken over for undergraduate bicycles, a knock-on effect of the requisition of the college bike shed.[115] Apollo University Lodge, the University's masonic lodge, which had moved from Frewin Court to Magdalen-owned 50a High Street in 1926, had to move again when these premises were requisitioned at the start of the war, occupied by the RAMC. From that point on, Apollo meetings moved into Magdalen itself (where college president Tizard rejoined the Brotherhood).[116]

Even the smallest nooks and crannies attracted the attention of the requisitioning authorities. 'Dear Sir, I hereby give you notice that the Ministry of Works has requisitioned the garage [on Savile Road] that you rent from Manchester College.'[117] The recipient, C. Noel Davis, who lived close by at 28 Holywell Street, protested the order:

I am a physician, who has been carrying on since April 1940 the practice of a young Oxford physician – Dr Patrick Smith – in order that he might be free to join HM Forces; also that I am a member of one of the Air Raid and Mobile Surgical Teams, appointed in connection with the Radcliffe Infirmary and Wingfield-Morris Hospital, for the care and treatment of Air Raid casualties.[118]

Therefore he needed his car and needed it nearby. Giving bureaucracy a bad name, within days the ministry had written to Noel Davis informing him that it was quitting the garage and delivering possession back to Manchester College and, consequently, its use to him.[119]

As the requisitioners went about their business and the University did its best to function in straitened circumstances, no one could ignore the fact that there was fighting going on. Threatened from the air, both city and university invested heavily in civil defence, while the army and Home Guard prepared as best they could to deal with the ultimate nightmare – German troops and fighting vehicles advancing over British soil following successful landings.

SIX

THREAT, WORRY
AND EVACUATION

'It was good to be alive even if the world was falling about our ears' wrote John Stokes, an Australian at Magdalen in Trinity 1940. 'While the men were coming back from Dunkirk we sat in the warm twilight on the lawn in front of the Library, listening to the *Water Music*.'[1] Francis Lloyd of St Hugh's mused that it was

> by contrast with the escalating World War that spring flowers and trees seemed so exceptionally lovely that year, but almost more memorable was the unearthly beauty of Oxford by night, in the black-out, with no other light than the moon and stars. And we went down on the day that France capitulated [22 June].[2]

Many contemporary accounts record similar reactions to the coming of war. Visiting American J.F. Fulton wrote:

> Oxford on a full moonlit night with all artificial illumination suppressed, presents a sight that is utterly unforgettable. The lights and shadows and glorious silhouettes of buildings against the autumn sky are sights that few have beheld ... and the thought of any injury befalling these landmarks is so disturbing that one banishes it completely from thought.[3]

A.L. Rowse would often see Christ Church's domestic bursar, Grant Robertson, emerge from the staircase where they both had rooms. He would 'feast his eyes on the lovely scene: the majesty of the Camera, St Mary's spire, All Saints' spire further off, framed by Hawksmoor's arcade'. On one such occasion during the war, wrote Rowse, 'when Oxford might have been bombed, I heard Robertson say, "If anything happened to this place, it would kill me".'[4]

As the war stretched and stretched again, from summer to winter and from year to year, people were obliged to normalize the abnormal. From what one ate, what one did and what one saw to what one thought about life, the war seeped into every day and was all enveloping. Millions shared worries about their own safety and that of loved ones. For the first year of the conflict at least, the prospect of fighting in the towns and villages of Oxfordshire and on the ancient city's streets was a real one. Carrying gas masks, training to pull corpses from ruined buildings, and mounting watch for enemy aircraft and the glow of incendiary fire became normal things for normal people. 'We had black-out curtains and strips of tape criss-crossing the windows ... Jeeps and tanks lined St Giles, and the ratio of men students to women changed dramatically', recalled Lorna Clish of St Hugh's.[5] 'RAF bombers zooming above' were 'a constant reminder of war' wrote Madge Martin following a walk to Boars Hill and Old Hinksey in October 1939.[6] They would become a backdrop of daily life: 'Basking in the garden', she wrote on 18 May the following year, 'the familiar bombing RAF planes roaring away in the blue sky.'[7]

Oxford people knew that their city's industrial district presented an attractive target to the German air force, and civil defence measures were taken as seriously here as they were in cities that ended up enduring significant raids. There were 'frequent false alarms, and German bombers could be heard throbbing their way through the night skies to the midlands and the north'.[8] At the time no one knew what was going to happen, and, as police reports on public morale show, people dreaded enemy action. There were 'persistent rumours' after the Luftwaffe's focus on Birmingham and Coventry in November 1940 that it would be Banbury's turn next, for instance, and the Oxford rumour mill predicted retaliatory bombing after it was reported that Heidelberg had been attacked by the RAF in May 1941 (it hadn't been).[9]

Preparations begun before the outbreak continued, further described here because they were so central to Oxford's war experience. The remarkable efforts of individuals, voluntary organizations, the city council, and college and University authorities defined everyday life. In this, of course, Oxford was just the same as everywhere else. As the author of 'The College in Wartime As Junior College Sees It' in the *Queen's College*

Record for 1939 wrote, squat dug-outs in the Fellows' Garden, boarded-up chapel windows, the blacked-out library, 'and the dislocations of normal life are not particular to Queen's but merely the application to us of nationwide changes'.[10] Exeter dug trenches in the Fellows' Garden, where there was also an air raid shelter. A concrete water tank appeared in the centre of the Front Quad lawn, and college treasures were sent to the Ashmolean and the National Library of Wales.[11] Oriel taped up the hall windows and sandbagged the ornate portico.[12] Fire equipment and forty tin helmets were procured, two rooms were converted to serve as air raid shelters, and attempts were made to secure an outdoor one in Merton Fields. Merton converted the wine cellar under the hall into an air raid shelter and 'a hideous shelter and a static water tank were erected in the Front Quad'.[13] Its treasures and medieval stained glass were removed to the New Bodleian. In October 1939 Manchester College's Warrington Window in the library and the chapel window overlooking Mansfield Road were boarded up as a precaution against bomb blast and splinter damage. In December 1940, oil paintings were stored in the chapel vestibule, and chapel and library stained glass was wired with expanded metal, normal windows screened with adhesive netting in case of blast damage. Static water tanks were installed in Trinity's Garden Quad and rose garden, and by the south wall of the main garden (for the New Bodleian's use).[14] The college fashioned air raid shelters in the cellars beneath the buttery and kitchens, but it was decreed that undergraduates were to use the shelter in the basement of the New Bodleian. 'We strongly suspected', wrote Harper-Nelson, 'that this was to preserve the college wine stocks which Philip Landon, the Bursar, would undoubtedly have regarded as more valuable than an undergraduate.'[15]

St Hilda's converted the basement of the Burrows Building into a shelter for the whole college, equipped with a piano and a radio.[16] Six hundred windows required blacking out, and a working party was got up to make curtains and black lampshades. Members of the SCR, old students and college maids were enlisted to help, five sewing machines whirring away on high table in the college hall, the curtains that fed them laid out and cut on the floor. The pictures from Christ Church's cavernous hall were removed to the SCR cellar and the basement of Kilcanon, valuables to the basement of staircase 9 in Peckwater Quad, and Renaissance drawings and the coin collection to the Ashmolean. The college's sandbagged barricades were said to be 'the most scientifically constructed in Oxford'.[17]

Some of this movement presented opportunities for restoration work.[18] In the case of New College's stained glass, the great Joshua Reynolds west window was plated and replaced by the Cotswold Casement Company of Moreton-in-Marsh. It was decided to plate some faces and other fragile glass and to conduct restoration, including the correction of details altered by the Victorians. The position of some of the figures, especially the prophets, was altered, along with saints' names and votive inscriptions.[19] The Reynolds window was replaced by clear glass. 'The light which then flooded the chapel seemed far too brilliant and brought home how marvellously the colour of painted glass enriches and softens.'[20]

Norman Heatley and other members of the team conducting research on penicillin excavated deep air raid shelters behind the Dunn School of Pathology. At Wadham,

> [t]he new Private Garden was converted to an allotment for growing vegetables for the College; there was also a .22 rifle range used by the Home Guard there. Three air-raid shelters were dug in the back quad while another three were excavated in the Fellows' Garden. These latter were later lined with concrete to make static water tanks.[21]

Wadham's quads were clad in wood to preserve the masonry. An air raid shelter was constructed beneath the hall, and, 'much to the general disgust, slit-trenches were dug in the Fellows' Garden, while essentially cosmetic protection was provided by the boarding up of key statues and the removal of the better Chapel windows.'[22] It wasn't just buildings that needed protection. Aware that they might have to destroy their work on penicillin at a few hours' notice if the Germans came, Howard Florey and his inner circle 'hatched a brilliantly simple plan': they rubbed spores of the mould that spawned the substance into their clothes, where they 'could lie undetected and dormant for years and then be revived for further study'.[23]

The threat from the air persisted long after the initial scares of 1939–40. If Hitler had marked the city as his seat of government, rumours to that end were of little comfort given the activity overhead and the knowledge that German aircrews used the Thames to guide them inland. And maybe the Luftwaffe wasn't apprised of the notion anyway; even if it didn't target central Oxford, which contained the bulk of college and University buildings, there was plenty more Oxford to bomb. The idea that Oxford was spared because of Hitler's designs on the place, or as part of some sort of 'agreement' about not (always) bombing each other's historic towns, remains unsubstantiated. The idea clearly gained currency after the war (it's probably the most well-known 'fact' about Oxford and the war, trumping even penicillin and the atom bomb work), though was in circulation at the time too. 'Hitler's keeping Oxford for himself', the dean of Somerville told Vera Brittain. 'He wants it to look as it always has when he comes for his Honorary Degree.'[24] There were other contemporary perspectives on this matter, too. Sir Reader Bullard recorded the jest that Oxford wasn't bombed because 'the Luftwaffe was run by Rhodes Scholars'. He also wondered whether it could have been because some colleges, in their First World War memorials, had commemorated the death of former German students.[25]

Christopher Hibbert, in his 1988 *Encyclopaedia of Oxford*, writes that the German *Stadtplan* or street plan of Oxford, commissioned by the high command and based on an Ordnance Survey map, 'crucially underestimated the extent of the Cowley factories'.[26] 'Purporting to show the city in 1937, it was actually about fifteen years out of date.' This can be verified by looking at an original copy of the map. 'Stadplan von Oxford mit Mil. Geo. Eintragungen' – meaning 'plan of Oxford with military geographical inscriptions' – was printed as a special issue (*Sonderausgabe!*) 'for official use only' in August 1940. The Cowley motor works are shown as being very small and are not highlighted in red – unlike the Cowley barracks and the railway stations and surrounding rail infrastructure running parallel from the bridge over the river in St Ebbe's to the end of Canal Street in Jericho. This map clearly did not accurately reflect the enormous extension of the Cowley works that had taken place since the map the Germans were working from had been printed. If one looks at the 'military edition war revision' Oxford and Henley-on-Thames Ordnance Survey map of 1940, the size contrast is clear.[27] As intriguing as the notion that the Germans were behind on their maps may be, it is probably a red herring; September 1940 Luftwaffe reconnaissance photos clearly show Morris Radiators and the Cowley works, and it might well simply have been the case that Oxford was not prioritized while the Germans still had the capacity to heavily bomb British targets.

Like the rest of Britain, Oxford wasn't just threatened from the air; bombing was a prelude for invasion, and Oxford was of interest to German authorities. As Caroline Shenton writes, persistent post-war rumours that Oxford was saved from bombing so that Hitler could use it overlooked

> the sinister interest shown in the city and the university in the *Information-sheft GB*, which makes specific mention not only of colleges and museums of note there but also of various academics who were on the Gestapo death list. If it were true that Oxford was intended to become a Nazi capital then it would have been purged not only of its intellectuals and other undesirables but also of its art, literary and historical treasures.[28]

Norman Longmate's fascinating counterfactual *If Britain Had Been Invaded* offers further perspectives on the theme of Oxford's potential fate had the country been conquered. The Gestapo advised that the 'English universities and colleges, Oxford, Cambridge, Eton, Harrow, etc., are exceptionally suitable for accommodating SS troops, [offering] large sports grounds, dormitories and community rooms [and a] favourable location.'[29] The enemy also 'had a particular score to settle with Oxford, which they regarded as a centre of British propaganda between 1914 and 1918'. 'Before the present war started', according to a Gestapo minute, the University 'began in spring 1939 to work on a new series of Oxford pamphlets against Germany'. Some of the OUP Pamphlets on World Affairs had given special offence, specifically *Mein Kampf*, *The Revision of Versailles*, and *The Law of Force in International Relations*. Their respective authors were marked down for early attention following a successful invasion.[30]

To meet the threat from the air, Oxford City Council built new shelters and enacted a range of other measures. Much had been achieved before the outbreak – such as the distribution of gas masks – and other plans were now taken off the drawing board and enacted. In 1940 the Ministry of Health established what would become the Churchill

Hospital 'as an Emergency Medical Service hospital for local air raid casualties'.[31] Emergency food distribution centres were established around the city. The water company 'prepared for the worst by acquiring mobile pumps to take water straight from the Thames, and installed twenty emergency drinking-water tanks in and around Oxford'.[32] People became used to using public and private shelters when air raid sirens began to wail. Born at Corpus Christi College in 1934, scout's son Denis Standen lived in college accommodation on Magpie Lane. He remembers being taken to the shelter during an air raid alert in 1941 just as he was getting ready for bed. Dressed in his pyjamas, he was ushered out of the house, aircraft 'wingtip to wingtip' overhead. He was led to a room below the college buildings, where he sat on the knee of a man who said he was a Russian Jew. This was Isaiah Berlin, a graduate of the college.[33]

From her family home in Kennington, just south of the city, Loraine Calvert 'could see the sky aflame at night when London was bombed as well as Coventry; we were always aware that we could have it happen to us'.[34] After the famous attack on Coventry on the night of 14–15 November 1940, speculation mounted as to whether it would be Oxford's turn next. The threat lingered. The following year, wrote Douglas Ross, 'a party of us solemnly and sentimentally promenaded through the centre of the city on a lovely evening in early summer, wondering whether it, and we, would be there to tell the tale next day.'[35] From the tower of Trinity's chapel, undergraduate firewatchers could see 'a wavering glow that lit the horizon as fires raged night after night in London and Birmingham'.[36] There were occasional reminders closer to home: on 22 March 1940 twenty bombs were dropped along a line from the Wildmoor Estate to RAF Abingdon, cutting Oxford Waterworks' service pipes. The Luftwaffe dropped leaflets across the county in August 1940, and Oxfordshire airfields were sporadically attacked. Malcolm Reeves's sister, recalibrating instruments salvaged from crashed aircraft at the Cowley works, 'found an airman's foot in a boot still in the plane'.[37] A bomb exploded in Littlemore on 9 April, and a Whitley bomber crashed into a house on Linton Road on 4 May 1941 'on a joyride from RAF Abingdon'. The crew had intended to 'wave to some of their chums' in the hospital at St Hugh's before deploying on active service. But the aircraft got too low. Attempting to land in one of Mrs Haldane's fields, it crashed into her lodge (now part of Wolfson College), catching fire. All three crewmen died as well as the lodge keeper's wife. Their son, just out of the bath, naked and engulfed in flaming petrol and oil, was taken to the burns unit at the Radcliffe Infirmary.[38] College properties beyond Oxford were also impacted by aerial activity. On 3 April 1945 a Lancaster crashed at a farm near Wantage owned by Worcester College, the detonation of its payload creating a crater 60 feet deep and 160 feet wide, causing extensive damage to the farmhouse and yard.[39] Houses in Southampton built on land given to Queen's by Edward III were damaged, presenting the college with considerable costs.[40] Manchester College's House Committee noted in February 1941 that there were reports of damage to college properties in Manchester, and that the Cross Street Chapel in the city had been destroyed.[41]

Preparations were evident across Oxfordshire as they were across the country, in suburbs, villages and fields. Harberton House, a red-brick, gabled town mansion on the Harberton Mead road, was taken over as an RAF code and cypher school, soon full of WAAFs learning how to operate technical machinery.[42] Servite priors formed the village of Begbroke's ARP team; Faringdon Folly was used as a lookout by the Home Guard; and the airport established by Oxford City Council at Kidlington in 1935 was taken over by the RAF (it was on a flight to Kidlington in January 1941 that aviator Amy Johnson crashed and died).[43] No place was unaffected: in Wytham Woods, parts of Radbrook Common went under the plough and sycamores on Common Piece were harvested by the Ministry of Supply.[44] At the Rollright Stones, the Royal Signals established a post on a hillock beside the King Stone and felled the ring of larches around the King's Men to allow 360-degree visibility. On the crest of the Cotswolds with commanding views, it was an ideal vantage point for spotting enemy aircraft.[45] Above and all around, war made its mark.

Invasion summer

The invasion threat was most acute following the Dunkirk evacuations (26 May–4 June 1940) and the subsequent French surrender (22 June). Then came the months of the Battle of Britain (July–October

1940), during which the prospects of German victory in the air and invasion by sea reached their height. Soldiers of the Oxfordshire and Buckinghamshire Light Infantry (OBLI), the regiment in which many local men served, formed part of the British Expeditionary Force (BEF) in France. Few returned home, because the OBLI battalions took part in the last-ditch defence mounted to protect the evacuation beaches. In the aftermath of those remarkable evacuations, thousands of British troops arrived in Oxford, quickly followed by thousands of Canadians planted in and around the city to meet invading German forces.

The summer of 1940 was lovely but ominous. Across the country,

> it was a time of anxious expectation and feverish activity. The invasion of Britain was the logical military sequel to the German victory in France; and the immediate means for combatting such an invasion were so slender that unlimited courage, ingenuity and effort were required to improve and supplement them.[46]

The possibility of airborne invasion gripped the public imagination, more so than the ancient – and far more realistic – threat of invasion from the sea. Coupled with this, the idea of the 'fifth column', a term borrowed from Spain, 'sanctioned a new and more pervasive concept of the dangers to be feared from the traitor or the secret agent'.[47]

Oxfordshire played its part that summer in what the War Office called the 'emergency evacuation across the Channel of a very large force' – the Dunkirk evacuations, otherwise known as Operation Dynamo. The plan required the preparation of reception and accommodation for up to 350,000 evacuated personnel as they were lifted off French beaches and landed on British soil. To facilitate this, existing military units in selected areas were ordered to prepare to receive up to 100 per cent of their own strength.[48] Banbury was earmarked as a reserve distribution control centre, and Oxford and Tetbury were designated as reception areas for 15,000 troops.[49]

No. 16 Infantry Training Centre at Cowley was the home of the OBLI. It also served as the South Midlands District (an army designation) Reception Camp, which meant that Oxfordshire's share of the Dunkirk evacuees would be sent there. Watching events unfold from Cowley that May, 'anxiety for the fate of the three battalions of the Regiment in France and Belgium was exquisite'.[50] On 28 May a telephone rang on the desk of the commanding officer, Lieutenant Colonel C.E. Whittal. 'Dynamo', said a voice. Replacing the receiver, Whittal opened a drawer, from which he took a sheet of foolscap. 'On it were details for the reception of the Depot's share of the BEF being evacuated.' Soon, soldiers only hours before on French beaches were pouring in, accommodated as best as could be arranged.

From 4 June, Phase 2 commenced as survivors of the 44th Division began to concentrate at the depot. They were accommodated in the barracks, in Headington Hill Hall, and in Brasenose and Magdalen woods, where large tented camps had been pitched. Port Meadow was also used for this purpose, Major Jarvis and a party of fifty soldiers working in four-hour shifts to extend available accommodation with yet more tents. It wasn't considered an ideal site but needs must.

> There is practically no concealment from the air, whilst digging for P.A.D. [passive air defence – meaning dug-out shelters in case of bombing or strafing] and security is impracticable as the water is only three feet below the surface. For this same reason there is no drainage and the bucket type latrines have been adopted. The whole area is liable to flooding.[51]

A camp capable of housing 5,000 men soon materialized on this plain beside the upper Thames.[52]

By 5 June, 1,400 Dunkirk evacuees had arrived in Oxford. The procedure upon arrival was to immediately feed the men, get them under canvas, equip them and pay them. A further 2,200 arrived the next day, 6 June, and 1,000 marched off to Port Meadow.[53] By 12 June, 283 officers and 7,962 other ranks were accommodated in Cowley and at Port Meadow. Stanley Lester, a member of the 5th Oxford St Michael's Troop Boy Scouts, recalls them arriving. They were

> tired and bewildered and being marched up to Port Meadow where there was a large bell tented area where tents as soon as they were erected were being camouflaged, this would be their homes until sent elsewhere. A very strange sight for us youngsters bringing the war even closer to home.[54]

St Hugh's student Monica Melles, returning to Holywell Manor after a seminar on *Paradise Lost*, saw 'a large group of soldiers, tired, hot, and travel-stained, being given tea and sandwiches by the main gate … Our academic efforts seemed a little out of place!', she wrote.[55]

Students and city residents did what they could to assist the survivors and provide comfort as they were shunted around the city. 'The most harrowing experience was in June 1940', recalled St Hugh's second year Mary Healey, 'when we helped at the canteens and reception centres for our troops rescued from Dunkirk. They came in an endless line, hollow-eyed and grey with fatigue and practically speechless from their ordeal'.[56] The Openshaw family, who lived on the corner of Polstead Road and Woodstock Road, organized social evenings for the soldiers in the hall at the St Margaret's Institute, the start of what became known as 'Maggie's Club'.

By 14 June all of the Dunkirk evacuees had been moved on, sent to divisional concentration areas to join units readying to repel an invasion. Despite their recent experiences, there was to be no let-up; France and a slew of other European countries were beaten, and it was Britain's turn next. Therefore, they were needed to reinforce other units if their own were not re-forming, there to fill gaps caused by what was euphemistically termed 'battle wastage' should the Germans arrive.[57]

How was Britain to be defended, and what was Oxfordshire's role? Clearly, the entire coastline could not be fortified and lined with troops and guns. It was decided, therefore, to concentrate resources to defend a series of inland 'stop lines' while at the same time holding in readiness mobile forces that could strike wherever the enemy appeared in number (stop lines were intended to 'enable the enemy to be held or at least delayed until our mobile reserve can counter attack and destroy them').[58] This is where Oxfordshire came in. It was covered by the mesh of subsidiary defensive strongholds and local stop lines emanating from the major ones (the GHQ 'Red' Stop Line ran to Abingdon – then in Berkshire – and included an anti-tank ditch west from Abingdon to avoid the loop of the Thames around Wytham, continuing along the Upper Thames). Oxfordshire was also identified as a good place to concentrate mobile forces, and this is what brought Canadians to the county on the heels of the Dunkirk evacuees.

Given British army losses of transport and equipment in the evacuation from France, at this crucial moment the 1st Canadian Infantry

Division, 'in point of training and equipment combined', was 'the strongest element in a very weak fabric' available to meet an invasion.[59] The division was effectively the only one in the entire country still equipped to fight as a single formation and with sufficient transport to reach any threatened point. It was therefore assigned a key role in the country's defence – that of a mobile reserve under the direct command of the Commander-in-Chief Home Forces, available to strike anywhere should a concentration of German forces develop.[60] With operations in France at an end and invasion seemingly imminent, the entire division re-formed at bases in southern England. The commander, General Andrew McNaughton, identified Oxford as offering a strategic advantage and, with the situation worsening, the South Midlands area of which it formed a part was accepted by senior British commanders as the most suitable 'position of readiness' for reserve forces.

'Canadian Force' was thus constituted as a self-contained formation on 20 June, and three days later moved from Aldershot to a new 'position of readiness' in the Oxford area, McNaughton establishing his Advanced Headquarters at Shotover Park. From here it could be sent wherever it was needed by the Commander-in-Chief Home Forces.[61] It was organized in brigade and battalion groups, forming mobile columns 'capable of rapid and flexible action'. As McNaughton put it, Canadian Force was 'a mobile reserve with a 360-degree front' prepared to operate from its Oxfordshire position of readiness 'anywhere in Great Britain from the south coast to Scotland, or in Wales'.[62] He had with him two of the division's brigades, the third awaiting re-equipment at Aldershot having served in France and lost its vehicles. The brigades were supported by the division's ancillary troops, including three artillery regiments, together forming an additional reserve group.[63]

Thus thousands of Canadians 'lay in the pleasant fields of Oxford-shire', encamped in locations such as Blenheim Park and the grounds of Eynsham Hall.[64] They prepared a 2-mile-long stop line and reconnoitred routes leading to likely points of attack. Off duty, the troops flooded the city centre, one poor journalist having his night's sleep at the Randolph disturbed by marauding Canadians. 'There were hundreds of them around in the streets last evening', he wrote, 'and without exaggeration half of them were drunk. They were yelling like redskins, breaking a certain amount of glass etc., and grabbing hold of women.'[65] Chief Constable Fox of the city police linked their presence to an increase in general drunkenness as well as the theft of bicycles and the 'borrowing' of cars.[66] Others were more appropriately impressed by the fact that these men from the other side of the Atlantic were here to defend them, Madge Martin writing that the Canadians gave 'a most reassuring atmosphere' after passing lorryloads of them on 25 June.[67]

The threat intense, rumours and strange reports abounded. On 1 July a detachment of Canadians sped to the village of Nettlebed in south Oxfordshire, the Observer Corps having reported a parachute apparently descending from an unidentified aircraft. They apprehended 'a young man with a furtive manner and an accent unfamiliar to them', carrying a map of Wales showing strange boundaries.[68] Soon under MI5 interrogation, he confessed to being a German spy, gave details of other spies dropped from the aircraft, and proffered the name of the chief German agent in Oxfordshire, to whom he was to report and receive the materials necessary for sabotage work. This person, James Florey, a farmer near Witney, was soon in a cell at Cowley Barracks. The C-in-C Home Forces no less, General Sir Edmund Ironside, was interested enough to come up to attend the interrogation.[69] But it proved a wasted journey: investigations and his own changed story soon determined that the 'parachutist' Franz Wilhelm Rutter was in fact Leslie Jones, a deserter from an anti-aircraft battery in Wales. The farmer, for whom he had once worked, was the only person in the locality known to him. 'He had confessed to being a spy partly because it seemed to be expected of him and partly because it offered the only readily available alternative to revealing his true identity and being court-martialled for desertion.'[70] Florey was released, Ironside ordering that he receive a personal letter of apology. His home and farm having been ransacked in the search following his arrest, Florey went to law and demanded compensation, eventually receiving £500 from the Treasury.[71]

Such alarms, farcical with hindsight, occurred across a nation on high alert. It was a time of stupendous flux, as troops prepared to face whatever might come, and peripatetic commanders sallied forth from their headquarters to inspect units in the field. Replacing Ironside as

C-in-C Home forces in July, General Sir Alan Brooke visited Oxford ('a good show but not enough troops').[72] He visited again on 17 September while touring 42nd Division's brigades, and on 20 December 'motored to Oxford to stop at New College' for the final day of an exercise involving 4 Corps, the formation responsible for British armoured reserves post Dunkirk. In the evening he 'dined with Dons' and bedded down in an undergraduate room.[73]

The Canadians' stay in Oxfordshire was short: as British formations such as 4 Corps came up to strength and were equipped, 'it became possible to plan for one two-division mobile corps north of the Thames and a similar one south of the river' – and it was south that the Canadians were sent, breaking camp on 2 July.[74] British forces building up in the South Midlands region now assumed the role of mobile defence should there be an invasion. They were also handed responsibility for the defence of aerodromes and the interception of enemy paratroops. This threat became a focus as the chance of seabourne invasion diminished with the strengthening of coastal defences. On 15 August Lieutenant General Sir Claude Auchinleck, C-in-C Southern Command, issued Operation Instruction No. 23 on 'Air Borne Attack'.[75] A recent increase in German air attacks in the Salisbury Plain area had drawn attention to the fact that across the region there were many places suitable for airborne landings. Salisbury Plain, the Berrow Flats, the Mendips, the Berkshire Downs, 'and a large portion of Oxfordshire' were identified as areas 'in which troop-carrying aircraft might land'.[76]

Preparing to meet landings across so large a region presented obvious problems. 'So extensive are these areas that any effective means of obstructing them against aircraft landing is not a practical proposition', meaning that the maintenance of highly mobile formations able to strike in any direction was essential. The plan was to attack landed forces as soon as possible – 'the enemy must NOT be allowed to establish himself'. Mobile columns in the Salisbury Plain and South Midland areas might be the first to contact landed enemy forces, in which case they would then be backed up by 'field formations' such as the 3rd Division and the 21st Tank Brigade. Not knowing where landings might take place, in what strength, and whether there would be multiple simultaneous landings, British forces had to be ready to move in all directions. The field formations were told that they might have to operate on the Severn beaches and in the Bristol area, 'the Salisbury Plain Area, in Oxfordshire, and on the Berkshire Downs'.[77] It was anyone's guess.

Across Oxfordshire anti-tank blocks were prepared on the main roads. Defensive construction work included pillboxes, which appeared in places such as Witney and Tadpole Bridge as key tactical points were fortified. Charges were stored near bridges in case they needed to be destroyed to prevent the enemy's passage. Preparations were made to place obstacles on potential landing grounds, and the Home Guard were ordered to ring church bells if twenty-five or more parachutists were spotted. Towns in Berkshire, Oxfordshire and Wiltshire were selected as anti-tank 'islands', including Bampton, Banbury, Bicester, Dorchester, Faringdon, Henley, Swindon and Witney. The vicinity of Wantage was identified as a likely site for airborne landings, and here and elsewhere the enemy would be met by roadblocks, mobile battalions and Molotov cocktails. Should the Germans reach Oxford, there were plans to halt or delay their advance towards the city centre. City Engineer Andrew Carstairs prepared a map marking roadblocks on the outskirts and 'strong points' of defence at Bury Knowle Park, St Edward's School, Pembroke, Christ Church and University College.[78]

Another core mission for forces stationed around Oxford was the protection of aerodromes and important communication and industrial sites. Battalions dedicated to aerodrome defence were stood up, including the OBLI's 70th Battalion, formed from a cadre assembled at Cowley Barracks in December 1940. In the Oxford area, their main task was to protect aerodromes at Abingdon, Bicester, Brize Norton, Chipping Norton, Kidlington, Little Rissington, Stanton Harcourt and Upper Heyford, new ones added to the list as they were built. Oxford-based army units also covered vulnerable points at Bletchley, Didcot, Islip, Leafield and Milton. For each of these places the OBLI was required to earmark 300 men, the working assumption that they would not all be attacked at once 'based on nothing but hope'.[79] Army units were also detailed to assist the civil authorities in the event of heavy air raid damage. Lieutenant General Nosworthy's 4 Corps was the higher formation covering the Oxford area, and in this role it allocated two groups, each comprising 500 infantrymen, fifty traffic control personnel, a field company, signallers and medics.[80]

Supporting the regular forces in all their tasks were the Local Defence Volunteers, formed in May 1940 and renamed the Home Guard in July. Oxfordshire's Home Guard was commanded by Brigadier-General Anthony Courage as zone commander, headquartered at the Territorial Army Association offices on Manor Road. It comprised the 1st (Banbury) Battalion; the 2nd (Bicester) Battalion; the 3rd (Chipping Norton) Battalion; the 4th (Bullingdon) Battalion; the 5th (Henley) Battalion; the 6th (Oxford City) Battalion; and the 7th (Oxford University Senior Training Corps) Battalion, in which students joining the army served as part of the 'war degree' arrangement before interrupting their studies and going off for regular service.[81] There were inevitable false alarms. On 7–8 September, as the launch of Hitler's Operation Sea Lion was expected, all troops were ordered to stand to by means of the code word 'Cromwell'. Mistaking it for the signal of an actual invasion, the Home Guard took the extreme step of ringing church bells, the signal for attack.[82] One can only imagine how all of these plans and all of these military formations would have fared if the Germans had managed to land significant forces in Britain. As it is, we leave them standing in readiness.

The worry of war

The stress of war ground worry into the soul, even if it was the done thing to make light of it and maintain the proverbial stiff upper lip. C.S. Lewis wrote that his housemate Janie King Moore believed that the Soviet invasion of Poland (17 September 1939) sealed 'the fate of the allies – and even talks of buying a revolver'.[83] Lewis remarked shortly after the outbreak that an 'unexpected feature of life at present is that it is quite hard to get a seat in church', people turning to God as danger closed in.[84] At the time of Dunkirk, the tension was palpable, and people were on high alert. Because of 'the immediate threat of airborne invasion', regimental belts with braces were worn by soldiers across Oxfordshire, officers 'ordered to carry pistols at all times'. The 'threat from without, coupled with the fear of treachery from within the gates, kept all, military and civilians alike, on tiptoes'.[85]

In the first week of July 1940 Oxford police reported four war-related suicides.[86] Albert Thomas was butler to the principal of Brasenose, a capable individual who (as he put it) had 'killed his fair share of Germans' in the last war. But on 'the most miserable day of my life', in May 1940, he devised a plan to kill himself and his family if Oxford fell to the enemy.

> Here were the Huns, within twenty-five miles of England, and we had nothing to defend ourselves with. It seemed to me that nothing could stop the Nazis. I thought of Rose and my two kiddies. The lovely [college] silver, the glorious wines in the cellar, all in the hands and power of the Huns. I felt simply full of despair, so I privately made plans ... If the Germans had come to Oxford, I will let you into one secret, rather than see them touch the 1800 brandy or the pre-war bottle of Green Chartreuse I should have doped the family with them. The brandy for Rose and me, the Green Chartreuse for the kiddies. Our shelter is in the vaulted cellars and what a glorious end it would have been.[87]

Artist Paul Nash also entered the slough of despond because of the worry of war. Suffering from chronic bronchial catarrh, he had fled the perils of the capital as soon as war broke out. Alighting in Oxford, where he would remain for the duration, he painted war scenes and helped enlist artists to chronicle the war effort, living in a flat at 106 Banbury Road. His correspondence reflected a guilt, shared by many people in places not getting bombed, that he was not suffering as others were ('not one bomb or incendiary' landed on Oxford, he wrote; 'never have we been short of food – except of course all here are underfed in valuable foodstuff like fats').[88] Nevertheless, the prospect was there, and he endured a 'black depression caused by the dark atmosphere of war, threatened invasion', and an illness requiring frequent visits to the Acland Home on Banbury Road (and which would cause the heart failure that killed him in July 1946).[89]

> I can sometimes be heard mumbling and intoning to myself as I wander the college gardens or thread my way through the Oxford streets jostled by the late British Expeditionary Force ... We have had the most awful time. I get very wretched and pray for death. What can come of such madness? I could not have dreamed of such horrid depths of the human mind.[90]

Even when the immediate danger passed, 'the war's pervading despondency combined with his own sense of isolation' fuelled Nash's depression, as did alcohol consumed as an antidote to boredom and intellectual inactivity. Honorary membership of Christ Church provided some relief from his 'ivory basement isolation', for here, as he told Betjeman, he could 'assume an aesthetic air and sit among my betters sipping madeira and enjoying it gluttonishly'.[91]

Nash was far from alone as the insecurity of war affected mental health. It contributed materially to a bizarre murder in the front quad of University College on 17 May 1940. John Fulljames took a Lee Enfield rifle from a friend's room and returned to his own, room 4 on staircase V. From the window, he opened fire on undergraduates leaving hall. Charles Moffat was struck in the abdomen, a second shot to the neck killing him. Dennis Melrose was hit in the chest, Pierre de Kock in the calf. Hearing gunfire, people still lunching in hall and in the Winter Common Room wondered if the invasion had begun. The perpetrator descended from his room and was intercepted at the lodge by the chaplain, John Wild, as he emerged from the SCR. 'Do you know who had the gun?', Wild asked. 'I'm afraid I did', Fulljames replied. 'What do you want me to do, Sir?'[92] He was soon sitting in the porters' lodge with the college's master, William Beveridge, awaiting the police. Beveridge asked him if he was ill. 'No', was the reply. Fulljames was evidently a confused young man. With strong pacifist leanings, he had nonetheless tried and failed to join the Territorial Army. He had taken a dislike to the boisterous set his victims belonged to, playing jazz and entertaining women. On the day in question he had had a heated argument about pacificism with his victims at breakfast.[93] He was described by his closest friend as being 'very worried about the war'.[94] Diagnosed as schizophrenic while in Brixton prison, he was tried in July; found guilty but insane, he was sent to Broadmoor.

Pressure on ordinary people was compounded by the threat of fifth-column activity and oppressive measures intended to maintain resolve and prevent the enemy from gaining valuable information. People needed to watch what they said, suspicion of anything unusual all-enveloping. Edmund Blunden had been outspoken about his hatred of war and admiration for Germany, and free with his criticism of the

British government's handling of affairs. He'd visited Germany before the war and had German friends. Tongues wagged; some thought he was a pacifist, others said he was a Nazi. By mid-1940, his Armenian wife Sylva had been shouted at while shopping in Oxford market, and called a fifth-columnist and a traitor.[95] The home of Blunden's sister was raided by the police, who removed all the letters he had sent her and went through his books looking for incriminating material. Blunden was summoned to a meeting with the warden of Merton, Sir John Miles, who said that he'd had reports about 'defeatist talk' and received protests and anonymous letters. 'I was supposed to be wanting the Germans to win and to have said that I hoped Hitler would come here', wrote a nonplussed Blunden.[96]

The country imperilled, in Trinity 1940 the *Oxford Magazine* considered whether or not the University would reopen at all for the new academic year. In order to quash rumours, members of St Hilda's JCR were assured that the University would only close if the Germans invaded.[97] Bowra, like many others, was convinced invasion was imminent, and lobbied his friend Lindemann, who saw Churchill on almost a daily basis, to get the University closed down so that all its students could join the forces. 'What is the good of looking after the College', he said, 'if, after the war, there is no College left?'[98] His fellow head of house, Micklem of Mansfield, reported to 'The Brethren of the Dispersion' (old Mansfield members) that though Oxford 'shade' was still 'inviolate', 'we have no idea how long one stone may be left upon another'.[99]

Some made sport of the situation. A.J.P. Taylor and his friends recalled it as a period of high spirits; 'we never laughed so much'. 'Strangers stopped me in the street and said, "Poor old Hitler. He's done for himself this time now he's taken us on".'[100] Beveridge bet Kenneth Wheare in the University College SCR betting book that there would not be a landing of more than 5,000 German troops on British soil.[101] In the Magdalen SCR betting book, Mr Stevens bet Mr Bazell that there would be 'a German sea-borne invasion' by the end of July.[102] The grim reality of the situation was obvious to all. By summer 1940 Blunden had 'yielded to the conclusion that invasion was likely'. To that end, he wrote, 'the speedy overthrow of other nations must have been considered a stage ... But whatever comes, let us hope that the true virtue and clear spirit of England will find their way into the new world.'[103] Because they were threatened, people looked anew at what they cherished most. For Rowse, the danger made very prominent the 'pride' and 'deep love' of 'English things',

> for our countryside and towns ... for places associated with names that are the very stuff of our tradition ... for our tradition itself and the literature in which it is expressed and handed on ... Something in the spirit of those things has helped us to survive the danger, so the danger to them has heightened our sense of their value, of their being very precious to us.[104]

While many worried about what was in store for them, the confidence and optimism of youth were also in evidence. In Alan Hackney's novel *Private's Progress*, Arthur Egan prepares to leave 'Apocalypse College' for the army, rather relishing the prospect. 'We've had the basic stuff, training, here at S.T.C. [Senior Training Corps]', he tells his roommate. 'Six weeks in the ranks, OCTU [Officer Cadet Training Unit], nice commission, off to see life, and back to Oxford again after.'[105]

Extraordinary circumstances elicited a cheerful insouciance and a 'live for the moment' spirit in the breasts of some people. Taking a turn around the University Parks one day, Albert Thomas saw

> young couples on the river quite gay in their sunbathing suits, young and healthy, clean in both body and mind (we hope); it sets you wondering how much longer they will enjoy the beauties and relaxations of Oxford before they are called back to their stern duties of the Services, to other obligations, or to the customs and traditions of their College life.[106]

'The most difficult thing to convey', wrote Larkin, 'was the almost-complete suspension of concern for the future'.[107]

> There were none of the pressing [career] dilemmas of teaching or Civil Service, industry or America, publishing or journalism: in consequence, there was next to no careerism. National affairs were going so badly, and a victorious peace was clearly so far off, that effort expended on one's post-war prospects could hardly seem anything but a ludicrous waste of time.[108]

'Careerism faded', wrote Kingsley Amis's biographer Zachary Leader, 'as no good news came from any war front'.[109] Young men returned to the city with stories of defeats in France and Norway, further foreshortening future horizons. For the first three years of the war, there was little good news to be had. John Ferris of Corpus Christi College exhibited 'an habitual air of depression'. War guilt among the non-combatants, he wrote, 'was heightened by the recurrent disasters to British arms. For me, the worst moment of the entire war was hearing, one lunchtime in hall, of the sinking of *Prince of Wales* and *Repulse*' (10 December 1941).[110]

The early years of war were a period of intense discomfort for Oxford's refugee community. Austrian and German nationals, regardless of whether they had fled Nazi persecution, were designated 'enemy aliens'. They might be required to attend tribunals and have restrictions placed upon their movements and had occasion to rely on friends and sponsors in Oxford and elsewhere to vouch for them. With the fall of France, the government ordered their mass internment, an aspect of the panic gripping a country faced with invasion and fearful of fifth-columnists, and, given the circumstances, a prudent measure taken to meet it.[111] Many were sent away, if only for a short time, to internment camps on the Isle of Man and in Devon and Shropshire. Italian philosopher Lorenzo Minio-Paluello 'was arrested at dawn at Oriel College'. His host Lady Ross, wife of the college provost, 'had to drag Minio-Paluello's wife Magda away from her husband as he was bundled into a lorry'.[112] The Austrian composer and musicologist Egon Wellesz, settled in Oxford since fleeing the Continent, was nevertheless despatched to the Isle of Man in June. It took the efforts of the University and prominent associates, such as Ralph Vaughan Williams and the music critic of *The Times*, to secure his return to Oxford in the autumn.[113] On 25 May 1940 *The Times* carried an article entitled '1000 Aliens in Oxford', in which Chief Constable Fox stated that he had made representation to the Home Office 'for the extension of the Enemy Alien Internment Orders to Oxford'.[114] Registrar Veale complained to the same newspaper that hundreds of aliens were at large in the city. They were 'a potential menace and we feel they should be interned'.[115] Other Oxford voices disagreed, Gilbert Murray condemning 'public hysteria' while All Souls fellow and barrister R.T.E. Leatham, on war release to the Foreign Office's refugee section, opposed the internment policy from inside Whitehall.[116]

Rooftops and trailer pumps

Oxford's student body, to a man and a woman, became a fire-watching and fire-fighting force benefiting the whole city as the University reacted to the Blitz and enacted the government order for compulsory fire-watching (February 1941). The University ARP (Fire-Fighting) Committee was chaired by the Bursar of St John's (or St John Baptist College, as his letterhead fashioned it more formally), and all colleges were involved. At Merton, which served as a control centre for the surrounding area, the fire-watching scheme required the continuous presence on duty of twenty men.[117] Some students joined the ARP; Bruce Montgomery, wearing 'an air raid warden's badge and carrying a walking-stick ... stalked aloofly to and fro in a severe triangle formed by the [St John's] College lodge (for letters), the Randolph bar, and his lodgings in Wellington Square'.[118]

New College's acting warden, Alic Smith, joined the Manor Road fire-watchers' group (every house along the road required to put a bucket of water outside each night).[119] 'Librarianship in time of war is an affair of stirrup-pumps and sandbags', wrote Bodley's Librarian Craster, 'of static water-tanks and trailer-pumps, and of the many activities that go by the name of ARP' (stirrup pumps were small and portable firefighting devices; trailer pumps were larger and required towing by a vehicle).[120] At the Bodleian, ARP cover was initially provided by staff, who formed a volunteer fire brigade and took turns on fire-watching duties at night, soon supplemented by teams of undergraduates. A University fire brigade was formed in 1940. Jesus undergraduates were enticed to stay up over Christmas 1940 vacation for fireguard duties with the offer of free board and lodging, and in May 1941 it became a requirement for all college members in residence to perform ARP duties.[121] With the regimentation of the Jesus student body – shelters in the cellars, ladders, trailer pump, and water tanks in both quads – it was felt that 'in a somewhat different sense the college had reverted to its position of three centuries earlier' when, during the Civil War, it was 'dismantled into part of a garrison'.[122]

St Hilda's was another college offering free vacation accommodation in exchange for fire-watching (see PLATE 25). In addition to college air raid duties, its students also fire-watched on the spire of the University Church of St Mary's on the High Street. A St Hilda's team won the

THREAT, WORRY AND EVACUATION   137

cup in the 1942 inter-college and University department trailer pump competition, though at a practice in the Meadow bursar Mrs Milroy got her fur entangled in the works.[123] Somerville built shelters for each of its main buildings, bricked up the library's loggia and secured the doors of Penrose and Maitland with further brickwork. A water tank, dubbed 'Mercury' (perhaps a joking reference to Christ Church's ornate statue, pond and fountain), appeared in front of the chapel, another in East Quad. The college trailer pump was dignified with its own shed, and college personnel cooperated with those of the Radcliffe Infirmary and OUP on firefighting and fire-watching rotas.[124] Four students slept each night in Queen's SCR Gallery, the college fire-watching team numbering fifty people. The roof was 'laid out with an ingenious series of ladders and gangways. A high-level bridge connects the Library with the north wing of the Back Quad, and on the roof above the Common Rooms there is a watcher's eyrie, complete with telephone and electric heater.'[125]

At the Ashmolean, an air raid shelter was opened in the basement and the Chantry casts dismembered, the busts saved but their plaster bodies used to fill sandbags.[126] Railings were placed around the building's extensive roof for the safety of those fire-watching at night. It was home to the Slade and the Ruskin schools of art (see PLATE 24); students 'slept in bunks, under scratchy grey blankets, in an area under the roof'.[127] To stop them disappearing in vacations, they were paid £2 a week for their efforts. Here Scottish artist Eduardo Paolozzi, a Ruskin student, fire-watched alongside the artist Yvonne Hudson and actor Rosalie Williams. Mr Ovenell 'remembers the eerie experience of lying awake on a camp bed in an office (the Tradescant Room) listening to the creaks in the building and wondering how he could fight a fire, with only the sand buckets which were dotted round the Galleries'.[128] Similarly, Ruth Parker, one of the 'penicillin girls' at the Dunn School of Pathology (see Chapter 9), was concerned that 'the place was full of inflammable materials. What could we have done with a stirrup pump and a bucket of water?'[129] At the Playhouse, four fire-watchers a night slept on improvised beds in the dressing rooms.[130] The climbing of college roofs, 'formerly a disciplinary offence, was now a patriotic obligation, with ladders provided'.[131] It presented an opportunity for the talents of the University Mountaineering Club, of both practical and comical value.

As Guy Fawkes Night approached in 1940, Balliol students hung a guy dressed in the uniform of an auxiliary fireman over the college gate on Broad Street. Next day it appeared hanging opposite the Randolph, its appearance embellished by a 'household utensil'.[132]

Fire-watching was one of the most prominent aspects of the wartime undergraduate experience (well described in Alan Hollinghurst's novel *The Sparsholt Affair*). Every night, recalled a student at University College,

> members of the College had to take it in turns to spend time sitting on the roofs of the College looking for passing aeroplanes. They even shared these duties during the vacation, with the College paying their board and lodging. Ladders were fixed to the towers, and it was easy enough to walk around the quads at rooftop level, even after a few drinks.[133]

Tony Phelps, reading Classics at University College, wrote that

> The occupants of my staircase regularly climbed to the roof of the tower and sat up there studying and plane spotting (very popular in those days). It was, perhaps, not entirely incongruous to be doing the latter while studying the tales of Troy or the wars of the 5th century BC.[134]

At Trinity, non-attendance at ARP drill 'was a serious disciplinary offence'. The students were divided into three 'divisions' covering the three main quads. As a resident of staircase II, John Harper-Nelson was in the 2nd Division, responsible for the protection of the chapel, Chapel Quad, Staircase 10, the Tower, kitchens, bathrooms and lavatories.

> The undergraduates were placed into four squads, armed respectively with hoses, stirrup pumps, ladders, and shovels ... Those of us detailed for duty had to be in college from 6 pm onwards and, if there was an air raid alert, to remain up and fully dressed until the All Clear. On the alert, two members of the section were to go up onto the top of the chapel tower.[135]

To get to the top of the chapel, they passed through the room housing the machinery that operated the tower clock and bell. 'The temptation to make the clock strike thirteen at midnight proved too much for some ... Even more fun was confusing people by adding a couple of chimes to four or five o'clock and watching the panicked rush for baths and breakfast.'[136] Fire-watching on the tower also afforded the opportunity to throw bottles onto Balliol's greenhouse. A joint Auxiliary Fire Service Unit for Balliol, St John's and Trinity was based in the last and regularly drilled in the Front Quad, practising firefighting with high-powered hoses.

Gerald Coombe went up to Exeter in 1943 on a special six-month war degree.

> As part of our RAF training we were required to learn the location of the principal stars, and in order to do this I used to climb through my bedroom window on to the ledge overlooking Brasenose Lane and gaze into the night sky ... very often as I did this I listened to a barrel organ which was frequently being played in the Turl.[137]

Nina Bawden of Somerville recalled an eerie weekend fire-watching in the University Museum, 'sleeping on a camp-bed between a mummy in a glass case and a stuffed alligator, and a more agreeable time playing planchette on the roof of the Bodleian'.[138] For University College's Thomas Morley, fire-watching was 'the single most distasteful aspect of wartime college life, not because of any inconvenience or discomfort but because of the boredom'.[139]

Douglas Ross recalls sand buckets and stirrup pumps positioned around Pembroke, and a gas detector in Old Quad. 'I remember parties of us being conducted on long scrambles through the roof timbers of the Old Quad and on to the leads. We probably saw more of the College's internal fabric than anyone other than the original builders and later surveyors and repairers', he remarked. Janet Gibbins of St Hugh's remembered fire-watching as a main contribution to the war effort – 'one spent uneventful nights on the roof of the Bodleian, and elsewhere, watching for incendiaries. I think we all worked hard, with a feeling that in war-time we were lucky to be in Oxford at all'.[140]

Hundreds of people attended stirrup-pump demonstrations, and houses with pumps displayed enamel plaques by their front doors to publicize the fact. Pressed Steel maintained a round-the-clock ARP control room, area wardens and about 400 volunteers including roof-top lookouts. First aid posts opened around the city, and a new ambulance depot was created at Cowley Place in case Magdalen Bridge was knocked out by enemy action, severing emergency access from the city centre. Five auxiliary fire stations were opened, and thirty trailer-pump fire-engine teams placed on standby. Madge Martin did 'Fire Guard's "wet" training' in the University Parks, 'crawling through the smoke, with nose pressed to the floor' to extinguish a blaze in the 'Fire Hut' with a stirrup pump.[141] June Coppock, working for Bletchley at Mansfield College, joined the Girls Training Corps and was taught how to extinguish incendiaries and move through huts full of smoke, to the accompaniment of simulated explosions.[142] She also volunteered for fire-watching to protect the college, returning to the premises at 7.30 p.m. on duty evenings.

In private homes people took measures to prevent injury from bomb blast. They taped or boarded up windows, or, in Madge Martin's case at 1 Wellington Place, stuck netting on in order to 'make splinters less likely to fly far'.[143] Shops in the centre of town, in Summertown and along the Cowley Road taped up their display windows.[144] The council opened more shelters, including one in the cellars under the Covered Market, and college and University buildings opened their doors too (a public shelter in the basement of Magdalen's New Library, and one in Jesus College cellars for residents of Ship Street).[145]

Among its numerous occupiers, the New Bodleian housed the Oxford Group Centre of the Royal Observer Corps, a clearing house for information phoned through by local observers, to be plotted on a gridded map and then forwarded to HQ Fighter Command. One of those reporting in was John Betjeman of the Uffington Observer Corps. From a corrugated iron hut in Parrott's Field, which he dubbed 'the urinal', his unit looked out for German parachutists in the Vale of the White Horse. His horsey wife, the Honourable Penelope Chetwode ('Propeller' to John), joined the Downs Patrol Division, cantering across the Downs at dawn each morning looking for the same intruders.[146]

Evacuation, of people and of things

European refugees continued to trickle in, and enemy POW camps opened on Oxford's outskirts. The city accommodated civilians evacuated from areas where heavy bombing was expected, such as London and Kent. By 6 September 1939, 20,000 evacuees were in Oxfordshire and the county council had 58 per cent more children on its books than it had in the summer.[147] Colleges, cinemas and municipal premises were used as makeshift accommodation when evacuees arrived by train at Oxford's Great Western Railway station, the women of Cripley Road next to the platform providing seats and refreshments outside their houses as the contingents came in. The Evacuation Officer had to buy 5 tons of straw to stuff emergency mattresses for the reception centre at the Majestic Cinema.[148] In late 1940, anywhere from 500 to 1,000 people were sleeping there each night, and disease outbreaks became a concern.

Other places chipped in. The babies expected by the provost of Queen's duly arrived, along with their mothers, but stayed only for a day before moving on. Rhodes House provided emergency accommodation for 112 women and children for the best part of a fortnight, and Christ Church similarly served as a halfway house for evacuees yet to be settled in homes. Students (the Christ Church term for fellows) and their wives received children from Kent, 'making sure they were fed and thoroughly bathed', the sub-dean attempting to ensure they were baptized before moving on.[149] St Hilda's took in children from St Swithun's in Winchester and Southover Manor in Lewes, and over a hundred from Ashford.[150] The Women's Voluntary Service (founded in 1938 for civil defence) looked after evacuees in the Town Hall and in the Plaza Ballroom at Holyoake Hall in Headington. Other volunteers catered for those billeted at the Majestic, including Reverend Martin, who conducted services for them. 'The poor things herd together in that dark stuffy hall with just a mattress and their few possessions around them', wrote his wife.[151]

Involuntarily uprooted, some people struggled to adjust to life in Oxford. Despite proximity to his friend C.S. Lewis and easy access to Inklings gatherings, Charles Williams missed the routine of his London life and his work at Amen House (though probably breathed a sigh of relief when he learned that the building had been hit by a bomb).[152] Reacting to Oxford's cliquey nature, he told his wife in October 1939 that 'Outside Lewis I never want to see anyone of Oxford or in Oxford again'. A 'London mother' wrote to the *Oxford Mail* complaining about being 'right in the slums of Oxford. When I think of my pretty little home in London, I feel I should get the next train back.'[153] Relations between landlords and evacuees could be fraught, and an appeals tribunal heard 200 cases within the first four months of its existence.[154] Toronto and Yale universities offered to accommodate the offspring of Oxford and Cambridge dons, causing 125 children and twenty-five mothers to begin an improbable journey from Oxford station in July 1940, bound for Liverpool and passage across the Atlantic ('Wouldn't it be fun if we were torpedoed!', said an excited Ellie Bourdillon to the horror of relatives bidding them farewell; 'Is this Canada yet?', asked Susan Lawson as the train pulled in to Banbury).[155]

University and college authorities were mindful of the threat of bombing and the misfortune befalling other institutions. The libraries of the British Museum and Liverpool University each lost some 500,000 items through enemy action; University College London's library lost around 100,000 volumes to fire and water; and thousands of King's College London's arts and law books, sent to Bristol University when the college moved there, were lost in the air raid that destroyed the Great Hall.[156] A bewildering array of rare and valuable items moved around Oxford, departed from Oxford or were brought into Oxford in an attempt to secure them. With war under way, wrote Registrar Veale, 'the University decided on a policy of dispersal of its irreplaceable treasures ... except for a certain number which could be put into the cellars of the New Bodleian, which we were advised were, for all practical purposes, bomb-proof.'[157] As collections went into storage, exhibitions and building developments were put on hold. The Ashmolean had recently acquired a 'highly interesting exhibition from Egypt – the shrine of Tirhakah [Taharqa], the Emperor of Ethiopia who reigned over Egypt in the days of Hezekiah'.

> [But when] the Hitler War broke out it halted many a development planned for the Ashmolean, including a new room for the Hills collection of musical instruments ... and other rooms in which the pictures and smaller treasures could be more adequately shown. The immediate concern of the officials was to place its chief possessions out of reach of Nazi bombs.[158]

Where to send treasures presented a dilemma. While deep under the New Bodleian might be considered a safe location, and Oxford was likely to be safer than London or Plymouth, no one had any idea where the enemy might strike. Theologian and clergyman Frederick Homes Dudden, master of Pembroke, reflected this in replying to a request from the Imperial War Museum for storage space for its library. He said that the college's unique treasures, 'which could never be replaced',

> have been sent away into the country. The treasures which are not unique, have mostly been retained here ... I should be inclined to agree with you that it had better be sent into the country, if suitable conditions for keeping it can be provided. No one can tell how long Oxford's immunity from bombing will last.[159]

As we have seen, the Ashmolean sent items to Chastleton House. Having made the necessary enquiries of its headmistress before war broke out, the president of St John's, Sir Cyril Norwood, oversaw the removal of college treasures to the girls' school at Westonbirt in Gloucestershire. Once 'a millionaire's mansion', it boasted a heated and air-conditioned cellar, in which the headmistress had agreed to house them.[160] But many treasures stayed in Oxford. Though Frank Dubber and his colleagues had already taken measures to protect valued items at the Bodleian, something bigger and better was needed. The matter was discussed with the New Bodleian's architect, Gilbert Scott, who suggested that a brick chamber be built in line with the bookstack tower, two floors underground on 'K' floor.[161] This facility, officially called the Treasure Chamber but more prosaically known as the Brick Room, was completed on 8 October 1939 and soon housed 60,000 Bodleian manuscripts and printed books. Other floors became available too, including newly fitted Roneo metal shelving on the floors above ground that could be used as larger deposits were received. Mainly in the vacations, books and manuscripts were transferred from the Old Library, the cellars of the Exam Schools, and the basements of the Radcliffe Camera and the Old Ashmolean. All the old books from Duke Humfrey's Library and the Arts End were also moved to the New Bodleian, 'where they would be much better protected in the event of enemy action'.[162]

The Bodleian received deposits from Oxford colleges and institutions. Most were books and manuscripts, but there was also the medieval stained glass from New College and Merton College chapels; masterpieces from Christ Church picture gallery; hundreds of manuscripts and the finely carved chapel reredos from Trinity; type plate and matrices from the Clarendon Press; cabinets of coins from the Ashmolean; and seeds from the Botany Department. There were rare manuscripts from Balliol and Merton and the libraries of the English School, the Modern History Faculty and the Hope Department of Entomology. Oriel sent manuscripts and deeds; University College portraits from the hall. Brasenose deposited incunabula, Mansfield sixty-seven desks and a lectern, and Corpus Christi a bust and some paintings. The Indian Institute deposited manuscripts, as did the Department of Botany – 4,000 of them, mainly from the Sherardian collection – as well as thirty-one specimen cabinets of herbaria. Minute books arrived from the Oxford Union, and the University Archives were transferred from the Tower of the Five Orders (it is interesting to think that muniment and other towers across Oxford, that for centuries had been associated with security, were now regarded as vulnerable given the aerial threat). There also arrived material from the University's School of Rural Economy, the Bureau of Animal Population, and the Edward Grey Institute of Field Ornithology.

Institutions queued up to send their valuables, eighty colleges, museums and other organizations sending packages, according to Chief Constable Fox.[163] There was material from the British Drama League, the Mineralogical Society, the Linnaean Society, the LSE, the Oxford and Cambridge Club, the Victoria and Albert Museum, the Royal Geographical Society, the Royal Society, the Royal Statistical Society, the Geological Society, the Victoria and Albert Museum's Dyce Collection, and botanical specimens from the Natural History Museum. The Blitz flushed out an ever-increasing amount of material, the bombing of Kew Bridge and Brentford Gas Works, for example, damaging the Royal Botanic Gardens' herbarium and library. Its director, Sir Arthur Hill, requested help, and Craster obliged. Items began arriving on 22 November 1940, ten lorries bringing cabinets and seventeen more bringing books. They came with their own Kew keeper, Dr William Turrill. The following February, Colsebourne Park was requisitioned by the Ministry of Aircraft Production and all the Kew material stored there had to be shipped out. The Bodleian, already considered 'full', agreed nevertheless to take in 600 feet of books.

THREAT, WORRY AND EVACUATION 145

On 23 September 1940 a bomb landed on the gallery housing the British Museum's priceless King's Library, destroying 124 volumes, a further 304 damaged beyond repair. The subsequent move to the New Bodleian took over a year to complete, the material travelling in 24-ton Great Western Railway containers and amounting to 80,000 volumes weighing in at sixty-four tons (1,572 boxes). Another massive deposit came from Somerset House, three railway containers bearing 471 boxes of registers to Oxford in August 1941.

The Librarian of Goldsmiths College, University of London, also contacted Craster, reporting that the University of London library in Senate House had been hit five times by high explosives. Craster sympathized but said his premises were full, though he could spare a few hundred feet-worth of shelf space. After the University of London librarian sent him a detailed report of the damage, Craster yielded further and offered 2,700 feet. The major part of the Goldsmiths Library began arriving in January 1941, sixteen lorry loads containing 50,000 volumes dispersed to J, G and E floors, shortly followed by sixteen more.

More large London collections were to come, Scott's Road Services of Turl Street bringing 40,000 volumes in twelve lorry loads from the Science Museum. It was clearly difficult for Craster to say 'no'; in July 1941 Vice Chancellor Gordon told him that he'd been asked on a visit to Eton if the Bodleian could house some of its material. Craster agreed, and 2,000 items were sent. That month, the keepers of the Court of Arches – the Archbishop of Canterbury's court of appeal – hurriedly packed 123 tea chests and five sacks, transported to Oxford in three lorries. From the Muniment Room of Westminster Abbey came the *Liber Regalis*, which contained the English coronation service introduced for the crowning of Edward II in 1308.

Non-university institutions and organizations around Oxfordshire availed themselves of the Bodleian's generosity too.[164] Boxes arrived from Kelmscott Manor, as did the archives of the city council and early churchwardens' accounts from St Michael at the Northgate. Gustav Holst's daughter, Imogen, brought in the score of the *Planets Suite*. Other private deposits included the papers of Lord Canning from the Earl of Harewood and the autograph manuscript of John Evelyn's diary. Valuables taken in ranged from solitary items – such as the charter of the Alfred Lodge of Freemasons – to the 64 tons-worth of the King's Library. At peak in 1941, deposits were received on 110 days. Everything was moved below ground level in a solitary passenger lift with a weight-bearing limit of 1,000 pounds. This amounted to 10,448 boxes and parcels, 9,683 of them from London collections; 7,000 of those boxes and parcels were unpacked and arranged on shelves as well as was possible. And all because of the fact that, when war broke out, the New Bodleian was just that – *new*, and empty.

Some arrangements for securing precious items were less successful than the Bodleian's monumental effort. A celebrated 'fail' involved the Museum of the History of Science.[165] The trouble began when the Museum's founder and curator, Dr Gunther, decided to place a number of extremely rare and valuable instruments in safekeeping and then died, without having told anyone their whereabouts, taking his knowledge to the grave. The missing items included Cardinal Wolsey's gilt brass sundial, ten astrolabes from around the world dating back to 984 CE, and several antique watches. The conundrum became the subject of table talk, the Bishop of Oxford recounting the tale to the king when visiting Windsor Castle to preach in St George's Chapel.[166] Veale wrote to the Home Secretary and Scotland Yard, reporting the loss of the 'unique set of astrolabes', the scrap value of which 'would probably be many thousands of pounds, some of the instruments being made of solid gold or silver'. The late curator, 'a person of rather unbusinesslike habits', he wrote, had left no clue as to their whereabouts and exhaustive internal enquiries had been 'unavailing'. The only lead was that they were probably sent to 'some country-house not very far from Oxford'. Arrangements were made for Gunther's successor as curator, Frank Sherwood Taylor, to call at Scotland Yard.

Advertisements were placed in *The Times*, and a watch kept on local auction houses. Gunther's widow could offer no assistance; the Museum janitor had recently died too, and his widow was similarly clueless. There was no record of the collection having been deposited in the New Bodleian. The end of the war brought an investigation by Inspector Somerset of Scotland Yard's Criminal Investigation Department. His twelve-page report could only conclude that the items were probably in Oxford or within a 30-mile radius. The affair reached its anticlimactic conclusion in summer 1948 when Sherwood Taylor sheepishly confessed to Somerset that the items had been found in the Museum's basement, 'in three quite small wooden fitted cases'. They had been concealed behind fifty or so other cases 'and evidently not opened by me. I feel that we ought to apologise to you for the very great amount of trouble you were put to in searching for something that was really in our possession though we did not know it.' No one was charged with wasting police time.

The threat of bombing took years to recede and people had to remain alert. It was not until February 1942 that Hitler officially released the forces earmarked for the invasion of Britain, and the so-called Baedeker raids of April–May 1942, targeting cities such as Bath, Canterbury, Exeter and York, brought renewed worry and redoubled civil defence endeavours. It was then that the Bodleian decided to move 2,000 of its greatest treasures out of the city. For the British Library and other national institutions, including the Bodleian, the government had found secure accommodation in the underground galleries of a stone quarry near Bath.[167] Bodleian treasures began leaving Oxford in June 1942, stowed in boxes provided by the British Library and conveyed in a secret Scott's Road Service convoy led by the Bodley Librarian's car. At the same time, the 'lowest floor of the new bookstack [in the New Bodleian] was converted into a public air raid shelter, with accommodation for 1,100 people, and put at the disposal of the City Council'.[168]

Even at this late date, in terms of the aerial threat, Oxford residents juxtaposed the city's tranquillity and beauty with the prospect of destruction. Balliol graduate Harold Nicolson dined at All Souls on 5 June 1942:

> We have coffee afterwards in the quad, and the sun sinks gently over St Mary's and the Bodleian. I gaze with love at those dear buildings, wondering whether they will be assailed by one of the Baedeker raids, and whether I shall ever see them again. We walk to Balliol, where I deliver an address on Franco-British relations ... I have a large audience and the speech goes well. There is a reception afterwards, and I return in the lovely warm night to the Randolph. Dear Oxford.[169]

Having reviewed the war threat to Oxford and the preparations to meet it, we now delve into the home front experience.

SEVEN

IN WARTIME OXFORD

> Wartime Oxford was a city in limbo, populated by students in their late teens awaiting call-up, a thinned-out cohort of dons who were either too elderly or deemed otherwise unfit to fight, and the motley assortment of émigré academics ... Almost untouched by air raids ... Oxford was an island of unreal normality between savagely blitzed cities – London to the south and, to the north, the industrial Midlands.[1]

Oxford's relative quiet could occasion a perverse sense of guilt, as experienced by Paul Nash and depicted by the main protagonist in Larkin's *Jill*, who leaves his family in a northern town regularly getting pasted by the Luftwaffe. The decline in road traffic contributed to the quietness. The requirement for student motorists to display green lamps was suspended, green lights being the prerogative of military convoys. Because of petrol rationing there wasn't much call for them anyway, registered student cars dropping from 415 in 1939 to zero in 1944.[2] Petrol shortages and frustration at increased military traffic in Oxfordshire caused Tolkien to give up driving altogether. As the number of cars on the streets fell away, bus travel increased, despite mileage reductions and service restrictions. In 1944, just shy of 40 million passengers were carried on Oxford's buses, a 30 per cent rise on 1939.[3] Declining car use did not bring a corresponding decrease in road-traffic accidents: 1940 saw the highest number of road fatalities ever recorded in Britain – 9,169 – a result of the blackout and often involving military vehicles. On 13 June 1940 Stuart Rowles was motorbiking to the Old Marston ARP post to get a steel helmet for a friend when he was killed by an RAF lorry towing a 'Queen Mary' low-loading trailer (used for moving salvaged aircraft) on Harberton Mead road.[4]

Less traffic, and the concomitant decline in tourists, contributed to Oxford's wartime atmosphere. 'Everything is so quiet and wonderful to-day' wrote Albert Thomas after a Sunday morning walk, 'for even the quads are nearly empty owing to the absence of trippers.'[5] 'Oxford was a university restored by war to a strange and timeless silence', wrote Nina Bawden.

> By edict, no bells rang and there was almost no traffic; the uncluttered curve of the High, the spires and towers of the colleges, slept in the clean, moist, quiet air as in some old don's dream of peace. After three years as an evacuee in the dusty confines of a Welsh mining valley and a final school term spent dodging flying bombs and sleeping in sandbagged shelters in London, I felt I had arrived in Arcadia.[6]

Having been on almost continuous duty with the Local Defence Volunteers at the height of the Blitz in central London, Harper-Nelson found the retreat into the tranquillity of Trinity College in October 1940 'like a transition from war to peace'.[7] Such sentiments were magnified for those who had escaped the Nazis, Austrian composer and musicologist Bojan Bujić writing that Oxford appeared 'as something other-worldly and idyllic'. It was like 'an island of the blessed'.[8]

Quieter in some ways perhaps, Oxford's human population nevertheless increased, and its dynamics shifted visibly. In line with the rest of the nation, everyone had a part to play in the war effort. Women's Institute branches across the county distributed soft fruit bushes and the Oxford Central Girls' School supplied hospital patients with flowers. The boys of the City of Oxford High School, Southfield School and Magdalen College School joined a schools' forestry camp that cut 1,224 tons of pit props for the coal mines. St Edmund Hall students spent summers on a forestry camp at Dulverton, felling spruce and Douglas firs, and at a harvest camp at Wilcote.[9] A team of women met weekly in the St Giles' Parish Rooms to darn socks and alter clothes for service personnel. Volunteers ran libraries for Oxfordshire's RAF stations and Women's Land Army hostels, and the Church Army operated a canteen at the Great Western Railway station providing food and beds for soldiers on the move. Members of the Women's Voluntary Services made it their business to support female service personnel 'in a city where women had not previously been catered for'. They made curtains for their hostels and washed bedspreads for those billeted in colleges without facilities for laundering large articles.[10]

Margaret Taylor, wife of the Magdalen historian, spent each morning making munitions in a factory. Women connected with Queen's knitted comforts for Queensmen at sea using wool provided by the New York mother of a former Rhodes Scholar.[11] Female students helped out in hospitals and nurseries and performed part-time munitions work. Hundreds of students and city residents answered the call of the Oxfordshire War Agriculture Executive to help bring in the county's harvest. Reverend Robert Martin of St Michael at the North Gate joined the ARP, his wife Madge helping at the War Supply Depot run by the Central Hospital Supply Service of the Red Cross and the Order of St John, headed by Lady Gertrude Bruce-Gardner. St Hugh's students also helped out here, such work being considered a feminine preserve.[12] Based high in the Provost's Lodgings at Worcester before moving down to the drawing room, they rolled bandages and made swabs, 'Air-Force socks' and 'Air-Force scarves', and responded to rush orders for items such as 'surgeons'-mask bandages' and 'slings for wounded Russians'.[13] The war affected people's businesses; City Motors won a contract with the Ministry of Supply to repair vehicles, and the draper's Cape and Company won an Air Ministry contract for blackout material.

War pervaded social life and recreational activities. There were dances in the Town Hall and the Holyoake Dance Hall in Headington, and concerts and lectures put on by the English Speaking Union and other organizations. People attended talks on 'What We Are Fighting For' and 'The Religion of National Socialism'. There were charitable concerts – one in Balliol's hall in aid of Finnish relief – and special services. These included a May 1940 Day of National Prayer that brought 2,500 people to the Town Hall, and Battle of Britain thanksgiving services. In April 1942 Principal Micklem conducted a German-language service in Mansfield chapel, featuring New College choir and broadcast to Germany by the BBC.[14] At a meeting in the University Parks attended by over a thousand people, the National Fire Service demonstrated how *not* to put out fires, followed by a comic football match between teams of firemen dressed as women.[15]

People were relentlessly exhorted to donate money – to the Spitfire Fund, War Weapons Week, the Norway Relief Fund, the Tanks for Attack campaign, the Mayor of Oxford's Air Raid Distress Fund, the Merchant Navy Comforts Service or 'Help for Russia' week, during which the hammer and sickle flew alongside the Union flag on Carfax Tower (the flag was, apparently, stolen by members of the University Mountaineering Club, delivered next day to the mayor made up as a smoking jacket, the hammer and sickle on the breast pocket).[16] A single week in December 1942 brought a Red Cross bazaar at the Cadena on Cornmarket and city-wide events for the Prisoner of War Fund. Reverend Martin's collection of toy soldiers was displayed for sale in the window of Morris Garages on Longwall Street, and there was an auction at the Randolph Hotel. Donations included jade scent bottles from the Duchess of Kent, a silver and turquoise cigarette box from the Duke of Marlborough, a flyable model aircraft made by the Oxford City Police, and two bottles of whisky from the Lord Mayor of London.[17] The Bishop of Oxford organized a fund to support the rebuilding of churches damaged by bombing in the dioceses of London and Southwark, which had raised nearly £4,000 when it closed in April 1941.[18] Ministry of Economic Warfare attempts to prevent imports into Nazi-occupied Europe raised the prospect of food shortages, and a number of famine relief committees were established around Britain.[19] One of them, the Oxford Famine Relief Committee (Oxfam), was founded at a meeting in the Old Library of the University Church on 4 October 1942, aimed at supporting famine relief efforts and with an initial focus on Axis-occupied Greece. A driving force was Australian-born Gilbert Murray, Regius Professor of Greek until retirement in 1936 and a leading League of Nations figure. Oxfam's 'Greek Week' raised £107,000 for the Greek Red Cross, 'an incredible effort from one city in wartime Britain'.[20] There were innumerable smaller collection efforts, Somerville raising £251 during the 1943 Wings for Victory week – enough for five parachutes, two dinghies for bombers and two for fighters, and one pair of chemically heated socks.[21]

War changed what people cooked and ate. The first ration books were issued soon after war began, and the Oxford Education Committee arranged cookery demonstrations to help people adapt to new ingredients and the loss of staple ones (showing them how to make sugarless puddings, for example). Initiatives such as 'Apple Week', supported by shop-front displays, encouraged people to consider the versatility of foodstuffs in plentiful seasonal supply. 'Many things are almost impossible to get hold of now', wrote Madge Martin in November 1940, specifying cheese, chocolate, biscuits, onions and lemons.[22] The list of things unavailable or in short supply grew; sweets were rationed as were towels, eggs became as rare as the proverbial hen's teeth, and corsets as well as stockings were difficult to come by. In the Warden's Lodgings in Wadham's front quad, Maurice Bowra felt keenly the shortages of soap, razor blades and cigarettes, and was reduced to using the *Daily Mirror* as toilet paper, finding it difficult to flush.[23] In the Trinity JCR it was suggested that the widely disliked *Daily Herald* be used 'to solve the difficulties of the Master of the Rolls', a comedy JCR post presiding over lavatorial matters.[24]

Even beer could be an issue, shortages causing licensees to limit opening times, sometimes to shut altogether, and forcing a reduction in alcoholic strength. Hook Norton beer decreased in strength from around 4.4 per cent alcohol by volume (ABV) in 1939 to 3.5 per cent in 1943 in order to cut down on barley and sugar consumption. The city brewer Morrells stopped producing strong ale and concentrated instead on two brews, dark and light (both coming in at about 3.2 per cent ABV) because of the cost of malt and scarcity of sugar.[25]

> In a wartime context of increasingly appalling food, long, cold hours of waiting, and the tendency of members of the armed forces to crowd out all available pubs when they could, the diminished strength of the beer went virtually unnoticed.[26]

With record demand, in December 1941 Hook Norton Brewery actually ran out of beer.[27] Morrells posted record sales that year and again in 1942.[28]

Oxford shared in the national 'grow your own' movement, no tennis court or sports field safe from the expansion of the legume. Vegetables were grown in the little Exam Schools quad opposite the Eastgate Hotel; allotments sprouted in the University Parks, Port Meadow and at Holywell Mill; and scores of plots were cultivated on Oriel's sports ground. Christ Church domestic staff were given allotments carved out of the old rugby pitch, while at St Hilda's part of the college garden by South Building was dug up, yielding the occasional luxury like asparagus.[29] Newly laid lawns in Oriel's First Quadrangle were converted to tomatoes and St Mary's Quad was devoted to cabbages and other vegetables.[30] Somerville grew vegetables along the south side of the Garden Quad, the sports field became allotments, and the students helped plant potatoes in the Parks.[31] The principal's private tennis court at Mansfield became a kitchen garden.[32] Plans to turn Manchester College's verdant quads into potato patches following an urgent appeal for cultivation from the city council in September 1940 were thwarted when rubble was struck less than a spade down.[33] Southfield golf course and Cutteslowe Park were turned over to the patriotic production of vegetables and North Oxford golf course was obliged to cede a field to the War Agricultural Executive Committee, though restrictive covenants thwarted city council plans to plough up South Park. Chickens roamed the gardens of the warden of Wadham and the provost of Queen's and milled around the Tolkiens' premises at 20 Northmoor Road. A.J.P. Taylor introduced poultry to his Holywell Mill home in Magdalen's grounds, and there were ducks in the president's Garden at Trinity. At a JCR meeting, the residents of staircase 9, whose rooms overlooked the garden, suggested that they 'be muzzled at all times and especially in the early morning'.[34]

Summoned home for consultations at the Foreign Office in summer 1942, Sir Reader Bullard, Britain's ambassadorial resident in Tehran, visited his family in Oxford. Though the Blitz was over, he wrote, it was 'painful to see how tight things were':

> My wife kept the family going by turning the garden into a home of twenty-two ducks and kept the ducks going by fetching two pails of swill every day, on the handles of her bicycle, from one of the boarding-houses of the Dragon School … Our house in Oxford was exempted from the billeting regulations because of the size of our family [five children], but in 1940 it had taken in a family of six, driven from the south by the

blitz. In the front garden there was a small contraption which I found was a field-kitchen. My wife was head of a small WVS group of women who were tied to their homes by age or family responsibilities and who undertook various local obligations such as the provision of tea and food during bombing raids and other crises.[35]

Patterns of employment changed because of the war. Women worked on factory production lines and drove buses. Hook Norton Brewery employed boys and women for the first time. College staff joined up, leaving jobs to be filled. At Christ Church, women were assisting the older male scouts by the end of 1939 and were taken on for the same purpose at Queen's too.[36] The 130-strong city police force called up 'war reservists' to plug gaps as regulars left for military service. Former porters and scouts were drummed out of retirement as the current crop left for the forces; at University College the aged scout Bateson regaled students with tales of 'young gentlemen' from the Edwardian era, and, meaningfully, of how generous they had been.[37] The conscription of women from 1942 meant that St Hilda's struggled for maids and 'Moabites' (its term for daily cleaners), meaning that students had to cater for themselves, making their own beds, cleaning their own shoes, dusting, and washing up their tea things.[38] Staff shortages led to an innovation at St Hilda's where, until 1941, visitors would ring a bell, which was answered by a maid. She would then enquire as to whether the person called upon wanted to receive the caller. Now, to save labour, a college lodge was opened in the South Building as an enquiry and communications centre.[39]

With over 250 members of staff joining the forces, OUP's general solution to the resulting labour shortage was massive overwork, employees at the mill sometimes pulling 66-hour weeks in addition to the compulsory dozen hours fire-watching.[40] Around fifty Bodleian staff were away from their positions – about half the strength – yet it remained open as normal.[41] The war 'significantly altered the composition of the staff', noted Craster, bringing to an end 'the recruitment of boys on whom the Bodleian had come to depend for the delivery of much of its day-to-day service'. They were replaced by women, those recruited since 1933 to work on catalogue revisions transferred to general library duties. There were other repercussions

IN WARTIME OXFORD 155

of shifting population, employment and accommodation dynamics. Eleanor Plumer, principal of St Anne's, used the 'gradual wartime disappearance of hostesses' accommodating students attached to what was a non-residential organization to persuade the delegates that the only possible solution was for it to run its own hostels. The first, at 11 Bradmore Road, opened in 1945.[42]

What people saw

War changed what people saw as they moved around the city. There was the kaleidoscope of uniforms and nationalities and different groups of evacuees and refugees. There was the Home Guard and ARP, British soldiers and airmen, naval officers and ratings, and members of the women's services. There were Americans, Canadians, and the occasional gaggle of New Zealanders and Poles. Khaki and air force blue were part of college life, as those *in statu pupillari* (students formally in residence) did their requisite stints in the Officers' Training Corp, University Air Squadron or Naval Division while at their books, and colleges housed service personnel on short courses as well as the staff of military departments. The nation was at arms, and uniforms and military manoeuvres became part of everyday life. Having matriculated in Convocation House in October 1940, Harper-Nelson and his fellow freshmen made the short journey back to Trinity. 'As we did so we were passed by a platoon of Royal Corps of Signals Officer Cadets crunching across the quad in battledress, boots and gaiters but wearing their black undergraduate gowns.'[43]

There were many other visual manifestations of war on the home front, one of them being queues. People lined up for cigarettes and cakes, and if you wanted to get into the theatres you queued or went early.[44] There were the taped-up shop windows and the sandbags, and armed sentries checking passes at the entrances to some buildings. Mansfield's sentries mounted guard with fixed bayonets and would offer the traditional 'Halt! Who goes there?' challenge. 'Dig for Victory' and 'Careless Talk Costs Lives' posters adorned noticeboards and advertising spaces such as the sides of double-decker buses. Sandwich boards on Cornmarket carried advertisements for blackout material.

There were events such as the fuel-economy exhibition in the Town Hall, waste-reduction displays in cinema foyers and war savings kiosks in workplaces.[45] Unusual signage appeared, directing American vehicles on the Carfax crossroads, warning road users that the traffic lights at the Holywell and Broad Street intersection were screened, or pointing servicewomen to the lavatories in Magdalen (a notice in the archway between St Swithun's and Longwall reading 'Conveniences, camp-followers, fem[ale]., for the use of').[46]

As well as college and University buildings, the military occupied other city spaces. The English Speaking Union established a free social club for servicewomen at 3 Cornmarket, and the Carfax Assembly Rooms became a forces' canteen with reading and writing rooms (Margaret Roberts spent an evening or two a week working here).[47] The Churchill Hospital was taken over by US Army medical services transferred from Park Prewitt Hospital in Basingstoke.[48] The Clarendon Hotel on Cornmarket became the American Red Cross Service Hostel and Club, where servicemen and women enjoyed 'shower baths and spacious rooms'.[49] Attending a lunch there, Madge and Robert Martin were shown over the 'beautifully appointed rooms, dormitories and kitchens' and the 'spacious canteen', which doubled as a ballroom.[50] The Church Army ran a hostel and canteen at 3 Cambridge Terrace along with a club and canteen on Station Approach providing food and accommodation for service personnel. The St Giles' Service Club and Canteen was at 43 St Giles, a branch of Toc H (an all-ranks Christian servicepersons' association founded in the First World War) in Norham Gardens, and Young Men's Christian Association (YMCA) establishments on Carfax and George Street. There was a YMCA Officers Club on Oriel Square and a Young Women's Christian Association (YWCA) hostel at 171 Walton Street. The St Margaret's Institute on Polstead Road, opened to entertain troops at the time of Dunkirk, sustained its operations.

> Entrance was free to members of the forces, and local people were also welcomed. Refreshments were served (tea, buns, chocolates, and cigarettes), and there was dancing to the music of Victor Sylvester. The club was a huge success … and 'Maggie's' continued in being, serving nurses and orderlies, as well as RAF personnel from nearby aerodromes.[51]

Adding to these military spaces, there was a Home Guard assault course on Jackdaw Lane, extensive facilities on Port Meadow and new barracks at the Slade Camp. Enemy prisoners of war were accommodated at Harcourt Hill in North Hinksey and Old Road in Headington on the fields of Wood Farm, many of them employed on the county's farms.[52]

Rationing and food shortages also had their effect on buildings and public spaces. A national level innovation was the 'British Restaurant' chain, its branches in Oxford known as 'Municipal restaurants'. These were communal kitchens with trestle-tabled refectories, intended to feed people rendered homeless by bomb damage and those fancying a meal off the ration (see PLATE 17). Popular with civilians and service personnel alike, Oxford's first branch opened in the Cowley Road Congregational Schoolroom in January 1941, followed by establishments at Rose Hill Community Centre, the Baptist Church on New Road (fronting onto today's Bonn Square), the Majestic Cinema on Botley Road and the Town Hall. Other municipal restaurants opened in prefabs on Canal Wharf and York Place in St Clement's.[53]

At these places, one could get a two-course lunch for as little as ninepence and work up from there: for a shilling, Madge Martin got meat, vegetables, a bread roll, pudding and a cup of tea at the New Inn Hall Street branch, which fed around 500 people a day.[54] Favouring branches at Gloucester Green and St Aldate's, for a shilling and three-pence Kingsley Amis was able to choose either shepherd's pie or sausage and mash as a main course and rice pudding or cake for afters, followed by a hot drink.[55] A county-wide Emergency Feeding Scheme extended communal restaurants beyond Oxford, Woodstock town council's communal feeding centre serving 1,550 meals in a single week in January 1941.[56] The Rural Pie Scheme took the 'British restaurants' concept to those unable to access the restaurants themselves. Pioneered in Oxfordshire and adopted by Minister of Food Lord Woolton as the basis for a national plan, the scheme delivered meals to labourers in the field.

Parading, marching and drilling became common sights. WAAFs paraded in Magdalen and the ATS drilled in Manchester (Balliol clas-sicist Bill Watt, working there for naval intelligence, met his future wife as he remonstrated with her for drilling her charges outside his window).[57] June Coppock and her Girls Training Corps unit 'learned how to march and we paraded past Lord Dowding who took our salute'.[58] The mayor held a Town Hall reception for 200 Canadians in April 1940, and in August that year a party of 300 New Zealanders was welcomed and conducted around the sights. The Band and Bugles of the OBLI performed in the Town Hall in February 1941 on the occasion of the 200th anniversary of the raising of one of its founding regiments. On 25 August 1941 a parade of tanks made its way down St Giles, accompanied by the OBLI band.[59] On 13 February 1942 Madge Martin watched 'kilted Cameron Highlanders marching up and down St Giles to the swirl of bagpipes' in aid of Warship Week.[60] On 21 February 1943 there was a parade of over 4,000 servicemen and servicewomen with nine bands in honour of the Soviet war effort. It was accompanied by an exhibition and shop window displays of photos showing scenes of life in the Soviet Union, Soviet forces in action, and Soviet women war workers.[61] On 9 April 1943 the Princess Royal inspected a hundred ATS servicewomen in Radcliffe Square, and on 26 July the band of the US Army's 102 Mechanized Cavalry Regiment performed in Brasenose hall for the Royal Armoured Corps.[62] In 1944 Major John Howard paraded an OBLI battalion on St Giles' for Salute the Soldier week, a fortnight before parachuting into France on D-Day at the head of a glider-borne company sent to secure the bridges over the Caen canal and the Orne river.[63]

There were then the military vehicles, a regular sight on Oxfordshire roads: jeeps and lorries, the occasional convoy of Bren gun carriers making its caterpillared way down Beaumont Street, a line of Morris reconnaissance cars or Cromwell tanks fresh out of the factory in Cowley, and torpedoes moving through Oxford by train destined for the south coast. Albert Thomas lived in a flat on the High Street.

One morning, a week after Dunkirk, and being an old soldier, I simply could not sleep thinking of our poor boys over there. Hearing a rumbling noise along the High going on for some time, I got up, slipped on my dressing-gown and went into the dining-room which overlooks the High. It was about three o'clock a.m. and I watched a convoy going to France consisting of every kind of motor from a dairy cart, furniture van and 'bus to a grocer's delivery van, all packed with something, though it was well covered.[64]

The convoy went on without interruption until 5.30 a.m. In June 1944 Glenys Parry 'waited an hour to cross the High as American armoured columns moved south' on their way to Normandy.[65] Military hardware could even be seen on the river, as Salter's boatyard built 'large numbers of landing and support craft, many of which took part in the D-Day landings'.[66]

Edmund Blunden, commissioned as a map-reading instructor, took his officer cadets 'on imaginative exercises in the more agreeable parts of the Oxfordshire countryside'.[67] The OTC moved around the city and county each week: in November 1942, for example, a mobile column struck out from Oxford for the village of Chiselhampton, 'quite attracting notice as we went, guns and tanks as well as common motor vehicles', passing through Garsington to a mock battle between the Baldons and Dorchester, 'the scene of victory over paratroops'.[68] Douglas Ross remembers driving 'all over the Berkshire Downs and out to the Cotswolds' in open 15-cwt military trucks, map reading and doing wireless telegraphy drill as part of his OTC service.[69]

Every now and then, Oxford residents would see or even participate in military and civil defence exercises. A Southern Region army exercise in April 1940 saw the Morris works and Pressed Steel 'attacked' with high-explosive bombs and Magdalen Bridge destroyed. As part of the exercise, many Oxford response units were declared unavailable, away dealing with an emergency at RAF Abingdon. This allowed civil defence units from around the county to be mobilized to support the city.[70] For Exercise Spartan in March 1943, British and Canadian troops advanced from 'Southland' to meet troops of Eastern Command representing the forces of 'Eastland'.[71]

The daddy of them all was the 'Battle of Carfax', a major city-wide invasion exercise in January 1943 involving thousands of civilians and members of the British and American armed forces. City residents were ordered to stay indoors, and all shops, cinemas and restaurants were shut. Two days of intense activity witnessed the simulation of a serious air raid and land attack, causing incidents across the city. The exercise was marked by the firing of dummy rounds, the liberal use of white paint and bags of flour to mark affected streets and buildings, and the sound of an assortment of exploding whizbangs (as the organizers had been instructed, for 'Thunder flashes, smoke bombs and practice incendiary bombs – applications should be made to Dr Coslett at the Electrical Lab.'). Reverend Martin donned his ARP kit and 'went through streets deserted by all but ARP people to the Church', where he took up station in the lookout post on the tower.[72]

Somerville students volunteered for role-playing parts in the exercise. One, 'whose realistic impersonation of a hysterical foreigner deprived of house and sense and all coherent speech had shown up some weak spots in the city organisation', was commended by the town clerk in a letter to Principal Helen Darbishire.[73] An unexploded bomb was reported in the drive of South Building at St Hilda's, and the enemy occupied the hall. Home Guardsmen stationed in the college garden sniped at enemy soldiers constructing a pontoon bridge below the island.[74] The RAF provided both friend and foe air support. 'It was very thrilling and rather frightening', Madge Martin wrote, 'to see the enormous planes "dive-bombing" and flying very low over the houses whilst being attacked by dummy anti-aircraft fire.'[75]

> Sharp and heavy explosions were heard in all parts of the City. Smoke bombs were also used and palls of smoke hung over the main objectives as the planes weaved and circled overhead. Wave after wave of attacking planes came over and the steady drone of their engines filled the air.[76]

Testing the emergency services as well as the readiness of military units, civilian 'casualties' required treatment, on the Banbury Road near Wycliffe Hall following gas attacks and elsewhere. There was a phosgene attack in George Street, and fires caused by incendiary bombs crept along Cornmarket. Cowley airfield was assailed and there was a tank battle on Cumnor Hill. An attack on the city by infantry and armour developed from the direction of Wootton near Abingdon, another put in from the Wheatley area, the enemy attempting to fight its way to the city centre through Headington, street fighting breaking out in the Rose Hill district. Magdalen Bridge was assaulted as the advancing enemy sought to cross the Cherwell. The city centre's riverine line of defence was probed elsewhere, Folly Bridge attacked by ground forces and dive bombers and Hinksey Bridge by infantry covered by tanks, with simulated shellfire. The exercise involved the Home Guard, batteries of Royal Artillery 25-pounder field guns in the University Parks, units of the Northamptonshire Yeomanry, the Rifle Brigade, 91 Group RAF, and the American 102nd Cavalry Regiment.[77] After the all-clear, Madge Martin ventured on to St Giles, 'to see the tired tank corps having a hot meal, looking very dirty and oily'.[78]

Large numbers of service personnel congregated in and around Oxford, an indication of this military sprawl provided by the Hook Norton Brewery's 'military trade' records. At Adderbury, it supplied Liverpool Irish, Liverpool Scottish, Yorkshire and Lancashire, and Cameron Highlander army units, as well as a Polish army transit camp. At Adlestrop House, its customers included a Worcestershire Regiment transit camp, a King's Regiment reinforcement camp, and US Army handling units. A NAAFI at Aynho stocked Hookie beer, and three officers' messes were supplied at Banbury. The officers' and sergeants' messes at Barford St John, where a Bomber Command training unit was based, were regular customers. Also supplied were messes, canteens and NAAFIs at Bodicote, Broadway, Burton Dassett, Byfield, Croughton, Byfield, Chipping Warden, Culworth, Daylesford, Edgecote, Moreton-in-Marsh, North Aston, Sarsden House, Shenington, Stow-on-the-Wold, Thorpe Mandeville, Upper Heyford, Woodford and Wykham. Business boomed as a result.

Scores of US Army and US Army Air Force units were based in Oxfordshire as American military power built up in Britain ahead of D-Day.[79] Courtesy of their presence, Oxford had its share of the 'overpaid, oversexed, and over here' phenomenon.[80] 'I danced a lot, and found myself doing the "conga" and other new American dances', wrote Madge Martin after a party at Rhodes House for Americans and Canadians on New Year's Eve 1942.[81] While some service personnel, American, British or otherwise, were resident in Oxford for a few weeks at a time doing courses, or stationed for longer periods at military facilities in and around, others were more transitory, staging through on their way to somewhere else. For them, Oxford was just another link in a chain, part of the labyrinth of holding camps and training establishments through which servicemen and women were shunted. Pam Dunnett of the Queen Alexandra's Imperial Nursing Service (QAINS) was recalled to Britain from Egypt ahead of D-Day. Disembarking at Southampton, her unit moved to a Nissen hut encampment in Wales before a spell at a military psychiatric hospital. It was then on to Oxford, billeted at Brasenose for a week awaiting deployment. All she remembered of her time here was being taught how to salute in the college hall and swapping the grey and scarlet uniform of the QAINS for khaki battle-dress and a Red Cross armband.[82] Neta McCallum was another one of these nurses, arriving at Brasenose on 3 June 1944 in preparation for onward movement to support the tented military hospitals established in Normandy on D-Day.[83]

> We were quartered in Brasenose, a sacred precinct where never a female foot had trod. Even at this stage of excitement and sense of urgency there were proctors and college servants making sure that none of our kit was dumped on the centuries old lawns.[84]

A few days and it was off again, borne on the fast-flowing tides of war. The nurses moved into tented accommodation alongside Americans massing in the New Forest before embarking for France, going ashore at Arromanches on D-Day+6.

People got used to the sight of military aircraft, in the skies above and occasionally on the ground, as crashed and shot-down machines were taken by road to the Cowley repair and salvage works. One such was the wrecked Messerschmitt Bf110 flown to Scotland by Deputy Führer Rudolf Hess in May 1941. Making its way by road to Cowley, it was put on public display in St Giles' before angry authorities had it whisked away. Air traffic was heavy because the county was a major centre of British (and, later, American) air power.[85] Airfields like Bicester and Upper Heyford, reopened in the 1920s, were joined in the following decade by new ones, including Abingdon, Benson, Brize Norton, Harwell and Kidlington. Fully functioning airbases, emergency satellite landing fields, and decoy airfields sprang up across the county. Their names illustrate how war imposed itself on the countryside: Akeman Street, Barford St John, Chalgrove, Chipping Norton, Edgehill, Enstone, Fawler, Finmere, Glympton, Grove, Kelmscott, Kingston Bagpuize, Mount Farm, Shellingford, Slade Farm, Stanton Harcourt, Starveall Farm, Watchfield and West-on-the-Green.

The creation of these airbases was part of an extraordinary expansion, 444 new airfields constructed across Britain during the war, 'the greatest civil engineering feat undertaken in the United Kingdom since the railways were built a century before'.[86] Oxfordshire was said to have more airfields per square mile than any other part of the country, and RAF aircraft based here rose from 450 in April 1939 to 1,250 in March 1940, growing further as the war progressed.[87] The county hosted glider, bomber, transport, training, photo-reconnaissance and test-flight squadrons, while battle casualties were brought by air for treatment in Oxford's hospitals. There was even a naval airbase, Royal Naval Air Station Culham, opened in November 1944. An Aircraft Receipt and Dispatch Unit, it was christened HMS *Hornbill*. The county's airbases included storage facilities, such as No. 6 Air Ammunition Park at Eynsham, part of a chain of air ammunition parks delivering bombs from underground stores to airfields. It could store up to 6,000 tons of bombs, with satellite facilities along the roads of the Eynsham Hall parkland.[88]

In the early years of the war, the sound of aircraft overhead often meant German bombers, though the 'noisy skies above Oxford were mostly threatening only in passing and were usually heralds of violent activity in London or further north'.[89] As the conflict wore on, the Luftwaffe visited less and less frequently, and by the time of the Normandy landings the Allies enjoyed virtual air supremacy and the enemy could no longer venture across the Channel. 'The never-ending roar (it wasn't a drone) of planes from the airfields all around Oxford' was a feature of life for Douglas Ross when he was at Pembroke, especially during the '1000 bomber' raids on Germany.[90]

The Betjemans found that after 'the silence of Ireland the noise of aeroplanes was deafening' when they returned to Garrards Farm in Uffington in autumn 1943.[91] After seeing a group of RAF gliders under tow, Penelope, 'whose grasp of modern science was non-existent' (according to her daughter), asked Bowra: 'Are the ones in front pulling the ones behind?' He replied in the negative: 'No, the ones behind are pushing the ones in front.'[92] In his 1942 painting *Oxford during the War* (PLATE 11), Paul Nash featured aircraft above the spires, leaving the viewer to work out whether they were friend or foe. 'The sky above the old university town', wrote Lord Berners in his 1941 novel *Far from the Madding War*, seemed to have become a rendezvous for aviators, a kind of non-stop meet; they were for ever circling, wheeling and diving overhead and the ancient walls never ceased to vibrate with their droning. To many this might be a promise of protection; to Emmeline, the sound was a reminder of the precarious age we live in.[93]

Another observable aspect of wartime Oxford was its changing population. The drop in male undergraduates was very noticeable and the inflow of academic exiles continued, augmented by refugee students. The University law school helped a Polish law faculty establish itself, its degrees awarded with the Oxford seal attached.[94] The University sponsored three Czech universities (Charles University in Prague, Cornelius University in Bratislava, and Masaryk University in Brno). The students were granted access to libraries and lectures, their degree ceremonies staged in the Sheldonian with the vice chancellor acting as rector.[95] Iris Murdoch described wartime Oxford as 'a gentle civilised city full of elderly German Jews with faun-eyes & Central European scholars with long hair & longer sentences'.[96] Rowse thought that Oxford had 'taken something of the place of Salzburg in pre-Anschluss days'. The 'café life of the town ... has become distinctly more Continental ... From the languages being spoken all around one, one might be inhabiting a bit of old Vienna or some Central European university town.'[97] Numbers grew; in September 1940 Oxford city police estimated the number of migrants in Oxford to be in the region of 15–20,000 and (in November) reported that the county's population had increased by about 50 per cent.[98]

As the year turned, the authorities reckoned that there were over 2,000 Austrian, German and Italian 'aliens' in Oxford.[99] So great was the 'influx of refugees into the town' that Berners' character Emmeline, 'obliged one day to visit the shopping centre, could hardly make her way through the streets'. Personifying common stereotypes of the time, Berners wrote that

Czechs, Austrians and Germans crowded the pavements. Chattering Frenchwomen were to be heard complaining in high staccato voices about the blackout and other inconveniences. Corpulent Jewesses in trousers, armed with string bags, descended on the food shops like locusts. Women from Whitechapel treated their perambulators as tanks and mowed down everything before them ... At first this alien population confined itself to the shopping centres and did not penetrate into the streets and sanctuaries of the collegiate portions of the town. Latterly, however, it had shown a tendency to overflow into the meadows, and Emmeline now took her daily exercise in the spacious garden of All Saints.[100]

Rowse expressed similar sentiments. The 'influx of academic refugees', he wrote, led to 'the first and most obvious difference' between peacetime and wartime.

> The life of the streets, even in the old centre of the town, has ceased to be dominated by the University. So many thousands of evacuees and refugees have flooded into the area, mainly from London: it is said that the population has gone up by some twenty per cent, perhaps twenty thousand people. Then there are all the men in uniform, who crowd into this convenient centre by all the bus routes from round about. So that the streets of Oxford that were calculated to accommodate a population of some twenty thousand with dignity and space, and had long ceased to serve modern Oxford adequately, now have an extra and almost impossible strain upon them. Pavements are incessantly crowded; shopping has become a torture (not that that much concerns dons and undergraduates); theatres are packed with unknown faces – as the war wears on it becomes rarer and rarer to recognise a friend, one greets a distant acquaintance with spontaneous effusiveness and genuine relief. The place is filled, one feels, with people who know not Joseph. The few decrepit old dons who are left, and crocks like myself, are driven to take refuge within their ample college walls, cross the High or the Broad furtively, looking neither to the right nor to the left, to scuttle for their daily constitutional into the cover of Christ Church Meadows or Addison's Walk at Magdalen, the gardens of Trinity or St. John's.[101]

A consequence of inward migration was a shortage of accommodation. Informing alumni that the annual 'Old Men's' get-together in Oxford would not take place, Mansfield's principal wrote that 'Oxford, as a city of refuge, is most uncomfortably overcrowded, and it would be quite impossible to arrange hospitality for you in private houses, in lodgings or hotels'.[102] Even finding lodgings for 'key workers' such as codemakers and firemen was a constant problem, triggering petty bureaucratic squabbles as heads of government departments and military units scrabbled to get hold of the personnel they needed. In September 1943 Company Officer Burton reported to the Inter-Service Topographical Department at Manchester College, where he was to join a section working out the vulnerability to fire of cities occupied by the enemy. Accommodation was arranged at the Main Fire Station on George Street, but he soon resigned and left Oxford on account of the cost of living. On an annual salary of £375, he was out of pocket to the tune of £2 a week, or around a quarter of his pay.[103] Given this situation, outfits such as the Bletchley Park section at Mansfield College liked to employ young local women, because they often came equipped with their own or their parents' homes.

European refugees acclimatized to the city. With support from the Quakers, Milein Cosman had enrolled at the Slade School of Art, moving to Oxford when it departed London in 1940. She lived in a bedsit in the shadow of the Ashmolean, lit by gas, with no running water and a privy in the garden. To supplement her income she taught for the Workers Educational Association and fire-watched.[104] She sketched people around the city (see PLATE 15) and socialized with members of the University, meeting her fiancé Philip Rawson at a concert in Balliol.[105] Bojan Bujić came to Oxford from Vienna, where he had been a professor of music, via the Netherlands. Now he had to reinvent himself and his discipline to gain a foothold, becoming a 'one-man music faculty' (Oxford didn't have one), 'instrumental in laying the foundations of a new academic discipline at the university after the war'.[106] Unknown in Britain as a composer, he was known to Lincoln classicists as a leading authority on the 'history and notation of Byzantine music'.[107] Consequently, the college offered him a three-year fellowship funded by the Society for the Protection of Science and Learning, and he moved with his family to 51 Woodstock Road (where he would spend the rest of his life).

Eighteen-year-old Ernst Eisenmayer was a sculptor, writer and painter who had twice attempted to escape Austria. Intercepted at the French border, he was arrested and sent to Saarbrücken prison and then to Dachau concentration camp. His release was secured by Professor Brierly, and Ernst landed at Harwich on 24 April 1939, granted permission to take up a trainee position at Lucy & Co.'s Eagle Iron Works in Jericho.[108] He lived in the Quaker hostel and studied at the Oxford Schools of Technology, Arts and Crafts, and Commerce in Church Street, St Ebbe's.[109] Eisenmayer was a founding member of the Oxford branch of the Young Austria movement, discussing Austrian history and culture and organizing Sunday afternoon bicycle rides in the city's environs. Despite his job and his studies, Eisenmayer's position became increasingly precarious after Dunkirk, and on 25 June he and all the other residents of the hostel were interned, police arriving at the Iron Works to collect him.[110]

Night skies and missing railings

At night, of course, it was all about what people *couldn't* see. There were no lighted phone boxes or public clocks and all workplaces had to be completely screened. Blackout was strictly enforced, especially after aerial observation in January 1940 had shown that the city's efforts were nullified by car headlights and traffic lights that could be seen changing at 2,000 feet.[111] Registrar Veale told heads of house that Hebdomadal Council's Committee on Air Raid Precautions 'has had brought to its notice a report that the civic authorities are not satisfied with the blackout in some Colleges'.[112]

Edmund Blunden was visited in his flat on several occasions because of blackout irregularities, unrepentant in his ignorance ('what can an airman see 6000 feet up at 250 mph? Glow-worms beware!').[113] It wasn't just the authorities who were on the case. When the dean of Balliol left lights showing at night, Trinity undergraduates on staircase 11 pelted his rooms with coal and bottles.[114] The door between the two colleges being unlocked because of fire regulations, the victim was able to sail through and apprehend his assailants. The president of Trinity received a letter from Tony Carson, a student who had observed 'a vast shaft of light pouring forth from the President's House' one evening.

> The door had not been left open by mistake for I soon discerned the magic words 'puss-puss' being chanted into the night ... Might I suggest that before the President's cat is put out, the light might be extinguished in the President's hall? Not only so that the said cat might be allowed a little privacy but also so that there should be no risk of something being dropped on the College by a Jerry who might be simultaneously performing his nocturnal operations overhead?[115]

Blackout returned celestial glories to city dwellers because of the absence of artificial light: 'The moonlit "High" and Radcliffe Square, with a star-strewn sky above, are a sight to dream of', thrilled the *St Hugh's Chronicle* in 1940.[116] Grace Hadow marvelled at the 'sight of Oxford in full moon, with no artificial light to disturb the peace, and with Magdalen Tower and St Mary's spire steeped in a radiance infinitely more radiant than floodlighting'.[117] But while blackout embellished the aesthetics of the night sky, it also caused accidents. Superannuated Brasenose scouts brought out of retirement as the college cast around for help found it a trial as they struggled to work, not helped by the unusual hours kept by the army officers who had annexed their college. For Tolkien, 'an evening out in town meant cycling in darkness down Banbury Road guided only by the white lines painted on the kerbstones' (perhaps to find 'that supplies had run dry and the pubs were shut' when he arrived).[118]

'We had to learn how to become blackout-conscious and navigate dark entrances and dimly lit halls' said Lorna Clish of St Hugh's, 'before reaching the utter blackness of our own room, across which we stumbled to draw the curtains before putting on the light'.[119] Trinity students suggested that the walls under arches and staircase entrances be painted white to help them find their way around in the dark.[120] Heidi Brønner, working in NID's Norway section at Manchester College, walked to her digs in the city centre each evening: 'on moonless nights I might as well be blind if I did not have the little pen holder light with me.'[121] In the hours of darkness, writes Ken Coombe, Worcester College could not be seen from Gloucester Green, 'the solitary gesture to its location being the dismal blue light inside the main gate, which cast its cold glow on the Porter's Lodge'.[122]

Mansfield's principal wrote that 'if you turn in at the College gates after dark, you must take care not to be punctured by a bayonet!'[123] Many libraries closed at blackout time, wrote the principal of St Hugh's, though the Radcliffe Camera was open until 10 p.m., and the introduction of 'daylight saving' through winter months helped (the Radcliffe Science Library's opening hours were extended given the amount of government-related research undertaken there).[124] To some denizens of Oxford, blackout brought more abstract concerns, the master of Pembroke, Homes Dudden, asking Hebdomadal Council 'what action was proposed to protect male undergraduates against the solicitations of prostitutes in the darkened streets'.[125]

Everyone noticed the absence of railings, removed from summer 1940 when the Ministry of Supply launched a national campaign for scrap iron and household metal goods that could, apparently, be turned into weapons. On 30 May the deputy controller of raw materials wrote to the treasurer of Christ Church, W. Austin Daft, asking if Keble's railings had been removed yet. 'There is grave need for all available scrap metal and I have no hesitation in saying it is essential to move as quickly as possible', said the official.[126] Austin Daft quickly passed the message along the line, writing to all estate bursars with 'urgent instructions' from the ministry to get a move on. St John's had already complied across its North Oxford estate, and bursars were requested to deliver their railings and any other scrap metal to T. Warburton at 17 Bridge Street, or to inform the firm as to where it could be collected or removed from.[127]

Railings vanished from the Martyr's Memorial and the churchyard on the Plain, the Botanic Garden, the subterranean toilets on Rewley Road and at St Michael at the North Gate. Christ Church lost iron fencing around the library, at the Meadow Gate and out front on St Aldate's.[128] Railings were spared around the Bodleian and Sheldonian for architectural reasons, and in Park Town lest pedestrians fall into basements. The University scrapped 'tons of iron railings from buildings and old iron bookcases from the basement of the Ashmolean', and by the autumn the city had yielded up a thousand tons.[129] Gardens 'have lost their railings now and are overrun by the town's dogs', wrote Albert Thomas disapprovingly. 'It would break my heart to see a garden of mine like that, so perhaps it is just as well that I have not got one.'[130] But others welcomed the openness. Reverend Martin wrote that many people 'consider that the appearance of a building is much improved by the removal of railings ... and it has been found that this does not lead to trespassing or desecration as some would fear'.[131] The front of his church was 'thrown open for beauty, and for the help of our country in its hour of need'. The railings around the Martins' home on Wellington Place, part of the St John's estate, were cut down on 29 June 1940: 'Our iron railings have gone to help feed the guns and so have many others', wrote Madge. 'It improves the look of places enormously and perhaps we shall be a less suspicious nation if we ever live through what is coming.'[132]

Entertaining the troops – and the people

While there might be fewer day trippers, there were more people in and around the town and sometimes from a bit beyond, visiting for 'staycation'-style breaks or resting from war work in bombed-out towns. The University and the British Council sponsored hospitality at colleges for foreign military personnel, and the city was a recreation hub for servicemen and women at bases across the county.[133] Stanley Lester, a former Oxford Boy Scout and Home Guard trooper, was stationed at Harwell near Wantage when he joined the RAF. From there he and his mates 'thought nothing' of cycling into Oxford 'for a Saturday night at the Stu in Walton Street'.[134] In addition to the various servicemen's and women's clubs and canteens around town, the city did its best to welcome its many military visitors. 'His Majesty's and Allied Forces Information Centre' was at 16 Turl Street, and several organizations produced dedicated guidebooks. *Around Oxford: Places You Will Visit* came out with Alden Press, and the English Speaking Union released *Oxford and What to See and How to See It*.

As part of its series of information pamphlets for American service personnel in Britain, the British Council published *Oxford*, a picture of Queen's and High Street and a message from Mayor R.P. Capel on the cover.[135] On behalf of its citizens, the mayor welcomed them 'to the ancient city of Oxford, with its world-famed University'. Sir Richard Livingstone, vice chancellor from 1944, added his welcome to a city 'whose University is the oldest in England, and has sent forth into the world many whose names are household words wherever the English language is spoken'.[136] The booklet sketched the history of the city and the University, underlining its national importance, and provided information on where to eat and sleep, transport, sport, shopping, places worth visiting in and near the city, places of worship and hospital facilities.

It wasn't all sightseeing, and large numbers of military males meant an increase in venereal disease. Magdalen Bridge became a 'lurking place' for military personnel and prostitutes, students of nearby St Hilda's advised to 'step hard on the toes' of any man who came too close.[137] Local newspapers carried warnings about sexually transmitted infections, but cases increased all the same. In 1939 the Radcliffe Infirmary's VD clinic treated 3,380 patients, a figure that had grown to 8,516 by 1943. The

Oxfordshire WVS expressed concern about the stationing of American troops in the county and their penchant for buying women drinks.[138] Drunkenness and crime were often blamed on troops, Chief Constable Fox lamenting the combination of servicemen and the increasing number of women frequenting pubs.[139]

Oxford became an inland holiday resort, serving not only the expanded local population but also people from further afield who were unable to visit coastal towns.[140] There was a six-week 'Bring the seaside to Oxford' programme, a dozen donkeys purchased for rides in Cutteslowe Park and extra paddle boats procured for the boating lake at Hinksey Park. Butlin's Fun Fair attracted crowds to the Botley Road Recreation Ground and Florence Park in East Oxford.[141] The *Oxford Mail* began a series of articles titled 'Around and About Oxford', encouraging people to walk and cycle in the countryside given that the use of cars was not permitted for leisure purposes.[142] Madge and Robert Martin frequently walked up to Iffley village or bussed out to Burford, Kingham, Lewknor or Henley-on-Thames for a stroll, home in time for dinner and a show. Albert Thomas would go out to Boars Hill with his family – 'only a sixpenny 'bus ride away and one of the prettiest places in England – and sit under a tree nibbling our lunch'.[143]

In 1941 Charles MacInnes, Reader in Imperial History at Bristol, organized the 'Holidays in Oxford' scheme for overworked and war-fatigued Bristolians – 'soldiers of the Home Front', as the *Daily Express* called them.[144] Approximately 7,000 people took advantage, placed in Oxford colleges for two-week breaks, sightseeing, playing games and relaxing. In all, the scheme cost nearly £20,000, though some colleges like Oriel were so happy to help that they refused to charge a penny. As MacInnes's told the president of Magdalen in October 1941, the scheme 'will help substantially to maintain public morale no matter what disasters may befall us ... Bristol will always be grateful to Oxford for what it has done.'[145]

Traditional forms of entertainment flourished. The New Theatre was playing to 20–25,000 people a week in 1941, and over the course of the war it entertained more than half a million members of the armed forces for free. Oxford venues thrived, particularly as London theatres were shut, meaning that big names toured the provinces. The Playhouse might have struggled to fulfil its pledge to remain open throughout the year had it not been for an audience swelled by soldiers, refugees and evacuees.[146] To overcome petrol rationing and restrictions on public transport, curtain up was moved, initially from 7.45 to 7.15 p.m., eventually settling at 6.15 p.m.

Art boomed. Paul Nash helped set up the Arts Bureau at the start of the war, based in Beaumont Street and recruiting creative artists of various types for a 'counter-imaginative thrust' and recording of aspects of British life and the war's impact on the nation and its people.[147] The Euston Road School of English painters, encouraged by Sir Kenneth Clark (Keeper of Fine Art at the Ashmolean 1931–33, now director of the National Gallery), put on a show at the Ashmolean, and there was an 'Art of War' exhibition at the Bodleian. Clark was also chair of the War Artists' Advisory Committee, which mobilized artists to record what might be lost to enemy bombing and what had been damaged already, aimed at representing national identity and steeling morale. He commissioned Nash to record scenes for the Air Ministry, his works including *Totes Meer*, based on the tangle of wrecked German and RAF aircraft massed at Cowley, and *Battle of Britain*, painted in Oxford and exhibited at the National Gallery in January 1942.[148] The War Artists scheme involved some of the country's leading artists and produced over 1,500 works, other Oxford subjects including Walter Bayes's watercolour of the cupola of Queen's College.[149]

Spanish painter Gregorio Prieto resided in the city, drawing students and local celebrities, Lady Margaret Hall putting on an exhibition of his work. Eduardo Paolozzi drew cycling students and American soldiers, and Milein Cosman sketched friends and strangers, including service-men deep in conversation at the Eagle and Child. The 'Younger British Painters' event at the Ashmolean in November 1939 was 'designed to help young artists who have suffered from wartime conditions', featuring over sixty paintings from artists under the age of 50.[150] The Austrian Centre organized a display of Otto Flatter's cartoons entitled *Mein Kampf Illustrated*, and Young Austria put on an event called *Austria Shall be Free*.[151] Romanian painter Arthur Segal's 'Painting School for Professionals and Non-Professionals' relocated to north Oxford.[152]

Though its collections were depleted by the removal of material to Chastleton House, the Ashmolean reopened on 16 October 1939 after its brief closure on the outbreak. It was felt that the public deserved to have access, given the circumstances, and the entrance fee was waived. Galleries were hung with facsimiles of the old masters and copies of Raphael's tapestry cartoons, and the Weldon Room was used for temporary exhibitions.[153] As well as exhibiting the works of the Euston Road group, it showed paintings by artists in and around Oxford, and organized events in conjunction with Warship Week and the Aid to Russia Fund. Annual visitor figures had risen to 78,000 by 1944.[154]

Music was another entertainment staple. The London Philharmonic under Malcolm Sargent performed on several occasions, audiences packed with young people, many in uniform. As Rowse enthused, Oxford had become a 'cultural centre' due to the 'presence of many distinguished cosmopolitans, but so far as this country is concerned, partly, no doubt, because of the winging of London. Never has there been such wonderful concerts, such an *embarrass de musique*, as Oxford has enjoyed in war-time.'[155] Across the county, the Entertainment National Services Association (ENSA) had staged 900 concerts for troops and war workers by the end of 1943.[156] Glenn Miller and his band played an open-air concert at the Churchill Hospital as well as at the American airbases at Grove and Mount Farm.

The full range of familiar 'home front' effects, as the chapter has indicated, were experienced in Oxford (save, of course, for bombing). The focus now returns to the University, and the ways in which students' and dons' lives were affected.

EIGHT

UNDERGRADUATES AT WAR

Because the war dragged on and intruded so much, it became the new normal. 'Behind the centuries of Oxford as a place and as a way of life, the war was always there as a black backdrop', said Stella Grove of St Hugh's.[1] For Roy Jenkins, 'the war, impending or actual, was a constant background to my years at Oxford.'[2] 'It was there, in the background', said Somerville's Nina Bawden, 'but we had grown up with it and were used to it, grumbling on over our heads like so much tiresome, adult conversation.'[3] Though it impinged on the everyday and brought risks, students still studied, colleges looked after them, and they enjoyed themselves. They served in canteens, fire-watched and drilled, and in the vacations might work on farms or in factories. John Mortimer described the wartime University:

> The Oxford of the twenties and thirties was still there, like college claret, but it was rationed, on coupons, and there was not very much of it left. The famous characters still behaved as though they lingered in the pages of *Decline and Fall*.[4]

Even in 'rationed, blacked-out Oxford, there were limitless hours for talking, drinking, staying up all night, even going for walks'.[5]

Harper-Nelson concurred. 'Perhaps the most remarkable thing about life in college during this time was that it was so unremarkable.'[6] There was a change in the political temperature; because international politics now encroached so egregiously, the ideological imperatives of the 1930s subsided. 'None of us was politically inclined', wrote Harper-Nelson, 'except in a rather woolly haze of idealism engendered in us by the Spanish Civil War, Gollancz's Left Book Club and Hulton's crusading new magazine Picture Post.'[7] The trick was to enjoy as much 'normal' life as possible before the war claimed you, and to get stuck in. Jenkins was 'almost as cast down by defeat for the Union presidency than by the fall of France'.[8]

Though they made the best of things, war-induced changes were inescapable. For example, one's college had been wholly or partly taken over by other people, and the impact on cohesion tremendous. St Hugh's third years, who had 'been living in splendid isolation', were 'viewed with something like distrust by freshers when they made their infrequent way to the Manor for JCR meetings'.[9] In the men's colleges, senior students disappeared into the military. 'The average age of the college had been much reduced', wrote Bruce Montgomery, 'and a sort of standard public-school prefect's common-room type had superseded the more adult eccentricities and individualities which had existed before the war'.[10] At Magdalen, observed history fellow Bruce McFarlane,

[t]he freshmen deprived of their seniors are failing to grow up & behave like schoolboys. The few surviving seniors withdraw in disgust & make no contact with them; & so the traditions die & the atmosphere becomes less and less civilized.[11]

'There are now schoolchildren, we are told', wrote a Queen's student in 1943, 'who would not recognize a banana if they saw one, so it may surprise no one to learn that there are now undergraduates at Queen's who would not recognize pre-war Oxford.'

Indeed, with the departure of the last stalwart in the summer, there is no undergraduate here now who was up before the war, and the memories of most of us go back so short a time that a respectful hearing is assured to anyone who can reminisce of Oxford in the first year of the war, when female bedmakers (we can hardly help calling them 'guides') were confined to Cambridge and second helpings were obtainable at dinner.[12]

The vagaries of war caused more subtle changes too. A former University College student wrote that relations with college servants 'were cordial if not close' (a normal state of affairs) but that there was a clear sense that scouts and porters 'who had fought in the previous war may have regarded some of us in reserved occupations as column dodgers'.[13]

If not rendered completely out of bounds by requisition, one's college was now shared with strangers – government clerks or military officers, a transient bunch of Canadian soldiers or Dutch naval cadets, a contingent in air force blue or a bunch of evacuees.[14] Exiled students from other colleges, even! Somerville offered high-table hospitality to its graduates now working in government departments in Oxford, and Merton gave common-room privileges to RAF officers from Abingdon. Then there were the children; a photograph shows William Beveridge surrounded by little evacuees in University College's front quad, another the incongruous image of children and mothers hanging out laundry in Radcliffe Quad.[15] Women's colleges adopted evacuated schoolchildren, undergraduates devoting weekends to their care.[16]

Eversley Belfield, returning to Pembroke in 1941 after his first stint in the army, was shocked to see how the college had been taken over: 'the whole place had altered – the only remaining staff seemed to be at the Porter's Lodge … I felt like some ghost haunting the place.'[17] This was Richard Hillary's experience too when an RAF mission caused him to 'fly down to Oxford'. He had had a tempestuous war so far, the reality of which had fallen far short of his 'kill or be killed' vision of aerial combat. He had killed but not been killed, and nothing could have prepared him for the disfigurement suffered when his Spitfire was shot down by a Messerschmidt in September 1940.[18] Extensive skin grafts and plastic surgery followed. Incredibly, though he could barely hold a knife and fork because of burn damage to his hands, he was allowed to return to service as a pilot. Hence the mission to Oxford. A friend who'd been back recently urged him not to visit.

> Richard, whatever you do, don't go back. It would take a book to explain
> how it's changed; but to sum it up in one sentence – in the Randolph
> Bar there is a notice saying: 'No unaccompanied ladies will be served
> drinks'.[19]

This didn't put Hillary off, and after circling the city a couple of times from the air, admiring landmarks such as the river, Magdalen Tower and Trinity's garden, he landed and jumped in a taxi to Trinity.

Superficially it was unchanged. Huckins, the porter, was still at the gate. 'Good evening, Mr Hillary', he said, in the same lugubrious tone in which he would announce that one was to be reported to the Dean. The window of my room still looked out on the Quad and caught the evening rays of sun, and a few old college servants raised friendly hands to their forelocks. But, apart from them, not a familiar face ... The place was tired; it had the left-over air of a seaside resort in winter.[20]

It was out of term time, though Hillary had at least expected to see some dons he knew. He wandered around the college, marking the rooms of friends now prisoners of war or killed in action. Leaving, he ran into the president's wife, who offered him a room in the Lodgings for the night, which he gratefully accepted before heading off to see what the city had to offer and if he could find anyone he recognized.[21] In January 1943, on a course for night fighter pilots, he was killed when his Blenheim crashed in Scotland.

Changes in college composition were striking. Christ Church men found they had the entirety of Brasenose living in their midst. In 1944–45 Trinity admitted only sixteen 'regular freshmen' but eighty-six service cadets. It also housed Balliol men, 'like Montagues fraternizing with Capulets', as Jenkins put it.[22] These things 'tended to increase the feeling of a club-like intimacy among undergraduates and dons alike', as people stuck to their own.[23] Corpus's student body was divided into three distinct groups. There were the 'natives', namely those undergraduates admitted in the normal way. Then there were the six-month short course cadets. Then there were the men of St Peter's. There was little mixing among the groups, and the circumstances brought the 'natives' closer together. In Christ Church's cavernous hall, Brasenose and Christ Church men dined at different tables, separated in turn from the RAF cadets (twenty-two on Christ Church's freshers list in 1941).[24] Trinity's JCR proposed that Balliol men resident in their college be allocated a separate table in hall (which they would surely have welcomed).[25] Separation impacted the SCR, too. Intelligence Corps officers got on perfectly well with their hosts at Pembroke, but there was hardly any contact between them. They fed at different times off different rations, and the fellows kept themselves to themselves: 'to them we were interlopers', wrote Cobban.[26] The master (Homes Dudden) was old and

178 OXFORD'S WAR

set in his ways and the two senior dons, Drake and Salt, were not easily approachable. This, Cobban reflects, was a great shame, especially as over a third of the depot's officers were academics or schoolmasters.

War was not conducive to the usual university 'experience'.

> [E]verything was unexpected and strange and an Oxford student could find herself digging up Portmeadow for cabbages, threading camouflage meshing for tanks in the Worcester Provost's drawing room and taking care of poor evacuee children from the East End … all this in addition to her regular duties of study.[27]

'The personelle [*sic*] of the university has changed tremendously', wrote Iris Murdoch. 'Everything here seems curiously the same – and yet I don't know why it should, for every month batches of men fade away into khaki, and Balliol is full of glossy civil servants from Whitehall.'[28]

> Myself, I continue my work in a faded, disintegrating, war-minded, uneasy, evacuee-haunted Oxford that likes me not. Everyone is younger & far more hysterical. Youthful dons & adult male undergraduates are as rare as butterflies in March. The halt the lame & the blind are left to us. I get moods when I want to rush out of Oxford, much as I love the place, & never look back.[29]

The atmosphere was palpably different. A Queen's student wrote that 'a more sober and responsible spirit prevails and, at the same time, there is a keen (and natural) sense of uncertainty and impermanence'.[30] 'All the time there was a special tension' wrote Stella Grove:

> We all felt guilty to be up at all and, as a result worked and played the harder … On the way to the college library, a glimpse of a stretcher case and their white attendants, or convalescents in hospital blue, could 'give us pause'.[31]

All St Hugh's students were conscious of the plight of the severely wounded servicemen occupying their college. It would have been different had they not been allowed to use the college library, and if the windows of some of the college houses did not overlook the hospital wards in the college gardens. 'From "The Lawn" [a large house at 89 Banbury Road leased from Lincoln] we could see everything', recalled Mary Healey:

sadly, perhaps those students in Holywell and other temporary accommo-
dations were better off in this respect for we could, from our windows,
see the Nissen huts smothering the rose-beds and tennis courts and
wonder whether things would ever be the same again.[32]

The prospect of military or some other form of war service over-
shadowed student life. 'After Oxford there would be the army (or some
other service) and there was not much point in thinking beyond that
thick barrier', wrote Jenkins.[33] Arriving at Pembroke in Michaelmas
1941, Douglas Ross felt that though 'one was now in Oxford and of
Oxford', there was no avoiding 'the elemental fact that everything one
did was affected and conditioned, to some degree, by the war', and an
'overwhelming sense of being there on borrowed time'.[34] Along similar
lines, Peter Anstey wrote:

> All of us, however, knew well that we had but a part-way course to
> run – Honours Mods in my case in four terms instead of five and little or
> no prospect of Greats to follow. Then the war would claim our undivided
> attention for the foreseeable future.[35]

Completing his short course cadet exams, Ken Coombe thought
the chance of returning to continue his studies was remote, aware of
the high casualty rate among RAF aircrew and of the fact that, even if
Hitler should be defeated, the war in the Far East awaited. 'We all went
down, to an unknown future, with little real belief in ever returning;
it seemed that the idyllic war for us was over, and the realistic stuff
was about to begin.'[36]

Guilt for being at university while there was a war on (and in a city
not getting bombed) was understandable but misplaced, for their time
would assuredly come. The majority of students also kept in touch with
other parts of the country, going home when term ended. As Stella
Grove recalled,

> vacations took some of us into the Blitz. As terms went by, brothers and
> friends were reported killed, missing, wounded or a prisoner. Men dis-
> appeared and reappeared in uniform instead of gowns ... Soon, Direction
> of Labour (ie unisex conscription) was announced, and we spent that
> night seeing an overnight end to our escapism.[37]

The prospect of military service was brought closer by obligatory
military training while a student. Anstey was called out to help build

a dummy airfield near Witney and dragged off in summer 1941 for a crash course in tractor driving and maintenance, in addition to weekly bayonet practice in Christ Church Meadow and night-time fire-watching duties. Patrick Benner of University College remembers life for undergraduates on service courses. Though the academic work was not very demanding, they had to undergo arduous training exercises, facilities including an assault course concocted on New College's playing fields on St Cross Road:

> I forget all the horrid details; but I know that one used amongst other things to go up over a high wall, scramble up the side of the pavilion, then traverse the front of the roof and drop down on the far side, and (with varying degrees of efficiency) cross a backwater of the Cherwell on a single pole. Afterwards, I would cycle back to college to change. My bedroom did not adjoin my sitting room, which I shared, but was part of the suite of a Fellow who lived out of College. As a result, his tutorials were regularly interrupted by a dishevelled post-assault course figure trudging through his room on the way to change, and then emerging again hurriedly to rush off to a lecture.[38]

Military training intensified in 1942 – perhaps, Harper-Nelson speculated, because of the mounting bad news as Japan entered the war and conquered allied territories in the Asia-Pacific region. 'Obviously someone in authority had decided that the fault lay in the general unfitness for combat of the Oxford undergraduate and so it was ordered that we should parade for Physical Training every Monday morning.'[39]

Stephen Cooper gave his parents a breakdown of a typical week: Sunday, free. Monday and Friday, 9.10 until 5:30, RAF work. Tuesday, three lectures and a tutorial. Wednesday, physics practicals. Thursday, three lectures and a tutorial. Saturday: three lectures.[40] Students 'do their studies', Rowse wrote, 'and a day and a half for OTC parades, [military] lectures, and [military] exercises in the country. In addition they have their college rotas for fire-watching and so on.'[41] He described the week of a male arts student: Monday: OTC all day, evening spent in preparation for a tutorial ('he has two a week, each due an essay'). Tuesday: filled with lectures and essay writing. Evening off, perhaps a concert or cinema. Wednesday: prep for the next essay; practice rugby match in the afternoon. Thursday: morning lectures, afternoon

OTC, evening reading for tutorial. Friday: essay writing for tutorial that evening. Saturday: away rugby match. Sunday: reading hard to catch up for next essay. A night or two a week fire-watching.[42] It was an incredible amount to fit in. As a student put it in the *St Catherine's Magazine*: 'When we [fire]watch through the night and march through the day, we begin to wonder when we are to work.'[43]

There was then civilian war work. Some Somervillians laboured alongside principal Eleanor Plumer of St Anne's at her fuse-testing 'factory' in the library of Hartland House. Having volunteered as a factory hand at the Cowley works, 'she conceived the idea of sub-contracting to her staff and students', trays of fuse-caps 'laid out on long tables to be tested'.[44] 'To our usual forms of exercise', wrote St Hugh's JCR president in 1941, the war added that of digging.

> A large number of people have taken this up, and have worked at allotments at Headington ... and on Port Meadow and in the Parks (where potatoes were grown). Nor did the work cease at the end of term, vacation activities have included nursing, tractor-driving, the sorting of Post Office mails, milk rounds, and all types of land work.[45]

Mary and her fellow undergraduates at St Hugh's tried to help out with the head injury patients, inviting 'ambulant' ones to tea, or taking them to the river.[46] Another St Hugh's student remembers the walk to the college library, 'through the grounds, full of pre-fab wards. The patients, desperate for company, always wanted to talk to us'.[47] Janet Gibbins recalled

> with horror washing endless greasy plates in the British Restaurant. A much more pleasant assignment was the 6–8 a.m. shift as a 'Red Cross nurse' at the Radcliffe Infirmary helping the hard-pressed night staff to complete breakfast and bedmaking before the day staff arrived.[48]

Stella Grove worked at the same British Restaurant on Gloucester Green, where she 'scraped the plates into a pig swill bin'.[49] Nina Bawden's 'particular duty'

> was listed as 'Entertaining American soldiers'. I found it no hardship. All I ever did for these polite, bewildered young men, kicking their heels in camps outside Oxford, was to serve as a waitress at the Red Cross Club in Beaumont Street.[50]

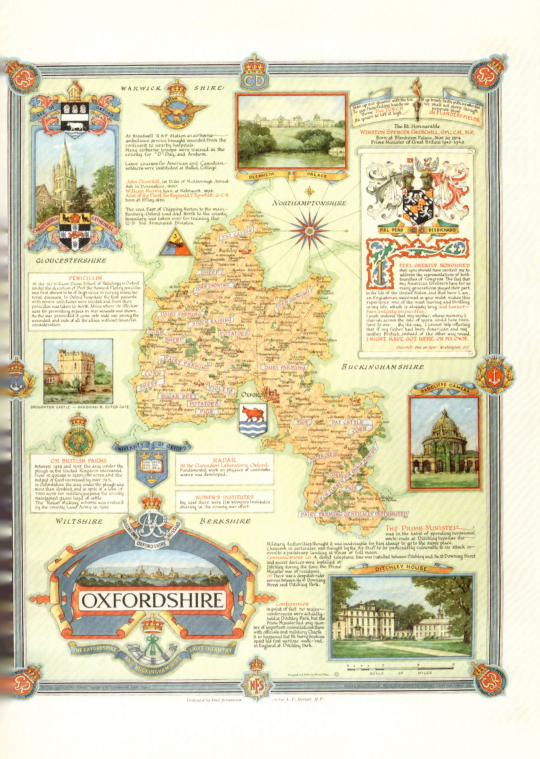

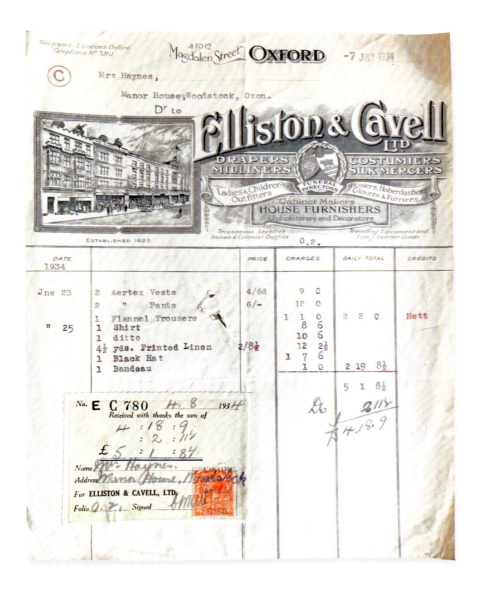

PLATE 1 (previous page) Ernest Clegg's drawing of Oxfordshire, showing Civil Defence and National Fire Services badges top and bottom and packed with information regarding the county's war effort. Issued by *The Countryman*, 1947, part of a series covering English counties.

PLATE 2 Telegram from the director of Military Training at the War Office telling the chair of the Joint Recruitment Board to start interviewing Oxford undergraduates for military service, 1 September 1939.

PLATE 3 A 1934 receipt from Elliston & Cavell's of Magdalen Street, queen of the Oxford department stores. At the time, all receipts had to pay 2d stamp duty.

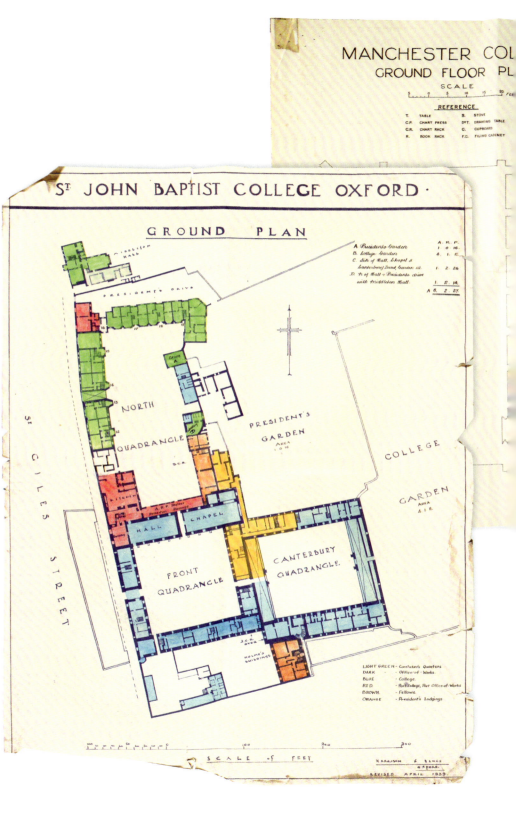

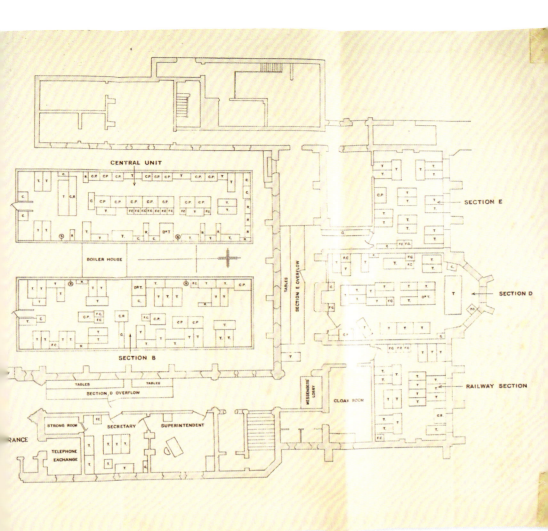

PLATE 4 This plan of the lower ground floor of St John's illustrates the way colleges shared space with government and military departments. Green is requisitioned Office of Works territory; red is part government, part college; blue is college.

PLATE 5 A plan of Tate Quad, Manchester College, showing the three huts erected to provide extra accommodation for Inter-Service Topographical Department personnel. The bottom right hut housed Section B, the Norway section. The plan also shows ISTD Superintendent Colonel Bassett's office and other ISTD sections, such as the Railway section.

PLATE 6 Colleges published annual 'records' or 'magazines', informing alumni of college life over the past year. Wartime editions, like this one from Mansfield College, detailed the military activity of college members and the conflict's impact on college life.

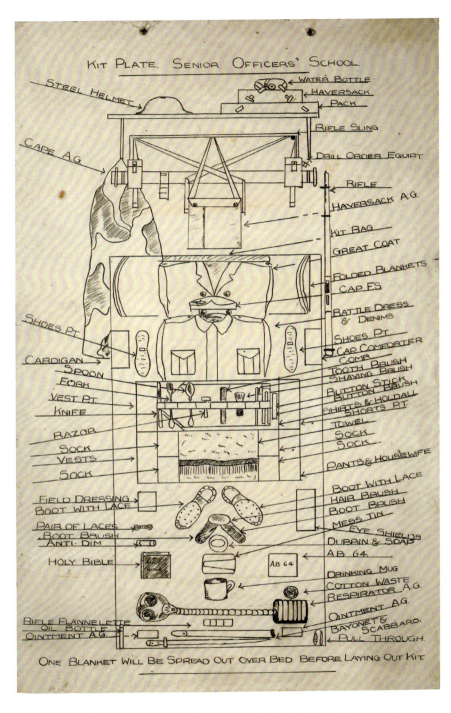

PLATE 7 A guide to laying out one's kit, issued to the Senior Officers' School at Brasenose College.

'England expects . . .'

JOIN THE OXFORD
HOME GUARD

TO-DAY

TO DEFEND YOUR HOME

TO-MORROW

All fit and willing men from the age of seventeen welcomed

FULL INFORMATION GIVEN HERE
SUMMERTOWN & WOLVERCOTE COMPANY

ALDEN PRESS

PLATE 8 Home Guard recruitment poster for the City of Oxford battalion, in which Maurice Bowra, Frank Pakenham and A.J.P. Taylor served.

PLATE 9 The Home Guard assault course at Aston's Eyot on the banks of the Thames, approached from Jackdaw Lane off the Iffley Road.

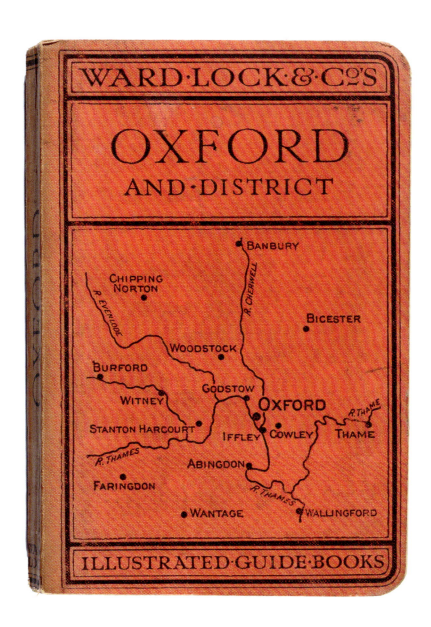

PLATE 10 Ward Lock's 1938–39 'red guide' to Oxfordshire.

PLATE 11 *Oxford during the War* by Paul Nash, 1942, oil on canvas. Nash was commissioned by former students D.B. Adams and A.D. Adams, the picture intended to hang above the south fireplace in the Worcester College JCR. It shows the Senior Training Corps' mobile column advancing westward and military aircraft above the city's spires (*Worcester College Record*).

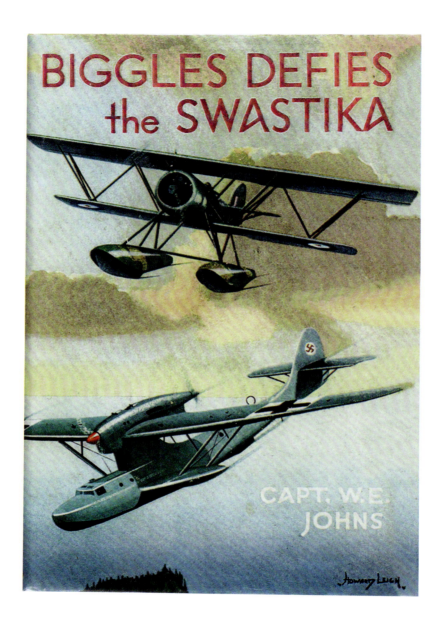

PLATE 12 William Johns added around a dozen titles to his series of *Biggles* novels during the war. This one, set against the backdrop of the Norway campaign, was published by Oxford University Press in 1941.

PLATE 13 *Totes Meer* (Dead Sea) by Paul Nash, 1940–41, oil on canvas.

PLATE 14 *London Evacuees at Oxford*, a watercolour by Ethel Hatch, 1942.

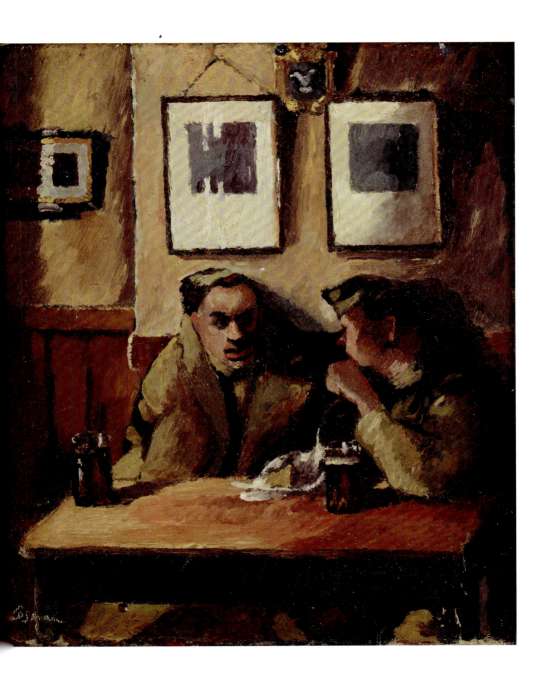

PLATE 15 *The Eagle and Child*, oil by Milein Cosman, 1942. Two British soldiers deep in conversation. Cosman did the sketches for this project in the pub itself, working on the painting by gaslight in her digs by the Ashmolean Museum.

PLATE 16 Evacuees in the Main Quad of University College, September 1940. The college master, Sir William Beveridge, is the hatted figure on the left. The large windows, those of the college chapel, show blast-damage protective screens.

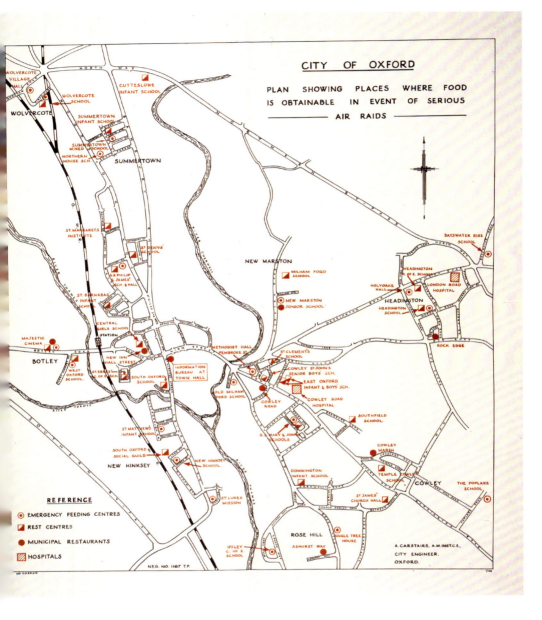

PLATE 17 A 1942 map showing emergency feeding centres, rest centres, Municipal Restaurants, and hospitals. Every British city had to devote enormous resources to civil defence and emergency services.

PLATE 18 British soldiers pass undergraduates outside The Queen's College.

PLATE 19 Uniforms on the streets: a knot of pedestrians outside the University Church on the High Street.

PLATE 20 The clean lines of the newly built New Bodleian, and white stripes painted on the kerb to aid visibility in the blackout. The Clarendon Building, where the recruitment board interviewed student volunteers, is on the left.

PLATE 21 The New Bodleian under construction.

PLATE 22 Allied troops being given a tour by a member of the English Speaking Union. Two parties pass beneath the Bridge of Sighs on New College Lane. The Sheldonian Theatre is directly ahead (*left*) alongside the Clarendon Building (*right*).

PLATE 23 *Troops at Balliol*, Richard Eurich, 1947, oil on canvas. Not just troops – there are navy and air force uniforms here, officers and other ranks. A game of bowls is in progress, drinks are being distributed and a cat observes the scene.

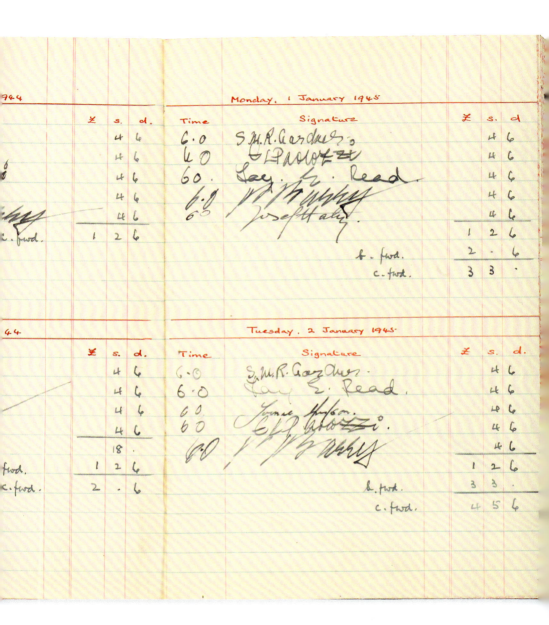

PLATE 24 Fire-watching at the Ashmolean: the fireguards' attendance book for Ruskin and Slade Schools, December 1944.

PLATE 25 St Hilda's firefighting: Hilary Allen and Denise Dudley hosing down South Building.

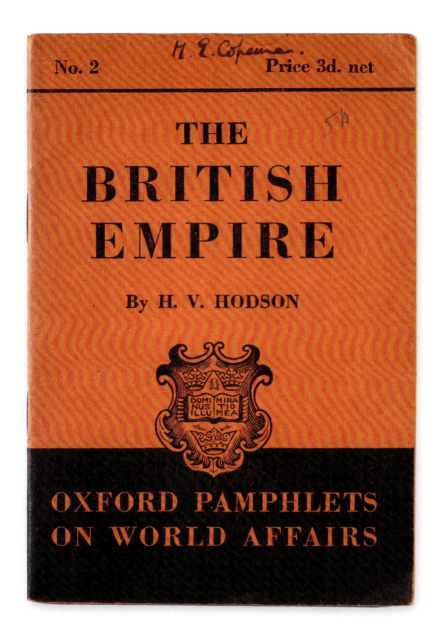

PLATE 26 The Oxford University Press 'Pamphlets on World Affairs' series. Over 6 million were sold, and they were intended as informational propaganda.

PLATE 27 Churchill Mark II anti-aircraft tanks with engineers and army personnel at the Morris works, 1944. They were used by the British and Polish armies in the Normandy campaign.

PLATE 28 Working in the old Map Room in the New Bodleian (first floor, windows on the left looking out onto the King's Arms pub): employees of the Inter-Service Topographical Department, part of the Naval Intelligence Division. Official photograph by Peter Bradford of the Admiralty Photographic Unit.

PLATE 29 An employee of the Inter-Service Topographical Department examining and cataloguing photographs and postcards, to be used for producing military intelligence. One of a series of official photographs by Peter Bradford of the Admiralty Photographic Unit, which was also based in the New Bodleian.

PLATE 30 A selection from the landmark 58-volume Naval Handbook series produced by Oxford and Cambridge geographers, working for Naval Intelligence Division 5. These four volumes deal with Italy. The open pages show maps and coastline detail, intended to help with the planning of military operations.

PLATE 31 Patients at the Combined Services Hospital for Head Injuries at St Hugh's College. Over 13,000 patients were treated here, in a hospital that achieved a bed capacity of 430.

PLATE 32 Food preparation in the St Hugh's kitchens

PLATE 33 Allied servicemen attending a short course at Balliol view the river from Addison's Walk in Magdalen College's grounds. The tower and buildings of Magdalen form the background. *c.*1942.

PLATE 34 One of the more unusual Second World War memorials: Pembroke College, Chapel Quad, John Wynne Harvey's *Mourning Women*, commissioned by the JCR in 1947.

Other Somervillians worked at the Red Cross Club too, it being suspected that one of their number, 'who changed from her drab working clothes into butterfly garments made from home-dyed cheese cloth when she left the college at six every evening, was not just setting forth to cut sandwiches.'[51]

The knitting parties held in the rooms of Somerville's principal after supper on Sundays produced brightly coloured blankets for the needy oversea, accompanied by a student read aloud (mostly Henry James). Somerville adopted an elementary school evacuated from Bow, students teaching the boys country dancing and Scottish reels. They produced plays for them to act in, a performance of *A Midsummer Night's Dream* in Trinity 1940 on the lawn outside Penrose arranged for wounded soldiers who were collected from the Radcliffe Infirmary.[52] In return, the boys and their schoolmasters helped transform the chapel lawn into a vegetable plot. Somerville students also volunteered as guinea pigs for an army malaria research unit testing new drugs, worked in munitions factories and helped bring in the harvest in vacations. St Hilda's students knitted, rolled bandages, looked after evacuees, helped out in the Toc H branch on the Plain, dug allotments at Headington Hill and in the Parks, did laundry and scullery work for the hospitals, knotted rags onto camouflage netting, sewed stretcher bags and rubbed out marginalia in books to be sent to POWs by the Red Cross Postal Book Service in the New Bodleian.[53]

Student activities and feeding

Normal undergraduate activities continued: sport remained a feature, there was still punting in Trinity, and clubs and societies of various stripes carried on meeting. Some college societies gradually ceased operating due to lack of numbers, but University clubs and societies continued.[54] Sport was no longer possible on a peacetime scale; annual varsity matches, races and competitions were suspended for the duration, and few colleges were able to field whole teams for inter-collegiate 'cuppers' competitions. So, combined college teams and crews were formed: Brasenose teamed up with Christ Church, Queen's with St Edmund Hall. Pembroke combined with neighbouring Campion Hall to form a rugby XV, and Univ clubbed together with Merton for a hockey team and rowing eights.[55] During Eights Week in 1941, Trinity teamed up with Balliol to produce a crew, Christ Church with Brasenose and Pembroke, and New College with Magdalen (thirteen crews competed; in 1939 there had been forty).[56] Four unofficial Oxford–Cambridge boat races took place, at Henley-on-Thames (1940), Sandford-on-Thames (1943, with the finish line at Radley College boat house), on Great Ouse (1944), and back at Henley in the final year of the war. The oarsmen didn't qualify for Blues, but despite their unofficial status the races 'were met with a large interest from both the public and the media'.[57]

The war situation had its plus sides: cycling, recalled Douglas Ross, was 'a delight with so few cars on the roads'.[58] Undergraduates, he continues, 'were an active lot. We walked for miles (often practising avoidance of air attack when the ground was dry underfoot).'[59] 'Of course, one had a bicycle', wrote Heidi Brønner.

> How could one otherwise get home at night time from friends in the outskirts after the last bus had gone? How could one otherwise get a night trip under the stars, undisturbed by lamps and lights, on winding country roads empty of all traffic? There is a grim irony in this; that only in such a war is it possible to find such peace out in the countryside.[60]

Music became more prominent in University life because of the war, said the *St Hugh's Chronicle*, and students established the Oxford University Musicians' Club to coordinate various activities. As in sports, some colleges combined their talents, Somerville partnering with Exeter Musical Society. The University College Music Society still had enough members to put on Fauré's *Requiem* in the University Church in February 1940, and town-and-gown choirs like the Oxford Harmonic Society and Oxford Bach Choir continued to function. Margaret Roberts (later Thatcher) sung *St Matthew Passion* with the latter in the Sheldonian. The glories of choral evensong, at Christ Church, Magdalen and New College, remained accessible: 'in drab wartime Britain', wrote a University College student, 'they were a very feast of beauty, peace and spirituality – and they cost nothing!'[61] At New College, Organist Herbert Andrews was determined to maintain the quality and frequency of choral services, believing that 'Hitler's sole objective was to disrupt the choral routine', which he took as 'a personal challenge'.[62] There

184 OXFORD'S WAR

was a general shortage of lay clerks, as those eligible to do so joined the forces. Evensong in winter months was moved to late afternoon, it being impractical to black out the cavernous chapel. The choristers dispensed with cassocks and Eton collars because of the war (except on Sundays). The choirboys were told by the headmaster of New College School that they could help in the war effort by making sacrifices like not wearing socks in summer. 'I wondered', wrote John Platts, 'how my going sockless was going to bring the Third Reich crashing to its knees, but was too timid to ask.'[63] The choir broadcast regularly for the BBC on Tuesday afternoons, alternating with King's College Cambridge. The BBC 'paid us in National Savings stamps and occasionally sent a large tin of toffees which HKA [Andrews] dispensed to those who deserved them'.[64]

The Oxford Union's doors remained open, but the war affected it in numerous ways. All four officeholders elected for the 1939–40 academic year were in the forces come the start of Michaelmas, and general numbers were down as the undergraduate population shrank.[65] With so many of the remaining undergraduates only in Oxford for a year before leaving for military duties, it was not possible to live out a full Union 'career'. Because of the wartime truce among the main political parties, it was difficult to get politicians to visit and speak against each other. Lively motions, therefore, were elusive, options further circumscribed by the fact that there was 'little appetite for purely frivolous motions' and that in the name of security, those proposed were subject to proctorial approval. Motions considered too controversial were vetoed, such as 'That in the opinion of this House lack of initiative rather than lack of resources is retarding the Allied prosecution of the war'.[66] Worthwhile debates still occurred, however, one moved by Victor Gollancz on 28 January 1943 considering whether the government should 'adopt a more energetic and practical policy towards the rescue of Jews in Europe' (the opposing team crossing the floor to support Gollancz following his moving speech).[67] But often the motions struggled to spark interest. Christopher Hollis writes:

> I remember returning home on leave shortly before the German surrender in Italy, to be confronted with an invitation to debate the rights and wrongs of the battle of Marston Moor. I did not feel strong enough for such an argument at such a time, nor, I imagine, did many others.[68]

Student newspapers felt the effects too. *Isis* ceased publication for the duration, editor Derek Mond dying in a flying accident, his co-editor twice wounded.[69] *Cherwell* functioned in a greatly diminished state. There were rumours that the Conservative Association would take it over, and a contributor to the *Oxford Magazine* predicted that the publication would meet its end. *Cherwell* responded by suggesting that the article's author seemed like 'a rather stupid and left-wing undergraduate' who did not realize that

> THE CHERWELL is not a Tory rag; we beg to present fairly the opinions of all parties who care to write, to present a selection of such literary talent as will contribute to us, and preserve the function of the paper in presenting university news of interest.

In the final Hilary 1942 issue, the editors promised that *Cherwell* would be back next term and 'continue to serve you on the twelve miserable pages allowed by Paper Control, with such talent as the Recruiting Board leaves us'.

Time-honoured discomforts of student life persisted: communal lavatories and no washbasins in rooms, jugs of water freezing in winter, a kettle on a gas ring per staircase for the heated variety. War just made them worse: a plimsoll line in the bath restricted water levels to a regulation eight inches, and coal rationing drastically reduced available heat. 'Oxford, in wartime, in winter, was damply, bone-achingly cold', recalled Nina Bawden.[70] Tony Palmer, who went up to University College in 1944, described the 'fierce cold' of his unheated bedroom: 'I was never so cold during 15 years in the Canadian West. I would put both my Army greatcoat and the bedroom carpet on top of the bedclothes.'[71] At St John's, coal shortages meant that only a single fire was allowed per staircase, leading students to work and entertain in the same room. It was the same at Pembroke, where there were communal fires 'and we shuffled around each other's rooms'.[72] At Trinity, Harper-Nelson and his friends would 'crouch around a fire pooling our meagre rations of coal'.[73] At St Hilda's, friends gathered in one room to keep warm, making toast around a single fire.[74] At the Union, the expense of maintaining the central heating could not be met, so stoves were brought in to the chamber during debates.[75]

Despite its reputation for high living and high table, Oxford endured an altogether drabber existence. College feasts and other festivities were largely suspended; though getting drunk was common, wrote Kingsley Amis, there were no lavish supper or drinks parties. 'HITLER STOPS THE FREE BEER', declared an *Evening Standard* sub-headline.

> Hitler has scored one victory. He has been the means of stopping the free beer which for centuries undergraduates of Brasenose College, Oxford, have received from Lincoln College on Brasenose Day. The custom started in the Middle Ages as penance after Lincoln College students had murdered a Brasenose undergraduate. This year the door between the colleges was opened, but there was no beer, as Lincoln College is now a Government institution.[76]

Like most colleges, Magdalen withdrew the privilege of holding private lunch parties in one's own rooms.[77] After Eights Week, there were no bumps suppers. Unable to muster sufficient numbers or resources on their own, all of the women's colleges joined together for a dance at Rhodes House in the first year of war. With no commemoration ball possible, Trinity JCR formed a dance committee. St Hilda's golden jubilee in 1943 went uncelebrated until 1946 and formal dinners were restricted to two a week, as the maids were unable to manage the blackout curtains and serve at table as well. Somerville held no gaudies and entertainment was cut to a minimum, though the tradition of the principal's Sunday tea party was retained.

Then there was the food. Students' rations were pooled, ration books handed in to the manciple or steward, those in lodgings surrendering them to their landlady or landlord. When dining in hall, they carried their rations of bread, butter and sugar with them in cake tins.[78] Along with the rest of the country, they got used to a range of dietary restrictions, including 'meatless nights' and new foodstuffs. At University College, students received a jar of jam or marmalade once a month.[79] While there might be jam today, there was no guarantee of jam tomorrow: as Allied troops were landing on Normandy beachheads in June 1944, Manchester College's House Committee discussed complaints about the jam ration. While it was resolved that each student would receive a pound of the preserve for the current month, from then on they would have to supply their own to spread on their bread or dollop on their steamed pudding.[80] Everyone became waste conscious, Nina Bawden 'appalled by the amount of delectable food left on plates and casually thrown away' at the American servicemen's and -women's club where she helped out.[81]

From January 1941 University College dinners dropped from three courses to two, while Pembroke gamely persisted with three-course repasts. Though suspended at St Edmund Hall, Worcester College retained the practice of sconcing 'for any solopsism' while at table.[82] Lunch at Univ was 'something of a disgrace – frequently no more than a bowl of soup or (not "and") a black pudding, supplemented by bread (unrationed) and one's own butter, cheese, etc'.[83] 'All I can remember of St Hugh's meals', wrote Lorna Clish, 'were the reconstituted dried eggs sitting like yellow rubber on the plates'. A reoccurring main course was 'soggy, watery bread and butter pudding with cheese sparsely sprinkled on it'.[84] Seared onto the memory of a University College student was the image of two thin slices of black pudding 'splendidly alone on a dinner-plate – with a roll. Another notorious dish was a thin soup which tasted of little else but pepper'.[85]

Meals came to feature fish, of which there was plenty, and dishes such as rabbit stew and spam fritter and chips. At Magdalen, the lunches deteriorated in quality, unfilled baked potatoes and soup featuring prominently. Tripe was served once – and once only – and there were walkouts caused by badly cooked offerings from the kitchens. At Jesus, 'squares of dried egg surrounded by baked beans' were standard, as were brown-coloured rissoles described on the menu as 'Cambridge steak'.[86] At St Hilda's, Bemax, a wheatgerm-based food supplement, was served, and the regular lentil cutlets were 'especially disliked'.[87] Arriving to a freezing room at Pembroke in Michaelmas 1941, Douglas Ross was 'cheered by a man from the Buttery bringing sardines on toast'.[88] But wartime realities – 'shortages of everything' – soon began to bite. Meals in hall were 'dreary', featuring powdered egg and Woolton pies (named after the Minister of Food), which Ross described as 'a mess of vegetables capped with mashed potatoes, like a vegan shepherd's pie'.

Kingsley Amis arrived at St John's in April 1941 'in impeccably proletarian style, driven over from my parents' house in Berkhamsted by the family butcher in his battered Morris'.[89] He was assigned a 'nasty little pair of rooms in the top corner of the front quad'. It didn't take long for his thoughts on college food to clarify. In an entry in the 'Kitchen and JCR Suggestion Book' he wrote that 'When I have potatoes in their jackets at home the jackets are worth eating. Here jacket and potato are fucking awful.'[90] He insinuated that the kitchen staff were profiting at the expense of undernourished students: 'Give us our cheese ration and stop making the bloody macaroni things. We don't think other members appreciated what a fucking hell of a lot of cheese they were missing.'[91] Perhaps those who had been at boarding school were better prepared than Amis: Ken Coombe wrote that 'coming from a provincial boarding school where the food in quality and quantity had reached its nadir, it seemed to me that Worcester fare was at its zenith, and I doubt if I ever dined so well.'[92]

Trinity seems to have fared better than most colleges. Here, the food was considered very good (and undergraduates retained the right to have guest lunches in their rooms). Harper-Nelson writes that he was never conscious of feeling that meals were inadequate, or of being hungry. There was plenty of bread and toast, and fried bread or 'piggy toast' were staples. Lunch was often soup, bread and cheese, and afternoon tea in student rooms was a feature. But then, he was able to afford extras that college provided at a cost. Trinity's ability to offer decent meals was due in no small measure to the efforts of the domestic bursar, Philip Landon, who took over the vegetable gardens on the college estate at Wroxton. He also persuaded the father of two undergraduates who owned a Scottish estate to send two whole deer each week. Ducks were introduced to the President's Garden, disturbing some undergraduates, as we have seen, and fifty hens took over the college sports field, under command of the groundsman.[93] Landownership brought benefits for other colleges too, Christ Church receiving eggs and vegetables from its farm near Cassington.[94] At Worcester, Coombe remembers 'deliciously hot new bread' and that 'butter could be purchased from the Buttery, dispensed under the aegis of the Manciple, the legendary Mr Drake, replete with winged collar and pinstripes.'[95]

As the war dragged on, restrictions intensified. At Trinity, Harper-Nelson noted some pretty disgusting substitutes for pre-war staples at the breakfast table. Tinned bacon from America and sausages called Soya Links, which had to be unrolled from grease-proof paper after being slid out of the tin, took the place of gammon slices and juicy pork skins.[96]

There was dialogue between JCR and SCR; a plea for hot puddings was put in, and the serving of 'lease-lend bacon' was compensated for by the appearance of fried potatoes at breakfast twice a week.

Despite dietary tribulations, Paul Addison warns against exaggerating the level of hardship. There was a war on, and everyone experienced rationing and culinary adjustments. Moreover, student needs were still attended by college scouts (if living in) and they ate rationed food that was more than sufficient to keep body and soul together. And there were always vegetables. 'Things are rather difficult now, I confess', wrote Albert Thomas of Brasenose. But 'even to-day things can be made rather comfortable if one goes about the matter properly ... A liberal helping of vegetables helps in these days to make up for the missing courses.'[97]

Preparing food was a challenge. Pressure on college kitchens was considerable, residents requiring feeding while catering staff left to join the forces. There were then the effects of the requisitioning of halls and, for colleges such as Lincoln, kitchens too. Due to the requisitioning of its hall, Pembroke stopped supplying food to undergraduates not in residence. Oriel, for similar reasons, limited to fifteen the number of undergraduates resident outside college able to eat within. At Queen's, extra staff were employed to carry food from kitchens to the JCR where meals were served, the hall having been requisitioned.[98] There was a great deal of quid pro quo: Pembroke's kitchen had not been requisitioned but the governing body allowed the army, who occupied other parts of the college, to use it freely. In exchange, the army allowed around twenty-five undergraduates to take their meals in the requisitioned hall, 'an important consideration to us', according to the bursar.[99]

It was possible, of course, to supplement the offerings of college kitchens. 'Peace-time delights, such as tea with cakes and crumpets in college rooms were still a part of undergraduate life', wrote Oriel's Peter Anstey, 'provided one was prepared to queue outside the North Oxford cake factory [Oliver & Gurden's at Middle Way Summertown] at 8 am and provided that a miniscule 2 oz butter ration delivered promptly each Monday by staircase scout had been kept intact' (St Hilda's students had to go and collect theirs, which also came on a Monday).[100] Lorna Clish and her friends at St Hugh's boosted their calorific intake

> by cycling to Summertown and queueing outside the cake factory for buns and cakes, the freshness of which compensated for their lack of such ingredients as butter and eggs, and which provided the wherewithal for a tea party, our only form of entertaining.[101]

The Oliver & Gurden 'cake factory' was known to all, including Margaret Roberts, who would queue for an hour. Some female under-graduates used the freshness of its products, when proffered by male suitors, to gauge their worth (had they got up at the crack of dawn to get the freshest stuff, or were the cakes past their best?). Roger du Boulay of New College wrote that while college meals might have been healthy, they were not filling.

> Who of my generation can forget the debt he owes first to Fuller's in the Cornmarket, but more importantly to the cake factory in Summertown, where day after day queues formed at first light and waited, studying Thucydides or Aeschylus, for the door to open at 7:30am?[102]

Meals in Jesus could be 'enriched by buns from the JCR store'.[103] At Pembroke, Frank and Fred, who ran the JCR pantry, supplied anchovy toast and cakes from Oliver & Gurden's.[104] Anthony Leatherdale (Pembroke) made use of the Municipal Restaurants, and patronized Del Nevo's fish-and-chip shop in St Ebbe's. Bawden remembers a good lentil curry for ninepence at the Taj Mahal, a pioneering Indian restaurant on Turl Street (also fondly recalled by Harper-Nelson). Parcels from home, 'preferably featuring large fruitcakes', formed another important element of the student diet.[105]

War had an interesting effect on differences of wealth and class. It brought higher taxes, so there was less money around. Even those who had it could not easily get around the fact that clothing was rationed along with petrol and food, although extras were always available to those with deep pockets. Well-heeled undergraduates forwent expensively decorated rooms, and poorer students were able to mix more easily with those who were better off. David Strawbridge, preparing to go up to Univ in 1939 from a grammar school in Dorset,

> was disconcerted to receive a letter from the College asking him to come equipped with a full dinner service for six (including two salt spoons), and then relieved to be told in a subsequent letter that, because of hostilities, all meals would be taken in Hall, and that he need only bring up a teapot and a couple of cups and plates.[106]

'Brideshead'-style high living largely disappeared writes Amis's biographer, 'a relief to scholarship and grammar school types'.[107] Relishing the war's levelling effects, Albert Thomas wrote:

> You never see to-day the hunters of the rich undergraduate in the High or the Broad, or the sporting dogs being led around, as you did in the old days. No 'swank' of the rich student. Everything is just as one would wish it. Sometimes, now taxis are a thing of the past, one sees couples walking along the High in their Glad Rags going to a dance.[108]

Bawden also noted the air of egalitarianism.

> The austerity of war concealed social and financial differences. Since we were all poor and shabby, neither poverty nor shabbiness troubled us. Since we expected to be recruited into the services when we went down, we were not fretted by personal ambition.[109]

Larkin wrote that wartime Oxford 'was singularly free' from traditional social distinctions.[110] Life in college was austere:

> Its pre-war pattern had been dispersed, in some instances permanently. Everyone paid the same fees (in our case, 12s. a day) and ate the same meals. Because of Ministry of Food regulations, the town could offer little in the way of luxurious eating and drinking, and college festivities, such as commemoration balls, had been suspended for the duration. Because of petrol rationing, nobody ran a car. Because of clothes rationing, it was difficult to dress stylishly. There was still coal in the bunkers outside our rooms, but fuel rationing was soon to remove it. It became a routine after ordering one's books in Bodley after breakfast to go and look for a cake or cigarette queue.

With new men coming up every term, as opposed to once a year, there was hardly any such thing as freshmen, and distinctions of seniority blurred. Traditional 'types' such as aesthete or hearty were pruned relentlessly back.[111] This was not, Larkin continued, the Oxford of 'Michael Fane and his fine bindings, or Charles Ryder and his plovers' eggs', but 'it had a distinctive quality' of its own.

> A lack of *douceur* [pleasure of life] was balanced by a lack of *bêtises* [foolishness], whether of college ceremonial or undergraduate extravagance ... and I think our perspectives were truer as a result. At an age when self-importance would have been normal, events cut us ruthlessly down to size.[112]

But it didn't cut everyone down to size and, as throughout the generations, world wars or depressions weren't going to stop those who wanted to do the Oxford 'thing' from doing it, regardless of their background. The Oxford 'characters' that Mortimer mordantly described lay by day

> naked in their rooms listening to Charles Trenet or Verdi's *Requiem*. By night they would issue forth into the black-out, camel hair coats slung across their shoulders like German generals, bow ties from Hall's settled under their lightly-powdered chins, to take the exotic dinner (maximum spending allowed under the Ministry of Food Regulations – five shillings) at the George Restaurant. What did it matter if the steak was whale (Moby Dick and chips) or the wine rationed Algiers or even black-market Communion? They still talked about Beardsley and Firbank and *Point Counter Point* and how, sometime in the summer vacation, they had been spoken to by Brian Howard, supposed model for the Waugh heroes, itching in his A.C. [RAF aircraftsman] Plonk's uniform in the downstairs bar at the Ritz.[113]

One gets the same impression of student excess and privilege from Harper-Nelson's wartime memoir: while Larkin's Oxford might have been drab, he was having a ball. For sure, the impositions of war featured heavily, but his recollections of gaiety, drunkenness, gramophone picnics, theatre and the drama society, bawdy songs and easy privilege spoke of an abiding side of university life in this gilded cage. Students reposing on chaises longues in smoking jackets, drinks cabinets and grand pianos in their rooms, 'trousering' drinking games and 'duckings' in the college fountain (or, in New College's case, the static water tank in the front quad), all featured.[114]

Home thoughts from abroad

All that as it may be, these things were left behind as the war claimed its due. For those going off to war, Oxford became a memory, one to be revived once normal life re-established itself, it was keenly hoped. But there was no guarantee. Bowra once described Oxford as 'a pause between one kind of life and another'.[115] He was thinking of peacetime days, but his description was doubly apposite for those who went up as youngsters fresh from school and then left the place, all too soon, for military service during a world war. Eversley Belfield left for an officer cadet training unit, a grim five months that contrasted sharply with the 'relatively easy-going, carefree, comfortable existence to which we had become accustomed at Pembroke'. The experience resembled 'being slung back into the harshest conditions of a boarding school while simultaneously trying to acquire alien skills and knowledge'.[116]

Oxford men and women found themselves posted all over the world, some destined for high-intensity combat, others gravitating towards headquarters jobs and staff work. Remembering home and the prospect of returning was important, Oxford part of the 'life before' they fondly remembered as military life consumed them. On embarkation leave in April 1940, doctor of philosophy student John Buxton visited New College. A day or two later, he deployed overseas. 'During the five years that followed, my thoughts often returned to New College, a reassuring symbol of the endurance of civilised values.'[117]

Oxford and the college to which one belonged were natural reference points in a topsy-turvy world at a profoundly dangerous time. As the war progressed, 'Oxford, Brasenose, and Sonners [nickname of Brasenose principal Stallybrass] in particular seemed to BNC men in uniform the very symbols of what they were fighting for.'[118] This sentiment was encouraged by the common practice of dons writing to their students, Stallybrass, for instance, sending 'literally hundreds' of letters to Brasenose servicemen. He would tell them about life in the dream city, and how the friendships forged there (as he put it to a student in the army in 1941) were its 'most precious gift ... even though our streets be darkened at night and crowded by day with uniforms and refugees from hard-pressed London'.[119] The college 'remained an oasis from which letters were sent out to members in the Forces and where a warm welcome was always ready for those on leave'.[120]

An assistant principal at the Treasury following graduation, Iris Murdoch commented to her Oxford friend David Hicks that 'Cairo must be a pretty rum joint by now; there must be almost as many Oxford men as Egyptians. God help Egypt.'[121] With normality on hold and uncertainty all around, Oxford was a mecca of the memory. In the heat and the dust of the Libyan desert, Leo Pliatzky had 'visions of floating in a punt on the rippling waters of the Isis, of dewy green meadows and long cool pints of beer'.[122] Oxford formed part of the mindscape against which servicemen and servicewomen compared new surroundings as they were sent hither and thither. From GHQ Middle East in June 1942, Frank Thompson wrote to Murdoch:

> I wish I could tell you about some of the places that I've seen – the individuality of each dirty & honorable city. I've seen a great many 'historic' rivers but only the Jordan is the equal of the Cherwell & Ichen. The bigger ones have water-meadows – even with yellow flag in them – but are nothing to the water-meadows that lie around St. Cross. It's not a bad place, England, when all's said & done.[123]

Frank, a wartime graduate of New College, did not see Oxford again: he was executed by the Bulgarian gendarmerie during an SOE mission in May 1944.[124]

John Betjeman, a Magdalen non-graduate, left his Uffington home, from where he had been able to keep up with Oxford and London cronies, to become press attaché at the British embassy in Ireland. While enjoying Dublin society, he missed home. 'Oh God to be in England', he wrote to Blunden on Advent Sunday 1942. 'Oh God for a nice whiff of paraffin oil and hassocks. Yes even for a glance at [C.S.] Lewis striding, tweed-clad to Headington' (Betjeman reserved an intense dislike for his former tutor, whom he blamed for having been sent down).[125] Later that year, he claimed that he would 'give ten years of my life for a month in a don's back garden in Cambridge or for a week's bicycle tour in North Oxford'.[126] Absence made the heart grow fonder, and it was while in Ireland that he began writing what he described as his 'epic', the blank verse autobiographical poem *Summoned by Bells* chronicling his life up to his premature departure from Oxford.[127]

UNDERGRADUATES AT WAR 195

There might be other reasons for wanting to revisit Oxford, affairs of the heart not least among them. J.D. James anticipated a visit during a couple of days' leave in his poem '48-Hour Pass (for A.C.B.)':

> To drip of trees the misty morning dawns,
> My schoolboy heart sings Oxford and I come.
> Rain falls in Manchester as I depart
> (A Forces ticket, via Birmingham)
> To print my studded boots on College lawns
> And tramp a hobnail love across your heart.[128]

For many, trips back to Oxford were not an option. James Thompson set his sensuous memoir *Only the Sun Remembers* against the backdrop of Trinity Term 1939, when he had been an undergraduate at Lincoln. In these halcyon days he had enjoyed idyllic weekends with his fiancée before Portsmouth barracks and a brutal little campaign in Norway changed things forever. As war bounced him around the globe (Bethlehem, Cape Town, Cairo, Haifa, Jerusalem, Basra, Colombo, Baghdad, the Maldives, the Seychelles, the Chagos Archipelago, Rangoon, Singapore, Bombay, Karachi), and into the arms of other women, it was to Oxford that his thoughts often returned. Oxford contacts enabled him to widen his experience of Ceylon (present-day Sri Lanka) during a lengthy posting to the island, an important British stronghold. On New Year's Eve 1941, arriving at Badulla in Uva province, he ran into his Oxford friend Raju Coomaraswamy, whom he had last seen on Turl Street in July 1939.

> [B]efore I arrived I had friends in Ceylon and through them other friendships came, Tamils, Ceylonese, Burghers; and Raju Coomaras-wamy, a friend from the Oxford years, who welcomed my arrival and whose kindness I can never repay. Through his friendship I climbed the glass strewn walls of racial prejudice and the intricate barriers of our colonisation.[129]

Thompson spent happy hours in Colombo's non-European Lawn Club, 'where Raju Coomaraswamy knotted the Centipede [the Varsity athletics club] scarf at his strong, black neck while we reminisced, easily dreaming of the Oxford days, picturing the quadrangle of All Souls, the Bodleian and the Camera against the soft skies of the Summer Term'.[130]

In all these matters, from maintaining psychological communities to preparing for incendiary bombs, the University's senior members were closely involved. They experienced the war in ways peculiar to themselves, a subject examined more closely in the next two chapters.

NINE

DONS AT WAR

Some dons left Oxford for the armed forces or became temporary civil servants working in home affairs and managing the war economy. Some did full- or part-time work in the fields generally labelled 'propaganda' and 'intelligence'. Scientists and medics contributed to advances in military technology and the treatment of casualties. As St John's philosophy fellow John Mabbott wrote, 'the physicists devised radar and counters for magnetic mines. The classicists went to use their linguistic skills at Bletchley, in decoding ciphers or learning Japanese ... [and] dons were enrolled in new or expanding Departments in the Civil Service'.[1] Staff at the Institute of Statistics monitored the British war economy, and its personnel were recruited by Whitehall departments.[2] Oxford academics joined the Statistical Branch established by Lindemann to support Churchill when he returned to government as First Lord of the Admiralty, following him to 10 Downing Street in May 1940.

For some, secondment to Whitehall brought 'the glamour and intellectual excitement of glimpsing government from within' and 'the reassurance of public usefulness'.[3] Some died on active service, others through war-related misadventure. Returning from a legal dinner in London, John Mortimer's tutor 'mistook the carriage door for the lavatory and stepped heavily out into the blackout and onto the flying railway lines just outside Didcot'.[4] H.A.L. Fisher, warden of New College, chaired an appeal tribunal examining the claims of conscientious objectors, and it was while he was in London to attend a meeting of the tribunal that he was knocked down and fatally injured by a lorry. Contrary to college legend, he was not a victim of the blackout – only of his habitual inattention to the physical world around him.[5]

War had a habit of finding uses for brainboxes and boffins and harnessing the talents of eminent people. As shown by the vice chancellor's pre-war survey of what senior members might do if war came, censorship, deciphering, propaganda, broadcasting, scientific research, information-gathering and -processing – as well as joining the forces and civil defence organizations – were likely areas of occupation. A rough taxonomy helps illustrate this. Older dons tended to remain in Oxford though might undertake war work; Alfred Emden, principal of St Edmund Hall, commanded the University Naval Division (his service as a Royal Naval Reserve lieutenant commander involving an anti-submarine patrol aboard a destroyer in the North Atlantic). Some younger dons joined the regular forces, including Christ Church philosopher A.J. Ayer, who served with the Welsh Guards before being recruited for SOE and MI6, indicative of the fact that, even if signing up for the war in a 'normal' manner, there was a good chance that people with certain aptitudes would find their way into certain occupations. The same was true of Trevor-Roper, who schemed to get into the army because he knew his eyesight would debar him if he went through the normal channels. He'd joined the Territorials before the outbreak and attended a Life Guards camp in summer 1939. Awaiting call-up when war began, he lectured the Oxford OTC four days a week on the use of the Bren gun and anti-tank rifle, despite having scored zero in his own firing tests because of his poor vision. It wasn't long before a friend got him a 'hush-hush job' that secured a commission in the regular army. That friend was the bursar of Merton, Walter Gill, who though in his fifties had wangled himself a position in a new outfit, the Radio Security Section of MI8, allowing him to use the wireless skills he'd developed in the army in the previous war and maintained as an enthusiast ever since.[6]

John Sparrow, fellow (and later warden) of All Souls, became a private in the Oxfordshire and Buckinghamshire Light Infantry. His logic, wrote his friend Harold Nicolson, was that 'a) he is not a good military man and that it is better to obey orders than to have to give them; [and] b) that it is less painful if one breaks entirely with one's previous life'.[7] Richard Holdsworth was a young fellow at University College, a former rowing Blue and popular rowing coach. On the outbreak he joined the University Air Squadron and a year later married the master's secretary, Mary Zvegintzov. He was killed in April 1942 while flying with an RAF Coastal Command squadron in Northern Ireland. Collin Dillwyn, Student of Christ Church, shot himself to avoid capture on the retreat to Dunkirk.[8] Stanley Casson, fellow in classical archaeology at New College and a First World War veteran, joined the Intelligence Corps. He served with the British military mission to Greece, and was present in both the Netherlands and Crete when they fell to the enemy. In 1944 he was appointed to advise the army on the protection of cultural artefacts in Greece as the Allies intervened in support of the resistance. He died in a crash on the flight out, becoming the first New College fellow to lose his life on active service. The Greek government gave him the honour of a requiem mass at the Orthodox cathedral in London.[9]

Dons with links to research of national importance stayed put in their labs and college rooms or were subsumed within larger organizations. Magdalen fellow Eric Moullin, Reader in Electrical Engineering, worked on 'the properties of dielectrics, the mechanisms of electrical noise and the characteristics of aerial systems'.[10] Like many others, he was determined to contribute in the most effective way possible, 'anxious to play a direct part in the development of new radio and radar devices'. He joined the Admiralty Signals Establishment at Portsmouth on the outbreak, taking his research team with him, later transferring to the Metropolitan Vickers research laboratory in Manchester.[11]

Some dons (and senior members of staff, such as laboratory researchers) had their paths to war service obstructed because of their nationality. Isaiah Berlin, prize fellow of All Souls and New College fellow, had a dodgy arm that precluded military service, and foreign birth (Riga) that debarred him from the type of intelligence work that he wished for. By accident, he found himself in America, working for the British Information Services, a propaganda outfit aimed at the American public, and providing the government in London with highly valued intelligence regarding American attitudes towards Britain along with pen portraits of key American movers and shakers.[12] At the start of the war, foreign nationals were prevented from working on radar in the Clarendon Laboratory, so they began working on nuclear fission. 'Naturally', writes the historian of Oxford's physics department, 'it was a big joke that this very highly secret work had been carried out by aliens or one-time aliens who could not be put on the highly secret radar work'.[13]

Dons connected to networks of power were utilized in a range of ways – commissioned to write reports, sit on boards and chair committees. Foremost among them, certainly in terms of fame, were Beveridge and Lindemann. The latter became Paymaster General with a Cabinet seat and was raised to the peerage as Lord Cherwell and made a privy counsellor, all within the course of the war (his Christ Church colleagues, pulling his leg, suggested 'Lord Christ of Church' as an alternative title). A scientific entrepreneur of national importance, possessing 'power greater than that exercised by any scientist in history' by dint of his appointment as the prime minister's chief scientific adviser, he recruited Oxford and Cambridge statisticians to provide the data prized by Churchill in his decision-making, as well as doing much to orchestrate, lead and support the Clarendon Laboratory's war effort.[14] He also sponsored individuals conducting important work, including R.V. Jones's research on infrared and radio beams, carried out in the Clarendon.[15]

Another distinct group of dons comprised those who continued about their duties while occasionally taking on informal, often unpaid, war-related work. Father Martin D'Arcy, master of Campion Hall, had preached and lectured widely in America in the 1930s and was requested by the Ministry of Information to continue his visits, also travelling to Spain and Portugal.[16] Others found employment in Oxford-based military outfits. Bill Watt, fellow of Balliol and a leading Latin scholar, was rejected for military service on account of defective eyesight. Instead, he joined naval intelligence as a temporary civilian officer, working twelve-hour shifts at Manchester College coordinating and editing data.[17] Other dons did war work on the side, working for the Political Warfare Executive or Chatham House and giving lectures and talks. This was not always out of choice; some wanted to do more, to be 'invited' more, but didn't get the call.

Dons willing to serve in some way but not recruited, or given only peripheral piecework, were frustrated. For Blunden, the 'lack of any specific activity was perhaps the most irksome thing of all'. 'It does *vex* me', he wrote, 'that this War did not employ me.'[18] Tolkien offered his services and was even interviewed at Bletchley Park, but was not called. Bowra said that he found it 'almost unendurable sitting here when the whole country is in deadly peril'.[19] His biographer writes that, in a sense, he 'had no war. He lived in a kind of suspended animation, with his patriotism rejected and his friends dispersed.'[20] Most of them 'had been recruited into one organization or another, but there was no invitation for Bowra'.[21] Thwarted by those who thought him 'unsuitable', he spent his time writing 'unreadable' books and going to the pictures, confiding to Lindemann that he was 'deeply anxious' to find a role. His perceived rejection hurt him, confirming a long-held conviction that he was an outsider.[22]

This was also, perhaps surprisingly given what he went on to achieve, the experience of Beveridge. When war broke out, he desperately wanted to be recalled to Whitehall, bombarding government departments with offers of assistance, all of which were rejected. This hurt him deeply, especially as he saw university people of similar age and standing finding roles. Thwarted though convinced he had a contribution to make at a high level, he spent the early part of the war attending meetings and giving talks for a movement proposing a future European federation, and writing letters disagreeing with J.M. Keynes's ideas on manpower or attacking the lack of planning machinery in Whitehall.[23] His biographer lists some of the reasons why politicians and civil servants weren't beating a path to the door of the 'Victorian Tudor manor-house' that served as his home at University College – reasons that applied to other senior university figures too.[24] There was the obvious fact that he was opinionated, forthright, and had fixed ideas which he wanted to impose on others, common traits in successful people used to leadership roles, though not ones welcomed by those who might have to work with them, including as their bosses. It was difficult to place (and to ensure subordination of) former high officials (Beveridge was an ex-permanent secretary). He lacked interpersonal skills and had annoyed big shots such as Attlee and Dalton by addressing them as if they were 'junior lecturers'. Finally, there was the view that he was an 'impractical visionary' and 'long in the tooth', which was Churchill's point of view.[25]

In contrast to the likes of Beveridge and Bowra, mustard keen to get involved, some dons felt, or professed to feel, that the war was 'none of their business'.[26] If asked why they were not in the fight to save civilization they might reply with the old jest that *they* were the civilization being fought for. Yet even those content not to have a direct role, like 33-year-old A.J.P. Taylor, could be made to feel awkward about it (as a contemporary ragged him, 'too young to serve in one war, and too old to serve in the other, eh?'). Even he, privately, was crying out to be given an attachment to Chatham House or some kind of role that would allow him to use his skills and be able to say that he was involved, even if he 'couldn't talk about it'.

Of course, some dons needed to remain in Oxford and mind the shop. What they did, after all, was defined as a reserved occupation. For those beyond military age, it was easier to view staying put as an obvious and important duty. Provost Hodgkin at Queen's, 62 when war broke out, told the registrar that

> in event of war I should feel it my first duty to reside in College and satisfy myself that the College and the various precious things contained in it were properly respected by those occupying the College, whoever they may be.[27]

As we have seen, Professor Brierly, in his late fifties when war came, used his expertise in international law to oppose the Nazis and aid refugees in their escape to Britain, as well as serving on government committees such as the Advisory Committee on Defence Regulation 18B, which reviewed the cases of British subjects who were interned. The clearly understood belief that university life should go on pleased Blunden, while at the same stirring 'a sense of guilt' as he was convinced that he could perform (once again) a useful role in uniform.[28]

Those left behind

Shrinking college fellowships had consequences. St Hugh's lost staff to the Ministry of Labour and Board of Trade. From Univ, Law fellow Richard Holdsworth and History fellow David Cox 'went off to fight', while Classics fellow Freddie Wells became a big wheel in naval intelligence.[29] By 1943 eighteen Magdalen fellows were absent having undertaken 'some form of National Service at home or abroad'.[30] The philosopher Harry Weldon was serving on 'Bomber' Harris's staff (advocating raids on German cities), while J.L. Austin was a lieutenant colonel and deputy chief of intelligence at Eisenhower's Supreme Headquarters Allied Expeditionary Force.[31] Godfrey Driver, who had served in the Middle East in the previous war, was responsible among other things for translating intercepted letters written in Aramaic by the Grand Mufti in Jerusalem, demonstrating in the process his contact with Axis figures, which led to his exile.[32] C.E. Stevens produced 'black propaganda', and it was said that it was his idea to use the opening notes of Beethoven's Fifth, which spelt *V* for victory in Morse code, on the BBC's European Service broadcasts. Trinity lost a fellow to the Ministry of Supply, one to the War Office, another to the Ministry of Information. One became a staff officer in the Middle East, one joined the RAF, and one the Royal Engineers. Two were absent for a while as part of the University delegation to Lisbon to confer Salazar's honorary degree.[33]

There were then the practicalities of increased workloads for those remaining behind. Wartime conditions 'profoundly depressed' Bruce McFarlane, who was having to take on more students and teach paired tutorials at Magdalen, which 'halves one's attention'. He felt that he should be doing more to hold the college together: 'It's just the moment when one ought to be busy & I haven't the time or the energy. I wonder what post-war Oxford will be like; I wonder.'[34] For Tolkien, war 'trebled official work, quadrupled domestic work'. Along with his ARP duties, he told his publisher, this meant that time with the manuscript of *Lord of the Rings* was at a premium. The situation was compounded by general labour shortages, the Tolkien household finding it extremely difficult to get domestic help, to find a gardener or even to get their bicycles repaired.[35]

At Univ, John Wild, medically unfit for service, was 'left in charge of most aspects of College life', the master, Beveridge, being something of an absentee (once he'd got his 'in' with government in summer 1940, he took up residence at the Reform Club, working in an office in New

204 OXFORD'S WAR

Scotland Yard). Wild therefore served variously as vice master, dean, domestic bursar and chaplain.

> Wartime members of College remember him with great affection, and recall his efforts to get to know them all, such as his regularly arranging evenings when the undergraduates could come and listen to his gramophone. No one appears to doubt that he was elected Master in 1945 [replacing Beveridge] precisely on account of his services to the College during the war.[36]

On top of the impact of their decrease in numbers, dons' experience of war was tangibly affected by the disruption of the venerable rhythm of University time, three terms of eight weeks, one following the other like clockwork. Now, undergraduates could matriculate in Hilary as well as in Michaelmas, and many did not stay for anything like the full lifespan of a normal degree. There were then the cadet courses, which ran at different times and extended into the vacations. All in all, it meant that colleges were nearly always full, and the terms ran into one another.

Those remaining in the depleted ranks saw change all around. C.S. Lewis wrote to a student in autumn 1939 describing 'the empty rooms with the names of the recently departed undergraduates still on the doors'.[37] 'All in all, Oxford was no longer the city of the young or the interesting', wrote Bowra. For him, 'lady typists in Keble fill no long-felt want'.[38] For the first time in his life he found that there was 'hardly anyone ... that one knows and likes' in the city.[39] At Corpus Christi College, 'the nightly procession to High Table was predominantly grey, stooped figures'.[40] Leaders of a socially conservative institution, they regretted unwanted change as matters far beyond Oxford intruded on normal life. Rowse wrote that 'the life of the streets, even in the old centre of the town, has ceased to be dominated by the University. So many thousands of evacuees and refugees have flooded into the area, mainly from London.'[41] Returning in December 1939 from a sabbatical spent in Uganda with a district commissioner friend, Mabbott entered 'a world from which most of my friends had already disappeared'.[42] Small, tight-knit college and University circles were disrupted as friends and colleagues moved away and newcomers arrived. Though given the circumstances few would sympathize with the proprietorial 'independent planet of Oxford' sentiments exhibited by the likes of Bowra and Rowse, one can understand the impact that war had on men of advancing years used to a cloistered life in a world they bestrode like colossi. Rowse put his finger on the root of their unease when he wrote that the 'inner life' of the University had been affected by the 'great influx of strangers from outside, and a great outgoing of the younger dons and third-year undergraduates to the war and to Whitehall'.[43]

It is difficult to assess the impact of this situation on the quality of Oxford teaching. It must have been significant, given the number of dons that left and the fact that among them were some of the best minds and, presumably, some of the most able teachers; certainly, the younger dons were, in peacetime, the most involved with the students. Larkin offers a clue as to the impact of their absence:

> The younger dons were mostly on war service, and their elders were far too busy or too remote to establish contact with us – often, in fact, the men of one college would share a tutor with another, whom they would never see socially at all.[44]

At University College, older dons remained in post until replacements could be found after the war, some, like A.S.L. Farquharson, dying in post during the conflict. Some undergraduates felt that this affected the quality of their teaching: one student was aware that his tutors had been appointed in about 1897 and 1907 respectively. They were 'not very well organized – giving essay subjects week by week in a haphazard way unrelated to any syllabus and one had to study the regulations carefully to see what the topics of the examination papers might be'.[45] At Oriel, Peter Anstey found himself 'farmed out to retired or semi-retired giants from the past'.[46]

As the previous chapter indicated, those remaining kept up with their scattered students, and tried to keep them connected, with each other and with their colleges. Hertford's chaplain Ian Thomson initiated a newsletter for current and old members, continuing it when he deployed overseas with the RAF. Letter number 9, written from the office of the assistant chaplain-in-chief, RAF, HQ Middle East, was sent home to be printed and distributed in February 1944. It offered news on the whereabouts of college men, presented in a jaunty tone. Thomson had met Bortolo on the ship coming out, and soon bumped into Orden in a Cairo cafe. Miller was expecting a commission in the RAF, and Campbell was in India. The last Mabbott Thomson heard, Oram was mentioned in dispatches in Sicily and Constable-Maxwell was 'covering himself with distinction' as commander of a fighter squadron which had recently been 'train-busting' over Nazi-occupied Europe. Constable-Maxwell had managed to get to Oxford in July 1943 to collect his MA: 'At 12:30 one day he was in the North Riding of Yorkshire. Two hours later he was in the Sheldonian collecting his degree, having flown to a 'drome near Oxford and motor-biked the rest.' Signing off, Thomson wrote that 'All is well at home, and the College carries on.'[47]

Letter number 10 was written from Hertford by bursar Dr W.L. Ferrar in July 1944. He distributed news sent in by students, and reported on SCR movements:

> Of the peace-time dons, Meade is (I think) in the Cabinet secretariat, Markham is an overlord of the nation's man power in one of the many departments of the ministry of Labour, Armstrong assists MAP [Ministry of Aircraft Production] and Denniston is in a branch of the WO [War Office].

'We have many visitors who spend a night or two in College during their leave', he wrote. ('A room can always be guaranteed to an old member in the Services provided he gives us 48 hours' notice'). The college carried on:

> There is still a number of men pursuing university degree courses, or patched up emergency courses, though but few of them are allowed to do more than two years and most only one; some even less. There is a steady flow of special courses, usually less than six months each, that disregard vacations, and keeps the College fairly full nearly all the year round.

On the whole, 'we flourish and remain very much a College, and your College at that. I mean that Hertford is still Hertford and not merely a set of college buildings that houses a floating population.'[48] Naturally, the business side of their relationship kept colleges in touch with their students too. Leo Pliatzky received a Corpus battels bill in the Western Desert while shells from an exploding ammunition dump screamed close overhead.[49]

Dons attended the college dead, too. Bowra read the daily casualty list in Wadham, and Pembroke's bursar, Salt, kept a handwritten list of the names of students and the units they were serving with, recording details of those killed or missing in action in red ink. The rector of Exeter corresponded with the parents of the fallen, maintaining a typescript list with handwritten additions.[50] College fellows corresponded with current and previous students, and with the parents of those killed or missing. Exeter Classics don Dacre Balsdon wrote to the parents of each college member who died.[51] When Merton's Keith Douglas was killed by mortar shelling in Normandy, Blunden wrote to his mother, initiating a correspondence similar to those he still maintained with the parents of friends killed in the previous war.[52] On a visit to Oxford, Trevor-Roper 'encountered an elderly don who could barely contain his tears, as he recounted the deaths of the young men who had made up his reading-parties'.[53] At Brasenose, Stallybrass wrote the obituaries of the college men killed in action.

John Bairsto's parents told Salt at Pembroke that their son had been lost at sea following a collision in the Atlantic. Austin Frost of Reading wrote to the master of Pembroke about his son: 'I regret to have to inform you that the War Office have informed me that my son HED FROST has been Killed in Action in the Far East on April 5th.'

> As he was a History Scholar of the College I beg to send you this sad news. He only attended lectures for one term and then decided that his country needed him more than his own personal problems did, and he joined The R. Berkshire Regiment as a Lieutenant. I had great hopes of a brilliant future but a higher destiny was chosen for him.[54]

Deaths brought poignant benefactions and articles left in wills made by young men before they went off to fight. R.M. Smith, killed in the retreat to Dunkirk in 1940, left his law books to Worcester College. Mrs Illius gave the college £500 to buy books for the law library in memory of her son, killed in action in 1943. F.H. Savory, who died of wounds the following year, bequeathed his books, and A.H. Dixon, who died of illness contracted on active service, left a sum of £100 per year to support new scholarships.[55] In 1944 Mrs Poyser gave 10 guineas to Brasenose in memory of her son P.R.W.

Poyser, killed in action. The Brasenose 'Benefactor's Book' records Mrs Brittain, mother of Lieutenant John Athron Brittain, killed in Italy in 1943, giving five silver tankards in his memory, a sixth given by his brother. Fulke Rosare Radice and Mrs Radice, parents of Captain Jocelyn Fulke Dalrymple Radice of the Queen's Bays, killed in France in 1944, presented the college with a silver mulling bowl dated 1773 in his memory.[56]

For dons remaining in Oxford, civil defence provided a means of contributing to the war effort. As well as doing some work for Chatham House at Balliol, Mabbott served as an ARP warden. Performing his duties from a post in the cellar of Rhodes House, he made new friends, soon enjoying conversations with Joyce Cary, the novelist and former colonial administrator, who lived on Parks Road, as they patrolled the city's streets. Tolkien found himself in the ARP, waiting by the telephone in a 'cheerless concrete hut in the grounds of St Hugh's'.[57] Other piecemeal war-related work came along, teaching short course cadets and organizing a syllabus for naval cadets in the English School, modifying lectures to suit less specialist audiences. He also rendered the Middle English lay *Sir Orfeo* into modern English for cadet lectures.[58] Colonel Wilkinson, commander of the OTC, arranged an honorary commission for Blunden in July 1940, satisfying his desire to at least get into uniform and 'do something' for the war.[59] His map-reading lectures, with their literary anecdotes and general history of cartography, were relished by the cadets, along with their forays into the countryside on exercises.

There were so many University men in the city's Home Guard battalion that the sergeant was able to issue the command 'Dons, fall out'.[60] Magdalen president and University vice chancellor (until his death in March 1942), Gordon became a private in the Home Guard; Registrar Veale and Dr Karl Parker, Keeper of the Department of Fine Art at the Ashmolean, lieutenants; while C.S. Lewis 'spent one night in nine mooching about the most depressing and malodorous parts of Oxford with a rifle'.[61] Alic Smith, acting warden of New College following Fisher's untimely death, joined the Home Guard and volunteered for fire-watching with the Manor Road team.[62] Lord Godfrey Elton, secretary of the Rhodes Trust, became a sergeant; and the head of the

Geology Department, J.A. Douglas, commanded the Oxford City Home Guard battalion, with the rank of colonel.

Even Bowra found a role in the Home Guard, commissioned as a lieutenant and second in command of South Company Oxford City Home Guard. He was put in charge of 150 postal workers and drilled them in Wadham's main quad.

> It is very agreeable and costs a great deal, as it means beer all round whenever we have a field day. The boys are almost entirely proletarian which I like a great deal. The few dons in it are kept down at the lowest rank, and not trusted with dangerous weapons. We are now armed with some fearsome American guns, and would certainly do a lot of damage (not necessarily to the enemy) on Der Tag.[63]

Frank Pakenham commanded the company. Scion of a distinguished military family, he had joined the Territorials as a private in 1939 and was a gazetted second lieutenant when war broke out. But after recurring bouts of influenza and a month in a nursing home he was invalided out, to his consternation and embarrassment.[64] He joined the Home Guard in 1940 and 'worked frantically as a company commander to atone for my failure in the real army. We were unbelievably belliger-ent – almost literally praying that the enemy would arrive in Oxford so we could give him a bloody nose.'[65] But he wasn't in luck in the Home Guard, either:

> One night there was a warning that the Germans were on their way – false as it turned out. We sprang to arms on the Abingdon Road. Eventually the order to unload was given. The Christ Church College cook, instructed by me in musketry, did not perform the operation successfully. He fired the last bullet into the ground and it ricocheted into one of my feet.[66]

Dons' war work: foreign and imperial policy

As well as the work of Bletchley Park (considered more thoroughly in the next chapter), a branch of intelligence involving dons was the collation of open-source material on countries or regions of interest to foreign-policymakers and military commanders. Information might be drawn variously from the international press, academic studies, and personal papers and correspondence. Once gathered and turned into digestible reports, it provided valuable information for those planning conventional or unconventional military operations in the regions concerned, and those whose job it was to consider the political context in which operations took place. Reports prepared by civil servants supported by experts drawn from other agencies of government, think tanks and academia could also contribute to the formulation of foreign and imperial policy, as offices of state (the Foreign Office, Colonial Office and India Office, for example) worked out what they should do in region X or Y when the war ended.

Based at Balliol, Chatham House's Foreign Press and Research Service worked closely with Foreign Office staff, producing press summaries and up-to-the-minute reports on historical and political matters relating to diverse parts of the world.[67] As Lord Gladwyn of the Foreign Office wrote, a number of 'excellent intellectuals were cooped up in Balliol under Arnold Toynbee and asked to define War Aims'.[68] Toynbee, director of studies and editor of the annual Chatham House *Survey of International Affairs*, was director of the Foreign Press and Research Service (from 1943, director of its Research Department). An example of the work conducted comes from Mabbott: following America's entry into the war there was a need for information on Liberia. The West African state was home to large Firestone rubber interests, and it was apparent that an American military base might be established there. This was a region of strategic and economic importance to Britain, and so the St John's don was tasked to compile a report, conducting research in the library of the British Museum and interviewing the Liberian ambassador.

Chatham House's horizon-scanning and preparatory work was important. Oliver Harvey, principal private secretary to Foreign Secretary Anthony Eden, repeatedly reminded his boss of the need to plan for the peace negotiations that one day would come, concerned that if the British government didn't have coherent plans it would be gazumped by the Americans.

> [W]e had a staff of professors at Balliol working on our behalf in close touch with the departments of the F.O. but they required a directive. If we hadn't our plan ready, Roosevelt would produce one of his own out of his pocket like the Atlantic Charter.[69]

Writing on British war aims for Chatham House, A.J.P. Taylor concluded that 'the British Government had no war aims nor indeed any idea of what they were doing'.[70] An order came from on high for the cessation of such work, regarded by influential elements within the Foreign Office as premature and undesirable. Drafts of work to date were to be destroyed. Taylor was wrong in his conclusion, the episode reflecting debates within government about post-war objectives and the urgency or otherwise of articulating post-war aims as opposed to simply getting on with winning the war, and a desire not to alienate the Soviets by naming them as likely post-war rivals. Lord Berners lampooned 'Cheatham House', describing it as 'a kind of sublimated branch of the Foreign Office'. Letters to the press, he wrote, complained of it as a waste public money.

> But the only signs of extravagance that were visible to the outside world were the lorries that were continually seen leaving the building with large quantities of waste paper ... If it wasn't doing much good, it wasn't doing much harm.[71]

Oxford research had long had an influence on imperial and colonial policy, informing colonial administration, constitutional reform, and development and welfare provisions. Expert knowledge and opinion on imperial affairs were more important during the war than they had ever been. Britain was fighting to retain its Empire, on battlefields in Africa and Asia and amid the shifting sands of international politics, where nationalism, communism and American anti-colonialism presented fundamental challenges. The political future of India and the modernization of Britain's relationship with the colonial empire were topics of great importance. Desperate to keep the Empire together – even anticipating India remaining within its orbit as a loyal dominion – civil servants in London and university experts sought practical solutions.

> The outbreak of war provided a powerful stimulus, intellectual and to some extent financial, for research in colonial government and economics. Academic help was mobilized to ward off transatlantic schemes for internationalizing control over all colonial territories – regarded in Britain as merely a euphemism for inserting American influence in place of British.[72]

Sir Reginald Coupland, Beit Professor of Colonial History and fellow of Balliol, was an authority on partition, having previously worked on the problems of Ireland and Palestine. He edited the influential think-tank-style journal *The Round Table*, which specialized in imperial and international affairs. He persuaded Nuffield College to fund a study on India's constitutional problems and embarked on a six-month period of field research. Returning to Britain in April 1942, he began writing his influential trilogy – *The Indian Problem, 1833–1935*, *Indian Politics, 1936–1942* and *The Future of India*, all published by 1943. As John Darwin notes, the affairs of the subcontinent had helped establish in Oxford the tradition of direct engagement with contemporary issues, including All Souls and the *Round Table*'s deep connections with imperial matters. Thus Coupland's wartime role in the search for a political settlement in India was a 'public advertisement of the University as a reservoir of expert knowledge and practical information in international affairs'.[73]

Margery Perham was the first official female fellow of Nuffield College and Reader in Colonial Administration from 1939, establishing a reputation as a leader in the field and an influential commentator on imperial affairs (for example, her famous 1942 contributions to *The Times* on the unsatisfactory state of British rule in South East Asia preceding the fall of Singapore).[74] Her wartime work illustrates the confluence of Oxford scholarship and governmental initiatives. A direct connection with government came in 1939 when Colonial Secretary Malcolm MacDonald included Perham in his private conference on the principles of future colonial policy. In 1941 the University's Higher Studies fund made a large grant available to Nuffield for research on colonial affairs, connected with the government's agenda for modernizing colonial rule. This supported Perham in her expanding work as she became director of the Nuffield Colonial Research Scheme, with offices at 72 High Street.[75]

In this role, she supervised research into imperial government and economics and edited the resulting series of Nuffield books. This work paralleled G.D.H. Cole's social survey of Britain, the two projects designed to assist the post-war rehabilitation of Britain and the Empire.[76] She contributed to the work of the Asquith Commission on higher education in the colonies in 1943–45 and the West Indies higher education committee of 1944. She also wrote reports on the post-war reconstruction of the colonial service to prepare officers for the widening demands that would face them, resulting in the Devonshire courses for colonial officials held in Oxford, Cambridge and London from 1945.[77] Another influential wartime government adviser on colonial affairs was New College fellow Christopher Cox, appointed to the newly created post of educational adviser to the Colonial Office. He became the key figure in determining future education policy in the colonies, including a prominent role in creating the Asquith Commission.

> Evidence from Cox, who was probably the most influential witness interviewed by the commission, was crucial in shaping the final report, which strongly endorsed the establishment of new universities, initially as at Ibadan, on the Oxbridge model.[78]

Post-war planning was an important strand of government activity on the domestic front too. Since the turn of the century, governments had been working their way towards provisions for social security; the welfare state erected following Labour's landslide 1945 election victory was not created out of thin air. Pressure for comprehensive social welfare schemes together with a programme of full employment and corporatist planning had mounted in the 1930s, foundering on both practical and philosophical grounds because they required the state 'to play a new and constitutionally illegitimate role in the direction of national life'.[79] But the war changed all that, creating energy and motion for planning. It vastly increased state intervention in all aspects of social and economic life, bringing command economics and centralization, and stoking belief in the power of the state to make society better. Men like Beveridge thought they could build a new social and political order by transforming the relationship between the individual and the state. Central committees on reconstruction were set up in all political parties, and a Cabinet Committee on Reconstruction was appointed in 1941 and a Ministry of Reconstruction created in 1942.

Beveridge could have written his famous report while director of the LSE, but instead he did so at Oxford for a number of reasons.[80] As an undergraduate at Balliol he had been influenced by his brother-in-law and friend R.H. Tawney, and the college's strong interest in social services nurtured his interest in social reform. This was reawakened when he returned to Oxford as master of University College in 1937, particularly through his friendship with Cole. As we have seen, initially Beveridge was spurned by government, and when his opening came, it was a small one. In July 1940 he was asked by Minister of Labour Ernest Bevin to prepare a short survey on wartime manpower requirements, and two months later was appointed to chair a Manpower Requirements Committee responsible to the Production Council, a body of Cabinet ministers.[81] He was assisted by Harold Wilson, who as a junior research fellow at University College had been helping Beveridge with his research into unemployment trends. This was all well and good, but it didn't offer Beveridge the scope that he sought, and the position he desired, which was the control of the workforce (or 'manpower' as it appeared in the language of the time, and in books for many years thereafter). It soon became clear that Bevin was very keen to keep him at arm's length, and by summer 1941 he was out to get rid of him. He did this initially by appointing someone else as director general of 'manpower', shunting Beveridge into the preparation of a report on the use of skilled manpower in the armed forces.[82] He was then offered the chairmanship of a committee on social insurance, which he rightly saw as being 'moved on'. But this was to be the opportunity for Beveridge to do 'what would prove the most important work of his life'.[83] Though it took him some time to turn his full attention to the inter-departmental Committee on Social Insurance and Allied Services, it led to a study advocating the reform of the entire system of social welfare. The report, Command Paper 6404, *Social Insurance and Allied Services*, appeared in November 1942, universally known as the Beveridge Report and a keystone document of the 'cradle to grave' welfare.

Selling 70,000 copies within a matter of days, the report pledged to tackle want, disease, ignorance, squalor and idleness in the reconstruction of post-war society (Harris writes that Beveridge was 'the purveyor of a portmanteau set of ideas offering all things to all men').[84] The report and its follow up, *Full Employment in a Free Society* (1944), 'proposed a great increase in state regulation of what had previously been seen as the essentially private concerns of the individual citizen'. It appeared at a time when the public was clearly expecting radical changes to take place after the war. Shortly after it came out, the Oxford Institute of

Statistics published its own analysis, *The Economics of Full Employment*, which agreed wholeheartedly with Beveridge's findings. Bringing together Fabian politics and Keynesian economics, Beveridge's work was hugely influential. While it 'would be misleading to suggest that Beveridge or the Institute determined government policy ... they did help to establish the conviction that mass unemployment could and should be avoided'.[85]

Other Oxford endeavours contributed to the welter of influential studies shaping the post-war state. Nuffield warden Sir Harold Butler and his half-dozen fellows managed to fashion for the college an important role in investigating national social and economic problems and planning for post-war reconstruction. In November 1939 Cole, the sub-warden, was appointed director of the Nuffield Social Reconstruction Survey. It had ambitious terms of reference, inquiring into the distribution of industry and population, the future of the social services and the efficiency of democratic institutions. A leading thinker and writer on social and economic policy, in 1940 Cole had returned to a position of political prominence when he was asked to assist Beveridge at the Ministry of Labour, drawing up plans for the effective use of manpower. A leading Fabian, his was one of the 2,300 names on the SS's 'Special Search List' of people to be rounded up after an invasion.

As part of the survey, Cole organized a series of conferences dealing with topics like post-war export trade, relations between education and industry, employment policy, female education, and teacher training.[86] They brought together academics, civil servants and industrialists, their exchange of ideas an important platform for post-war planning. Data from the survey was deployed to advocate for widespread social reform.[87]

William Adams, warden of All Souls, was one of many senior Oxford figures with a foot in both academic and government camps, having worked in various ministries and as principal secretary to David Lloyd George during his premiership. In the 1930s he had helped bring academic refugees from Europe to Oxford, and early in the war worked with Max Grünhut, whom he had helped leave Germany in 1939, in composing a survey of the consequences of the evacuation of children to Oxford.[88] Adams sat on the Nuffield Social Reconstruction Survey, and, starting in 1941, convened the All Souls Group. This created a network of leading educationalists in close contact with R.A. Butler, president of the Board of Education, whose 1944 Education Act was to transform secondary schooling and become a key part of the post-war consensus.[89] The All Souls Group's deliberations were of 'seminal importance in helping shape the pattern of wartime educational legislation and postwar educational developments'.[90] Further exploiting Oxford expertise in the educational field, Butler appointed a committee under St John's president Norwood to examine the secondary school curriculum, its 1943 report arguing in favour of a tripartite system of grammar, technical and modern schools, shaping national policy until the 1960s.

Writing and broadcasting

While scholars were considered to be good at administrative tasks and therefore suited to government service, they were also of significant importance in the media.[91] The government enlisted propagandists from the intelligentsia, attaching them to organizations like the Ministry of Information, the Army Bureau of Current Affairs, the Political Warfare Executive (PWE), the Crown Film Unit and the BBC.[92] Many academics felt the need to do what they could to boost public morale (whether it needed it or not) through journalism, broadcasting or lecturing service personnel. They explained the origins of the war and Allied war aims, and conjured roseate visions of what peace would look like. Jose Harris writes that historians of old and young generations – including R.C.K. Ensor, H.A.L. Fisher, E.H. Carr and A.J.P. Taylor – were in constant demand as lecturers and commentators on the war, 'while Professor Neale's 1942 Ford lectures on the Elizabethan parliaments helped to consolidate highbrow national identity in a manner comparable to Olivier's Henry V' motion picture (1944).[93]

Speaking and writing in the national cause, from the sententious to the inspiring, Oxford dons wrote books and pamphlets and took to the airwaves, offering factual talks or spiritual guidance. A.J.P. Taylor worked part time for the Ministry of Information and PWE while performing his college duties. His house at Holywell Ford 'was a centre for writers young and old, wayward musicians, and the grander Slav refugees clustered in north Oxford as well as his pupils coming on leave', as well as providing an occasional berth for the rabble-rousing Dylan Thomas.[94] Taylor took tutorials at home, Magdalen's bursar having told him that college rooms were unavailable because the Judicial Committee of the Privy Council was moving in.[95] This suited Taylor, living in a world of his own surrounded by meadowland and not nearly as fastidious about Oxford tutorial traditions as the college's senior history don. Much 'to the disapproval of my colleague Bruce McFarlane', as he put it, Taylor relished the freedom enforced by war. One-on-one tutorials might be good for a 'really able pupil', but 'the others are far better handled in threes and fours. As soon as I found my way about, I cut down on individual tutorials and operated in pairs.'[96]

Taylor's most obvious contribution came through lecturing. With an army chauffeur and unlimited petrol, he addressed military units in Oxfordshire, Berkshire and Buckinghamshire on European history. The idea was to explain and offer commentary on world affairs. Becoming something of a pundit, Taylor also featured on the BBC's 'Home Talks'. He gave history classes to civil affairs officers recruited to administer Italy and Germany upon their eventual defeat and offered his services to Chatham House. In 1943 he was asked by PWE to help prepare a handbook on Hungary for British troops who might occupy the country, taking leave from Magdalen and moving to London to work in Bush House for a period. He also became an unofficial adviser to the Czech government-in-exile, and was 'taken up by the Yugoslavs'.[97]

Taylor also found time to work on his book *The Course of German History*. Published in summer 1945, it was strongly influenced by the circumstances of the day and reflected prevailing feelings towards Germany, a partisan indictment with 'Alan the prosecuting council'.[98] Many other academics had their work shaped by the war. While working for MI6, Trevor-Roper's friend and boss Dick White led him to an academic study for which he was to become famous. In autumn 1945 he

> began a systematic investigation into the circumstances of Hitler's death, including interrogation of eyewitnesses, and compiled an official report on the subject. After returning to Christ Church as a Student (fellow) in 1946, he expanded his report into a book, *The Last Days of Hitler*, which was published to high acclaim in 1947. It was never out of print in its author's lifetime.[99]

War led to a revival of Christianity, and Oxford scholars contributed to debates made urgent by the struggle against fascism, producing important works on the nature of faith. As we have seen, Mansfield's principal Micklem had visited Germany in the 1930s, bringing back clandestine literature from the German Confessing Church, the movement opposing state attempts to roll all Protestant churches into a single pro-Nazi entity. In contrast to 1914, he supported the war given the nature of the situation within Germany.[100] *National Socialism and the Roman Catholic Church*, commissioned by Chatham House, was published by OUP in 1939.[101] In the same year he also published *May God Defend the Right!*, a guide to Christians at a time of moral crisis, and spoke on European Christianity on the radio.[102] Bishop of Oxford Kenneth Kirk, who had been Regius Professor of Moral and Pastoral Theology until 1937, delivered a sermon before Encaenia in 1940. Subsequently published by OUP as *The Menace to Faith*, it described Hitler's threat to civilization as a whole and the Christian faith in particular.[103]

C.S. Lewis, enjoying new celebrity following the publication of *The Screwtape Letters* in 1942, lectured on Christian belief at RAF stations from Abingdon to Cornwall. The head of religious broadcasting at the BBC admired *The Problem of Pain* (1940), in which Lewis argued for faith in God. He invited him to give a series of broadcasts on Christian belief, episodes including 'What Christians Believe', 'Christian Behaviour' (also a 1943 book) and 'The Christian View of God'.[104] The BBC recognized religion as 'an integral and important aspect of the national fabric', believing that it had 'a duty to offer both religious instruction and inspiration in the darker moments of the war'.[105] As Lewis remarked in a sermon, although 'all individuals face the ultimate realities all the time',

> war quickens and sharpens our awareness. When everyone in the country lives with the prospect of having their house destroyed by a bomb during the night, the Christian talk of Armageddon seems less fanciful than in the 'weak piping times of peace'.[106]

Works such as *Screwtape* and *The Problem of Pain* 'appealed very strongly when there was so much suffering and evident evil about'.[107]

F.M. Turner asserts that Lewis was the single twentieth-century Oxford religious figure 'whose influence extended far beyond the

University', even though he was neither a member of the faculty of theology nor a theologian. Generally 'opposed to modern culture and secularism', along with the other Inklings, he personified the 'increasingly religious character of Oxford during the late 1930s and early 1940s', which was 'due less to the clergy than to the laity'.[108] He emerged as a major apologist for Christianity through his broadcasts and books, which represented a spirited defence of the Christian faith in modern times, and a rejection of secularism. Lewis's influence was evident in much wartime and post-war Oxford poetry, 'which frequently linked the blitz, Communism and Fascism to such themes as Arthur, Beowulf and the tramp of the troll kings'.[109]

War contributed to the character of post-war British literature and, like the 1914–18 war in which they had been directly involved, shaped the writing of established authors such as Lewis and Tolkien. It helped inspire Narnia and cast a shadow across Middle-earth, their creators writing late at night after the day's work was done, supping pints in pubs and reading aloud to each other in college rooms. The Inklings were more peripatetic than usual during the war, as American servicemen crowded favoured haunts, which were subject to occasional beer shortages (temporarily closing the Eagle and Child).[110]

Tolkien, Professor of Anglo-Saxon and fellow of Pembroke, spent the war about his academic duties in Oxford while also working on what would become *The Lord of the Rings*, vigorously encouraged by Lewis.[111] Its 'centre', he told Charles Williams, 'is not in strife and war and heroism (though they are all understood and depicted) but in freedom, peace, ordinary life and good living.'[112] The war, for Tolkien, seemed to signal an end to cherished things. He had considered writing a sequel to *Farmer Giles of Ham* (1937), but, as he told his publisher, the sequel was 'plotted but unwritten, and likely to remain so. The heart has gone out of the Little Kingdom [inspired by the Oxfordshire and Buckinghamshire countryside], and the woods and plains are aerodromes and bomb-practice targets.'[113] Man's destruction of the landscape moved him 'to profound anger', and he was sensitive to the damage 'inflicted on the Oxfordshire countryside by the construction of wartime aerodromes and the "improvement" of roads'.[114] Until the start of the war he'd run a Morris, though ceased driving when petrol rations came in. 'By this time Tolkien perceived the damage that the internal combustion engine and new roads were doing to the landscape, and after the war he did not buy another car or drive again.'[115] Though safely published before the war, even *The Hobbit* (1937) did not escape its tentacular reach, going out of print in 1942 when the warehouse stock was destroyed in the Blitz.[116]

The war, it can be claimed, played an important role in the creation of *Brideshead Revisited*, written between December 1943 and June 1944 as Evelyn Waugh recovered from a cracked fibula sustained during parachute training. Personal injury combined with the oppression of wartime led him to hyperbolize the Oxford he'd known before the war. Written in 'a bleak period of present privation and threatened disaster – the period of soya beans and Basic English' – the result was, he said, a book 'infused with a kind of gluttony, for food and wine, for the splendours of the recent past, and for rhetorical and ornamental language'.[117] In writing *Brideshead*, 'the recollection of a more elegant past still alive in the 1930s was particularly piquant', contrasted with the regimented, rationed travails of a world at war.[118] As Waugh put it, not knowing then that the English country-house era was not, in fact, doomed by war, 'I piled it on rather, with passionate sincerity'. As a result, the book stood in his mind as a 'souvenir' of the war, 'rather than of the twenties and thirties, with which it ostensibly deals'.[119]

Visiting Oxford

Oxford's place in national life had long been buttressed by communication with, and visits to and from, London. It was a nodal point on a national network of power and influence, an ideas bank to draw upon for those in power, and a platform from which they might speak or trial new ideas. Parliamentarians and civil servants seeking a break from the hurly-burly of the capital and the pressure of work found in Oxford an oasis. Others, such as editor of the *New Statesman and Nation* Kingsley Martin, visited because influential members of their intellectual circle lived and worked there. As they were often Oxford (or Cambridge) graduates themselves, a trip to the alma mater was a tonic, perhaps affording the opportunity, through high-table chatter or a stroll in the fellows' garden, to tap into sources of knowledge as they honed their thinking on matters of state or policy details. 'You may run into a number of eminent figures on the international scene, not merely experts, but statesmen, almost daily crossing the Broad', wrote Rowse.[120] Leo Amery, Secretary of State for India and a distinguished graduate of Balliol, visited Oxford in June 1942, reconnecting with the band of academics who had long championed a form of imperial federation. During the visit he addressed the Oxford Union, which remained a pulpit of national importance despite its more circumscribed wartime activity. The following year, Colonial Secretary Oliver Stanley visited, his pugnacious Union speech one of the war's key statements on the future of the British colonies.[121] In February 1940 Rab Butler spoke at a Union banquet held in honour of the Polish ambassador, and on 16 February 1943 there was much excitement in the House of Commons following a speech made by Harold Balfour at the Union the previous evening.[122]

Kings and queens visited Oxford to receive degrees, and representatives of foreign and dominion governments were feted, such conferments and visits indicating the manner in which the University engaged with the state. Having recently hosted Amery and Sir Edward Bridges (secretary to the War Cabinet), in January 1942 All Souls stalwart Lionel Curtis entertained the Australian diplomat Alfred Sterling and politician Sir Earle Page, until recently a party leader and, briefly, Australian prime minister.[123] Page was in Britain as 'resident minister', representing his country in the War Cabinet. The manner in which his invitation to Oxford came about illustrates its connection with the salons of power. Page had corresponded with Curtis regarding his ideas for improving imperial cooperation. Curtis liked them, and suggested a visit to All Souls, where he would assemble '20 of the best minds of the time to thrash out the best way of making real progress' (as Page put it).[124] A fortnight later, he was dining alongside warden Adams, Major General Sir Ernest Swinton (until recently Chichele Professor of Military History) and Geoffrey Dawson, editor of *The Times*. Curtis gave the Australians a tour, which included Magdalen Tower and Addison's Walk, and on the radio that night Page learned of the retreat to Singapore island.[125]

People often 'dropped in' on Oxford to meet people and visit old haunts. In May 1943 Chips Channon called at Blenheim to show the place to Field Marshal Sir Archibald Wavell, then stopped at Oxford 'to call on an old general, Sir Something Swinton'. They were joined by Sir Harold Percival, steward of Christ Church, for tea.[126] Home Secretary Herbert Morrison was often invited to tea at Christ Church by Lindemann.[127] A frequent wartime visitor was John Martin, Churchill's principal private secretary, snatching weekends away from the high-tempo routine dictated by his boss's antisocial work habits and the sheer volume of business that had to be transacted.[128] A Corpus graduate, Martin would stay with friends at Magdalen, put up at the Mitre Hotel or stay at Coupland's Boars Hill home. But his regular haunt was Oriel, where he was a guest of his fiancée's father, Sir William Ross, provost and vice chancellor (1941–44).

During his visits Martin met influential people such as the American-born professor of jurisprudence and friend of Roosevelt, Arthur Goodhart. As he dined and tea'd his way around Oxford, he epitomized the manner in which the University was informally connected to government.[129] He attended plays and church services, went shopping, and courted Rosalind Ross, to whom he proposed after a picnic walk from Boars Hill to Bablock Hythe. They wed at the University Church in 1943, traffic halted on the High Street as the party, which included Clementine Churchill, processed back to Oriel.

The visits of Lord Halifax, Chancellor of the University and ambassador to Washington, to Oxford illustrate the incidental connection between academia and those in positions of power. In September 1943 he met Coupland at Balliol. 'I dined in Common Room, and talked with Coupland and Oman and Swinton and others … Coupland thinks he can solve India, and is writing a book to tell us how to do it.'[130]

Halifax valued Oxford as a place to recharge the batteries and gain a sense of perspective on turbulent international affairs. Visiting in April 1943 to lecture to a 'General Mixed Course for Americans, Canadians and British of all ranks that is going on in Balliol', he enjoyed

a delightful walk round Christ Church Meadow with [All Souls warden]
Adams … It was a most perfect afternoon, and Oxford was looking at
its best. The Balliol business did all right, although rendered as alarming
as possible by being called 'The Brains Trust'. The following morning,
by arrangement, Stanley Baldwin [former prime minister and serving

chancellor of Cambridge] came to Oxford, and we drank old sherry together on the Warden's lawn, and talked unceasingly.[131]

While Oxford had its place on the network of national power and influence, London was the fount of power. Those drinking at it did not always value the opinions of academics, no matter how eminent, as much as those academics thought they did, or should. To these London-based movers and shakers, Oxford might be a diverting backwater, though not a place in which politically ambitious people should tarry. In August 1940 Hugh Dalton, Minister of Economic Warfare, spent the night at All Souls. 'It is quite a pleasant break from the Ministry and they are much interested in political gossip but, somehow, one feels from their comments that they are far out of touch with any of our real problems.'[132] In March 1944 Richard Crossman called on Dalton, now President of the Board of Trade. Crossman had been leader of the Labour group on Oxford City Council, and now worked for PWE. He was thinking about accepting the principalship of Ruskin College but Dalton advised against it, on the basis that a parliamentary career beckoned: 'He thinks he could win Coventry next time' (which he did, at the 1945 election).[133]

Whitehall and Westminster types could be dismissive of Oxford dons and academics in general. Dalton thought Sir Arthur Salter, Gladstone Professor of Government, fellow of All Souls and MP for Oxford University, self-important. He had a habit of writing long letters to the prime minister, simultaneously infuriating and boring him.[134] Dalton didn't think much of the other University MP, either, sneering at Quintin Hogg and at Sir Hubert Henderson, Treasury adviser and fellow of All Souls, who 'hangs about the fringes of Oxford'.[135] Beveridge was kept at arm's length by Downing Street, Churchill telling him that he was too busy to see him until after the war, which must have rather dented his ego.[136] In June 1943 Dalton had dinner with the civil servant Douglas Jay, who had been invited to stand as the Labour candidate for Oxford University. 'He says he met the most frightful lot of people, dim and wildly eccentric and totally out of touch with all reality, at Oxford last week, when the matter was broached.'[137]

Harold Nicolson advised John Sparrow, who had ambitions to become warden of All Souls, not to apply for the librarianship of the Bodleian.

I said that this was not the moment to make such a decision. Without realising it, he was probably overtired and overworked, and that through the cold of London the firelight playing on the books acquired a disproportionate beauty. But to be Librarian at the Bodleian meant much more than firelight on books. It meant dining at Worcester high-table on Sunday off cold pork; it meant walking in the Parks with the sub-Librarian; it meant a little house in North Oxford, and a bicycle. Wouldn't it be better just to go back to the Chancery Bar, to hunt books in the Charing Cross Road, to stand for Parliament, to become Solicitor- or even Attorney-General, or even Lord Chancellor Hawke or Sparrow Hawke if he liked? He could always end up in North Oxford if the worst came to the worst.[138]

Nicolson himself recoiled at the prospect of becoming master of Balliol when it was suggested by his friend Jasper Ridley in late 1944.[139] In the minds of such people, Oxford was not a place to make one's name, though it could be an attractive retirement berth. Field Marshal Montgomery, wrote the King's private secretary Sir Alan Lascelles, was 'quite serious in his wish to be considered for the headship of an Oxford college after the war'.[140]

Having considered in this chapter the war's impact on Oxford's senior members, and their connections with the war and affairs of state, the next chapter develops this theme by looking in detail at the University's association with certain types of intelligence, and its endeavours in the fields of science and medicine.

TEN

INTELLIGENCE, SCIENCE AND MEDICINE

Dons and graduates joined the intelligence services, some recruited by the Government Code and Cypher School (GCCS) at Bletchley Park (renamed Government Communications Headquarters – GCHQ – in 1946). They came from universities across the country but overwhelmingly from Oxford and Cambridge, London a distant third. This reflected, among other things, the engrained biases of Bletchley's parent organization, the Foreign Office.[1] Paul Addison writes that the theme of academics and intelligence 'ought not to be laboured', because 'intellectuals were a transient minority in the world of secret intelligence'.[2] But, equally, their participation should not be overlooked, certainly in a study of Oxford and the war and given Bletchley's preference for 'professor type' recruits.

Beyond Bletchley, there were other organizations dedicated to the gathering, processing and dissemination of intelligence, and Oxford people made a hefty contribution to their work. Widening the net beyond GCCS and the attempt to break into and understand foreign nations' secret communications allows us to embrace open-source intelligence (that derived from extant and generally available sources) and to examine the work of Oxonians involved in its production, and reveals one of the most important uses to which Oxford real estate was put.

The Oxford buildings and institutions involved in the production of various types of intelligence were Balliol, Mansfield and Manchester colleges, the School of Geography, the New Bodleian and Oxford University Press (OUP) – as well as Oriel and Pembroke, which housed the Intelligence Corps. Intelligence work conducted in Oxford was crucial to national security and the planning and conduct of military operations: during a spat with the Ministry of Labour over the billeting of female workers in Oxford, Commander Edward Hok, superintendent of Section 47B at Mansfield, said that while his unit might not appear to have the 'urgent sound of "Munitions" or "Aircraft Production" ... I can assure you that unless our own production carries on side by side with theirs, they might as well shut down for all the use it would be'.[3]

First, a sketch of the Bletchley aspect of Oxford's war. A good deal of GCCS's work involved wireless or written communications requiring translation. An example would be the signals intelligence derived from the 'Y' station network which intercepted enemy radio traffic and located its point of origin. Interpreting the data that it yielded required linguists, and when messages had been encrypted they needed decryption. While mathematicians and linguists were of obvious utility, specialists in many other fields possessed relevant aptitudes. Classicists 'were thought suitable for such research as they were used to collating defective scraps of evidence, their pedantic exactitude was seen to be worthwhile when lives were at stake, and they had a reputation at that time for writing concisely and clearly'.[4]

Bletchley also recruited specialists in economic history, Russian studies, English literature, comparative philosophy, Egyptology, international relations, art history, theology and papyrology.[5] Oxonians at Bletchley included the Camden Professor of Ancient History, Hugh Last; Michael Dummett, who took the Japanese course at the Bletchley outstation in Abbottabad, known as the Wireless Experimental Depot; Christ Church classicist Denys Page; and the philosophers Gilbert Ryle (also of Christ Church) and Stuart Hampshire (All Souls). Peter Twinn, after leaving Brasenose in 1938 with a first in maths and now engaged in postgraduate research, answered the first advertisement put out by Bletchley's directors as they grappled with the Enigma code. He is credited with the first break into Enigma, and in 1942 became head of the Abwehr Enigma section. Walter Ettinghausen, a don at Queen's, ended up in charge of the translator's group of Z watch in the German naval section in Hut 4 after joining the army and then being ordered to Bletchley in February 1941.[6]

INTELLIGENCE, SCIENCE AND MEDICINE 227

Bright students, or those with a knowledge of foreign languages, were likely candidates for Bletchley, and the 'right type' was often to be found from among those with cosmopolitan family backgrounds. This was true, for example, of Jewish students at Oxford and Jewish families in Oxford. Joshua Goldberg was headhunted while reading Classics at Corpus Christi College, joining the Intelligence Corps and then Bletchley's Japanese translation section.[7] Sub-Lieutenant Laurence Cohen was reading Greats at Balliol in December 1941 when Japan entered the war. 'His college master asked him if he would like to learn Japanese, but he had no idea of the purpose until he reached Bletchley.'[8] Ann Mitchell was reading maths at Lady Margaret Hall when recruited by the Foreign Office. Clueless as to what she had signed up for, upon graduation in 1943 she found herself in Hut 6 working on German army and air force codes.

While the picture is fragmentary regarding Oxford dons and graduates at Bletchley, some research has been conducted, and a taste of it helps us comprehend their contribution and the value of their degree studies. Six St Hugh's graduates are known to have worked in Hut 6: Auriol Burrows (Modern History), Stella Castor (Classics), Heather Harris (Classics), Anne McDougall (PPE), Pamela Smith (Modern History) and Helen Watts (Classics).[9] Working alongside Hut 6 was a specialist section known as SIXTA (Signals Intelligence and Traffic Analysis). Its job was to examine 'facets of the messages such as volume, direction, broadcasting patterns, call signs and other relevant characteristics, separate from the message content'. Seven St Hugh's graduates worked here: Mary Baker (Modern Languages, French), Dorothy Davie (PPE), Mary Gilbertson (Modern History), Marianne Rigby (PPE), Eleanor Luscombe (Modern Languages, French and German), Helen Wilton (Modern History) and Marion Whittaker (PPE).

Hut 8 specialized in German naval Enigma messages (it was here that Alan Turing worked). About 130 women worked here supporting the cryptographers. Hut 4 provided it with similar traffic analysis to that provided by SIXTA for Hut 6. Five St Hugh's graduates worked in huts 4 and 8: Peggy Maclean (PPE), Eleanor Harris (Modern Languages, French and German), Diana Colbeck (Modern Languages, French and German), Monica Daniels (Modern Languages, French and German)

228 OXFORD'S WAR

and Alison Fairlie (Modern Languages, French). Hut 7 staff worked on Japanese naval codes, and included four St Hugh's graduates: Zaidee Garrett (Maths), Constance Senior (Maths), Alice Bishop (Modern Languages, French) and Rosemary Johns (English Language and Literature). Hut 3 concentrated on deciphered German army and air force Enigma messages needing translation from Hut 6, moving later into strategic intelligence. Working here from St Hugh's were Margaret Brittain (Modern Languages, French and German) and Mary Darwall (Modern Languages, French and German). Hut 9, an administrative section, and Hut 10, dedicated to air intelligence and then MI6, were the workplaces of four St Hugh's graduates: Elaine Reynolds (English Language and Literature), Adaline Parker (Modern Languages, French and German), Doreen Foster (Modern Languages, French and Italian) and Daphne Moss (Modern Languages, French and German). Finally, in Hut 11, where the Bombe machines were housed, worked two St Hugh's women, Pamela Gibbons (English Language and Literature) and Patricia Duke (PPE).

Oxonians contributed to other intelligence and counterintelligence activities. John Cecil Masterman, novelist, sportsman and Christ Church history tutor, oversaw the double-cross system for MI5 as chairman of the Twenty Committee, turning German agents against Berlin before returning to Oxford at the end of the war as provost of Worcester. In December 1939 Trevor-Roper was recruited by Dick White to interpret Abwehr radio traffic for MI8, the Radio Security Service of the War Office. Its function was to detect radio signals sent from German spies in Britain, to be rounded up by MI5 if discovered. Finding that they were also reading the radio transmissions of the Abwehr, the Radio Security Service expanded work to cover enemy wireless communications anywhere in the world.[10] When the unit transferred to MI6 and counter-espionage work, Trevor-Roper became head of the radio intelligence section and developed expertise in underground resistance within Germany and preparations for Britain's post-war occupation.[11] A future head of house, Daphne Park, went up to Somerville in 1940, becoming president of the University Liberal Club and only the second woman to speak at the Union. Upon graduating in 1943, she joined the First Aid Nursing Yeomanry, soon coming to the attention of SOE because of her knowledge of ciphers. From then on she supported SOE activity on behalf of resistance movements in occupied Europe, and shortly after the war was sent to Austria with the Field Intelligence Agency, tracking down Axis scientists before the Soviets could get their hands on them. In 1948 she joined MI6.[12]

Naval intelligence and the Inter-Service Topographical Department

Oxford's star turn on the intelligence front was the work of the several outfits clustered along Mansfield Road. Mansfield College had been occupied by Bletchley before war broke out. Then, in autumn 1940, Naval Intelligence Division (NID) 5 and NID 6 moved into the School of Geography. In 1941 the larger of the two, NID 6, began operating as the Inter-Service Topographical Department (ISTD).[13] A year later it took over Manchester College, soon erecting huts in the Arlosh and Tate quads (see PLATE 5). Still more space was needed. Huts appeared on Mansfield's land (where today's John Marsh building stands), and on the Master's Field of Balliol's sports ground on Jowett Walk. ISTD also used New College's Old Library, rooms in the Ashmolean for draughtsmen and mapmakers, and a large part of the New Bodleian, where it also oversaw the work of NID 11, the Admiralty Photographic Library. Along with Section 47B at Mansfield, NID 5 and ISTD were the main source of OUP's government work throughout the war.

What were these organizations? NID 5 was all about geographical intelligence for military operations. As early as June 1939 Rear Admiral John Godfrey, director of Naval Intelligence, had visited Cambridge to meet the vice chancellor and the director of the Scott Polar Research Institute. A similar visit was made to Oxford, and in 1940 Godfrey and his assistant, Lieutenant Commander Ian Fleming, contacted Professor Kenneth Mason, head of the School of Geography, requesting confidential reports on some regions of interest to the navy. As a result, a new series of naval handbooks for tactical and strategic purposes was commissioned to update the geographical material used by staff officers planning operations. This would be conducted by research sections in both Oxford and Cambridge, and a memorandum of collaboration was drawn up on 8 December ('The Collaboration of Oxford and Cambridge Universities in the Production of Topographical Information'). Here was an important and niche task for the geographers of Oxbridge and other universities, working alongside specialists from government and the armed forces (see PLATE 30).

NID 5 specialized in the production of detailed long-range information on all aspects of locations where military operations were likely to take place. Among other things, this led to the publication of the enormous, 58-volume Naval Intelligence Handbooks series, a feat that still ranks as one of the greatest achievements of academic geography.[14] They contained over 5,100 maps and diagrams and almost 6,400 photographs. Some ran to 700 pages in length, and print runs of up to 4,000 copies were ordered (for example, the handbooks on France, Belgium and the Netherlands). Even the handbook prepared on tiny Corsica warranted a respectable 1,750 copies. The handbooks were classified, intended for the use of service personnel only. When the restriction was lifted in 1955, they 'assisted a generation of British university teachers who were required to deliver lectures on regional geography that figured largely in most undergraduate syllabuses in the 1950s and 1960s'.[15]

The work of these geographers was essential as politicians and military planners took into account 'the influence which known geographical factors would have on strategic plans or military tactics'.[16] For example, knowledge of beach gradients and tidal movements in planning for the Normandy landings, or of the water content of German soil before Anglo-American armoured formations rolled in during the terminal days of the Reich, was of immeasurable value. Academic geographers worked alongside surveyors, cartographers, climatologists in the meteorological services, explorers taking on active roles in special operations, political geographers contributing to colonial, dominion and Foreign Office activities, and economic geographers supporting economic warfare.[17]

Relating to geographers, though embracing other Oxonians and the peculiar ways in which they contributed to the war, those with experience in harsh and remote lands helped provide specialist knowledge for military operations and economic warfare. Mason had a background in exploration, having co-founded the Himalayan Club. University expeditions in the 1920s to Spitzbergen and the Arctic fed into wartime operations to obtain ball bearings from Sweden, and expeditions to Greenland furnished individuals with experience and knowledge that could assist SOE missions in Scandinavia and the study of sea ice pertaining to the Arctic convoys. Members of the 1932 University Expedition to Borneo provided ideas, intelligence and personnel for Australian-led special operations as the Allies laid plans for the recapture of the giant island from the Japanese.[18] The 1935–6 University expedition to North East Land, organized by the University's Exploration Society, enabled David James to hone skills that equipped him to contribute to British operations in Antarctica.[19]

Also operating out of the School of Geography and Manchester College, the Inter-Service Topographical Department (ISTD) came into being as NID 6 in April 1940, Colonel Sam Bassett of the Royal Marines and University College Classics don Frederick Wells working out of a disused toilet at the Admiralty. It moved to Oxford in autumn 1940. Whereas NID 5 focused on the production of general handbooks for long-range planning, ISTD specialized in the production of bespoke reports, maps and other outputs related to specific military missions. Unlike NID 5, it might be instructed to produce material with a very short turnaround time.

The catalyst for the growth of both NID 5 and ISTD was the realization, early in the conflict, that British intelligence had atrophied since 1918. The Norway campaign rammed this home, British forces obliged to rely on outdated publications such as Baedeker's 1912 guide to Scandinavia for topographical and climatological intelligence. It also became evident, as Germany conquered much of Europe, that British attempts to push its forces back were going to depend heavily on hazardous amphibious operations involving air, land and maritime forces. Much of ISTD's work, therefore, as its superintendent, Bassett, put it, involved the study by experts of 'how to get on a beach and get off it again'.[20] With Churchill actively involved, in May 1940 the chiefs of staff instructed the Joint Intelligence Committee (JIC) to investigate the state of topographical intelligence across the armed forces. The result was the creation of ISTD, which, though remaining under Admiralty control, was there to be indented on by all three armed services.

232 OXFORD'S WAR

ISTD's responsibilities were set down by the JIC on 8 February 1941. It was to act as a centre for the collection and collation of the best available topographical information in the possession of the armed services or of outside sources. From this it was to produce reports and publications that gave military commanders the topographical intelligence they required. It was also to supply information required by the Joint Planning Staff and the director of Combined Operations either in the form of printed publications or ad hoc reports, and to provide the armed forces, on request, with such topographical intelligence as they might require. It generated detailed intelligence on the geography, geology, climate, vegetation and built environment of locations around the world where British and Allied forces were (or were likely) to conduct military operations.[21]

ISTD became an integral element in the planning and execution of military operations, including the Dieppe Raid, the invasion of Madagascar, the Anglo-American 'Torch' landings in North Africa, the decisive Normandy landings, and planned assaults against Japanese-occupied Malaya. It was tasked by a diverse range of military 'end users', helping to direct commando raids, sabotage operations, major amphibious landings and targeted air attacks. It identified terrain on which gliders might attempt safely to land, onto which paratroops or supplies might be dropped, and where airfields might best be established. It indicated where fresh water might be found as Allied forces took over an area or moved through it, and assisted those planning for the reconstruction of German oilfields upon their capture.

The work required a host of specialists, in soil and sand, water tables, tides and currents, the weather, mining, engineering and the built environment. ISTD had a transportation section, an engineering section and a geological section.[22] Data was derived from a range of sources, including books and articles (in plentiful supply in Oxford), aerial photographs supplied by reconnaissance flights from nearby airbases, information provided by servicemen inserted into enemy-held territory by small boats, and photos and information obtained from private companies with overseas interests (such as steamship companies, Lloyd's of London and Thomas Cook). A contacts register of people known to have recent experience of living in or visiting overseas locations employed fifteen people.[23] The register they built and maintained listed the names of scholars, explorers, geographers, travellers, businesspeople and refugees. There was then the information provided by the Admiralty Photographic Library, operating from the New Bodleian's basement (see PLATE 29). This monument to exhaustive research and information management contained photos from NID and other military and official sources, as well as from shipping companies, commercial firms, magazines, newspapers, technical and trade publications, tourist and photographic agencies, geological, geographical, and other university departments, and private collections. Its stock of images was boosted when Bassett and Wells received permission from Godfrey to appeal to the public via a BBC radio broadcast, yielding around 10 million postcards and holiday photographs. The press took up the appeal, and responses flooded in. According to Bassett, 'One lorry turned up at Oxford loaded with tins of cine-film – the result of several travel series. In this consignment alone we estimated that there were over *three million* single pictures.'[24] Processing this required painstaking sorting, involving sixty processes.[25]

ISTD also maintained a Library Research Unit, it being realized that the answer to almost any technical question asked by military planners existed within Britain, including in English and foreign-language publications of all different types. It was calculated that in the London region alone there were ninety libraries collecting periodicals relevant to some specific interest. With the rich research resources of the contact register, the Photographic Library and the Library Research Unit, it was soon 'possible to obtain recent photos or the names of recent residents of almost any place, coastal or inland, in the world'.[26] As a practical example of how things worked, information requested by the military about an obscure river crossing on the Somme was eventually derived, when the collections had been scoured, from a photo forming part of an illustrated advertisement for a French dredging company placed in a technical periodical.

As well as preparing written reports, maps and illustrations, ISTD furnished information to aircrew and military commanders in other ways. Models manufactured by an in-house model-making unit communicated information in an accurate and memorable manner. One of the earliest produced was for the amphibious attack on Dieppe in

234 OXFORD'S WAR

1942, photographs of the model taken at appropriate angles used to produce hundreds of silhouette booklets for the raiding forces. Coastline silhouettes – concertina panoramas comprising continuous, horizontal strip images printed in booklets or albums – were one of ISTD's most innovative products, used extensively to facilitate beach recognition during the D-Day landings. ISTD commandeered the only Graber machines in the country, which could reproduce glossy pictures in big copy runs.[27]

ISTD provided intelligence for many of the war's most famous operations. For the 'Dambusters' raid, it calculated the flow of feeder rivers and the maximum capacity of the reservoir before overspill, a botany expert using the state of vegetation shown on aerial reconnaissance photos to assess when it was at its highest. It also identified a suitable Scottish loch for practice runs. In another famous operation, ISTD provided intelligence for the RAF sorties that eventually sank the German battleship *Tirpitz*, constructing a scale model of the Norwegian fjord it was hiding in as part of its efforts to instruct the aircrew.

ISTD also contributed to the raid on German ships anchored at the French port of Bordeaux, made famous by the 1955 film *The Cockleshell Heroes*. The attack was to be conducted by canoeists, who would enter the Gironde estuary, find their way to the mouth of the Garonne river, canoe up it, and attach limpet mines to their targets. ISTD's job was to provide detailed information to help the brave souls who had volunteered for this potentially suicidal mission, which required them to paddle for 80 miles. It supplied them with data on tides and currents and pinpointed safe hiding places where they could lay up during daylight hours. To do this, over 2,000 ground and aerial photos of the region were studied and more than 600 silhouettes composed to enable them to identify their position while moving under cover of darkness. ISTD staff worked out the heights of landmarks and natural features, even describing distinctive smells the canoeists would encounter, emanating, for example, from a brewery and a chemical factory.

A new ISTD section was created following a February 1943 meeting between the scientific adviser and the Army Council to discuss 'the fire problem likely to arise when a BEF [British Expeditionary Force] invaded the continent'.[28] The Fire Vulnerability Intelligence Section's job was to tell the armed forces where the major urban fire risks were

INTELLIGENCE, SCIENCE AND MEDICINE 235

in Europe and other parts of the world where they would operate as they went on the offensive. The section produced hundreds of brightly coloured and information-laden maps, covering conurbations across the world where the Allies might drop bombs or deploy land forces. It established which parts of cities were most susceptible to firebombs or 'blockbuster' bombs (no point in dropping incendiary bombs on areas that were unlikely to go up in flames, or blockbusters on areas where there were few buildings susceptible to blast damage).

While assisting Allied targeting of towns and cities to be attacked, the Fire Vulnerability section's primary purpose was to provide information useful for commanders once these places had been *captured*. Not least, the Section could provide intelligence concerning the parts of town most vulnerable to enemy bombing (it being prudently anticipated that the enemy would attack Allied forces once they captured European conurbations). Thorough details about a port or inland city would allow commanders to orientate themselves as they moved in, informing them, for example, where *not* to store ammunition in case of retaliatory bombing or shelling, where fresh water could be found, and where it might be safest to billet troops.

As part of its organizational structure ISTD had sections dedicated to particular regions as well as particular areas of expertise. Personnel from countries of interest – France, the Netherlands, Norway and so on – were on the staff, as were Americans given their intimate involvement in Allied planning for Europe's reconquest and their early recognition of the value of the work being done in Oxford. Wren Pam Braham had worked in the Admiralty Photographic Library in the New Bodleian before transferring to the Norwegian department of Section B in a hut in Manchester's Tate Quad early in 1944.[29] Under Lieutenant Commander Edward Clowser, she worked alongside Norwegian soldiers, sailors and Wrens, Americans and civilians (including Wolmer Marlow, the governor of Svalbard, and Finn Dahl, cousin of Roald).[30] Her main task was to make mosaics out of aerial photographs, contributing to the missions to find and destroy the *Tirpitz*.

Norwegian Wren Eleonore Fredrikke Knudtzon moved to Britain from Stockholm in 1942.[31] She also worked in Section B, gathering and processing intelligence for military operations in Scandinavia. She described Section B's hut as a 'single long room with a jungle of writing tables, drawing boards, archives, map drawers, bookshelves, dressboys, chairs and stools'. Long tables ran along the inner walls, large maps of Norway spread across them, with Clowser's table at the far end, bearing telephones and a scrambler. The hut and its chilly concrete floor were inadequately heated by two coal-burners. Here, seven days a week, laboured twenty-five people. The work was so secret, Eleonore recalls, that those in Section B did not know what went on in Section A, the other hut on the Tate Quad lawn.

Heidi Brønner was another Norwegian in Section B.[32] Her job was to produce marked maps and detailed images of targets to be attacked, constructing mosaics made from glued-together photos in order to do so. 'A target at Skien river is to be attacked by Mosquito planes from low altitude', she wrote of one such operation. Only the day before, RAF photo reconnaissance aircraft had flown over the area, and now, as a result, Heidi had before her two heaps of photos, rushed to Manchester once the aircraft had landed. Heidi then put the photos under a stereoscope, a device that allowed the viewer to see a three-dimensional image, essential for accurate readings of heights, depths and features.

> Now I look down through the lenses for the first time. For a few seconds my eye muscles are opposing, then the terrain jumps up towards me in three dimensions, so suddenly that I jump. There is snow on the ground, all mixed up colours and tints have gone away. And there is sunshine. Trees and houses pop up so alive that you want to touch them with your finger, and by the shadows on the snow you may study the vertical forms as if you were standing there yourself. One of the most important things we find is a cable which is stretched over the river between two tall masts, and on the mosaic this is marked by white ink and a warning text added [for the benefit of the pilots who would attack at low altitude].

For ISTD's extensive D-Day preparations, Bassett himself made a clandestine visit to the landing beaches, inserted from a submarine. His organization, presided over from his office in Manchester College, provided Eisenhower's SHAEF with vital intelligence, including invaluable maps for the invading forces and detailed knowledge of the topography and geology of the invasion beaches.[33] Bassett's memoir captures the drama as well as the sheer scale and significance of the work carried out in Oxford. In the thick of the planning, the reproduction of photos of the assault beaches was crucial and ISTD was asked effectively to mass-produce them. More Graber photo reproduction machines were installed in the New Bodleian. A roll of photo paper passed over a glass frame, behind which were placed a negative and a high-powered lamp. The roll then went through developing tanks, fixing tanks and washing tanks. Next, it was passed over electrically heated drums and was guillotined to the required size when it emerged.[34] At one point, a rusty tank leaked chemicals through the floor, damaging 'beautiful veneers of precious inlaid wood' in a room below which had been 'kept back' from the military. Registrar Veale asked Bassett to come over from Manchester College to inspect the damage. Fortunately, it being a new building, the Ministry of Works was able to find the original craftsmen in order to repair the damage.

To produce images of the invasion beaches, a special squad of Spitfires took zero-height obliques of the whole Normandy coastline. The pictures were joined together with tape to produce a panorama and taken to SHAEF, where they were shown to Admiral Sir Bertram Ramsay, Allied naval commander-in-chief. He said that he only wanted force commanders and planners involved to see the material, so asked for forty copies. Fine. Bassett scurried back to Oxford and visited John Johnson at OUP. He duly produced the required prints, and they were sent off to SHAEF. It wasn't long before Ramsay called Bassett on the scrambler. He had wanted forty *thousand* copies! They were so good that it had been decided that gunnery staff could make targeting grids to fit the pictures, allowing ground forces to call in gunfire support by grid number reference. Therefore, all ships involved in the landings needed a copy, as did the landing craft conveying the troops onto the beaches and land force commanders down to unit level.

The request dumbfounded Bassett. It was abundantly clear that ISTD did not have the paper, the time or the equipment to fulfil the order. He did the maths; ISTD would need to print 2 million photos and would need 737 miles of photographic paper and 10 tons of chemicals every second day. He told SHAEF that it was impossible. This prompted Eisenhower to call the Admiralty, unprepared to accept this outcome. Bassett was to be told to list exactly what was required, and bombers

238 OXFORD'S WAR

would fly the material over from America. Within three days, the first of them had touched down in Oxfordshire. With the materials coming online, ISTD now had to overcome the time factor. It did so by using continuous processing machines, which were commandeered from around the country and brought to the New Bodleian, protests overcome by a priority order from Eisenhower.

This vital but intensely secret work was attended by inevitable security headaches. Anyone even glimpsing the material would know exactly where the invasion was to take place, potentially blowing the elaborate deception operation undertaken to convince Hitler that it was the Pas de Calais, not Normandy, that was the target for the invasion that he knew was imminent. Bassett could 'turn the New Bodleian into a kind of fortress, locking everyone up until after D-Day – which meant keeping almost a thousand people behind locked doors for several weeks'. In the end, he decided to give his staff a 'jolly good talking-to on the question of security'. As part of the security equation, the enterprise demanded the destruction of waste material, particularly as the Graber machines homed in on prints matching the negatives. Bassett therefore incinerated all scrap material, lighting 'a bonfire four times a day on the tennis ground attached to Manchester'.[35]

ISTD's work, Bassett writes, involved around 6,000 people. Frustratingly, the figures aren't explained.[36] Records mention that ISTD was employing 750 by 1944, one assumes in Oxford, an assumption corroborated by Bassett's aside on D-Day security that one option was to 'lock up a thousand people' (though this figure might refer to *all* those working in that particular building). What is clear is that ISTD was a quite extraordinary organization, up there with the top 'hidden' contributors to Allied victory. Further along Mansfield Road, another nest of military personnel and civilians, most of them women, also laboured on clandestine tasks aimed at foreshortening the prospects of Hitler's Reich.

Mansfield College and Oxford University Press

While Bletchley is best known for codebreaking, it was also responsible for code-*making*. The production of 'communications security materials' – meaning the printing of requisite forms and codebooks – was

Mansfield's remit when in August 1939 Bletchley's Code and Cypher Production Unit moved in.[37] Known as the 'construction section', it was responsible for 'constructing' British codes and ciphers. Generally referred to as Section 47B, on the outbreak it came under the Naval Intelligence Division, specifically NID 10. This was because the Royal Navy was by some distance the main consumer of the forms, codebooks and ciphering tables that it produced, given the very large number of ships and shore establishments that it was responsible for (the army and air force mainly used code machines and had fewer units and establishments).[38]

To start with, NID 10's Edward Hok presided over the labours of thirty-eight women at Mansfield, though by the end of 1939 the figure was just shy of a hundred. Hok wrote in January 1942 that his unit's role was the preparation and printing of codes, cyphers, recoding and recyphering tables, call signs, direction-finding verification tables, key memoranda, and kindred books in connection with the communications arrangements of various government departments. The section also analysed and vetted Admiralty signals traffic, as it was responsible for code *security* too. The 'detailed analysis of all signals In and Out of the Admiralty or passing through the Admiralty, together with the records of traffic from foreign stations is carried out at Oxford'.[39] The work was led by NID 10 officers assisted by a staff of 'girls' provided by the Foreign Office.[40] Advising the Admiralty 'in matters relating to coding and cyphering', it examined over half a million messages in the calendar year 1941, and was soon printing millions of documents.

Given the severe lack of accommodation in Oxford, local women were recruited where possible. One of them was June Coppock, a pupil at Milham Ford School on Marston Road. Leaving school in 1940, she was approached indirectly by the head of OUP and sounded out. In January 1941 at the age of 16 she was taken on as a typist ('though I never did any typing while I was there') in the Code and Cypher Production Unit. She would remain at Mansfield until September 1945, working seven days a week, 9 a.m. until 6.30 p.m., with an hour and a half for lunch.

> Our job in Room K was to record every Naval message, whether sent by cable or wireless, from Royal Navy or Merchant Navy ships, or shore establishments. We recorded them in lead-weighted books, the same as

on-board ships, which in an emergency could be ditched overboard, and sink. Where we would sink them if they had to be disposed of in Oxford I don't know – the Isis probably! ... Our main purpose was to ensure that no code was used too often. We would send the information off to Bletchley Park and they would probably arrange for a different code to be issued ... For each message we recorded the time and origin, the time that the message ended, and, in a special column, which code had been used ... Each day's tally of messages was taken to BP by courier each evening.[41]

Barbara Roxby was in the same unit and recalls the tight security. The core working area featured a strongroom and an 'inner citadel'. The college was kept under armed guard, and the combinations on the safes in the tower were changed three times a day. Two Bank of England employees on site

supervised the collection of all scraps of paper, blotting paper, etc that were used in the production of the Aircraft Reporting Codes and Bombe codes and they took it all away, under an armed guard of soldiers, in a lorry to Wolvercote Paper Mills where it was all pulped.[42]

Coppock and Roxby's section worked in the spacious room beneath the library (today's JCR), where 'there were lots of trestle tables and the Foreign Office ladies sat at one end of the room and told everyone what to do'. There was a telephone exchange on the top floor of the tower. By 1941 the Mansfield establishment comprised 149 staff in the code and cypher section. There were also fourteen office keepers, watchmen and 'women cleaners', six military guards, an office-keeper, van driver, courier, and Hollerith punch-hole tabulating machine mechanics.[43] By October 1944, there were about 350 women employed at Mansfield.

As Chapter 4 explained, OUP's war work was dominated by government printing, and ISTD and Section 47B were its major 'customers'. The majority of confidential printing was done by OUP and HMSO Press in Harrow, both working at capacity and struggling against rising demand. By the end of 1941, OUP undertook

a small amount of letterpress work and a large amount of lithographic work for NID 6, and their remaining work is placed by Section 47B of the Foreign Office, Mansfield College, Oxford, and consists of Recoding and Recyphering Tables, Syko Cards and Key Memoranda for the 3 Fighting Services, but mainly for the Admiralty, also Naval Codes and Cyphers for various Admiralty documents related to Signal matters.[44]

INTELLIGENCE, SCIENCE AND MEDICINE 241

Forms printed included wireless traffic logs, Greenwich Meantime time grids, recyphering tables, and forms for Bletchley and intercept stations detailing frequency and call signs.[45] There were General tables, Home tables, Middle East tables, and Far East tables, as well as One-Time 'Three' Pads and One-Time 'Two' pads for IPI.[46] They also produced aircraft reporting codes.

Printed matter from Mansfield (for which purpose the library was controversially taken over) and OUP was used in faraway places, in India and Kabul, by the Consul General in New York and the British High Commission in Ottawa.[47] It wasn't a matter of 'just' printing things; there were many requirements associated with this extraordinarily complex business. The binding of documents and photographs was a major feature of the work required to produce the outputs ordered by ISTD and Section 47B, including weighted covers designed to sink if aircrew or sailors had to ditch secret documents. At one point, Hok arranged for Pitmans of Bath to produce 52,000 weighted covers.[48]

There were all sorts of practicalities to be considered in terms of typeface and ink type too. As an exasperated Hok noted, if the font size for in-aircraft reporting codebooks is reduced, 'we are told that the light in a bomber is very bad and that the type is too small. If we increase the size of the book we are told that the navigating officer's table is too small to hold so large a book.'[49] There was then the matter of solubility; ink needed to be resistant to moisture in extreme conditions and to being handled by damp hands, but it would be ideal if the 'print should entirely disappear after immersion in water for about twenty-four hours'.[50] Experiments were conducted, though some desired requirements proved to be unrealistic. John Johnson had occasion to write to Godfrey in May 1942 arguing against the adoption of 'fugitive printing', a technique involving the use of security ink that would run if tampered with or dampened. This was because the technical challenges of doing so mid-war were too great. 'It would be necessary', Johnson explained, 'to provide specially coated paper at a rate of at least 180,000 sheets, or 10 tons, per week.' Special ink would be required 'in very considerable quantities', and thirty machines at OUP – more than half of its machining plant – would have to be equipped with rubber rollers.[51]

It is apparent that Oxford real estate played a little-known but important role in the intelligence war. The work of Bletchley and its Oxford outposts, and of ISTD and NID 5, involved Oxford graduates and dons, peripherally in some cases, intimately, as in the case of the geographers, in others. Taken together with the activities of Chatham House and the piecemeal contribution of dons to the preparation of political intelligence for agencies such as PWE, the picture that emerges is intriguing. In the fields of science and medicine, Oxford real estate also played a significant role in the war effort, and Oxford staff were deeply involved in a range of war-related advances. It is to this aspect of Oxford's war that we now turn.

Of laboratories and hospitals

The British government was 'far more dependent on academic expertise in the scientific conduct of the war' than had been the case in 1914–18.[52] Now, war

> gave priority to scientific and technological goals, and for the first time in Oxford's history the largely invisible scientific departments and laboratories came into their own as publicly acknowledged centres of theoretical innovation and advanced research.[53]

Jack Morrell argues that 'many of the Clarendon's researchers were saved for physics and for Oxford by the convulsive outbreak of the second world war and their subsequent employment as boffins'.[54] In addition to physics, the war 'reinforced the existing strengths of Oxford science in chemistry, zoology, ecology and genetics at the very moment when the national importance of basic research at the universities was about to receive fuller public recognition than ever before'.[55] Oxford scientists conducted research in three areas of strategic importance: the atom bomb, radar and penicillin. But there were significant contributions in other fields too, as we will see.

Some researchers found that what they were already working on had immediate utility in terms of the war effort, while others changed tack in order to address emerging requirements. Some found themselves and their research simply 'taken over', as government and war industry devoured laboratories and research teams (see the example of Moullin in the previous chapter). Wartime conditions, wrote Edward Milne, Rouse Ball Professor of Mathematics, fellow of Wadham and president of the Royal Astronomical Society, necessitated 'team rather than individual work', demanded 'results rather than principles', and sometimes required the withholding of 'secret' research. Milne's own bag was ballistics, working on armour-piercing munitions and sound ranging for the Ordnance Board.[56]

The endeavours of Oxford scientists were subject to wartime constraints, as well as the usual skirmishing involved in trying to attract support and its most valued manifestation: funding.[57] This came variously from government departments such as the Department of Scientific and Industrial Research (DSIR), agencies such as the Medical Research Council, charities such as Rockefeller, and companies such as ICI. They had to deal with shortages of raw materials and lab equipment and the demand that civil defence placed upon their time. The University Museum's fire brigade established a night patrol of the Science Area, and air raid shelters were constructed between the University Observatory and the biochemistry department. Professor of geology James Douglas, commander of the Oxford City Home Guard, and most of his department's staff were involved in military or civil defence duties.[58] Oxford medical departments lost staff to military service, 'but three groups of people were available to make up the shortages: elder statesmen of medicine who had emigrated to Oxford; refugees fleeing from Fascism; and women, who could at last assume positions of real responsibility'.[59]

Some scientists spent time away from Oxford on war committees or defence projects. Robert Robinson, professor of organic chemistry, served on numerous bodies concerned with chemical defence, explosives and chemotherapy. Lindemann was mostly absent in London, and R.V. Southwell was on the Ministry of Supply's advisory council and chaired several committees concerned with wartime engineering research. Sir Henry Tizard had chaired the government's Committee for the Scientific Survey of Air Defence since 1934 (the Tizard Committee) and led the eponymous mission to America in September 1940 that shared British research on vital technologies such as radar and the bomb. A leading international conduit of scientific intelligence and exchange, member of the Air Council and adviser to the Minister of Aircraft Production, he became president of Magdalen in 1942. During his presidency, he spent three months away advising the Australian government (urged to accept the invitation by Churchill). There he visited defence establishments and advised on scientific developments in relation to the Pacific war. In 1944 he took up the chairmanship of a committee created by the chiefs of staff to assess the impact of new weapons on defence policy. When his proposal for a new chiefs of staff subcommittee under a scientific adviser was accepted by Attlee's government shortly after the war ended and he was offered the job, he resigned from Magdalen, because while some fellows were happy for him to accept and carry on as president a minority opposed the idea.[60]

The main effort of the inorganic and physical chemists was the improvement of military respirators, contracted to the Ministry of Supply. This was the preserve of Cyril Hinshelwood, Dr Lee's professor of chemistry, and his colleagues working at the Inorganic Chemistry Laboratory on South Parks Road.[61] 'Activated' charcoal was employed in respirators to neutralize poison gas, and Hinshelwood visited America as collaboration developed. Dr Harry Irving of St Edmund Hall was part of his anti-gas team and also worked on War Office research on 'preserving the efficiency of signal-flares and photo-flashes during storage under conditions of tropical temperature and humidity' (acting at night as deputy head warden of ARP Area 'A').[62] Oxford chemists also contributed to the work of the Inter-Services Research Bureau under chemical engineer Professor Dudley Newitt, designing gadgets for SOE and resistance movements from its base at a mansion near Welwyn. There was also a contract for work on the suppression of gun flash, and some Oxford chemists worked on the 'spectra of the fuels in the tanks of German aeroplanes shot down over Britain, from which it was possible to deduce much about the sources of the fuels'.[63]

Radar used radio waves to detect and measure the distance of objects and could be crucial in providing early warning of air attack or, at sea, the presence and location of enemy submarines. The prototype 'Home Chain' radar system on the English coast was operational by summer 1939, and the chase was on to establish a parallel system of radar sets able to 'see' ships as well as low-flying aircraft at short distance.[64] In this pursuit, chance played a role in creating a role for the physicists of the Clarendon:

> The fact that the new laboratory became ready for occupation within weeks of the beginning of hostilities proved to be an extraordinarily favourable coincidence. Once talk of requisitioning the building as a military hospital had passed, the way was open for the empty space to be allocated for war-work. Already in the summer of 1939 ten or so of those working in the laboratory who had experience of electronics had been initiated in the early development of radar at Pevensey on the Sussex coast, and by January 1940 they were engaged back in the Clarendon on research on microwave components intended for use in operational radar.[65]

Lindemann offered the Clarendon's facilities to the Admiralty, and its team worked mainly on the design and development of microwave radar for ships and aircraft, funded by DSIR. In the newly built part of the Clarendon, later to be named the Lindemann Building, 'the majority of the research staff remained; most of them started work on devices for centimetre waves and the far infrared. Reflex klystrons for 32 mm and 12.5 mm were developed, together with magnetrons and methods for determining receiver sensitivity.'[66] The Clarendon played a decisive part in the development of centimetre radar, which was all about focusing the radio wave down in size, so that it didn't pick up everything (such as waves on the sea) but things that might be of interest (such as the conning tower of a submarine). It led to new radar sets being fitted to ships from late 1941, and, later, to the aircraft of Coastal Command. As part of the team Arthur Cooke, future warden of New College, designed the 'transmit–receive' cell, which was to be used in all radar equipment.

Alongside Birmingham, Oxford made the crucial discoveries and solved many of the peripheral problems resulting in the first U-boat kill attributable to centimetre radar, which occurred in April 1942. The success of this research contributed greatly to the eventual defeat of the U-boat menace, particularly by providing 10-centimetre radar sets that were not detectable by the enemy's systems, unlike the previous 1.5-metre sets, meaning that enemy submarines did not have time to dive once detected.[67] After the war, it was accepted by the Germans as well as the Allies that the key factor in winning the Battle of the

Atlantic had been centimetre radar.[68] Oxford physicists also worked on confusing enemy radar and protecting Allied ships from magnetic mines. They played an important part in developing acoustic mines, such as those laid at the entrance to the Seine ahead of D-Day in order to bottle up enemy torpedo boats that might otherwise seek to prevent the Allied landings.

Elsewhere in the Clarendon Laboratory, other highly secret work was going on. The team working on radar on the north side knew that work was going on under Francis Simon on the south side, walking passed the windows on their way to work, looking in and wondering what was going on in there.[69] But, as in the New Bodleian and other college and University buildings, secrecy shrouded the activity. Apart from the scientists themselves, everyone else (including undergraduates) was kept out of the Clarendon research areas, wooden barriers erected and 'naval pensioners scrutinising passes'.[70]

What was going on in the Clarendon's south side was work of global importance conducted by low-temperature physicists, related to the production of atomic weapons. Lindemann had been interested in low-temperature physics for some time; thanks to his efforts, within five months of Hitler coming to power a nucleus of exceptional scientists was established in Oxford.[71] He contacted the chairman of ICI, who persuaded his board to offer contracts to scientists recruited from Germany, some starting as early as 1 May 1933. When the Academic Assistance Council was established in the same month, another source of assistance came on stream. Francis Simon moved to Belbroughton Road with his family, and from 1936 held a readership in thermodynamics. K.H. Mendelssohn arrived in April, and Nicholas Kurti, Heinrich Kuhn and H. and F. London came later. They lived on their contracts until other openings came along, Kuhn finding a college appointment in 1938, Kurti financed by the 'Tube Alloys' project when it began. The Breslau physicists soon became the dominant research sector at the Clarendon. Simon, rated the 'finest low-temperature physicist in the world', began a programme of nuclear-weapons research, which became urgent as Germany raced towards the creation of its own bomb.[72]

Under the direction of the government's MAUD Committee, established in March 1940 to investigate the feasibility of an atomic bomb, four universities were involved in Britain's research (Birmingham, Cambridge, Liverpool and Oxford).[73] Birmingham was the theoretical engine room, with Liverpool and Oxford working on isotope separation. The Clarendon team became part of the government's 'Tube Alloys' research programme funded by DSIR. In collaboration with Otto Frisch and Rudolf Peierls at Birmingham (both refugees from Germany and the researchers behind the MAUD Committee's creation), in Oxford Simon together with Kurti, Kuhn (both also refugees from the Nazis) and American Henry Arms laid the groundwork for the gaseous diffusion method of separating uranium 235, the isotope responsible for nuclear fission. Involving some thirty scientists and thirty support staff, it proved to be the most promising method. The Oxford team demonstrated that it was feasible to separate fissile isotopes, influencing the American decision to launch its own atomic bomb project.

Oxford medicine was also boosted by war. Largely through Lord Nuffield's generosity, the fortunes of the city's hospitals had been restored to such an extent that 'by 1939 the Oxford region was seen as the model for hospital coordination for the whole nation'.[74] Nuffield money had extended the Radcliffe Infirmary, purchased the Observatory and its grounds, rebuilt the Wingfield-Morris orthopaedic hospital in Headington, and established new professorships and a medical trust.[75] Though Oxford did not yet have a separate medical school, powerful figures such as the Regius Professor of Medicine and the University Registrar aspired for it 'to become a great centre, perhaps the centre, of medical progress', and the war presented an opportunity to establish a full medical school.[76]

> This otherwise controversial move was presented as the only responsible reaction to the demands of the wartime emergency. Dispersal of the London medical schools meant that London students needed training elsewhere, while Oxford students were denied the usual clinical facilities in London.[77]

Oxford medical research contributed to the war effort in several distinct ways. Physiologists studied British drug plants in an attempt to replace Continental supplies cut off by German conquests. Dr W.O. James of the Department of Botany set up the 'Oxford Medical Plant

Scheme' after the public had been asked to 'help collect wild medical plants that could subsequently be processed by the pharmaceutical industry', part of a national Medical Plant Collection Scheme established by the Ministry of Health in March 1941.[78] The war wasn't all about modern drugs, plants no longer viewed just as 'old drugs' but instead appearing at 'the forefront of British wartime medicine'.[79] The Oxford scheme's initial aim was to 'grow, dry and market specific medicinal plants requested by the Ministry', though soon found itself 'leading research efforts on behalf of the national scheme'.[80] James also chaired the Oxfordshire and Buckinghamshire Herb Committee, which produced two films on herb collection from desirable plants (belladonna and foxgloves), and gave five talks on BBC radio.[81]

C.S. Elton's research was diverted to the protection of food through rodent control. Dr Janet Vaughan, Somerville's principal from February 1945, was an expert in blood diseases and transfusions who earlier in the war had played a major role in blood supply for London. The closing stages of the war found her in Belgium working on starvation, and she was one of the first scientists to enter the Belsen concentration camp. Herbert Seddon, Nuffield Professor of Orthopaedic Surgery, fellow of Worcester and head of the Wingfield–Morris hospital, set up a Peripheral Nerve Injuries Centre, which as part of its work studied nerve surgery required for gunshot wounds.[82] The biochemistry laboratory researched the treatment of burns, the blood signature of the antimalarial drug mepacrine, nutrition and the effects of toxic substances. Oxford biochemists developed dimercaprol (also known as British anti-Lewisite), which was an antidote to arsenic poisoning and the chemical warfare gas Lewisite.

The work of the inaugural Nuffield Professor of Anaesthetics, New Zealander Robert Macintosh, illustrates how pre-existing research became interwoven with collaborative wartime initiatives. Before the war he had anaesthetized for an American plastic surgeon treating the wounded in the Spanish Civil War, working with very primitive equipment. The experience convinced Macintosh that there was a need for a simple portable vaporizer suitable for battlefield use. Returning to Oxford and with the aid of Clarendon physicists, the prototype Oxford vaporizer no. 1 was the result.[83] This portable device delivered a rapid and even flow of ether to the patient, and by 1945 over 4,000 had been manufactured at the Cowley works and delivered to Allied field hospitals. More sophisticated vaporizers and other items of equipment, including the Macintosh laryngoscope, were developed too. Together with the superbly illustrated textbooks written by Macintosh and other members of his department, they had a major impact on the practice of anaesthesia. Mackintosh was made an air commodore and put in charge of the RAF's anaesthetic services. His department provided training courses for military anaesthetists, and was 'deeply involved in hazardous physiological research into the provision of respirable atmospheres in submarines, survival during parachute descent from high altitudes, and the evaluation of life-jackets, using an anaesthetized volunteer submerged in a swimming-pool'.[84]

The Catalan plastic surgeon Josep Trueta, a professor of surgery in Barcelona, had developed pioneering techniques during the Spanish Civil War. He argued in his influential book *Principles and Practice of War Surgery* that patient outcomes 'were greatly improved by minimising the elapsed time between wounding and surgery'.[85] The book was translated into English and influenced Royal Army Medical Corps practice during the war. A staunch republican, his life consequently at risk in Spain when Franco triumphed, Trueta emigrated with his family to Britain in 1939. Here he was in demand as a lecturer on air raid surgery and practical air raid precautions because of his experience, and he began advising the Ministry of Health. In September 1939 G.R. Girdlestone, Nuffield Professor of Orthopaedic Surgery, heard him lecture on air raid casualties and invited him to Oxford. From 1942 to the end of the war, Trueta was surgeon in charge of the busy accident department at the Radcliffe Infirmary. In spite of a heavy clinical workload, his research continued, particularly in the field of kidney neurovascular physiology, and he also wrote on the use of penicillin in bone infection. His collaboration with Girdlestone led to the establishment of the Oxford School of Orthopaedics.[86]

Other Oxford research contributed to medical advances. To monitor the effects of rationing, the government commissioned physiologist and nutritionist Dr Hugh Sinclair to undertake the Oxford Nutrition Survey, which began work in May 1941.[87] One survey group consisted of 120 pregnant working-class women selected from the maternity hospital in Ruskin College and 253 'mainly' working-class pregnant women from the Radcliffe Infirmary's maternity hospital. The surveys revealed deficiencies in protein and vitamin A. As a result, the ministries of Health and Food adopted a food supplement programme, entitling pregnant women to extra rations of fruit and dairy produce as well as cod-liver oil tablets.[88]

Undoubtedly Oxford's most renowned wartime medical advance emanated from the Dunn School of Pathology, where penicillin was transformed into a crucial antibiotic.[89] In collaboration with a team that included biochemist Ernst Chain and Margaret Jennings, Australian Howard Florey, professor of pathology and head of the Dunn School, obtained penicillin in stable form, the first to isolate, purify and apply to on-patient treatment what would become the world's most widely used antibiotic. Chain had left Germany shortly after Hitler's accession, 'disgusted with the Nazi gang'.[90] Florey had been investigating lysozyme, an enzyme found in mucus known to have anti-bacterial properties, continuing research he'd been conducting at the University of Sheffield before his Oxford appointment. Chain's team had documented how the lysozyme worked, and commenced work on other antibacterial substances, including penicillin.[91] They used a culture of Alexander Fleming's strain of penicillin that had been maturing for some time at the Dunn School, but it was not until late 1939 that the work was taken up 'vigorously'.[92]

On 25 May 1940, with the situation in Europe looking bleak, the first experiment took place to see if penicillin 'exerted any protective effect on infected mice'.[93] The team demonstrated that it could protect the unfortunate laboratory inmates against infection from the deadly streptococcus genus of bacteria; those given penicillin survived, the others were dead come the morning.[94] These experiments sped things up considerably, leading, Florey wrote, to 'the immediate realization of the possible therapeutic value of penicillin in man, especially in the war-wounded'. It was at once decided, he continued, 'to explore every possible means of obtaining enough material for preliminary trials of the drug in infections in man'.[95] Struggling to get external support, his team had no choice but to prepare the material in the Dunn laboratory.

INTELLIGENCE, SCIENCE AND MEDICINE   251

Florey asked one of Professor Witts's junior associates, Dr Charles Fletcher, to help with clinical trials. His first task was to find a patient in a terminal condition in order to test the substance in case of 'some unique adverse reaction in man' – or, as it happened, woman.[96] Fifty-year-old Elva Akers, in the Radcliffe Infirmary with inoperable breast cancer, agreed to be the guinea pig. With Florey and Witts looking on, on 17 January 1941 she offered Fletcher her arm and became the first person to be injected with penicillin, suffering no adverse reaction.[97] From 12 February the first sustained treatment took place. The previous December, City of Oxford police constable Albert Alexander was scratched on the face by a thorn while pruning roses, a chance accident that presented the opportunity to move the penicillin trials 'from mice to men'.[98] His badly infected scratch had become life-threatening, and he now languished in the Infirmary. Abscesses had spread across his face and an eye had been removed. Fletcher administered an initial 200 mg dose, then 100 mg every three hours.[99] Alexander's urine was taken to the Dunn School by bicycle to extract the unused penicillin for readministration. Within days he had made a remarkable recovery, despite the penicillin being very impure. His condition stabilized and the swelling went down as he received 220,000 units over five days. But supplies of the drug ran out, and he died in April. It was clear that Florey and his team could not conduct convincing clinical trials while they were still struggling to produce sufficient quantities. Nevertheless, the experiments had demonstrated the enormous potential of penicillin in wartime.[100] In order to conserve the meagre amounts being produced, following the treatments of Alvers and Alexander trials continued on children with localized infections. They took place at the Radcliffe and were conducted by Fletcher, Florey and his scientist wife, Mary Florey.[101]

Wartime strictures made the research difficult: to conduct the necessary programme of animal experiments and clinical trials, for example, the team needed to process up to 500 litres of mould filtrate each week. Courtesy of biochemist Norman Heatley's experiments, they 'began growing it in a strange array of culture vessels such as baths, bedpans, milk churns and food tins' before a customized fermentation vessel was designed for ease of removing and to save space, renewing the broth beneath the surface of the mould.[102] A team of 'penicillin girls' was employed to inoculate and generally look after the fermentation process as the Dunn lab became a penicillin factory. Heatley solved the riddle of penicillin's instability and refined an automated extraction machinery following his Heath Robinson experiments. He found a way to harvest it from huge volumes of filtrate coming off the production line by extracting it into amyl acetate and then back into water, using a countercurrent system. Another biochemist, Edward Abraham, was employed to help step up production.

Like other pioneering British research, realizing the full potential of penicillin required American horsepower. Unable to produce enough penicillin for use in general treatment, Florey and Heatley crossed the Atlantic in July 1941 with a small amount of the purified and stabilized drug. Florey wrote that he felt 'like a carpetbag salesman trying to promote a crazy idea for some ulterior motive' as he touted his way around America attempting to drum up interest.[103] One material aid provided by the Americans to the British programme was the dispatch to Oxford of corn steep liquor for growing the penicillin in, which increased the yield. A second series of trials were conducted in Oxford from January 1942, and the first treatments in America took place in March. In April 1942 Oxford's work was taken into the army, a quantity given to the War Office and dispatched to Cairo. In May 1943 Florey went to North Africa in company with Professor Hugh Cairns (see below) to inspect and oversee trials.[104]

After considerable effort, Florey managed to convince powerful figures in the American academic and research establishment that the drug was important. Forty large organizations, including government outfits such as the American War Production Board, universities, and pharmaceutical companies such as Pfizer, gradually became involved. Around a thousand chemists were eventually engaged in classified research on the drug's chemistry and production. This led to penicillin becoming available in America on a scale larger than was possible in Britain, and after the initial logjam caused by obstacles to production in commercial quantities the floodgates opened. First used in the Pacific in April 1943, it was the accepted treatment for servicemen with pus-producing infections in the theatre by the end of the year.[105] In the first five months of that year, 400 million units were produced

INTELLIGENCE, SCIENCE AND MEDICINE 253

in America – enough to treat 180 severe cases. In the following seven months, 20.5 billion units were produced. By D-Day, 100 billion units were being turned out each month, and by the end of 1945 Pfizer was making more than half of global production.

Though Oxford's penicillin research 'effectively gave rise to the modern antibiotics industry', the drug

> was not patented because leading medical bodies in Britain then thought it was unethical to do so, and also perhaps because it might have been difficult to specify patents of lasting value. Several American firms, by contrast, did take out patents on their own discoveries in penicillin and profited enormously from them.[106]

Somerville biochemist Dr Dorothy Hodgkin solved the riddle of penicillin's structure in 1945, allowing for its synthetization and mass production, thus making the antibiotic era possible.[107] In this manner and set against the backdrop of war and driven by the need to treat its victims, penicillin was brought to the world by the endeavours of a relatively small team of dedicated scientists on South Parks Road. Florey's Australian compatriot Hugh Cairns not only helped introduce the drug to the field of battle but led another innovative and dedicated team bent on saving lives blighted by war, this one based just up the road at St Hugh's College.

St Hugh's and the Combined Services Hospital for Head Injuries

Cairns went to Balliol as a Rhodes Scholar in 1919, later marrying the master's daughter, Barbara Smith. In 1934 he considered taking his 'growing neurosurgical service to Oxford, where there was room for expansion and where he had friends and influence'.[108] A rising star and sought-after specialist (attending T.E. Lawrence after his ultimately fatal motorcycle accident in May 1935 and permitted to retain his brain), Cairns was set to transform neurosurgery.[109] Soon after moving to Oxford he had meetings with Vice-Chancellor Lindsay and Registrar Veale, and produced a memorandum for the Regius Professor of Medicine on the 'desirability of establishing a complete School of Clinical Medicine at Oxford'.[110] Cairns founded the neurosurgical unit at the Radcliffe Infirmary, and met with Lord Nuffield, helping persuade him to invest heavily in Oxford medicine. Cairns's appointment to one of the accompanying endowed professorships, that of surgery, was announced in January 1937, and he became a fellow of Balliol and head of the Department of Surgery.

By the time war broke out, Cairns was an established Oxford figure and renowned in his field. He was also known and trusted by the army, consultant to the Queen Alexandra's Military Hospital, a RAMC facility at Millbank.[111] On the outbreak of war he became adviser to the Ministry of Health on head injuries and neurosurgeon to the British Army, joining the RAMC as a colonel and head of its neurosurgery operations, soon rising to the rank of brigadier. He was a look-ahead man: as the situation in Europe worsened and anticipating the steel shortages that war would bring, he convinced the War Office to procure all surgical instruments likely to be needed, meaning that there was a plentiful supply throughout the conflict.[112] The national Emergency Medical Service was formed before the outbreak and many hospitals were built to treat the heavy casualties expected as a result of German bombing (including, as we have seen, the Churchill). A military neurosurgical base hospital was also planned to serve all of the armed services, largely on the initiative of Cairns, and Oxford seemed like the ideal place to host it.[113]

Oxford was considered a good location because it was unlikely to be heavily bombed and was near to London. Within the city's precincts, St Hugh's was thought a suitable site for a number of reasons. There was the spaciousness of its grounds, which would allow for the construction of extensive wards. There was then the fact that the college buildings were relatively new (erected during the First World War or after) and based on *corridors*, not pokey little staircases as was the norm in older colleges, and therefore suited to the movement of patients on beds and stretcher. The use of brick and plaster in the construction, as opposed to stone, was helpful too, rendering surfaces easier to clean and sterilize. Finally, St Hugh's was close to the Radcliffe Infirmary, the epicentre of Oxford's medical provision and research, and Oxford was surrounded by airbases to which battle casualties could be flown.[114]

In this way war came to St Hugh's, with an intensity unrivalled in any other part of the University. In February 1940, the heavily converted college opened for business as the Combined Services Hospital for Head Injuries, aka the 'Nutcracker Suite', a neurological facility of the 'first importance' and the only head-injury centre in Britain exclusively for service patients and run as a military hospital.[115] It was soon filled with neurosurgeons, neurologists, anaesthetists, theatre sisters, ward sisters and patients (see PLATE 31). Its primary work was treating servicemen who had been shot in the head or received a brain injury in another way, perhaps from shrapnel or bits of ordnance, armour plating, or metal displaced when a shell penetrated a tank or an aircraft or when a position was shelled.

The hospital's commanding officer, Lieutenant Colonel Greenway, would do rounds with the matron and a retinue each day, dressed in full uniform including peaked cap, swagger stick and yellow crocheted gloves. In spite of the frightful nature of the wounds being treated, a 'cheerful, bantering camaraderie persisted throughout the place'.[116] An officers' mess for military doctors was located at 80 Woodstock Road, 'run on boarding school lines by a fierce, but kindly-at-heart (if you could get there) old Major' who had been 'dug out of retirement' by Cairns and wangled a commission. Comprising mainly neurologists, it was, surgeon John Potter recalls, an essential escape 'from the procession of horribly wounded men that we would be facing again when we got back to the wards and the operating theatres'.[117]

Hospital administration occupied the upper floors of the college buildings, and the main operating theatre was constructed out of part of the garden and the corridor leading from the old building to the Gray Allen building. What became the SCR cloakroom was constructed for the theatre staff, and a NAAFI was built in the courtyard leading to the main entrance on St Margaret's Road.[118] Part of the college library was used for those who were delirious, known as the 'Noisy Boys' Ward'. It 'smelt continuously of paraldehyde, the best and safest tranquiliser available to us'.[119] Fifty beds soon rose to a normal establishment of 300 when a warren of big huts spread across the capacious gardens, opened on 1 March 1941. The number of new cases admitted during the calendar year 1941 was 2,153, the majority from the army, 507 from the RAF (186 of them flying personnel).[120] To cope with the scale of this patient throughput, convalescence hospitals were opened to take men on when they could be moved, relieving bedspace in St Hugh's (see below). St Hugh's achieved its peak bed capacity of 430 during the battles in Normandy, a period during which, Potter writes, casualties were pouring in and the staff barely had time to sleep. Over 13,000 military personnel were treated at St Hugh's during the course of the war.[121]

Another Cairns initiative, extending the reach of the St Hugh's hospital, was the creation of mobile neurosurgical units to perform operations on the battlefield, training staff and equipping them with 'diathermy and power suction and lighted brain retractors for use from Benghazi to the Rhine'.[122] Just as he had been swift to stress the advantage of air evacuation for battle casualties, Cairns recognized that to save the greatest number of patients, immediate expert care after a wound had been received was crucial.[123] Each mobile unit comprised a neurosurgeon, a neurologist, an anaesthetist, two general-duty RAMC officers, two QAINC sisters, four RAMC orderlies and two Royal Army Service Corps drivers.[124] Each unit carried enough equipment and supplies to conduct 200 operations without replenishment, and patients were handled through the various stages of their journey, from regimental aid post to casualty clearing stations, via field ambulance and base hospitals eventually to St Hugh's, by doctors and nurses who had trained at the college and were known to each other.[125]

The original mobile unit, along with its patients, was captured in 1940 during the fall of France. New units were then dispatched to North Africa as the fighting concentrated there. They were remarkable essays in improvisation: No. 4 Mobile Neurological Team, supporting the 8th Army in North Africa from a forward position close to the fighting and also maintaining a rear position, worked from a captured Italian bus converted into an operating theatre, a pre-operative ward with an eleven-stretcher capacity located in a large attached awning.[126] The results of rapid post-wound treatment were tremendous.

> Even those who were sent from the forward to the rear section were treated within 48–72 hours after being wounded. By these means the incidence of infection, brain abscess, meningitis and brain fungus was reduced from about 25% to 5%; over 90% of wounds healed by first intention and it was rare for any further operation to be needed unless it was of a reparative nature.[127]

A striking photograph from the St Hugh's archives brings home the benefit of these facilities. It shows a scene from No. 6 Mobile Neurological Team, commanded by Surgeon-Major Jack Small. An operation is being performed upon a patient with a horrific-looking skull wound on the beach following the Normandy landings, a line of trees visible through the open side of a tent.[128] Altogether, the nine mobile neurological teams deployed overseas treated over 20,000 battlefield casualties, and an estimated 80 per cent 'of the soldiers and airmen with head injuries in all theatres of war passed through their hands'.[129]

In conjunction with the work of the mobile units, Cairns and St Hugh's played a key role in taking penicillin to the battlefield. Back in early 1941 when Florey and his team were beginning tests and clinical trials involving humans, Cairns had experimented with the drug on meningitis cases. As we have seen, in 1942 a limited amount of penicillin was sent to Cairo, and from April 1943 it became available for the treatment of meningitis at St Hugh's. The results were striking.[130] College librarian Philippa Hesketh-Williams remembers a doctor wandering around her office as if in a daze. 'It's a miracle', he kept on saying, 'they are dying the night before and next morning their temperatures are down to normal.'[131] In May 1943 the War Office sent Cairns and Florey to North Africa and Sicily to study potential field usage and dosage in the treatment of penetrating brain injuries, and set up clinical trials, coordinated with the mobile units and the results sent back to Oxford. As part of these trials, No. 4 Mobile Neurosurgical Unit attached to the 48th General Hospital at Tripoli and No. 5 attached to 71st General Hospital at Sousse during the Sicilian campaign were used.[132] Fifty gunshot wounds and twenty-three head wounds due to blunt injury (often caused by road accidents) were treated. The trials during the Sicilian campaign 'proved so incredibly successful that a new phase in medicine had evidently arrived'.[133]

The St Hugh's hospital had satellite facilities where patients no longer requiring intensive care could rehabilitate, close enough so that they could return if acute care or further surgery were needed. One was the Military Auxiliary Hospital at Tusmore Park near Bicester, a facility 'for patients with severe brain damage'.[134] Patients were also sent to the hospital opened by the Red Cross, as part of its enormous national war effort, at Middleton Park near Middleton Stoney in Oxfordshire. This establishment, for officers and other ranks, was 'exclusively devoted to head cases and to treatment of injuries of the brain'.[135] The major St Hugh's satellite was Headington Hill Hall, historic home of the Morrell family, which had been requisitioned by the government in 1939 and earmarked as a satellite of the St Hugh's hospital (remaining in use as a rehabilitation hospital until 1958). As nurse Joan Staniforth explained, many patients had a very prolonged stay in the recuperation hospitals given the nature of their injuries, and were visited regularly by Cairns.[136] At the Headington facility, where she worked, patients had the use of workshops as part of their treatment and rehabilitation. Some could not move parts of their body, some needed speech therapy, and some had visual problems such as depth perception. A huge programme of care was built around their needs.

As well as being a working hospital, St Hugh's functioned as a major training establishment for 'a whole generation of neurosurgeons, neurologists and specialist nurses', its graduates including Dr Diana Beck, the first full-time female neurosurgeon.[137] It also functioned as a training centre in neurology and neuropsychiatry for junior medical officers with the objective of diffusing information of practical value throughout the armed forces.[138] However busy, staff were expected to attend evening sessions, when the brains of those who had died were examined by Dorothy Russell and Peter Daniel, to see what could be learnt. The hospital innovated in the use of in-theatre medical artists and kept extensive records (still used to this day – for example, in sports injuries research). Cairns ensured that key staff described their work in detail, and many papers appeared in the *British Journal of Surgery*, the *British Medical Journal* and the *Lancet*, contributing to professional and scholarly advances.

A major campaign on Cairns's part that warrants acknowledgement concerned motorcycle accidents. In the first year of the war three motorcyclists were killed each day, two of them army riders. In the first twenty-one months of war, 2,279 riders or pillion riders had been killed in road traffic accidents (two-thirds of them from the army), recklessness and the blackout among the chief causes. Seeing so many army dispatch riders killed or maimed and profoundly moved by the experience of treating Lawrence, Cairn's 'carried out a vigorous campaign publicizing the advantages of crash helmets in papers published in 1941, 1942, 1943, and 1946'.[139] As a result of his research and lobbying, the army made crash helmets compulsory in November 1921.

Cairns was also involved in the establishment of the National Spinal Injuries Centre at Stoke Mandeville, realizing that service personnel with spinal injuries required specialized care. It was established by Ludwig Guttman, who had fled the Nazis in 1939 and worked for the next five years under Cairns at St Hugh's and the Radcliffe Infirmary. With D-Day approaching, a specialist unit was supposed to have been set up at Oxford's Nuffield Orthopaedic Hospital, but its director refused to release bed space and it was opened instead at Stoke Mandeville, with Guttman in charge.[140]

Because of the St Hugh's hospital, Oxford was the 'leading neuro-surgical center in Great Britain just before, during, and for 5 or 6 years after World War II'.[141] The four key developments were 'expert neurosurgery in the battlefield; antibacterial therapy, notably penicillin; speed of evacuation, especially by air; and the specialism of the Combined Services Hospital for Head Injuries at St Hugh's'.[142] The statistics pay testament to the value of the work done at St Hugh's and by its mobile units overseas. Surprisingly, bullet wounds of the brain are rarely immediately fatal, death usually caused later by infection. Missile wounds of the brain had resulted in 50 per cent mortality in 1914–18; in 1939–45, the new techniques developed at St Hugh's had reduced the figure to 5 per cent.[143]

The inspiring medical work conducted in Oxford is as good a place as any to draw things to a conclusion. Having examined many aspects of the war's permeations in Oxford, it is time to reflect on whether the experience changed the institution, and to look ahead to the post-war world.

ELEVEN

THE POST-WAR WORLD

The Allied situation improved as the war dragged on, though no one knew when it would end. The British government believed that the Japanese war might continue for another year or two after Germany's defeat, and was preparing to swing the Empire's main weight eastwards once Hitler had been vanquished. But the sense of danger on the home front dissipated. Though German V1 and V2 missile attacks, a few of which affected Oxfordshire, began in June 1944, the prospect of invasion and further blitzes dwindled to naught. Compared to the despair of summer 1940, when he had considered killing himself and his family if the Germans entered Oxford, by the time Brasenose butler Albert Thomas was putting the finishing touches to his book in early 1944, things had changed dramatically. '[T]he Huns missed the 'bus when they had us beat', he wrote.

> [T]hey have not got a cat in hell's chance now. I have just watched sixty-three Fortresses, flying very high, pass over Oxford ... and my spirits are as high as they are. How grand it is to feel (despite our politicians) that we are a wonderful nation who simply refuse to know when we are beaten.[1]

The German surrender took effect on 8 May 1945, Victory in Europe (VE) Day. The bells of Oxfordshire's churches and colleges joined peals across the nation. St Mary's in Woodstock marked the occasion, and in Blenheim the 'double doors in the Duke's dining room were thrown open and [MI5] staff allowed on to the palace terrace to listen to the bells'. It was 'a very tremendous occasion ... a real thanksgiving.'[2] There were thanksgiving services in Manchester College chapel and over the road at New College. Magdalen and New College floodlit their towers and St John's and Lincoln their quads, as did St Edward's School on Woodstock Road. The New Theatre on George Street illuminated its blunt facade, and Madge Martin wrote of the 'glory of Merton College chapel, flood-lit against the deep blue sky'. 'How thankful we must be, for ever, that our lovely Oxford Buildings have been spared bombing raids.'[3]

Enormous crowds thronged the streets, shouting and cheering, singing and dancing. Reverend Martin recovered flags and bunting from the tunnel where they'd been stored since the Coronation. There were, wrote Madge,

> huge bonfires fed by ARP properties, magnesium bombs, great logs of wood, chairs, tables, ladders etc with dancing rings of young people circling them, beautiful flood-lit buildings, lighted windows, torch-light processions, and a good-humoured gaiety with no rowdy-ism. We all got parted in the singing throngs at Carfax but Robert and I went about together, happier than for years, remembering it all for ever, light after darkness! Our own house was beautifully bedecked with flags and every window a blaze of light – after 5 years and more. We all met at last for cups of tea before going to bed at 1.00am. Thank God for this day of days.[4]

Sergeant J.T. Quirk of the Royal Electrical and Mechanical Engineers, a patient at St Hugh's, heard the bells. 'Recovering from having a Tantulus metal plate [made at Cowley] inserted into my head'; there were quite a number of soldiers in the ward recovering from similar operations.

> The 'Head Cases' were quite distinctive because we all wore a white muslin cap ... [The] Duty nurse kindly turned her back, and about 6 of us went through an open window and down into Oxford. People recognized us for who and what we were and made quite a fuss of us.[5]

'The bells rang like water cascading out of the air', recalled a St Hugh's student:

> [T]here was dancing and drinking in the streets, there were bonfires on the High. It was both an historic occasion and a continuous party. The Principal of St Hugh's, Miss Gwyer, chose to take a high and mighty line

about undergraduates returning to the College and their beds by 11 pm. We all signed in decorously and then slipped out of College over the walls and carried on with the party.[6]

Mrs Warner was in Webber's department store on the High Street buying material for a wedding dress when she heard the bells, and people emerged onto the streets cheering and shouting.[7] One student was having a cup of tea when she heard the news.

> We all poured out of the café, doing the conga and picking people up as we went, until we had an immense line of people dancing from St Giles to Carfax. We formed a cordon across Magdalen Bridge and every vehicle entering Oxford was given a piece of lavatory paper which they had to give up at Carfax. The GIs thought they'd entered a mad house.[8]

The *St Hugh's College Chronicle* recounted the day's events:

> There is not one of us who will not remember as long as she lives the spirit of goodwill and joy which filled the College and united it still more firmly with the whole University on that day of sunshine and showers, breakfasts in boats on the peaceful Cher., greeting from undergraduate to undergraduate, known and unknown, thanksgiving made with all England at the three o'clock broadcast, and a more personal thanksgiving for the peace that had never been disturbed, as the hymn of praise rose in college chapels. Then a night of bonfires and singing, of dancing on Magdalen Bridge under the soaring, floodlit spire, and of weary, contented home-coming on the first starlit night of peace.[9]

Shop windows were illuminated for the first time since September 1939. Magdalen Tower 'was beautiful', wrote June Coppock, 'after walking past it every day in the darkness, when you could not even put a torch on'.[10] The 'only outward sign of rejoicing' at the Ashmolean on VE Day 'was that the statue of Apollo on the roof ... above the Front entrance was suddenly seen to be sheltering under an umbrella'.[11] An effigy of Hitler burned opposite the Martyrs' Memorial, and over sixty bonfires flamed across the city that night, in Glanville Road, where people danced the conga, and in Mansfield College, where 'worn-out articles of furniture from our temporary JCR were thrown, to the accompaniment of war-like shouts and dances by members of both Common Rooms'.[12] An enormous pyre at Carfax corner yielded thirteen hundredweight of scrap iron when council engineers cleared up the following day.[13]

'My mother, who'd been out celebrating, came home in the evening', recalled Christopher Prior.

> She dragged my brother (seven) and I (eight) out of bed saying, 'You must see this moment of history!' Bleary-eyed, we left our house in Bainton Road and were further dazed when we reached St Giles by the street lighting and the crowds. Nothing like this during the war! I don't remember much but have a vivid memory of a string of bonfires down the middle of St Aldates and a man wrapped in the Union flag running and leaping over every one of them. My other recollection was the acrid smell of burnt rubber in Cornmarket. The fires had scorched the rubber bricks that were laid to suppress the traffic noise in those days.[14]

Jenny Standen lived in Headington, her bedroom facing towards Southfield golf course and Cowley. She looked out of her window and thought there were a lot of stars out that night. Her mother 'nearly cried because it was the first time her daughter had seen streetlights, which had been turned off during the war'.[15] Martin Gilbert, who would one day become Churchill's official biographer, remembered the day well. Eight years old and residing just outside Oxford, he

> listened to the King's victory broadcast and then hurried up the hill to watch the burning in effigy of Hitler and Mussolini. On the following day my friends and I solemnly stuffed our model aeroplanes with cotton wool, lit the wool with matches, and threw the planes up into the air to their destruction.[16]

A.J.P. Taylor's son Giles had a holiday from the Dragon School to mark the day, so together they cycled out to Blenheim for a picnic with John Betjeman. The poet, whose British Council outfit had migrated there, gave them a tour over 'Housemaid Heights' and the palace's roof, incensing the duke.[17] In the evening, Taylor joined other Magdalen fellows for champagne in hall before dancing round a bonfire in the meadow.[18] As well as the chapel service and illuminated Bell Tower, New College drank the king's health at dinner that night, though couldn't find enough fuel for a bonfire in Garden Quad.[19] The future judge James Pickles lost his virginity in Christ Church after drunken celebrations around the fire at Carfax.[20] Nina Bawden remembered the night because

264 OXFORD'S WAR

of 'the tumbling bells, the joyful streets full of people, but chiefly because I met an undergraduate at Carfax and fell in love'. Climbing back into Somerville after the gates had closed, she was caught by Principal Darbishire, who overlooked her misdemeanour and advised her to get down off the wall before she caught a chill and go and have a hot bath.[21]

Members of Queen's College joined with Ministry of Home Security staff for a short service in chapel. In the evening, the last barrel of Chancellor ale, kept since 1939 for the occasion, was broached, wrote the provost; 'wine was served, and we drank the ancient College toasts'.[22] When darkness fell, the college was illuminated by a bonfire on the High Street, men of Merton and University Colleges its most active stokers, demanding Queen's bring out its wood. Speeches were delivered on the college steps, and raiders carried off the college flag, found later flying from the flagstaff of the dean of Christ Church.[23]

Tolkien wrote that when peace finally came, 'I actually went out to an Inklings on Thursday night and rode in almost peacetime light all the way to Magdalen for the first time in five years'. The Inklings planned to celebrate victory by taking over a whole pub in the countryside for at least a week, to be spent 'entirely in beer and talk, without reference to any clock!'[24] But Charles Williams collapsed and died a week after VE Day, and the Inklings were never the same again.

Further ceremony and celebration greeted news of the final defeat of Japan in August, the atom bombs bringing an unexpectedly swift end. St Giles was ablaze with light, wrote Madge Martin, the war memorial floodlit. Bishop Kirk, preaching at a Thanksgiving Service in Christ Church Cathedral, grappled with the moral issues surrounding the use of the revolutionary new weapon that Oxford scientists had helped create.[25]

Tallying up and derequisitioning

The war over, it was time to try to get back to normal. One of the first things colleges needed to do was get in bids as the hardship pool's remaining funds were dished out. A.H. Murray, rector of Lincoln, said that the college's claim would include recompense for loss of conference income.[26] Trinity was in the hunt too, 'continually occupied by students' throughout the war, including during the vacations, 'with necessity to maintain a staff in the Domestic Bursar's Office costing £540 pa'.[27] From Keble, H.J. Carpenter wrote that 'our buildings were totally occupied for 5 years by a Government Department, and during that period our undergraduates were dispersed to 2 other colleges and for part of the period in 4'. Despite 'a large intake of freshmen this term and return into residence of war service men our dispersal during war means we are left this term with a third of our rooms unoccupied'.[28] Queen's was also preparing a claim, as was Somerville, its treasurer, M.B. Stonedale, writing that the college buildings had not been derequisitioned in time for students to come into residence for Michaelmas.[29]

There was also the matter of damage to college estates, furniture and fixtures. Stallybrass of Brasenose said that he would claim from the hardship pool if the government didn't satisfy the 'legitimate claims' of the college 'for the damage done by the Military'.[30] St Peter's had had its playing fields requisitioned by the army, said master R.W. Howard as he applied for funds. 'They were used as a tank depot and have been completely ruined'.[31] St Edmund Hall's vice principal, John Kennedy, said that if the college claimed, it would be for damage due to having had so many cadets in residence for four years ('They certainly messed the place up pretty badly').[32]

No college had a better claim than St Hugh's. 'Throughout 6 years of War', wrote the principal to the secretary of the University Chest,

> St Hugh's has been living under very difficult and cramped conditions in seven buildings. Expenses incurred in the management of these scattered buildings were heavy in spite of the congestion and lack of amenities. College will claim compensation from the Hardship Pool for rent and rates on houses which had to be acquired to accommodate undergraduates.[33]

There had been significant loss of conference income and heavy expenditure incurred in the hastily arranged move back to college, a process which had required the purchase, regardless of cost, of a substantial amount of furniture in order to provide minimum requirements for incoming students. The college had had to move back into buildings just left by the War Office, no 'reinstatement work' having been undertaken.[34]

Less well-heeled colleges that had been requisitioned thought that the hardship pool worked against them. As Pembroke's bursar told his opposite number at St John's, the reception colleges did better out of the rates than the requisitioned colleges, getting unwarranted 'bonuses'.[35] In signalling his college's intent to apply for hardship money, Pembroke's master wrote that

> the working of the Pool appears to us to have been a much better bargain for the Reception Colleges than for those commandeered. We as a college largely requisitioned appear to have paid into the Pool about £1230 more than we have received from it; and this, in proportion to our total contribution and receipts, seems to be (with three or four notable exceptions) amongst the most unfavourable results to an individual College.[36]

A handicap for requisitioned colleges, it was argued, was making the refund of rates in respect of commandeered property a matter for the pool. It was clear that reception colleges had incurred no greater expenditure on rates than in a normal period, but benefited from the rebate. Requisitioned colleges, on the other hand, had been paying rates on premises they continued to use as well as those taken over by the government.

Others disagreed. The bursars of Magdalen and New College teamed up to write a memorandum for the Bursars' Committee. It seemed, they said, that 'hardship' was always interpreted as a college having lost more money through being put in one category – reception or requisitioned – as opposed to the other, whereas the University (they thought) meant it to be general hardship, not necessarily 'losses', and that this could be experienced by a reception college as well as one that had been requisitioned.

> We are not at all sure that behind this objection to the use of the word 'losses' there does not lie a fallacious conviction that it is only possible for the requisitioned Colleges, and not for the reception Colleges, to suffer 'hardship', and that if, for instance, it appeared later that there was a great shortage of undergraduates owing to the war and the reception Colleges suffered a disaster, this disaster should not be attributed to the category in which they were put, but would be deemed a general result of the war and not a matter for compensation from the Hardship Pool.[37]

Dissenting from this view, the two bursars argued that it was impossible to say that requisitioned colleges suffered greater hardship than reception colleges.

In *not* applying for hardship-pool funds, some gently bemoaned the system's inequalities and just wanted to move on. President Norwood of St John's told University authorities that his college would not claim but was conscious that it had paid in far more than it would get out, representing 'very rough justice'.[38] Merton's domestic bursar, E.W.B. Gill, posted a 'no claim' return and said that he hoped the pool would be shut down before the end of the year. 'I have had six years dealing with people who take six months to do what any intelligent man could do in a week, and I hoped to find Oxford free of such dithering.'[39]

Slowly, the civil servants, staff officers and cadets departed Oxford, leaving damage in their wake as well as welcome cast-offs, such as refrigerators in the huts on Balliol's sports ground. When Registrar Veale alerted the Domestic Bursars' Committee to an opportunity to claim American army surplus, many colleges responded, Pembroke putting in a request for carpets, hearth rugs, bedsteads, mattresses, blankets, sheets and pillow slips.[40] Derequisitioning took time, as bureaucratic wheels turned slowly and military and civilian organizations in colleges waited for other accommodation to become available before they moved out. Pembroke's master said that it would take until at least the middle of 1946 to get the college fit and available for occupation by undergraduates. The Oxfordshire War Agricultural Committee remained in residence until April that year, the Ministry of Works finally relinquishing its rooms in September.

Lincoln, requisitioned on 8 September 1939, struggled to get its War Office guests out – the registrar going so far as to draft a letter of complaint to *The Times* for the rector to send, if he so wished.[41] The burden of its content was that slow handovers were a breach of public faith. This was especially so when there seemed to be no possible good reason for foot-dragging. In Lincoln's case, the presence of a mere eleven nurses was holding up all plans to get the place ready for the 1945–46 academic year. When the college finally regained possession of its buildings, it had a rush to get ready and make good wartime dilapidations and damages. The Ministry of Works was asked to pay for 197 yards of ticking to be purchased from Webber's on the High Street for the re-covering of mattresses and pillows which had been in constant use by the army and military nurses for nearly six years.[42] Furniture was in a terrible state and lots of new items would be needed, including nine chests of drawers, fifty easy chairs, twenty-six cupboards, twenty-six desks, seventeen tables and twenty-four book cases.[43]

Merton was still part-occupied well into Michaelmas 1945. 'The College is seriously perturbed to hear on good authority that the Civilian Repair Organization is to retain approximately 20 sets of rooms and one or two lecture rooms until March 29 1946', wrote warden John Miles. 'Is there still nothing that you could do to rid the College of Government Departments?', he implored Veale.[44] Anticipating full repossession, the college took stock of repairs and alterations that would be necessary to turn it back into a college. W. Holland-Hibbert wrote to the Ministry of Works to say that when its workmen had constructed ARP shelters in the St Albans Quad basement, they had removed 'certain circulating pipes for the hot water system to the baths' and made 'extensive alterations' to the bathrooms.[45] He was now asking if he could get it all repaired, at government expense, in order to make the place habitable for students.

Manchester retook possession of its premises in April 1946, though the huts in its grounds were still needed by the military.[46] As late as March 1947, said the principal, there was still lots to be done, including planing and polishing of the library and hall floors, the cleaning of stonework, and the breaking up of the concrete foundations of the now-removed huts, to be followed by the restoration of the lawns.[47] A detailed 'schedule of dilapidations' was produced in June 1947 as the college sought compensation for damage and wear and tear, prepared in great detail, as for other colleges, by the University of Cambridge's Department of Estate Management. The Carpenter Library needed reglazing, there were noticeboards to be removed, holes in walls to be plugged, floor damage to be made good, and new lino to be laid. The mosaic floor in the library lobby needed specialist attention, and the SCR required the renewal of the brass sash lifts for the windows and repairs to the cord cleats. Yale locks fitted to doors throughout the college needed to be removed, and someone had to pay for a new WC pan for the ladies' lavatory.

THE POST-WAR WORLD   269

John Marsh, bursar of Mansfield, sought to pull strings in order to secure the earliest possible return of the college buildings. In June 1946 he wrote to Harold Wilson, who had not only won a seat in Parliament in the previous year's Labour landslide but been appointed parliamentary secretary to the Ministry of Works. In replying, Wilson said that the staff now occupying Mansfield were due to replace some War Office staff in buildings at Eastcote. In that month this Bletchley outstation in Middlesex became the main home of GCHQ, the new name for the Government Codes and Cipher School. Wilson said that the move should take place by the end of the month, though '[c]onsiderable adaptations at Eastcote will be necessary before the Foreign Office can move in'.[48] The college would just have to be patient.

It wasn't until 1947 that the principal was able to report:

> This summer we shall say good-bye without over-mastering regret to the Government department which has been occupying our buildings since 1939. We look forward with great eagerness to returning home. We have indeed already established 'a bridgehead' in our own premises by receiving back the use of the kitchen, which has made a small lecture room for most of this year.[49]

Yet, at the time of writing, the college was 'still cumbered about by sheds and concrete erected by the Government'.[50] It was not until August 1947 that the last government workers left, and the library books were returned from New College.[51] A new chapter in the college's history now began, for the decision had been taken to become a residential college and, to begin with, accommodation for ten students was created in what today is the JCR.

Things took even longer at St Hugh's, though a Herculean effort as Michaelmas 1945 began meant that scattered students and staff were able to move back into their college. They

> had uncertainty hanging over us all through the Long Vacation, and then at a few weeks' notice (with promises of help in the struggle which did not all 'come off') were obliged to remove ourselves, our furniture and our books, into a College which needed cleansing in every corner, filled with broken furniture and worn-out equipment, and the essential services in dangerous disarray. Ready in a month? The first feeling of all who looked on the spectacle was of utter incredulity, but, by a feat of

organization for which the Bursar deserves the greatest credit, it proved just possible to receive students 'not earlier than 2 pm' on October 13th (the first day of term).[52]

When that day came, sentries still manned the college gates on St Margaret's Road as dozens of undergraduates waited to be let in. Over a hundred volunteers, including German POWs, had helped get the place ready, cleaning and clearing broken furniture. Some jobs would take longer to complete, such as repairs at the point at which the original 1916 buildings joined the Mary Gray Allen wing, where 'the apparatus for the operating theatre had been ripped from the walls'.[53] Marion Graham wrote that the college still 'smelled of hospitals, having been vacated by the army about 10 days before term'.[54] 'That first dinner', recalled Merrill Brady, 'the whole establishment was pervaded by the clinical breath of antiseptic, and, indeed, there was still a large hand basin in Hall itself.'[55]

A year and a half after returning to the college buildings, the principal wrote that 'for those of us who watched with some anxiety the disintegrating effects of six years of scattered existence, the rapidity and completeness with which we have regained our sense of corporate entity has been a matter for rejoicing.'[56] This was essential for re-establishing college cohesion, which had suffered because of the dispersal of the student body over so many years. A complete redecoration was well under way by summer 1947; the walls were finished but the floors and furniture still showed 'unmistakable signs of their six years of exceptional wear and tear'. Some of the stores and huts in front of the main building had been removed, but it was not possible to demolish the six wards and their ancillary corridors. They were not 'huts', the principal was at pains to emphasize, despite the word being commonly used to describe them. Rather, they were 'well-constructed buildings of brick and concrete', which had now been let to the University on a three-year tenancy and converted into offices. The Institute of Statistics had moved in, as had the Bureau of Animal Population and the Edward Grey Institute of Field Ornithology.[57] A year later, all of the 'huts' spreadeagled across St Hugh's' gardens had been occupied following the arrival of Maison Française, installed in The Shrubbery, and the Department of Zoological Field Studies. A new bicycle shed was under

THE POST-WAR WORLD 271

construction (the pre-war one having been demolished by the military), and when this was completed the college could 'dispense with the unsightly corrugated iron erection', built for the hospital staff.[58] During the academic year 1951–52, St Hugh's – 'at last' – obtained a licence to do away with all the wartime buildings. 'The great event of the year', wrote the principal in summer 1952, 'has been the demolition of the huts in the garden'.[59] For the first time, in *thirteen years*, the college community was in full possession of its grounds and buildings.

Loss of life

The most profound impact of war on university life across Britain was the unnatural death of students past and present. Second to that, perhaps, was the 'serious educational loss' experienced by young people, their time in education 'shortened, circumscribed or impoverished as an immediate consequence of the war'.[60] Larkin's 'Poem About Oxford' (1970) characterized the 'blacked-out and butterless days' of wartime university life, and acknowledged the fact that, for him, Oxford for the rest of his life would be associated with 'the depths of the Second World War'.[61]

Many never returned to convert war degrees into the finished honours article. The Union flag that had draped the coffins of prisoners of war at Batu Lintang POW camp in Sarawak before they were laid to rest was placed in All Saints Church on the High Street, together with two wooden memorial plaques. Throughout the city and the county, new rolls of honour were inscribed, and memorial plaques, tablets and sculptures erected, or added to those bearing the names of the previous war's dead. Colleges went to considerable efforts raising money and commissioning their memorials. At Jesus, the original intention was to replace the First World War memorial brass plaque in the chapel with an updated one. But the JCR objected to this location – many students being chapel- not churchgoers – and so it was agreed to set up a new memorial in the JCR (today's Harold Wilson Room).[62] Exeter launched an appeal supported by a pamphlet, commissioned sculptor H. Tyson Smith, and held an unveiling ceremony.[63] Pembroke's war memorial, featuring three mourning women, was commissioned in 1947, and the governing body ordered two new hall windows bearing the service insignia of the fallen, installed in 1955. Some colleges published books offering biographies of the dead, including Queen's *Liber Vitae Reginensium Qui Pro Patria Morten Obierunt, MCMXXXIX–MCMXLV* (1951) and Magdalen's *The Undone Years: Magdalen College Roll of Honour, 1939–1947* (2004). In terms of Oxford graduate deaths overall, Paul Addison acknowledges that the *Oxford Magazine*'s figure of 1,719 killed was 'clearly an underestimate', one college alone having 100 names to add to the roll at the time of the article's publication in 1947.[64]

The 1947 *Pembroke College Record* – the first for eight years – featured the college's roll of honour, bearing the names of 51 men killed in the war. This was a large number, considering that in 1938–39 there had only been 140 students in residence.[65] Corpus Christi's roll of honour records 415 students and alumni as having served in the armed forces, 51 losing their life. Christ Church dead numbered 215 and Brasenose lost 124, including a German Rhodes Scholar killed on the Eastern Front.[66] Jesus lost 38 and Exeter 81, while 43 names were inscribed on Merton's memorial plaque beneath the Fitzjames Arch.[67] The war memorial on Oriel's gateway leading onto the High Street bears 72 names.[68] The Queen's tablet names 80 former students and one member of staff. The stone on the cloister wall in New College lists 159, and Trinity's roll of honour was 133. Hertford records 71 Second World War dead in the chapel portico. Worcester's memorial records 92 students and two members of staff, Balliol's 122. Keble's chapel tablet bears 52 names, the University College war memorial 89. College archivist Robin Darwall-Smith writes that of the Univ men who matriculated in 1937 and 1938, the names of 'no less than one-eighth' are listed.[69]

Brasenose's losses were higher than in the First World War, writes the college historian, largely because the college ethos – 'athletic, loyal, light-hearted, physically courageous – matched only too well the ethos of the Royal Air Force'. It wasn't just Brasenose; Trinity's losses were four-fifths of those sustained in the First World War, and over a third of the dead had been in the RAF, flying having 'seemed to have particular appeal to sportsmen'.[70] Six of Trinity's 1938 First VIII were killed on active service, four of them with the RAF. Brockliss writes that the death rate 'reflected the fact that so many Oxford graduates served with the RAF with the chance of survival much less than in the other two services'.[71]

Returning warriors and other undergraduates

College life in the immediate post-war years was shaped by the return of those who had interrupted their studies either to join the forces or to undertake civilian war work. Dons' positions had been kept open for them. While some had died on active service, 'more typical of the times were the many dons who enjoyed a "good war" and returned in 1945 as more substantial figures, the coming men of postwar Britain.'[72] The demographic effect was more noticeable in the JCR. The Pembroke of the immediate post-war years was still a small college of around 150 men, nearly all ex-service. Many had come from responsible administrative posts in different parts of the world, wrote Eversley Belfield. They 'were serious and anxious to get on with life and careers interrupted'. Student life continued in an atmosphere shaped by lingering austerity; rationing persisted (St Hugh's was receiving food parcels from America and Australia), as did coal shortages. A University College student 'recalled that lunches in 1945 consisted of not much more than soup and one boiled potato', another that 'you could blow off the meat helping from the plate'.[73] Rook pie found its way onto the menu in the Union dining room.[74] Freezing cold winters were a feature, students huddling in the library because it was heated. 'To keep warm all the strange thick garments acquired during the war were dug out and the place looked like a beaten army on the move'.[75] Demob suits and remnants of military kit became part of Oxford's wardrobe, along with the sportswear, dinner jackets, tweeds and flannels. Many ex-servicemen relied for everyday purposes upon what 'they had managed to loot from His Majesty's Government, from string vests ... to tattered anoraks in faded camouflage and the ubiquitous duffle-coat or, for the grander ex-officers, a "British Warm" greatcoat in all its glory'.[76]

Returning to Oxford was a welcome aspect of homecoming and the resumption of lives shaken by war. The main protagonist in *Private's Progress* returns to his college after three years in the army:

> In the garden quadrangle of Apocalypse undergraduates were coming
> back from the Buttery with their little white jugs of ration milk. Some of
> them had military moustaches now, and wore their former service dress
> trousers without turnups, dyed green or brown.[77]

On Broad Street he is stopped by his former tutor, who corrects him on a small error in an essay submitted before he enlisted, carrying on as if he'd never been away. This return to the familiar was just what many would have wanted. Peter Anstey had left Oriel in 1942 for the Royal Navy, returning for the start of Michaelmas 1945.

> One day I was a junior administrative officer at a naval air station in
> southern Ceylon. Barely 72 hours later, having unbelievably been ac-
> corded the privilege of an air passage home, I was once more an under-
> graduate, dining in Hall on the first day of term.[78]

Even the gloomy Bowra perked up with the return to normal. As he wrote to Edith Sitwell, 'We are settling down again, with grave, war-scarred undergraduates, who are very modest and charming and terribly eager to learn. It is rather wonderful to be at it all again.'[79]

The war contributed to a dilution of the idea that colleges were *in loco parentis*, and to college attempts to regulate personal lives. Compulsory chapel disappeared over the next decade and a half. Though students were still expected to return to college by midnight and restrictions on visitors remained, age-old regulations were increasingly contested. Ex-servicemen found restrictions on going to the pub and the need to wear gowns out after dinner irksome, and these requirements were 'tacitly relaxed'.[80] Student drinking, which had followed a pattern of exclusion before 1939, changed. 'Before the Second World War proctors banned students from local pubs, but after the war some became recreational outlets attached to particular colleges (Trinity and the White Horse, Wadham and the King's Arms).'[81]

The student body of the immediate post-war years presented a striking juxtaposition, 'hardened ex-servicemen' rubbing shoulders in the same year groups with 'callow schoolboys'. John Harper-Nelson resumed his studies at Trinity in 1947. Life, he thought, was grimmer than in wartime, rationing stricter and winter worse. 'But we worked and played with all the vigour of ones reprieved. We had survived.'[82]

Returning ex-servicemen were 'enjoying their first flush of civilian freedom', and they were joined by 'those we called the school-boy undergraduates'.[83] Michael Bradley was one of them, 18 years old when he arrived at University College in 1946. 'The great majority of my contemporaries', he recalled, 'were WWII veterans, mature, self-confident, and in some cases battle-hardened.'[84] 'Ex-majors with MCs, wives and moustaches had little in common with 17-year-old boys who carried green ration-books entitling them to extra bananas.'[85] Harris writes that post-war Oxford was full of undergraduates of a different cast to any seen before. Mature men, and a sprinkling of women, 'who had fought battles, managed government departments, traded in espionage and lived through bombing, but who (in marked contrast with undergraduate veterans of the First World War) seemed remarkably unscathed by their experiences'.[86]

For those students who had *not* been away, the returning servicemen and women were a strange new element in their lives, and not an entirely welcome one. Nina Bawden felt returning servicemen intruded on 'her' Oxford. They were sophisticated, 'older than years, stern, purposeful men … taking over our university and reducing us, by their middle-aged presence, to the status of schoolchildren'.

> Our cafes, our streets, our societies – the whole of our playground was invaded by demobbed soldiers and sailors and airmen; colleges where we had previously known almost everyone were full of strangers; the Radcliffe Camera, so comfortably adequate for its reduced, wartime population was busy as a mainline station at rush hour.[87]

The dust settled. The New Bodleian was finally put to its intended use, formally opened in October 1946 when King George VI turned a silver key (which broke) in its main door on the corner of Broad Street and Parks Road.[88] The king spoke of his pleasure at learning of the building's wartime use as a 'temporary refuge and safe shelter'.[89] Awards and honours were distributed in recognition of war work. Bodley's Librarian was knighted in 1945, and such was OUP's contribution that Registrar Veale asked the prime minister for an award for printer John Johnson. Sir Alexander Cadogan, permanent undersecretary of state at the Foreign Office, endorsed the recommendation, and the director of Naval Intelligence 'strongly supported' the idea.[90] A CBE was duly awarded, also in 1945. In the same year Frank Dubber was made an honorary MA in recognition of his role in making the New Bodleian a stronghold for national treasures. Stanley Dorrill, owner of the New Theatre, earned an MBE for his role in entertaining the forces; Arthur Cooke picked up an OBE for his work on radar; and Florey, appointed Knight Bachelor in 1944, was awarded the Nobel Prize in 1945, jointly with Chain and Alexander Fleming, 'for the discovery of penicillin and its curative effect in various infectious diseases'.[91] Colonel Sam Bassett added the OBE to the other awards that the work of ISTD had earned him, and Hugh Cairns was knighted in 1946.

Changes in town?

War changed British higher education because it was a forcing house of deeper social, political and economic shifts. Even in the war's most dire period, the government made clear that it wanted things to return to normal in the university sector as soon as possible, announcing that this would happen from the start of the 1944–45 academic year – regardless of the length of the war, and with a pay increase for academics thrown in.[92] As the war progressed, pressure to release arts students from military service mounted.[93] In 1943 the vice chancellors and the UGC discussed the resumption of normal university activity, including the release of premises occupied by government departments and the military, which had particularly affected Oxford, Cambridge and London. The motion agreed at the meeting was amended by Tizard to say that 'in the interests of the nation, it is urgently necessary that the universities should be able to return to more normal activities in October 1944, irrespective of the duration of the war.'[94] In 1945 the minister of labour – now R.A. Butler – told Cabinet colleagues that there had been a loss of about 30,000 men who would have had arts degrees had it not been for the war, 'and this was very serious for the higher posts in the public services and in industry'.[95]

Few areas of academic inquiry were unaffected by the war and the social changes gathering momentum. As well as highlighting the importance of university research for military, industrial and economic affairs, the war stimulated educational reform and rising demand for university places.[96] The relationship between universities and society was undergoing drastic change. 'To some extent this was designed as a consequence both of the reconstruction of the education service and of the trend towards a more "planned" society with the apparent need for a larger university system.'[97] Anderson writes that the war 'created a new mood of social expectation, and post-war policies led into a continually rising curve of growth', as higher education left the stagnation of the 1930s behind.[98]

There's no doubt that the war had had an enormous impact on Oxford – the loss of a huge percentage of its normal student body as well as its teaching staff, incoming droves of service cadets, and the requisitioning of buildings guaranteed this. Normal university life had been suspended, college life 'profoundly dislocated by almost six years of war'. Many colleges witnessed an 'almost total suspension of an independent communal life of the kind which had been maintained throughout the centuries'.[99] But these were factors that could be redressed or that, like the division of the post-war student body into those who had served and those who had not, would level out over time. The question is, were there deeper changes?

In many ways the University returned to normality with surprising speed, despite the inconveniences of derequisitioning and reminders of war such as rationing. Unsightly water tanks and air raid shelters were removed from quads and gardens, and groups of college students who had been billeted elsewhere returned to their own staircases and common rooms.[100] The military informed the proctors that they could resume the use of green lights for undergraduates' cars shortly after VE Day, and the Christ Church and New College beagles returned to action following wartime confinement in Garsington.[101]

To what extent were changes that were already under way acceler-ated – rather than caused – by the conflict? Addison writes that, viewed 'from a distance, the outstanding characteristic of Oxford's wartime was adaptability', including a new model of college and University administration, a new structure of degrees and a new, improvised way of life.[102] 'The Oxford of the later war years was no longer a provincial town but a cosmopolitan crossroads.'[103] Utilitarian wartime Oxford 'was

278 OXFORD'S WAR

no place for the swells of peacetime. In the new Cromwellian Oxford a more egalitarian time prevailed.'[104]

But did the war simply dent the closeted, class-divided Oxford portrayed in works such as Masterman's *An Oxford Tragedy* (1933), Dorothy L. Sayers's *Gaudy Night* (1935), Mavis Doriel Hay's *Death on the Cherwell* (1935) and Crispin's *The Case of the Gilded Fly* (1944)?[105] How much of Waugh's over-the-top Oxford, of puking through ground-floor windows and lunching with the Georgoisie in shantung ties and pastel shirts, survived beyond 1945? Rather a lot, it would seem. Certainly, this would be a forgivable conclusion if taking soundings from literature of the post-war period, observing, for example, the insularity portrayed in Masterman's *To Teach the Senators Wisdom, or, An Oxford Guide-Book* (1952), Davre Balsdon's *Oxford Life* (1957), and further Oxford-based 'whodunnit' fiction such as Crispin's *The Moving Toyshop* (1946).[106] Having described the austerity of wartime Oxford, Larkin wrote of his 'shock' during a visit after the war when he saw 'an undergraduate in a sky-blue cloak and with hair down to his shoulders, and of realizing that all that was starting again'.[107] Paul Johnson remembers watching Kenneth Tynan arrive at the Magdalen lodge at the start of his second year in 1946, 'awestruck' by

> this tall, beautiful, epicene youth, with pale yellow locks, Beardsley cheekbones, fashionable stammer, plum-coloured suit, lavender tie, and ruby signet-ring ... 'Have a care for that box, my man [Tynan told a servant] – it is freight with golden shirts![108]

Sisman remarks that the worst wartime hardship for Magdalen fellows was 'the reduction from four to three courses'.[109] Speaking to the idea of small as opposed to seismic change brought about by war, Mabbott recounts an anecdote from St John's SCR. Here, the basic drink was vintage port, 'in which we toasted "Church and King" every evening'. Bought from Croft and Dow in vintage years, it was then laid down in the college cellar for at least fifteen years, much longer if possible.

> Our great twentieth century hope was the 1912. During the war years (1939–45) we could not import supplies, and the few Fellows in residence steadily continued to drink 'Church and King' every night. When the Steward of our Common Room came back from his post in

the Ministry of Shipping in 1945, the first thing he did was to go down to the cellar and count the bottles of port. He came up greatly shaken and summoned an emergency meeting of his Fellows. He said 'Gentlemen, I regret to inform you that there is only seven years' drinking left in the cellar.'[110]

Yet beyond indications of continuity conveyed by such vignettes, and the undoubted survival of much that was familiar, significant changes were afoot at the national level. As the blackout curtains came down and the uniforms disappeared from streets and staircases, some things affecting the University's fibre had certainly changed, chief among them the ramifications of the 1944 Butler Education Act. It created, through the 11+ exam, the grammar school and state studentships, a new clientele for universities, drawn from across society, indicating a shift towards the state-funded expansion of higher education. The Act abolished fees in secondary schools and introduced secondary education for all, thus expanding the pool of school-leavers seeking to go to university. While some resented it, others welcomed it unreservedly. One such was Bowra, who had long advocated an aristocracy of intellect. 'By securing that the state financed all who were able to profit by a university education', he wrote, 'the Act entirely altered the character of Oxford, and demolished the all too justifiable charges that it admitted only the rich.'[111] Looking back later in life, he viewed the war as a turning point in the University's fortunes. In his opinion the 1944 Act not only rescued the University from growing financial difficulty but raised academic standards by multiplying the number competing for places. Thus while the end of the war brought a period of restoration, in which the revival of the collegiate system took pride of place, it was a restoration that ultimately was to be subsidized by the Treasury and adapted to the requirements of national education policy.[112]

The wartime and post-war admission of military and ex-service students presaged greater changes. The admission of military cadets and probationers during the war had brought to Oxford a higher proportion of boys from assisted schools than ever before, though recruitment from the independent schools revived when the war ended.[113] Oxford sociologist A.H. Halsey writes that the old class-based conceptions of education so strongly associated with Oxbridge were challenged after 1945, and the need to compete for and cultivate all talent became pronounced. During and immediately after the war the intake of army and air force cadets – together with ex-servicemen on Further Education and Training Scheme grants – helped sustain interwar trends of increasing numbers of working-class sons and daughters.[114]

The Further Education and Training Scheme, launched in early 1943, had stimulated demand for university entrance. It offered grants covering the full costs of a university education, including allowances for dependents, to everyone on war service whose post-school education had been interrupted or deferred, meaning that the financial barriers to Oxford entry were abruptly removed. For men and women in the services who had never qualified for university, but who now wished to do so, a common services entrance exam, conducted by the civil service commissioners, was instituted.[115]

> The post-1945 growth in numbers stemmed almost entirely from ex-servicemen taking advantage of the government's Further Education and Training Scheme grants. Oxford made it easier for them to get in by relaxing admission requirements and making shortened honours schools available.[116]

The most immediate challenge for college and University authorities in post-war Oxford, therefore, came from rising student numbers. There was a flood of ex-servicemen returning to complete their degrees, coinciding with new provisions for the public funding of students. The government decided to finance a rapid, two-year programme of university expansion, part of a deal whereby universities agreed to reserve 90 per cent of their places for ex-service candidates in 1946 and 1947.[117] It being in the interest of colleges to maximize student numbers, there was a spectacular rise in the volume of undergraduates admitted. Between the wars, Oxford's undergraduate population had risen very slowly, from 4,163 in 1923–4 to 5,023 in 1938–9. In 1949–50 there were 7,323 students, an increase of nearly 50 per cent.[118] Figures from the college level bring home the scale of change. In the years immediately preceding the war and those during it, St Edmund Hall had 80–100 students in residence, graduates never numbering more than nine and usually only one or two. In 1946 it had 182 students in residence (thirty-three of them graduates), the following year 243 (forty graduates).[119]

New or repurposed buildings were urgently required to cope, the limited availability of space in Oxford one of the reasons why it lagged behind the rate of growth at other universities (between 1945 and 1950, redbrick universities and colleges increased their numbers by 130 per cent). Colleges did what they could. St Edmund Hall had recently obtained the leases of 46–48 High Street and during the war purchased the lease of the masonic buildings forming the east part of the little inner quadrangle behind the shop fronts.[120] Together, they formed the nucleus of what would be opened in the early 1950s as the Besse Building, modestly extending the Hall's capacity to accommodate students 'on site'. Balliol and New College pressured Manchester to keep the huts in its quads for use as student accommodation; New College turned the Founder's Library into a dormitory when its wartime occupants departed.[121] Wadham's returning warriors 'rarely complained of being crammed into double or even treble sets, however uncomfortable, especially as lodgings [outside of college] were an available alternative now that the wartime migrants from bigger cities began to go back home'.[122] A sensible pooling of information about accommodation across the University was maintained, courtesy of the work of the registrar, Council and inter-collegiate committees. In Michaelmas 1945, for instance, Council recorded that as a result of the 'release' of St Hugh's from requisition, ninety-seven sets of rooms would become available at Holywell Manor and Savile House.[123]

In Michaelmas 1945 New College warden Alic Smith reported that his college was negotiating for the acquisition of the Clarendon Hotel when it was vacated by the American army, to be used as an undergraduate hostel (though he feared that the negotiations were likely to break down).[124] As late as 1947, the college was accommodating students in large prefabricated huts in Holywell Quad.[125] St John's was more successful in the hotel game, and had some hefty advantages. As Mabbott wrote,

> [w]e immediately put in for planning permission for a new building. It was given, but we were warned that materials were scarce and we would come well down the queue created by bomb damage. Our Bursar had

anticipated this and had stacked in our Bagley Wood enough timber cut before 1940 and therefore now well seasoned. He had also bought from Rutland quarries enough of their lovely blue streak Clipsham stone for a new building leaving it stored there until required. So we could build at once.[126]

The result was the Dolphin Building, designed by Edward Maufe and named after the inn that had stood there three centuries before. But it would not be ready for occupation until 1947, so other measures were needed to cope with a 30 per cent rise in student numbers. St John's happened to be the ground landlord of the Oxenford Hotel on Magdalen Street, diagonally opposite its porters' lodge. At the end of the war the 'old ladies' who ran it decided to close it, so the college took back the lease and bought the entire contents, furniture, linen, pictures, curtains and all, so that forty returning undergraduates could walk straight in. 'It was a popular residence, and its occupants appreciated the watch kept over their slumbers by such guardians as *The Monarch of the Glen*, *Dignity and Impudence* and *The Soul's Awakening*.'[127]

So desperate was the accommodation situation that the possibility of converting the Exam Schools into a hostel for 110 students was investigated. This caused quite a stir, the Schools' curators, led by acting curator G.D. Parker, predictably opposing the idea. Examining in wartime had been difficult without the Schools; overcrowding had been common, and complaints from students, examiners and proctors frequent. No venue in Oxford, the curators said, was large enough to replace the three large schools inside the Exam Schools (the North, South and East Schools). Those supporting the idea looked to the use of college dining halls as alternative examination spaces. Colleges were canvassed for their opinions, the weight of them siding with the opposition, and Hebdomadal Council rejected the proposals in March 1946.[128]

Increasing student numbers put pressure on staff as well as accommodation. In September 1945 the master of Pembroke wrote to the officer commanding the 16th Battalion of the Royal Army Ordnance Corps at Bicester, asking for the release of Corporal E.V. Organ of the Catering Corps. He was the college's former cook, and they were desperate to have him back. Homes Dudden explained that he had been told it was permissible to make the approach as the Ministry of Labour had asked the college to accommodate some undergraduate officers, and they could only do this with more staff. Currently, only one person was running the college's entire catering operation, and with the additional students and much larger numbers of undergraduates expected in Michaelmas, Corporal Organ was desperately needed.[129]

The war's impact on the academic world

The war was 'a vector of academic change, but on a more far-reaching scale and with different consequences' than the First World War.[130] In medicine, Lord Nuffield's donation in 1936 had ensured that Oxford researchers were firmly ensconced at the Radcliffe Infirmary by the outbreak of war. Under the National Health Service Act a decade later, the Infirmary, the Churchill Hospital and certain other local facilities were designated a teaching hospital and amalgamated under a board of governors, the new group known as United Oxford Hospitals.[131] War revolutionized the position of science and technology in relation to British universities given the new need for scientists, engineers and doctors in ever greater numbers.[132]

Before the war, the growth of Oxford science had been suppressed by several factors, not least the view shared by many dons that it was primarily a centre of humane learning, and a consequent reluctance on the part of the colleges (that those dons controlled) to take on more science undergraduates. The world wars 'helped to produce mounting recognition on the arts side that the achievements of natural science were necessary to the survival even of humane culture'.[133] The war was a watershed, marking 'the onset of a period of more than thirty years in which public support of scientific research at British universities was recognized as a major priority of the government and indispensable to Britain's survival as a great power'.[134] Academic physics was shown to be vital to national well-being, and this only increased in the decade following the Axis defeat, for with the onset of the Cold War the 'future prospects of civilisation on both sides in the nuclear arms race [seemed] to depend on a higher level of expertise' in this subject.[135]

Connections between Oxford science and national industry were strengthened in the post-war years, the latter becoming more science-based and therefore absorbing more graduates. Oxford's wartime medical and scientific achievements provided it 'with a firm base from which to respond to the post-war worldwide expansion in science', and student numbers in natural sciences grew rapidly.[136] Serendipitously, Oxford science benefited as national and international scientific projects – notably at Harwell, home of the Atomic Energy Research Establishment from 1946 – 'located the University within an area of major scientific investment'.[137] As the *Oxford Magazine* noted in 1945, 'future historians will point to Harwell as a crucial point in the industrialisation of Oxford science [and] the nationalisation of learning'.[138] Oxford nuclear physics cooperated closely with Harwell, which generously made its much larger facilities available to Oxford researchers. If certain areas of science at Oxford had been somewhat introverted between the wars, writes John Roche, this situation now changed dramatically. 'Oxford after 1945 involved itself fully in the national and international expansion of science through collaborative projects with British and overseas universities and institutions', hosting conferences, publishing and editing international journals, and pumping out research publications.[139]

War and post-war social change brought a blossoming interest in more applied social-science disciplines and their capacity to solve practical problems, and many new social-science posts were created in a brief phase of post-war academic expansion, including the permanent establishment of the Oxford Institute of Economics and Statistics.[140] As John Darwin writes, war greatly increased the prestige of specialized knowledge of Europe's recent history and contemporary politics, raising its value in the eyes of government. Strengthening Britain's academic expertise in key regions now became a priority, and the creation of St Antony's College and the Maison Française was part of Oxford's turn to wider world knowledge.

Despite wartime expansion in science and medicine, Oxford's position as a centre for the study of the humanities remained undiminished.

> The power and prestige of the classics survived with remarkable tenacity into the post-war world. Indeed, the collapse of humane studies in central Europe under Hitler's regime, and the flight of many mid-European

classical scholars to Oxford, meant that in the 1930s and 1940s Oxford was more than ever before the acknowledged international capital of Greek and Latin learning. [141]

The history faculty, meanwhile,

> resumed its portmanteau role as a training ground for a small handful of outstanding scholars, a nursery for the nation's statesmen, and – in the words of one returning undergraduate veteran – a repository for the 'deadweight of people for whom history is just the easiest subject to read'. [142]

The entry of many arts and social science dons into work of national importance during the war encouraged a widespread feeling in Oxford circles that the war had not undermined but confirmed the intellectual advantage of an Oxford generalist education.[143] The rudiments of classical learning were still seen in the 1940s and 1950s as 'indispensable for any Oxford matriculant in whatever discipline', though they were to be progressively dismantled in the 1960s. Oxford's intellectual life – 'still in 1939 powerfully hallmarked by classics, Englishness and Christianity – became increasingly secularized and international'.[144] As the wheel turned, much that was familiar in the intellectual climate of the interwar years, in the way history was written and stories of nations were told, was changing. New College warden H.A.L. Fisher, writes Alan Ryan, had 'presided over a late flowering of an educational style and of educational ideals that the Second World War swept away'.[145] But all of that, come 1945, lay in an unknown future.

As discussed in Chapter 1, the war had delayed many building projects, including the completion of Nuffield College, not commenced until 1949, a dozen years after its foundation. Regulations enforced by the war had prevented 'almost any extensive building work', contributing to a 'crisis' for Oxford stonework because 'regular maintenance had been impossible'.[146] Oxford avoided some of the enthusiasm for urban planning, such as the proposal for a motor highway through Merton Field and Christ Church Meadow, linking the Plain with St Aldates and taking traffic off the High Street (proposed in the 1930s and resurrected after the war).[147] Thomas Sharp's 'Merton Mall' scheme, published in

1948, aroused huge controversy, and debates about this and other road schemes punctuated the city's post-war years. Sharp's scheme aimed to preserve and enhance Oxford's historic core, but in so doing he envisaged a massive clearance of hundreds of supposedly 'outworn' houses and the erection of blocks of buildings in new streets. Most of his proposals were rejected, but the city council applied the principle of clearance quite ruthlessly in the south-western quarter of the city. Wartime and post-war concerns converged with those already evident before the war, and serious (as opposed to lunatic) discussion about moving the car industry away from Oxford did not subside until the 1950s.[148] The interwar growth of the Cowley works and new housing had administered a shock from which the University continued to reel. It

> bred fears that Oxford's identity might be swamped by factories. The slogan 'Oxford – home of Pressed Steel' had been repeated with unease as well as amusement. This feeling chimed in with national concerns after 1945 to contain urban growth and so fostered the protection of open spaces and the development of a 'green belt' policy.[149]

Remnants of war can still be found in Oxford and the wider county. St John's placed a gold-lettered Latin inscription on the wall by the buttery to the men and women 'who devoted their energies to the provision of and distribution of food for the support of the people during almost six years of crisis. They did good in a moment of evil and preserved hope in times of danger.' At Magdalen, the RAF left a plaque on the archway under Founder's Tower in St Johns's Quad 'in gratitude for the good fellowship they enjoyed and for the privilege of being allowed to worship in the College Chapel'. In 1988 the Burma Star Association's Oxford and district branch presented St Michael at the Northgate with the Burma Star Memorial Window.[150] A plaque in the entrance to Manchester's Arlosh Hall, unveiled by Princess Anne in 2014, marks the preparation for D-Day that took place there.

Blue plaques identify buildings where notable wartime discoveries were made; apparatus for the production of penicillin is displayed at the Museum of the History of Science; and blackout pelmets and curtains lived on in colleges such as Mansfield and Magdalen for many decades. Graffiti, some of it obscene, still adorns the basement of

Ditchley House, the work of soldiers detailed to guard the premises during prime-ministerial visits. The initials of Canadian soldiers can still be observed on Blenheim trees. The chimneys of Cowley works retained their camouflage paint until the 1990s, and the grain silo built by the Ministry of Food at Water Eaton remained a familiar landmark for commuters until its demolition in 2013 to make way for Oxford Parkway station.

Oxford's research had helped forge war-winning weapons, while the development of penicillin 'liberated medicine from its ineffectiveness against disease and brought a cure for the lethal common infections of pneumonia, meningitis and septicaemia'.[151] Florey and his team's break-through heralded the beginning of the antibiotic age, and 'transformed doctors' and society's perceptions of medicine's properties'.[152] Work conducted in Oxford helped the Allies win the intelligence war, shaped the foundations of the welfare state, and influenced debates about the future of the British Empire. Landmark wartime projects in Oxford were aided and sometimes led by people who had fled fascist Europe, the city's status as a sanctuary for scholars benefiting its research and hastening the defeat of the states from which they had fled.

These achievements, and the consultation and cooperation between government and universities that had nurtured them, was in sharp contrast to the situation in enemy states. Hitler's flagrant disregard for higher education set the tone for the Nazi state's relationship with universities – including their unheralded closure in 1940 – and their consequent failure to help Germany prosecute the war as effectively as it might have done. While British universities and their students were expected to play a part, they would be protected, not interfered with, in contrast to the forceful and sometimes violent state interventions that came to warp higher education in Germany, Italy, Japan and the Soviet Union.[153]

It would be absurd to inflate Oxford's wartime significance; it was not the country's only centre of academic expertise, and though London might look to it for assistance in numerous ways, the capital, as a global centre of research and hive of war-related activity, dwarfed provincial cities, even those housing venerable universities. While Oxford contributed to work leading to the creation of the atom bomb, other universities played larger roles. Reflecting the manner in which Britain's war effort was eclipsed by that of America, it was on the other side of the Atlantic that the full realization of the project came about. As Christopher Brooke writes of Cambridge science during the war, but with greater application to Oxford, 'to compare the tiny works of the Cavendish [Laboratory] and the mighty Manhattan project is like setting a bicycle beside an articulated truck.'[154] With penicillin, Oxford played a key role in developing the drug, discovered by Fleming at a London hospital, but it was American companies that brought it to market. This in itself tells us a lot about the role of universities during the war, and the benchmarks of success: achievements depended on international contacts and on teamwork, their realization part of a process linking wartime research to that which had gone before. Acknowledging the lineage of such discoveries and advances allows us to appreciate Oxford's role in both perspective and proportion.

The Second World War forms a distinctive layer of Oxford's historical archaeology. Unique unto itself, as things always are in their own time and place, it was intimately bound to happenings elsewhere in the county and the nation, and distant lands beyond the shire.

A NOTE ON SOURCES

Sources on Oxford during the war aren't difficult to come by because books written by people who were around at the time – novels, autobiographies, memoirs, diaries – abound. So, too, do biographies of Oxford people and general books about the University and the city. There is then the proliferation of books that examine all sorts of aspects of the war, such as the threat of invasion, civilian evacuation, the plight of refugees and the development of the atom bomb, from which material on Oxford can be gleaned. There are published accounts of Oxford institutions, be they books or articles in in-house journals and on institutional websites. They include the Ashmolean Museum, the Bodleian Library, the Forestry Institute, the physics laboratories, the Union and the University Press. Especially, there are the many published histories of Oxford's colleges, even though some seem to gloss over the war years. This, perhaps, is because it was an abnormal time in which, for many of them, normal college life ground almost to a halt due to the requisitioning of buildings and arrival of military personnel on six-month courses, further thinning out the number of 'normal' undergraduates, already reduced by military service.

There are some excellent general texts for those interested in Oxford during the war, and they have provided essential scaffolding for this work. Malcolm Graham's *Oxfordshire at War* (Stroud: Alan Sutton, 1994) is a fantastic study, written by the then head of Oxfordshire Studies at Oxfordshire County Council. Another work warranting special mention is the twentieth-century volume of *The History of the University of Oxford*, edited by Brian Harrison and published by Oxford University Press, also in 1994. While Paul Addison's chapter on the Second World War was the obvious starting point for this study (along with Graham's book), most of the volume's contributors offer material relating to the 1930s and 1940s, from which this work has benefited enormously.

In terms of archival material, use has been made of the University Archives, and material held in the Union Library such as back issues of the unofficial University magazine the *Oxford Magazine* and the student newspaper *Cherwell*. Most archival material has come from the splendid archives of Oxford's colleges, including runs of in-house college publications. The National Archives at Kew have provided intriguing information on the use to which some colleges were put on behalf of government departments, and snippets have been gleaned from King's College London's Liddell Hart Centre for Military Archives and the wonderful BBC People's War oral history archive project. Some material from the Oxford City Council archive has also been used. Nevertheless, while a lot has been looked at, in terms of secondary and primary material, as readers will see, the surface has only been scratched!

ABBREVIATIONS
AND ACRONYMS

ABV	Alcohol by volume
ATS	Auxiliary Territorial Service
BCA	Balliol College Archives
BEF	British Expeditionary Force
BNCA	Brasenose College Archives
C-in-C	Commander-in-Chief
DSIR	Department of Scientific and Industrial Research
ECA	Exeter College Archives
ENSA	Entertainments National Service Association
GCCS	Government Code and Cipher School
GCHQ	Government Communications Headquarters
GPO	General Post Office
HMCA	Harris Manchester College Archives
HMSO	His Majesty's Stationery Office
ICI	Imperial Chemical Industries
ISTD	Inter-Service Topographical Department
IWM	Imperial War Museum
JIC	Joint Intelligence Committee
LMH	Lady Margaret Hall
LSE	London School of Economics
MCA	Mansfield College Archives
MI5	Military Intelligence 5
NAAFI	Navy, Army and Air Force Institutes
NID	Naval Intelligence Division
OBLI	Oxfordshire and Buckinghamshire Light Infantry
OCTU	Officer Cadet Training Unit

OHC	Oxfordshire History Centre
OTC	Officers' Training Corps
OUP	Oxford University Press
PCA	Pembroke College Archives
POW	Prisoner of War
PPE	Politics, Philosophy and Economics
PWE	Political Warfare Executive
QAINS	Queen Alexandra's Imperial Nursing Service
QCA	The Queen's College Archives
RAMC	Royal Army Medical Corps
SEHA	St Edmund Hall Archives
SHAEF	Supreme Headquarters Allied Expeditionary Forces
SHCA	St Hugh's College Archives
SIXTA	Signals Intelligence and Traffic Analysis
SOE	Special Operations Executive
SPSL	Society for the Protection of Science and Learning
TNA	The National Archives
UGC	University Grants Committee
Univ	University College
UOA	University of Oxford Archives
UOTC	University Officers' Training Corps
WCA	Worcester College Archives
WVS	Women's Voluntary Services

NOTES

EPIGRAPH

1. William Bell (ed.), *Poetry from Oxford in Wartime* (London: The Fortune Press, 1945), p. 8.

INTRODUCTION

1. Alister McGrath, *C.S. Lewis: A Life* (London: Hodder & Stoughton, 2013), p. 192.
2. Demolished in 2013 to make way for Oxford Parkway railway station, this rail-served silo was designed to resolve the problem of drying, storing and transporting extra crops. Across Oxfordshire, war arrested the move away from arable to pasture. Between 1939 and 1944 the area of the county under permanent grassland fell by 44 per cent, from 215,000 acres to 140,000. The production of wheat, oats and barley grew massively as a result. Malcolm Graham, *Oxfordshire at War* (Stroud: Alan Sutton, 1994), p. 112.
3. Christopher Tyerman (ed.), *New College* (London: Third Millennium, 2010), p. 118. Procuring underwear was almost as difficult as securing a cadaver for the operation, featuring a fictitious Royal Marine's staff officer carrying 'secret' papers in a briefcase.
4. During the war, 'escaping from an unwelcome sermon', Lewis 'noticed a strange, double-sided wardrobe, converted out of the Principal's private entrance to the antechapel. Here was a trigger for imagination: here the kingdom of Narnia was born.' J. Mordaunt Crook, *Brasenose: The Biography of an Oxford College* (Oxford: Oxford University Press, 2010), p. 357. Mordaunt makes the point that the wardrobe episode echoes an E. Nesbit short story, 'The Aunt and Annabel', that Lewis used to tell evacuees at the Kilns. The wardrobe story was recounted by A.N. Wilson on BBC Radio 2 in 2006. Images of fauns and the like, encountered in childhood reading, also formed part of Narnia's lineage.
5. Founded by MP for Abingdon Sir Ralph Glyn. See 'The Upper Thames Patrol', at www.thamesatwar.co.uk/3.html. The Patrol came to number 6,000 men and women, its units divided into sections along the Thames's 125 miles, checking its many locks and road and rail bridges.
6. Peter Lester, 'Wartime Memories of 1435021 AC Stanley Lester', BBC World War Two People's War oral history archive, A8867965, www.bbc.co.uk/history/ww2peopleswar/stories/65/a8867965.shtml. Pakenham was a Student of Christ Church, and had been invalided out of the army early in the war. He contested and lost Quintin Hogg's Oxford seat in the 1945 election, though later

that year Attlee's government made him Baron Pakenham so that he could enter the Lords. He became Lord Longford, an Irish title, upon his brother's death in 1961.

7. Andrew Stewart, 'Ten Days in Oxford: How Canadians Troops Defended Britain', King's College London Second World War Research Group blog, 27 March 2017, www.swwresearch.com/post/ten-days-in-oxford-how-canadian-troops-defended-britain-in-1940—part-1.

8. Robin Darwall-Smith, 'Univ. during the Second World War', *University College Record*, 2005, www.univ.ox.ac.uk/wp-content/uploads/2020/04/Record-2005.pdf.

9. Duff Hart-Davis (ed.), *King's Counsellor: Abdication and War: The Diaries of Sir Alan 'Tommy' Lascelles* (London: Weidenfeld & Nicolson, 2020), p. 101, diary entry 25/2/42, on observing Beveridge at the National Gallery opening a Royal Institute of British Architects exhibition on post-war housing designs.

10. There was no varsity athletics for seven years. Graham Tanner and Laurence Chandy, *The History of the Oxford University Athletic Club* (Oxford: OUAC, 2010), p. 53.

11. Detail from Christopher Hibbert (ed.), *The Encyclopaedia of Oxford* (London: Macmillan, 1988), p. 15, and St Edmund Hall archives (hereafter SEHA), *St Edmund Hall Magazine,* 1943—48. Presumably the drink in question was ale.

12. On the deer cull, see McGrath, *C.S. Lewis*, p. 196. For Queen's beer, see 'The Queen's College' in H.E. Salter and Mary Lobel, *A History of the County of Oxford*, Volume 3: *The University of Oxford* (London: Victoria County History, 1954). For the St John's port crisis, see John Mabbott, *Oxford Memories* (Oxford: Thornton's, 1986), p. 114.

13. P.H. Sutcliffe's history of Oxford University Press, quoted in Fran Lloyd, 'Becoming Artists: Ernst Eisenmayer, Kurt Weiler, and Refugee Support Networks in Wartime Oxford', in Sally Crawford, Katharina Ulmschneider and Jaś Elsner (eds), *Ark of Civilization: Refugee Scholars and Oxford University, 1930—1945* (Oxford: Oxford University Press, 2017), p. 247 n.44.

A TOUR ROUND TOWN

1. James Stephens Curl, *The Erosion of Oxford* (Oxford: Oxford Illustrated Press, 1977), p. 3.

2. The reference is to the Oxford cityscape presented in Philip Pullman's famous *His Dark Materials* trilogy and its follow-up, *The Book of Dust* (the third novel in the trilogy yet to be published), which is at once entirely recognizable as well as phantasmagorical. A short introduction to it can be found in Pullman's *Lyra's Oxford* (Oxford: David Fickling Books, 2003), including a pull-out map, 'Oxford: By Train, River, and Zeppelin'.

3. The figures are 57,036 (1921), 80,539 (1931) and an estimated 107,000 in 1941 (no census because of the war). Christopher Hibbert (ed.), *The Encyclopaedia of Oxford* (London: Macmillan, 1988), p. 331.

4. Evelyn Waugh, *Brideshead Revisited* (London: Penguin Classics, 2000), p. 25.

5. In contrast, Wytham, because of the terms by which Raymond ffennell handed the Abbey and 3,000-acre estate over to the University in 1943, was to be preserved, and thus remains pristine. Curl, *The Erosion of Oxford*, p. 110.

6. Peter Collison, *Oxford Town and Gown* (Stroud: Amberley, 2011), p. 84, figure from 1948.

7. 1931 figure referring to 100 out of 2,000 streetlights. 'Public Services', in Alan Crossley and C.R. Elrington (eds), *History of the County of Oxford*, Volume 4: *The City of Oxford* (London: Victoria County History, 1979).

8. Curl, *The Erosion of Oxford*, p. 95.
9. John Harper-Nelson, *Oxford at War: An Undergraduate Memoir, John Harper-Nelson, 1940–42* (Northbridge, Western Australia: Access Press, 1996), p. 146. His belongings were conveyed in a cabin trunk, a heavy leather suitcase and an old wooden school tuck box.
10. Hibbert (ed.), *The Encyclopaedia of Oxford*, p. 360. The northern bypass bit was built in the mid-1930s as an unemployment relief exercise, extending from Headington to Eynsham and moving the A40 traffic out of Oxford. The Botley–Hinksey section opened in 1938.
11. John Betjeman, *An Oxford University Chest* [1938] (Oxford: Oxford University Press, 1979), p. 97.
12. Many of those buildings were covered in ivy or Virginia creeper, a practice adopted as a partial antidote to mounting concerns about stone decay, and to conceal Roman cement-faced stonework 'scored to imitate blocks of stone'. Experts advising colleges were coming round to the opinion that these plants damaged the stone, leading to vigorous post-war pruning that would reveal the disastrous condition of some of Oxford's stonework. To the decay of ages had been added the 'deposit of chemicals on the stone' from industry and motor vehicles, and the peril of traffic vibrations. W.F. Oakeshott (ed.), *Oxford Stone Restored: The Work of the Oxford Historic Buildings Fund, 1957–1974* (Oxford: Trustees of the Oxford Historic Buildings Fund, 1975), p. 4.
13. See the photo of waggons loaded with kit outside Walter's in the 1920s, and the picture of colonial kit from the company's 1936 catalogue, in Charles Allen (ed.), *Tales from the Dark Continent: Images of British Colonial Africa in the Twentieth Century* (London: André Deutsch/BBC, 1979), p. 92.
14. *Alden's Guide to Oxford* (Oxford: Alden and Company, 1938).
15. R.A. Denniston, 'Publishing and Bookselling', in Brian Harrison (ed), *The History of the University of Oxford*, Volume 8: *The Twentieth Century* (Oxford: Oxford University Press, 1994), p. 452.
16. Anna Nyburg, 'German-Speaking Refugee Publishers in Oxford: Phaidon, Bruno Cassirer, and the Oxford University Press', in Sally Crawford, Katharina Ulmschneider and Jaś Elsner (eds), *Ark of Civilization: Refugee Scholars and Oxford University, 1930–1945* (Oxford: Oxford University Press, 2017).
17. 'Martyr's hygienic hair-dressing rooms' occupied the floor above, offering facial and scalp 'vibro massage' and permanent waving.
18. *Alden's Guide*. See Harper-Nelson's description of the tearoom: *Oxford at War*, p. 55.
19. Zachary Leader, *The Life of Kingsley Amis* (London: Vintage, 2007), p. 95.
20. The Noted Café was at 129a High Street, and the Shamrock Tea Rooms – 'a restful corner where conversation can be enjoyed – yet in the centre of the City' – at 6–8 St Michael's Street. The Oriel Restaurant and Private Hotel stood opposite Brasenose at 106 High Street, the Town and Gown Restaurant at 135 High Street, and the Jewish Restaurant at 95 Walton Street. Harper-Nelson writes that the Noted and the Town and Gown were frequently overcrowded in the evenings.
21. '"Oxford Will Never Be the Same": The Last Days of the Glorious Cadena Café', *Oxford Mail*, 22 July 2013; Hibbert (ed.), *The Encyclopaedia of Oxford*, p. 67. Memorably referenced in Betjeman's 1941 poem 'Myfanwy at Oxford'.
22. *Alden's Guide*.
23. Montgomery wrote under the name Edmund Crispin, and the novel was published by Gollancz in 1944, the first of his Gervase Fen whodunnits. The more well-known *The Moving Toy Shop* appeared in 1946. Quotations from Philip

Larkin, *Jill* (London: Faber & Faber, 2005), p. xv, and Harper-Nelson, *Oxford at War*, p. 50.

24. It apparently boasted the 'fastest shove-halfpenny board in England'. Harper-Nelson, *Oxford at War*, p. 50.

25. Leader, *The Life of Kingsley Amis*, p. 95.

26. Humphrey Carpenter, *The Inklings: C.S. Lewis, J.R.R. Tolkien, Charles Williams* (London: HarperCollins, 1997), p. 185.

27. *Alden's Guide*.

28. Betjeman, *An Oxford University Chest*, p. 90.

29. St Catherine's Society existed, with new premises on St Aldate's, but it was not a college of the University.

30. Some of which, and aspects of Beef Street's character, were pleasingly incorporated into the new quad's design.

31. St Peter-le-Bailey Church had been moved down New Inn Hall Street to widen the road in 1874 (now St Peter's College chapel).

32. *Alden's Guide*, p. 28. See the photograph in Stephen Blundell and Michael Freeman (eds), *Mansfield: Portrait of an Oxford College* (London: Third Millennium, 2012).

33. 'The Isis' is a name given to the River Thames as it passes through Oxford in particular and, in general, from its point of rising in the Cotswolds until its confluence with the Thame at Dorchester (in Oxfordshire). Most of the buildings that now dominate Gloucester Green (around the bus station and the market square) are late twentieth century. At the time of the war, a large Halls pub, the Greyhound, stood at its westernmost edge, facing on to Walton Street. The old Welsh Pony pub is one of the few original buildings bordering Gloucester Green (named for the animals that once graced the market outside its windows). A plan to build a multistorey car park on Gloucester Green was rejected in 1936 on grounds of cost. Hibbert (ed.), *The Encyclopaedia of Oxford*, p. 154.

34. As shown to great effect in the 1944 amateur film made by American soldier James R. Savage, a flight surgeon of the 14th Photo Reconnaissance Unit. Savage was based at RAF Mount Farm airbase (3 miles north of Dorchester) as part of the US 8th Air Force. His film, made for family back home, shows scenes of Oxford street life, a boat trip from Salter Brothers of 78 Folly Bridge down the Thames to Wallingford, and trips to nearby Abingdon, Dorchester and elsewhere. See 'Oxford at War 1944', http://podcasts.ox.ac.uk/oxford-war-1944. City of Oxford and District Motor Bus Services ran services to Woodstock, Dorchester, Burford, Abingdon and Faringdon, and offered 'Excursions to Stratford-upon-Avon, Warwick, Whipsnade Zoo, Windsor, Malvern, and Sulgrave ("for Washington's ancestral home")'. South Midland Motor Services, its offices at 118 High Street, ran daily coaches to London. Outlying attractions advertised in *Alden's Guide* included Chastleton House and Gardens near Moreton-in-Marsh (Blenheim did not open to the public until 1950, though the park was open daily and its gardens open three days a week from noon until 4 p.m., entrance price 6d. *Oxford and District Illustrated Guide Book* (London: Ward, Lock, 1938), p. 187).

35. The outbreak of war in 1939 saved the Broad Street/Ship Street block from demolition. Malcolm Graham and Laurence Waters, *Oxford Yesterday and Today* (Stroud: Alan Sutton, 2002), p. 5.

36. Preserved and relocated at the Buckinghamshire Railway Centre.

37. Graham and Waters, *Oxford Yesterday and Today*, p. 107.

38. *Alden's Guide*. This edition was priced at a shilling, the 1946 edition twice as much. The pocket-sized guide contained advertisements for this bygone Oxford. It was edited by Henry Alden from his company's 14 Broad Street premises,

from where 'postcards, view books and souvenirs' were sold. The handy little guide contained 'notes on the district and rivers', a 'key-plan of the University and city' and a folding map of central Oxford. A fruit-and-veg handcart is to be seen in Savage's film. See note 34, above.

39. On the site of today's Thames Valley Police headquarters. The animals were moved to Dudley Castle. See 'Lion Was Pride of Short-Lived Oxford Zoo', *Oxford Mail*, 1 December 2010.

40. The roundabout of today was installed in 1950, the city council's traffic improvement schemes delayed by the war. The statue was moved during this redevelopment to Cowley Barracks. When that was scheduled for closure, it was moved to the Slade Territorial Army base in Headington, and then, in 2008, to the new TA centre in Abingdon.

41. Larkin, *Jill*, p. 71.

42. Fascinating 1935 photographs of condemned houses and streets can be viewed at www.pictureoxon.org. Curl writes that the designation of the term 'slum' reflects 'a middle-class attitude to terrace-housing where grand values are applied to humble situations'. Curl, *The Erosion of Oxford*, p. 108. See also Graham and Waters, *Oxford Yesterday and Today*, p. 5, and the distinctly 'Victorian' 1938 picture of Friars Street and Commercial Road, with horse-drawn delivery cart and tightly packed terraced housing on p. 75. Wholesale clearances led to the destruction of historic as well as substandard houses. The pre-war clearance scheme was much less drastic than what was eventually carried out, and involved much more rehousing on site.

43. Dorothy Erskine Muir, *Oxford* (London: Blackie, n.d. [c. 1951]), p. 24. The area is behind the Jam Factory and encompassed parts of Osney. She is referring to the cattle market on Oxpens Road. Many houses in the area were cleared in the 1930s.

44. E.A. Greening Lamborn, 'Architecture', in *Handbook to the University of Oxford* (Oxford: Clarendon Press, 1932), p. 70.

45. Figure from Curl, *The Erosion of Oxford*, p. 9.

46. A major period of development, there were other buildings planned in the 1930s that didn't come to fruition. They included a Balliol scheme for a new hall and building fronting on to Broad Street; the extension of Exeter College over the site of Parker's bookshop; and All Souls plans for an enlarged common room, home for the manciple, and new fellows' rooms. See Howard Colvin, *Unbuilt Oxford* (New Haven CT and London: Yale University Press, 1983).

47. In 1932 Mrs Hartland had purchased the freehold of a site between the Woodstock and Banbury roads, the site of this new building and of today's college. Giles Gilbert Scott had been commissioned to design a building that could be erected in stages. Also in the 1930s, St Anne's was left the remaining lease on 1 South Parks Road, and from 1936 this became the society's administrative, tutorial and social home. Hibbert (ed.), *The Encyclopaedia of Oxford*, p. 375.

48. '[M]ore kindly described "as a home for unfortunate girls", run by an Anglican sisterhood'. John Jones, *Balliol College: A History, 1263–1939* (Oxford: Oxford University Press, 1989), p. 266. Accommodation when opened in 1932 for thirty-seven students, and two sets for fellows.

49. 'The Ashmolean Museum Conservation Plan' (University of Oxford Estates Services, 2012), p. 22.

50. Ibid., p. 23.

51. Vicky Simon and Richard Pollard, *Oxford Central (City and University) Conservation Area Boundary Review Consultation Report*, appendix report (London: Alan Baxter,

2019), and Anthony Croft, *Oxford's Clarendon Laboratory* (Oxford: Department of Physics, 1986), p. 82. Commissioned in 1935 to prepare a scheme for the development of the Science Area, T.A. Lodge singled out the Clarendon Laboratory as being in 'an advanced state of obsolescence'.

52. Hibbert (ed.), *The Encyclopaedia of Oxford*, p. 213.

53. John Buxton and Penry Williams (eds), *New College Oxford, 1379–1979* (Oxford: The Warden and Fellows of New College Oxford, 1979), pp. 257–8. New College's War Memorial Committee raised the funds, and the building featured squared Bladon rubble for the walls and dressed Clipsham stone for the window surrounds.

54. Edmund Craster, *History of the Bodleian Library, 1845–1945* (Oxford: Clarendon Press, 1952), p. 265.

55. In May 1932 the Rockefeller Foundation offered to contribute up to three-fifths of the estimated total cost of £400,000 for the new library on condition that the University found the remainder within four years, which it managed to do within a year. Mary Clapinson, *A Brief History of the Bodleian Library* (Oxford: Bodleian Library Publishing, 2015), p. 142.

56. Elsewhere on that most 'traditional' of Oxford streets, the warden of Merton's lodgings at its eastern extremity did not then exist either. Designed just before the war, it wasn't completed until the 1950s.

57. L.W.B. Brockliss (ed.), *Magdalen College Oxford: A History* (Oxford: Magdalen College, 2008), p. 650.

58. *Worcester College Record, 1939–44.*

59. Jeffery Burley, Roger Mills, Robert Plumptre, Peter Savill, Peter Wood and Howard Wright, 'A History of Forestry at Oxford University', *British Scholar*, vol. 1, no. 2, 2009, p. 240. It was part-funded by a £25,000 gift from the Rajah of Sarawak. The separate School of Forestry and Imperial Forestry Institute were merged in 1939 to form the University's Department of Forestry.

60. The pub's name reflected barge horses that had been stabled nearby. Historic Urban Character Assessment, 'Western Suburb: Castle Mill Stream and Fisher Row', Historic Urban Character Area 7 (2013), Users/stsbo918/Downloads/ HUCA-7-The-Western-Suburb-Castle-Mill-Stream-and-Fisher-Row.pdf. The Scala is today's Phoenix Picture Palace.

61. Don Chapman, *Oxford Playhouse: High and Low Drama in a University City* (Hatfield: University of Hertfordshire Press, 2008), p. 5.

62. They joined a number of other Oxford cinemas: the Electra on Queen's Street, which opened as a theatre in 1911 (the building demolished in 1978 on the site of today's Marks & Spencer); the Majestic in Botley (1934); the Super on Magdalen Street (opened in 1924 and until closure in 2023 an Odeon cinema); and the (now demolished) New Cinema in Headington (1923). On the city's outskirts and reflecting another popular leisure activity of the period – as well as the growth of Oxford's working-class population – the newly built Oxford Stadium opened for greyhound racing in 1939 (speedway following soon after the war). New recreation grounds were laid out at Five Mile Drive, Florence Park and Bury Knowle, joining those established by the city council in the 1920s. An ice rink in a new art deco building was opened on Botley Road in 1930, though in 1934 it became the Majestic cinema. In 1947 Frank Cooper turned it into a marmalade factory. The building was demolished in the 1980s.

63. Cowley and Headington were the main areas of expansion in the twentieth century before 1939, with smaller residential developments at Botley and Cutteslowe. See the map of phases of urban expansion 'Modern Oxford' in Crossley and Elrington (eds), *A History of the County of Oxford*, vol. 4.

NOTES 299

64. R.C. Whiting, *The View from Cowley: The Impact of Industrialization upon Oxford, 1919–1939* (Oxford: Clarendon Press, 1983), pp. 5, 196.
65. Laurence Brockliss, *The University of Oxford: A History* (Oxford: Oxford University Press), p. 528. Quotation from Curl, *The Erosion of Oxford*, p. 8.
66. Map 'Modern Oxford', in Crossley and Elrington (eds), *A History of the County of Oxford*, vol. 4.
67. Oxfordshire County Council, *The Story of Oxford* (Stroud: Alan Sutton, 1992), p. 45.
68. 'The whole economic situation of the town was transformed.' Ruth Fasnacht, *A History of the City of Oxford* (Oxford: Basil Blackwell, 1954), p. 210.
69. A.L. Rowse, *Oxford in the History of the Nation* (London: Weidenfeld & Nicolson, 1975), p. 245.
70. Christopher Hobhouse, *Oxford: As It Was and As It Is To-day* (London: Batsford, 1941–42), p. 109.
71. Colvin, *Unbuilt Oxford*, p. 179. 'Totally contemptible' was how Colvin summarized the science area buildings erected in the period. Ibid., p. 178.
72. Ibid.
73. Sheldonian detail from *Alden's Guide*, p. 3. New Bodleian and Rhodes House quotations, Colvin, *Unbuilt Oxford*, p. 178.
74. Hobhouse complained that the architect had 'banished proportion along with symmetry' in his design, and regretted that the New Bodleian had 'taken the place of a charming row of houses'. Hobhouse, *Oxford: As It Was and As It Is Today*, p. 109.
75. Rowse, *Oxford in the History of the Nation*, p. 221.
76. Ibid., p. 252. In contemplating a sorely needed extension to the Bodleian, wrote Wadham's warden Maurice Bowra, the 'reformers wanted an up-to-date library on the American model'. Giles Scott 'with bland complacency refused to listen to criticisms and produced a building which pleased nobody but himself'.
77. C.M. Bowra, *Memories, 1898–1939* (London: Weidenfeld & Nicolson, 1966), p. 341.
78. Ibid.
79. Betjeman, *An Oxford University Chest*, p. 104.
80. Ibid., p. 8. Betjeman was able to overcome his horror and accept employment with Shell, producing films about the English countryside designed to encourage people to drive through it.
81. Ibid., p. 9.
82. Arthur Mee, *Oxfordshire: County of Imperishable Fame* (London: Hodder & Stoughton, 1942), p. 8.
83. Fasnacht, *A History*, p. 213. I'm not entirely sure whether this remark indicates condescension towards the 'requirements' of what she considered working-class people (surely all types of people went to the new cinemas and theatres and used the shops, and working-class people did not form the general clientele of the soon to be demolished Clarendon Hotel). Fasnacht also seems not to account for the range of reasons for buildings being 'modernized' or 'demolished'.
84. Muir, *Oxford*. Bill Bryson writes that Oxford is 'a beautiful city that has been treated with gross indifference and lamentable incompetence for so long'. *Notes from a Small Island* (London: Black Swan, 1995), p. 157.
85. Jeremy Catto (ed.), *Oriel College: A History* (Oxford: Oxford University Press, 2013), p. 743.

OF UNIVERSITY AND COLLEGES

1. A.H. Halsey, 'Oxford and the British Universities', in Brian Harrison (ed.), *The History of the University of Oxford*, Volume 8: *The Twentieth Century* (Oxford: Oxford University Press, 1994), p. 577.
2. *Oxford and District Illustrated Guide Book* (London: Ward Lock, 1938), p. 9.
3. Arthur Mee, *Oxfordshire: County of Imperishable Fame* (London: Hodder & Stoughton, 1942), pp. 177, 11.
4. Ibid., p. 195.
5. W. Roger Louis, 'Reassessing the History of Oxford University Press, 1896–1970', in Louis (ed.), *The History of Oxford University Press*, Volume 3: *1896–1970* (Oxford: Oxford University Press, 2013), p. 13.
6. Associated with the 'received pronunciation' English favoured by the BBC (though viewed as separate by its first director-general, Lord Reith). Essentially, the 'Oxford accent' was a general term equating to upper/upper-middle-class speech, potentially tinged with affectation.
7. Ten of these universities were independent, the other ten university colleges affiliated to the federal University of London.
8. Christopher Brooke, *A History of the University of Cambridge*, Volume 4: *1870–1990* (Cambridge: Cambridge University Press, 2004), p. 540. In 2022 there were around 2.6 million people studying at Britain's approximately 170 higher-education institutions.
9. Leslie Mitchell, *Maurice Bowra: A Life* (Oxford: Oxford University Press, 2010), p. 234. See also Asa Briggs, 'Preface', in Charles Fenby, *The Other Oxford: The Life and Times of Frank Gray* (London: Lund Humphries, 1970).
10. The 1932 *Handbook to the University* (predating Nuffield's foundation) specifies nineteen men's colleges and Keble (a 'new foundation'); All Souls; four women's colleges; the two non-residential bodies; and St Edmund Hall (p. 98). It doesn't mention colleges such as Mansfield and Manchester, not yet Permanent Private Halls (PPH), or St Peter's Hall, a PPH since 1929.
11. A new gabled building for non-collegiate students was erected on the corner of Merton Street and High Street at the eastern end of the Exam Schools range in the 1880s. This was to give these students and the Delegacy that administered them a home, equipped with a reading room and JCR, helping foster a common identity and social centre. L.W.B. Brockliss, *The University of Oxford: A History* (Oxford: Oxford University Press, 2016), p. 370. In 1937 the Society's headquarters moved to newly erected premises on the east side St Aldate's, and the Bureau of Statistics moved into the building thus vacated. *Alden's Guide*, p. 41. The Delegacy of Extra-Mural Studies based at Rewley House, forerunner of the Department for Continuing Education, continued the work in the field of adult education that it had commenced in the 1870s.
12. B. Harrison, 'College Life, 1918–1939', in Harrison (ed.), *The History of the University of Oxford*, vol. 8, p. 89. Harrison mentions 198 'male tutorial fellows' in 1937 (p. 85), and it is known that the women's colleges had small fellowships and relied on male colleagues for much of their tuition. It's difficult to clarify the numbers. Many figures quote 'tutorial fellows' but seem not to account for other University staff (such as demonstrators), and more casual workers such as college lecturers – mentioned, but not incorporated in the figures I have seen. On page 106 of this Harrison chapter, a figure of 407 'fellows of men's Oxford colleges' in 1937 is given. Addison gives a figure of 504 'academic staff in September 1939'. P. Addison, 'Oxford and the Second World War', in Harrison (ed.), *The History of the University of Oxford*, vol. 8, p. 171.
13. H.E. Salter and M. Lobel, 'The University of Oxford', in Salter and Lobel (eds),

A History of the County of Oxford, Volume 3: *The University of Oxford* (London: Victoria County History,1954), pp. 1–38.

14. C.S.L. Davies and Jane Garnett, *Wadham College* (Oxford: Wadham College, 1994), p. 75.

15. QCA, *Queen's College Record*, vol. II, no. 7, 1939.

16. J. Catto (ed.), *Oriel College: A History* (Oxford: Oxford University Press, 2013), p. 742. Mansfield in 1939 had eight people in the SCR – a principal, vice principal, bursar, chaplain, three tutors and a research fellow. Pembroke had eight fellows on the strength plus a bursar and a master, Univ seventeen fellows and a master, Exeter thirteen fellows, Brasenose fewer than twenty.

17. In 1939 the median governing body size across the University was fourteen. Harrison, 'College Life', p. 85.

18. J. Jones, *Balliol College: A History, 1263–1939* (Oxford: Oxford University Press, 1989), p. 265. New College figures from 'Epilogue', in J. Buxton and P. Williams (eds), *New College Oxford, 1379–1979* (Oxford: New College Oxford, 1979), pp. 366–7. In December 2021 the smallest Oxford college (as opposed to Permanent Private Hall) was Harris Manchester, with 314 students (graduate-only Nuffield had 96). www.ox.ac.uk/about/facts-and-figures/student-numbers.

19. Brockliss, *The University of Oxford*, p. 341.

20. Margaret Thatcher, *The Path to Power* (London: HarperCollins, 1995), p. 35.

21. P. Collison, *Oxford Town and Gown* (Stroud: Amberley, 2011), p. 19.

22. A.S. Faiz, 'A Flight from Self, to Self', *Worcester College Record*, 1992.

23. Collison, *Oxford Town and Gown*, p. 7.

24. Douglas Ross, 'A War Year: 1941–42 (Part 2)', *Pembroke College Record*, 1993.

25. L. Brockliss, 'University Life', in Harrison (ed.), *The History of the University of Oxford*, vol. 8, p. 450.

26. Adam Sisman, *Hugh Trevor-Roper: The Biography* (London: Phoenix, 2011), p. 46.

27. Ann Thwaite (ed.), *My Oxford* (London: Robson Books, 1977), p. 134.

28. C.M. Bowra, *Memories, 1898–1939* (London: Weidenfeld & Nicolson, 1966), p. 334.

29. Thwaite (ed.), *My Oxford*, p. 144. Mortimer's time in residence at Oxford was cut short by revelations about a correspondence with a schoolboy.

30. J. Harper-Nelson, *Oxford at War: An Undrgraduate Memoir, John Harper-Nelson, 1940–42* (Northbridge, Western Australia: Access Press, 1996), p. 97.

31. E. Clare Friedman, *Strawberries and Nightingales with Buz: The Pioneering Mathematical Life of Ida Busbridge, 1908–1988* (Createspace, 2014), pp. 71–2.

32. Thwaite (ed.), *My Oxford*, p. 158. For her part, Bawden craved the company of young men, partly to evade the need to join in-college 'groups', the beautiful and confident on the one hand, the dowdy on the other.

33. J. Mordaunt Crook, *Brasenose: The Biography of an Oxford College* (Oxford: Oxford University Press, 2010), p. 336.

34. Penry Williams, 'The Life of a Don', in Christopher Tyerman (ed.), *New College* (London: Third Millennium, 2010), p. 106. C.S. Lewis, when asked if someone was a don, replied, 'Oh no, he was a *learned* man'.

35. Tyerman (ed.), *New College*, p. 121.

36. Both Edward Heath and Denis Healey make this point.

37. J. Harris, 'The Arts and Social Sciences', in Harrison (ed.), *The History of the University of Oxford*, vol. 8, p. 217.

38. *Handbook to the University of Oxford*, p. 89.

39. Tyerman (ed.), *New College*, p. 71.

40. Brockliss, *The University of Oxford*, p. 383.

41. Laurence Brockliss, 'Welcoming and Supporting Refugee Scholars: The Role of

Oxford's Colleges', in S. Crawford and J. Elsner (eds), *Ark of Civilization: Refugee Scholars and Oxford University, 1930–1945* (Oxford: Oxford University Press, 2017), p. 61.

42. For the costs of studying at Oxford, see Brockliss, *The University of Oxford*, from p. 439. Also the colleges section of the 1932 *Handbook*, which offers college-by-college information.

43. Thomas Charles-Edwards and Julian Reid (eds), *Corpus Christi College Oxford: A History* (Oxford: Oxford University Press, 2017), p. 379.

44. Harper-Nelson, *Oxford at War*, p. 34.

45. Most dons' households had servants in the 1930s, a study showing an 'enormous preponderance of females' in Summertown and Wolvercote wards of North Oxford. Collison, *Oxford Town and Gown*, p. 71.

46. A wider social issue of course. The type of books I mean are novels such as those of Edmund Crispin, J.C. Masterman's *An Oxford Tragedy* and *To Teach the Senators Wisdom, Or An Oxford Guide-Book*, and 'insider' travelogue-cum-histories, such as Dacre Balsdon's.

47. Christopher Hobhouse, *Oxford: As It Was and As It Is To-day* (London: Batsford, 1941–42), p. 105.

48. Harrison, 'College Life, 1918–1939', p. 85.

49. Ibid.

50. Tom Harrisson, *Letter to Oxford* (Wyck: The Hate Press, 1933), p. 15. Harrisson's extraordinary ramble defines Oxford as 'a swell place to live in' (having abandoned Cambridge to move there) but one that 'has certain effects on the minds of people who live in it'. Those effects 'are towards a special sort of unreality, time-sense, and consequent inaction: life is too pleasant, and nothing is quite real'. Ibid., p. 17.

51. Christopher Hibbert (ed.), *The Encyclopaedia of Oxford* (London: Macmillan, 1988), p. 474.

52. Harper-Nelson, *Oxford at War*, pp. 15, 55.

53. Jones, *Balliol*, p. 270.

54. J. Harris, 'The Arts and Social Sciences', in Harrison (ed.), *The History of the University of Oxford*, vol. 8, p. 217. The Oxford Association (soon renamed the Oxford Society) was created in 1932 to address this issue and to promote the cause of Oxford graduates and keep them in touch with what was going on in the University. Brian Harrison, 'Government and Administration, 1914–1964', in Harrison (ed.), *The History of the University of Oxford*, vol. 8, p. 716. Despite the focus on college, the University side of things came into sharper relief for those inclined, upon leaving Oxford, to retain links with others who had attended the place. This is how informal networks thrived, the link to Oxford (never mind one's college) being a sufficiently narrow and exclusive bracket. One often comes across references to Oxford alumni meetings in diaries and memoirs; off the top of my head I can recall Henry 'Chips' Channon dining in London with a group of Oxonians calling themselves 'The Cloisters'; the Governor of Ceylon attending an Oxford dinner in Colombo; and the Resident Minister in Iran attending a dinner where Oxonians, many from Balliol, had been gathered together. The Oxford and Cambridge Club on Pall Mall played a role in sustaining and developing Oxbridge links.

55. Mordaunt Crook, *Brasenose*, p. 377.

56. Timothy Weston, *From Appointments to Careers: A History of the Oxford University Careers Service, 1892–1992* (Oxford: Oxford University Careers Service, 1994), p. 15.

57. The Appointments Committee established a Women's Sub-Committee in 1932.

58. Angela Edward, 'Object Biographies – A Green Car Lamp in Oxford', British

Archaeology at the Ashmolean Museum, britisharchaeology.ashmus.ox.ac.uk/east-oxford/ob-green-car-lamp.html.

59. Brigid Allen, *Morrells of Oxford: The Family and Their Brewery, 1743–1993* (Oxford: Oxfordshire Books, 1994), pp. 115–16.

60. On brewing, see 'Liquid Legacies: Beer and Brewing at the Queen's College', at www.queens.ox.ac.uk/liquid-legacies-beer-and-brewing-queens-college. Also Harper-Nelson, *Oxford at War*, p. 34. Allen writes that Queen's was in 1939 still producing a 'token' thirty barrels a year of College Ale, and in October only a small quantity of the very strong 'ceremonial beer' known as Chancellor's Ale (at 1100 specific gravity, being around 11 per cent alcohol by volume). Allen, *Morrells of Oxford*, p. 115. By the 1930s Morrells was supervising the college's twice yearly brewings in the antiquated college brewhouse.

61. Hobhouse, *Oxford: As It Was and As It Is To-day*, p. 100. This second edition, published in 'winter 1941–42', noted that Hobhouse had joined the 'Fighting Services soon after the publication of this book' and 'was killed on active service in England early in 1940'. Ibid, p. viii. Hobhouse writes condescendingly and dismissively of Oxford's female students. See pp. 101–3.

62. John Betjeman, *An Oxford University Chest* (Oxford: Oxford University Press, 1979), p. 17.

63. Hibbert (ed.), *The Encyclopaedia of Oxford*, p. 64.

64. Harper-Nelson, *Oxford at War*, p. 52.

65. Jones, *Balliol*, p. 271.

66. The war made things easier in the Balliol–St John's–Trinity quarter because doors between colleges had to be left unlocked in case of fire.

67. Jonathan Bate and Jessica Goodman, *Worcester: Portrait of an Oxford College* (London: Third Millennium, 2014), p. 74.

68. Philip Larkin, *Jill* (London: Faber & Faber, 2005), p. xv.

69. Robin Darwall-Smith, 'Univ. during the Second World War', *University College Record*, 2005.

70. Thwaite (ed.), *My Oxford*, p. 86.

71. St Edmund Hall archives (SEHA), *St Edmund Hall Magazine*, 1943–48.

72. Clare Hopkins, *Trinity: 450 Years of an Oxford College Community* (Oxford: Oxford University Press, 2005), p. 391.

73. Keith Thomas, 'College Life, 1945–1970', in Harrison (ed.), *The History of the University of Oxford*, vol. 8, p. 201.

74. Harper-Nelson, *Oxford at War*, p. 28.

75. Margaret Rayner, *The Centenary History of St Hilda's College, Oxford* (London: Lindsay Ross Publishing, 1993), p. 80.

76. Ibid., p. 83.

77. Brockliss, *The University of Oxford*, p. 462. Female colleges had adopted corridors for student rooms, not the traditional staircase.

78. J. Alan Thompson, *Only the Sun Remembers* (London: Andrew Dakers, 1950), pp. 8–9.

79. Pauline Adams, *Somerville for Women: An Oxford College, 1879–1993* (Oxford: Oxford University Press, 1996), p. 220.

80. Davies and Garnet, *Wadham College*, p. 75. More two-bedroom sets were broken up with the coming of the boom in student numbers after the war.

81. 'Oaks' are second doors that if shut meant that the inhabitant was not to be disturbed (hence 'sporting one's oak').

82. Harper-Nelson, *Oxford at War*, p. 6.

83. Thwaite (ed.), *My Oxford*, p. 132.

84. Harper-Nelson, *Oxford at War*, p. 8.

85. Jones, *Balliol*, p. 269.

86. Ibid., p. 270.
87. Davies and Garnet, *Wadham College*, p. 75.
88. Daisy Dunn, *Not Far from Brideshead: Oxford Between the Wars* (London: Weidenfeld & Nicolson, 2022).
89. Thomas, 'College Life, 1945–1970', p. 109.
90. D.J. Wenden, 'Sport', in Harrison (ed.), *The History of the University of Oxford*, vol. 8.
91. 'Dining societies' is a common euphemism for drinking societies often with arcane rules and rituals governing membership, exclusion and activity.
92. SEHA, *St Edmund Hall Magazine*, 1939.
93. Richard Ollard (ed.), *The Diaries of A.L. Rowse* (London: Penguin, 2004), p. x.
94. Barry Webb, *Edmund Blunden: A Biography* (New Haven CT and London: Yale University Press, 1990), p. 234.
95. Carleton Kemp Allen, 'College Life', in *Handbook to the University of Oxford*, p. 118. The author's rather fanciful take captures something of the metropolitan–periphery condescension of Oxford towards the surrounding countryside – and most things beyond Oxford – that has been a long-standing aspect of its character.
96. Quoted in Diane Kay, 'Architecture', in Harrison (ed.), *The History of the University of Oxford*, vol. 8, p. 501.
97. Brooke, *A History*, p. 287.
98. Harrison, 'College Life, 1918–1939', p. 102.
99. Thomas, 'College Life, 1945–1970, p. 212.
100. Quoted in Jan Morris, *The Oxford Book of Oxford* (Oxford: Oxford University Press, 1984), p. 380.
101. Thwaite (ed.), *My Oxford*, p. 15.
102. Ibid., p. 128.
103. Betjeman, *An Oxford University Chest*, p. 51.
104. I can't trace the quotation, but someone once wrote something along the lines of 'Oxford only prepares you for Oxford'.
105. Selina Hastings, *Evelyn Waugh* (London: Vintage, 2002), p. 81. Of her subject, Hastings writes that 'as though attempting to recapture his lost youth, to evoke a longed-for golden age, Evelyn returned again and again to Oxford' (ibid., p. 139).
106. Michael Barber, *Anthony Powell: A Life* (London: Duckworth Overlook, 2005), p. 33.
107. Ibid., p. 35. Interview for *Isis*, 1973. As he reminds us, Waugh didn't overlap with Betjeman.
108. Collison, *Oxford Town and Gown*, p. 95.
109. Denis Healey, *The Time of My Life* (London: Michael Joseph, 1989), p. 25.
110. In 1944 the Oxford colleges were responsible for 504 church livings. F.M. Turner, 'Religion', in Harrison (ed.), *The History of the University of Oxford*, vol. 8, p. 302.
111. Noel Annan, *Our Age: The Generation that Made Post-War Britain* (London: Weidenfeld & Nicolson, 1990), p. 5.
112. Humphrey Carpenter, *The Inklings: C.S. Lewis, J.R.R. Tolkien, Charles Williams* (London: HarperCollins, 1997), p. 162.
113. P. and R. Malcolmson (eds), *A Vicar's Wife in Oxford, 1938–1943: The Diary of Madge Martin* (Woodbridge: Oxfordshire Record Society/Boydell Press, 2018), diary entry, 28 May 1938, p. 43n.
114. Humphrey Carpenter, *J.R.R. Tolkien* (London: HarperCollins, 2016), p. 205. Isolating her further, some 'terrifying' dons' wives served only to confirm her belief that 'the University was unapproachable in its eminence', and she became known as someone who 'did not call'. Ibid., p. 206.

NOTES 305

115. Adam Sisman, *A.J.P. Taylor: A Biography* (London: Sinclair-Stevenson, 1994), p. 134.
116. There was nevertheless an insularity about Oxford despite its many national and global connections, Leslie Mitchell observing of Bowra that he 'performed on a narrow stage. His beliefs and concerns were largely Oxford in character and provenance. The tribe which inhabited that city had its own rituals and codes which were not always those of the outside world.' Mitchell, *Maurice Bowra*, p. x.
117. Ibid., p. xi.
118. Geoffrey Dawson, editor of *The Times* until 1941 was a fellow. Annan quotation from N. Annan, *Our Age*, p. 5.
119. These conversations also 'infiltrated inter-college salons run by cultivated dons in search of undergraduate talent, Bowra, Boase, Platnauer, or more raffish rivals such as Kolkhort or Dawkins'. Harrison, 'College Life 1918–1939', p. 78.
120. Harrison, 'Politics', p. 382.
121. 'Gowns-Woman', in Thatcher, *The Path to Power*; 'Balliol on the Brink', in Roy Jenkins, *A Life at the Centre* (London: Papermac, 1994); 'The Approaching Storm, 1937–39' and 'Fighting for Freedom, 1939–43', in Edward Heath, *The Course of My Life* (London: Hodder & Stoughton, 1998). Thatcher had a rough time; pursuing her burgeoning interest in politics in a University environment that was male-dominated, she endured the condescension of female peers because of her unfashionable conservative convictions, and was later beasted by eminent tutors of the time who didn't like what she had become and chose therefore to emphasize her averageness as a student (writing as if they were assessing the credentials of a Nobel prize entrant as opposed to an undergraduate). For this and the 'snobbish condescension' of the liberal establishment, see John Campbell, *Margaret Thatcher*, Volume 1: *The Grocer's Daughter* (London: Vintage, 2007). The experience hardened her heart and forged a lifelong sense of being an outsider. Ibid., p. 50. Staying on for a fourth year as a chemist, she became president of the Oxford University Conservative Association in Michaelmas 1946.
122. Harrison, 'Politics', p. 382.
123. David Walter, *The Oxford Union: Playground of Power* (London: Macdonald, 1984), p. 107.
124. Harrison, 'Politics', p. 382.
125. In a humiliating vote, he lost 750 to 138, one of the biggest Union majorities in history. See Joe Thompson, 'Atonement, Scapegoats, and the Oxford Debating Society', *The Kentucky Review*, vol. 5, no. 2, 1984.
126. Churchill was to claim during the war and in his history of the conflict that the vote had a significant impact on Italian and German decision-making, though historians have found little evidence to sustain this view. Martin Ceadel, 'The "King and Country" Debate, 1933: Student Politics, Pacificism, and the Dictators', *The Historical Journal*, vol. 22, no. 2, 1979.
127. *Oxford* (1941), part of the 'Films of Britain' series, film.britishcouncil.org/resources/film-archive/oxford.
128. Brockliss, *The University*, p. 342.
129. *Oxford and District Illustrated Guide Book*, p. 161.

RISING FASCISM, APPROACHING WAR

1. William Hayter, 'New College between the Two World Wars', in J. Buxton and P. Williams (eds), *New College Oxford, 1379–1979* (Oxford: New College Oxford, 1979), p. 109. Hayter was a New College undergraduate 1925–29, and warden from 1958.
2. Richard Hillary's chapter 'Under the Munich Umbrella', in *The Last Enemy*

(London: Macmillan, 1942), offers an excellent flavour of the student mood as he encountered it, made all the more penetrating by the fact that it was written in 1940–41.

3. Denis Healey, *The Time of My Life* (London: Michael Joseph, 1989), p. 34.
4. Ibid.
5. David Walter, *The Oxford Union: Playground of Power* (London: Macdonald, 1984), p. 73. Walter's chapter on the 1931–40 period offers an excellent overview of political Oxford at the time, and he offers a detailed analysis of the 1933 'King and Country' Union debate.
6. *New York Times*, 20 February 1934, www.nytimes.com/1934/02/20/archives/oxford-students-aid-hunger-march-several-hundred-carry-red-flags.html. For a picture of students heading the march through St Clement's, see www.getty-images.ae/detail/news-photo/oxford-undergraduates-join-lancashire-hunger-marchers-24-news-photo/1360181496.
7. R.C. Whiting, *The View from Cowley: The Impact of Industrialization upon Oxford, 1919–1939* (Oxford: Clarendon Press, 1983), p. 72.
8. Ibid., pp. 74–5. In contrast, Morris Motors was almost strike-free.
9. Chris Farman, Valery Rose and Liz Woolley, *No Other Way: Oxfordshire and the Spanish Civil War, 1936–39* (Oxford: Oxford International Brigade Memorial Committee, 2015), p. vii.
10. Felicity Heal (ed.), *Jesus College Oxford of Queen Elizabethes Foundation: The First 450 Years* (London: Jesus College and Profile Editions, 2021), p. 64.
11. Farman et al., *No Other Way*, p. 5.
12. Ibid., p. 32.
13. See the website of the Association for Basque Children, at www.basquechildren.org/colonies/aston.
14. Farman et al., *No Other Way*, pp. 32–3, and Meirian Jump, 'The Basque Refugee Children in Oxfordshire during the Spanish Civil War: Politically Charged Project or Humanitarian Endeavour?', *Oxoniensia*, 2007, p. 63.
15. This was organized by Denis Healey to raise funds for the cause. T. Buchanan, 'Foreword', in Farman et al., *No Other Way*, p. vi.
16. Edward Heath, *The Course of My Life: My Autobiography* (London: Hodder & Stoughton, 1998), p. 52.
17. Ibid. Lord Nuffield's pro-Franco position.
18. Hayter, 'New College', p. 109.
19. Farman et al., *No Other Way*, p. 37.
20. L.W.B. Brockliss, *The University of Oxford: A History* (Oxford: Oxford University Press, 2016), p. 341.
21. Kantorowicz was a historian of Germany and held a visiting professorship at Oxford in 1934. He visited again in 1938 when, in the aftermath of Kristallnacht, he decided he had to leave Germany, going on to establish himself in America. Of course, on personal matters such as Bowra's relationship with Kantorowicz, information is thin on the ground. I am informed here by Elisa Rolle's 'Queer Places' blog, www.elisarolle.com/queerplaces/ch-d-e/Ernst%20Kantorowicz.html.
22. Fran Lloyd, 'Becoming Artists: Ernst Eisenmayer, Kurt Weiler, and Refugee Support Networks in Wartime Oxford', in S. Crawford, K. Ulmschneider and J. Elsner (eds), *Ark of Civilization: Refugee Scholars and Oxford University, 1930–1945* (Oxford: Oxford University Press, 2017).
23. S. Blundell and M. Freeman (eds), *Mansfield: Portrait of an Oxford College* (London: Third Millennium, 2012), p. 21.
24. Ibid., p. 50. This is in a section by Alma Jenner, 'Mansfield at War'.

25. See Tom Buchanan, *Britain and the Spanish Civil War* (Cambridge: Cambridge University Press, 1997).

26. C. Hobhouse, *Oxford: As It Was and as It Is To-day* (London: Batsford, 1941–42), p. 105.

27. Brockliss, *The University of Oxford*, p. 435.

28. J. Winter, 'Oxford and the First World War', in B. Harrison (ed.), *The History of the University of Oxford*, Volume 8: *The Twentieth Century* (Oxford: Oxford University Press, 1994), pp. 24–5.

29. D. Walter, *The Oxford Union: Playground of Power* (London: Macdonald, 1984), p. 97.

30. Richard Freeman, Michael Foot, Frank Hardie and Keith Steel-Maitland, *Young Oxford and War* (London: Selwyn & Blount, 1934).

31. B. Harrison, 'Politics', in Harrison (ed.), *The History of the University of Oxford*, vol. 8, p. 391.

32. Lord Longford, *Avowed Intent: An Autobiography of Lord Longford* (London: Little, Brown, 1994), p. 71.

33. From the account of the meeting in the student magazine *Isis*. 'Statements following Oswald Mosley's meeting in Oxford', *Isis*, 27 May 1936, isismagazine.org.uk.

34. Quoted in the entry for 62–65 Cornmarket on the Oxford History website, www.oxfordhistory.org.uk/cornmarket/west/62_65_hsbc_bank.html.

35. Addison, 'Oxford and the Second World War', pp. 167–8. For an interesting perspective, see the section 'Spain, the 'Intellectual' Left, and the 1938 By-Election', in Whiting, *The View from Cowley*, p. 170.

36. P. and R. Malcolmson (eds), *A Vicar's Wife in Oxford, 1938–1943: The Diary of Madge Martin* (Woodbridge: Oxfordshire Record Society/Boydell Press, 2018), editor's note.

37. Ibid., p. 21.

38. Communists had swamped the Oxford Labour Club meeting and helped bring about Gordon Walker's withdrawal, those favouring this action believing that only a single 'anti-Munich' candidate running against Hogg would have a chance of overturning the Tory majority. Healey, *The Time of My Life*, p. 37.

39. 'Lord Lindsay and the Election of 1938', Keele University, www.keele.ac.uk/thekeeleoralhistoryproject/lordlindsayandtheelectionof1938.

40. The 1988 television drama-documentary *A Vote for Hitler* dramatized the events surrounding the by-election, John Woodvine playing Lindsay.

41. C.M. Bowra, *Memories, 1898–1939* (London: Weidenfeld & Nicolson, 1966), p. 350.

42. P. and R. Malcolmson (eds), *A Vicar's Wife*, diary entry 28 September 1938, p. 22.

43. D. Chapman, *Oxford Playhouse: High and Low Drama in a University City* (Hatfield: University of Hertfordshire Press, 2008), p. 117. The old Playhouse's last productions in Hilary 1938 included John Masefield and Nevill Coghill's *Oxford Summer Diversions*, featuring an appearance from Tolkien, with beard and robe, reciting Chaucer's 'The Nun's Priest's Tale'. Ibid., p. 110. The Oxford Playhouse had been here from 1923 until its move to the new theatre on Beaumont Street in 1938. The building had been built and opened in 1906 as the Big Game Museum, which shut in 1923.

44. P. and R. Malcolmson (eds), *A Vicar's Wife*, p. 22.

45. St Hugh's College archives (hereafter SHCA), *St Hugh's College Chronicle*, 1938–39, p. 9.

46. Ibid., pp. 9–10.

47. Farman et al., *No Other Way*, pp. 45–6.
48. Peter Conradi (ed.), *Iris Murdoch: A Writer at War, Letters and Diaries 1939–45* (London: Short Books, 2010), p. 81.
49. Winston Churchill, *His Father's Son: The Life of Randolph Churchill* (London: Phoenix, 1996), p. 166.
50. Ibid.
51. Ibid. See M. Ceadel, 'The "King and Country" Debate, 1933: Student Politics, Pacifism and the Dictators', *Historical Journal*, vol. 22, no. 2, 1979.
52. Barry Webb, *Edmund Blunden: A Biography* (New Haven CT and London: Yale University Press, 1990), p. 217.
53. Willis Nutting, 'The British Case', *The Review of Politics*, vol. 2, no. 2, 1940, p. 238. The titles published before the war in addition to Zimmern's concerned the British Empire and colonial raw materials (answering charges of British exploitation), a critique of *Mein Kampf*, economic self-sufficiency, 'encirclement', race in Europe, Versailles and the Fourteen Points, 'living space' and population problems, the 'refugee question', and the affairs of Turkey, Greece and the eastern Mediterranean and the 'Danubian basin'.
54. J. Darwin, 'A World University', in Harrison (ed.), *The History of the University of Oxford*, vol. 8, p. 612.
55. Ibid., p. 622.
56. J. Medawar and D. Pyke, *Hitler's Gift: Scientists Who Fled Nazi Germany* (London: Richard Cohen Books, 2000).
57. Anthony Grenville, 'The Jewish Scholars Who Found Safety among the Spires', *Jewish Renaissance*, October 2019, p. 22.
58. L. Brockliss, 'Welcoming and Supporting', in Crawford et al. (eds) *Ark of Civilization*, p. 62.
59. Ibid.
60. Beyond our scope, but through its work and other contacts Lindemann and Tizard fell out.
61. P. Adams, *Somerville for Women: An Oxford College, 1879–1993* (Oxford: Oxford University Press, 1996), p. 244.
62. Blundell and Freeman (eds), *Mansfield*, p. 50.
63. Thomas Charles-Edwards and Julian Reid (eds), *Corpus Christi College Oxford: A History* (Oxford: Oxford University Press, 2017), p. 371.
64. Buchan was a novelist and governor-general of Canada 1935–40. An Oxford graduate, he lived in the nearby village of Elsfield.
65. A.L. Rowse, *Oxford in the History of the Nation* (London: Weidenfeld & Nicolson, 1975), p. 222.
66. L. Brockliss, 'Welcoming and Supporting Refugee Scholars', in Crawford et al. (eds), *Ark of Civilization*, p. 69.
67. F. Lloyd, 'Becoming Artists', in Crawford et al. (eds), *Ark of Civilization*, p. 261.
68. The figure quoted in the *Jewish Chonicle*. Ibid., p. 262.
69. Farman et al., *No Other Way*, p. 39.
70. It is worth reflecting on the magnitude of the Academic Assistance Council's work in the 1930s and early war years. Today known as the Council for At-Risk Academics, its website offers a powerful summary: 'In all, some two thousand people were saved in those early years, and helped to build new lives. Sixteen won Nobel Prizes; eighteen were knighted; over one hundred became Fellows of The Royal Society or The British Academy. Their contribution to British scientific, intellectual and cultural life was enormous.' See www.cara.ngo/who-we-are/our-history.
71. Grenville, 'The Jewish Scholars', p. 22.

72. SHCA, *St Hugh's College Chronicle*, 1938–39, p. 26. Dunn writes that it assisted 2,600 Jewish scholars over a six-year period.
73. Brockliss, *The University of Oxford*, p. 524. See this section for information on the scholars assisted.
74. R.A. Denniston, 'Publishing and Bookselling', in Harrison (ed.), *The History of the University of Oxford*, vol. 8, p. 462.
75. Kate Lowe, '"I Shall Snuffle About and Make Relations": Nicolai Rubinstein, the Historian of Renaissance Florence, in Oxford during the War', in Crawford et al. (eds), *Ark of Civilization*.
76. See Anthony Grenville, 'Academic Refugees in Wartime Oxford: An Overview', in Crawford et al. (eds), *Ark of Civilization*. When Einstein left for Princeton, he requested that his stipend be used to help other refugee scholars. Judith Curthoys, *The Cardinal's College: Christ Church, Chapter and Verse* (London: Profile Books, 2012), p. 309.
77. Editors' introduction, 'Oxford's Ark: Second World War Refugees in the Arts and Humanities', in Crawford et al. (eds), *Ark of Civilization*, p. 2.
78. P.H.J. Gosden, *Education in the Second World War: A Study in Policy and Administration* (London: Methuen, 1976), p. 144.
79. Ibid., p. 170. Of further significance in preparing the ground, the Universities and Colleges (Emergency Provisions) Act of September 1939 enabled Oxbridge to make freer use of endowment income. Ibid., p. 150.
80. Oxford University Archives (hereafter OUA), Bodleian Library, Oxford, UR6/CQ/11/4, file 1.
81. P. Hennessy, *Whitehall* (Lonon: Secker & Warburg, 1989), p. 97.
82. Gosden, *Education in the Second World War*, p. 143.
83. King's College London went to Birmingham, Bristol, Cambridge and Edinburgh; University College London to Aberystwyth and other locations; Goldsmiths to Nottingham, the London School of Economics and Birkbeck College; Queen Mary's College, the School of Oriental and African Studies, Bedford College and St Bart's to Cambridge; and Westfield College and the Slade School of Fine Art to Oxford.
84. This was a considerable achievement, as was the fact that 'once war broke out he ensured that Oxford did not close down as it had in 1914, but rather offered short courses for students before they were called up'. Robin Darwall-Smith, 'George Gordon', *Dictionary of National Biography*.
85. Paul Addison, 'Oxford and the Second World War', in Harrison (ed.), *The History of the University of Oxford*, vol. 8, p. 169.
86. OUA, UR6/CQ/11, 13, file 1, minutes of heads of colleges meeting, 9/2/39.
87. Jones, *Balliol*, p. 278.
88. A. Sisman, *Hugh Trevor-Roper: The Biography* (London: Phoenix, 2011), p. 67.
89. The Board, appointed by Congregation, is responsible for overall supervision of the Museum.
90. 'Jesus College', in H.E. Salter and M. Lobel (eds), *A History of the County of Oxford*, Volume 3: *The University of Oxford* (London: Victoria County History, 1954); and Heal (ed.), *Jesus College Oxford of Queen Elizabethes Foundation*, p. 64.
91. Jeremy Catto (ed.), *Oriel College: A History* (Oxford: Oxford University Press, 2013), p. 692; and Charles-Edwards and Reid (eds), *Corpus*, p. 378.
92. SHCA, *St Hugh's College Chronicle,* 1938–39.
93. Robert Bruce, 'Deposits in the New Bodleian during the Second World War', *Bodleian Library Record*, vol. 26, no. 1, 2013. Luckily, in 1964 Dubber wrote a detailed account of what he and his colleagues had done. See 'War Deposits in the New Library, 1939–1945', 5/4/64. Library Records d. 1747.

94. Edmund Craster, *History of the Bodleian Library, 1845–1945* (Oxford: Clarendon Press, 1952), p. 342.
95. Malcolm Graham, *Oxfordshire at War* (Stroud: Alan Sutton, 1994), p. 6.
96. Ibid., p. 28.
97. OUA, UR6/CQ/11/3X, file 1, Oxford and District Joint Hospitals Board, Hospital Organization Committee memorandum, 5/6/39.
98. Pembroke College archives (hereafter PCA), PMB/J/1/68, Wartime requisition, 5/8/39–18/12/45.
99. Leslie Mitchell, *Maurice Bowra: A Life* (Oxford: Oxford University Press, 2010), p. 238.
100. At the same time, the Balliol Players, Roy Jenkins among them, toured a production of Aristophanes' *Birds* around a dozen schools and historic sites. Roy Jenkins, *A Life at the Centre* (London: Papermac, 1994), p. 33.
101. Launched in a BBC broadcast by the former prime minister (now chancellor of Cambridge) in December 1938 to raise money for the resettlement of Jewish children needing refuge from Nazism.
102. Conradi, *Iris Murdoch*, p. 21.
103. Ibid., p. 22.
104. Ibid., p. 68.
105. Ibid.
106. Bowra, *Memories*, p. 354.
107. Ibid., p. 355.
108. Ann Brown and Ruth Flanagan, 'The Ashmolean at War, Part One, 1939–1940', *The Ashmolean* 19, 1990–91, p. 19. Other material was packed and sent to Aberystwyth, transferred in February 1941 to Filkins Hall near Lechlade. Though moving its own treasures out, the museum accepted valuables from various colleges for safekeeping.
109. P. and R. Malcolmson (eds), *A Vicar's Wife*, p. 49.
110. Ibid., p. 50.
111. Humphrey Carpenter, *The Inklings: C.S. Lewis, J.R.R. Tolkien, Charles Williams* (London: HarperCollins, 1997), p. 68.
112. Ibid., pp. 67–8.
113. Ibid., p. 68.
114. W. Roger Louis, 'Reassessing the History of Oxford University Press, 1896–1970', in Louis (ed.), *The History of Oxford University Press*, Volume 3: *1896–1970* (Oxford: Oxford University Press, 2013), p. 24. It retained its premises in Neasden and the music department in Soho Square.
115. Sisman, *Hugh Trevor-Roper*, p. 76.
116. OUA, UR6/QC/11/1, file 1.
117. Frances Cairncross and Hannah Parham (eds), *Exeter College: The First 700 Years* (London: Exeter College and Third Millennium, 2013), p. 90.
118. 'Jesus College', in Salter and Lobel, *A History of the County of Oxford*, vol. 3.
119. Adam Sisman, *A.J.P. Taylor: A Biography* (London: Sinclair-Stevenson, 1994), p. 128.
120. Graham, *Oxfordshire at War*, p. 2.
121. P. and R. Malcolmson (eds), *A Vicar's Wife*, p. 51.
122. James Tobin, 'Hook Norton Brewery: A Brief History, 1849–2019', unpublished paper, 2019.
123. Ibid.
124. Eric Waldram Kemp, *The Life and Letters of Kenneth Escott Kirk, Bishop of Oxford 1937–1954* (London: Hodder & Stoughton, 1959), p. 83.
125. In 1941 Brander joined the Empire Department of the BBC as Eastern Intelligence Officer.

126. Webb, *Edmund Blunden*, p. 219.

127. Ibid.

128. Sisman, *A.J.P. Taylor*, p. 128.

CONSCRIPTION AND REQUISITIONING

1. Margaret Rayner, *The Centenary History of St Hilda's College, Oxford* (London: Lindsay Ross Publishing, 1993), p. 79.

2. P. and R. Malcolmson (eds), *A Vicar's Wife in Oxford, 1938–1943: The Diary of Madge Martin* (Woodbridge: Oxfordshire Record Society/Boydell Press, 2018), p. 52.

3. James Tobin, 'Hook Norton Brewery: A Brief History, 1849–2019', unpublished paper, 2019. The brewery hosted other units during the course of the war, including troops from the Royal Artillery, the Royal Corps of Signals, the Royal Pioneer Corps and the Gordon Highlanders.

4. Brigid Allen, *Morrells of Oxford: The Family and Their Brewery, 1743–1993* (Oxford: Oxfordshire Books, 1994). pp. 118–19. From stately home security, the Morrells then living at the Hall 'experienced a sudden adjustment to a world in which solid Victorian comforts could no longer be taken for granted'. The accumulations of a prosperous manor house were rapidly flogged off as an era in one wealthy family's history drew sharply to a close: the glass cases of stuffed birds, the satinwood drawing-room furniture and Axminster carpet, grand piano and oriental china all went, as did the billiards table, oil paintings of hounds and horses, the landau, the brougham and the bath chair.

5. Humphrey Carpenter, *The Inklings: C.S. Lewis, J.R.R. Tolkien, Charles Williams and Their Friends* (London: HarperCollins, 1997), p. 69. A week after moving all his books Lewis was told his rooms wouldn't be needed after all, so he had to move all of his belongings back.

6. Jeremy Catto (ed.), *Oriel College: A History* (Oxford: Oxford University Press, 2013), p. 74.

7. Roy Jenkins, *A Life at the Centre* (London: Papermac, 1994). p. 34.

8. P. and R. Malcolmson (eds), *A Vicar's Wife*, p. 53.

9. Edmund Craster, *History of the Bodleian Library, 1845–1945* (Oxford: Clarendon Press, 1952), p. 341.

10. A.L. Rowse, *Oxford in the History of the Nation* (London: Weidenfeld & Nicolson, 1975), p. 260.

11. Malcolm Graham, *Oxfordshire at War* (Stroud: Alan Sutton, 1994), p. 100.

12. Robin Brooks, *Oxfordshire Airfields in the Second World War* (Newbury: Countryside Books, 2001), p. 189.

13. Nigel Dawe, *Tubney Wood at War: The Hush-Hush Factory* (Kingston Bagpuize: Thematic Trails, 2014).

14. Dora Saint, aka Miss Read, based her Thrush Green novels on Witney and its surrounds, living there during the war with her husband, who was in the RAF.

15. When the Ministry of Aircraft Production was formed with the coming of the Churchill administration, its head, Beaverbrook, removed control from the Air Ministry (and Nuffield) to ensure that the vital matter of repairing damaged aircraft and engines – by civilian companies as well as the RAF itself – all came under that Ministry's umbrella, something he pushed through within six weeks. See Anne Chisholm and Michael Davis, *Beaverbrook: A Life* (London: Hutchinson, 1992), p. 377. He also took over Nuffield's aircraft factory at Castle Bromwich, which ended up producing 11,500 Spitfires between June 1940 and November 1945. Ibid., p 386.

16. Brooks, *Oxfordshire Airfields*, p. 205.

17. Graham, *Oxfordshire at War*, p. 99.

18. It also made Centaur tanks as well as Salamander and Neptune amphibious fighting vehicles and Sherman Firefly anti-tank tanks.
19. PCA, PMB/J/1/68, Wartime requisition, 5/8/39–18/12/45.
20. P. Addison, 'Oxford and the Second World War', in Brian Harrison (ed.), *The History of the University of Oxford*, Volume 8: *The Twentieth Century* (Oxford: Oxford University Press, 1994), p. 145.
21. Ibid., p. 169.
22. OUA, UR6/QC/11/1, file 1, Vice-Chancellor's note on national service, 2/3/39.
23. PCA, PMB/J/1/68, Wartime requisition, 5/8/39–18/12/45, message from George Gordon, 7/9/39.
24. Addison, 'Oxford and the Second World War', p. 167.
25. The University Archives has a number of files on this subject.
26. Addison, 'Oxford and the Second World War', p. 167.
27. Denis Healey, *The Time of My Life* (London: Michael Joseph, 1989). p. 44.
28. Ibid., p. 45.
29. I'm not entirely sure if it was the same place, but Yeomanry House, Manor Road, was the address used in correspondence by Major J.D.T. Eve, No. 2 Sub Area Quartering Commandant. The UOTC was sometimes known as the Senior Officers' Training Corps, the 'junior' ones being the OTCs that large numbers of undergraduates had been part of at public school.
30. He produced pocket-sized anthologies of literature and poetry that were popular with soldiers (*Diversions* and *More Diversions*).
31. PCA, PMB/v/1/2/6, World War Two roll of service, general papers, 1940–45.
32. Douglas Ross, 'A War Year: 1941–42 (Part 2)', *Pembroke College Record*, 1993.
33. Eversley Belfield, 'Further Pembroke Recollections', *Pembroke College Record*, 1983.
34. Other sources suggest that the University Air Squadron was based on St Cross Road and used Kidlington aerodrome.
35. Richard Hillary, *The Last Enemy* (London: Michael O'Mara Books, 2014), p. 18. First published by Macmillan in 1942.
36. John Harper-Nelson, *Oxford at War: An Undergraduate Memoir, John Harper-Nelson, 1940–42* (Northbridge, Western Australia: Access Press, 1996), p. 85.
37. Ibid.
38. Ibid., p. 127.
39. Nathan Stazicker, 'Memories of 1939: Lieutenant Tom Roberts', *Hertford College Library & Archives Blog*, 10 November 2021, hertford.ox.ac.uk/library-archives/tom-roberts.
40. PCA, PMB/P/6/4/3, 'University of Oxford War Decrees'.
41. Addison, 'Oxford and the Second World War', pp. 171–2.
42. Philip Larkin, *Jill* (London: Faber & Faber, 2005), p. vii. The introduction was written in 1963.
43. Rowse, *Oxford in the History of the Nation*, p. 263.
44. Addison, 'Oxford and the Second World War', p. 169.
45. Ibid., p. 177.
46. Ibid., p. 176.
47. Ibid., p. 175.
48. Ibid.
49. Hebdomadal Council had a Committee on the Financial Arrangements for Royal Navy, Royal Corps of Signals, and RAF Probationers' Courses.
50. *Worcester College Record*, 1939–44. This edition, published in 1944, was the first since 1938.

51. Clare Hopkins, *Trinity: 450 Years of an Oxford College Community* (Oxford: Oxford University Press, 2005). Over 3,000 probationers and cadets had matriculated by 1942. Daniel Greenstein, 'The Junior Members, 1900–1990: A Profile', in B. Harrison (ed.), *The History of the University of Oxford*, vol. 8, p. 48.
52. Addison, 'Oxford and the Second World War', p 180.
53. Ken Coombe, 'Undergraduate 1945, Graduate 1981: An Adventure', *Worcester College Record*, 1982.
54. Ibid.
55. Anthony Croft, 'Oxford's Clarendon Laboratory' (Oxford: Department of Physics, 1986), p. 89.
56. Robin Darwall-Smith, 'Univ. during the Second World War', *University College Record*, 2005.
57. P.H.J. Gosden, *Education in the Second World War: A Study in Policy and Administration* (London: Methuen, 1976), p. 154.
58. UOA, UR6/CQ/11/2a, file 1, Vice-Chancellor to senior members, 29/4/39.
59. Denniston was a founder of the 'Room 40' codebreaking unit in the previous war and was now deputy head of the Government Code and Cypher School.
60. UOA, UR6/CQ/11/2a, file 1, Vice-Chancellor to senior members, 29/4/39.
61. Ibid.
62. PCA, PMB/J/1/68, Wartime requisition, 5/8/39–18/12/45, 7/9/39.
63. Ibid.
64. Addison, 'Oxford and the Second World War', pp. 170, 192.
65. Ibid., p. 175.
66. Gosden, *Education in the Second World War*, p. 142.
67. PCA, PMB/v/1/2/6, World War Two roll of service, general papers, 1940–1945, press cutting, 11/9/40.
68. Addison, 'Oxford and the Second World War', p. 173.
69. J. Harris, 'The Arts and Social Sciences, 1919–1939', in Harrison (ed.), *The History of the University of Oxford*, vol. 8, p. 220.
70. Gosden, *Education in the Second World War*, p. 147.
71. Ibid., p. 148.
72. Ibid.
73. Ibid., pp. 150–51.
74. Ibid., p. 156.
75. Ibid., p. 157.
76. Michael Heffernan and Heike Jöns, 'Degrees of Influence: The Politics of Honorary Degrees in the Universities of Oxford and Cambridge, 1900–2000', *Minerva*, vol. 45, no. 4, 2007, p. 396.
77. Ibid., pp. 397–8.
78. 'The President Sends a Message to the Special Convocation of the University of Oxford Held at the Harvard Commencement on the Award of the Degree of Doctor of Civil Law, June 19, 1941', Franklin D. Roosevelt Presidential Library and Museum, Box 61, Master Speech File', www.fdrlibrary.marist.edu/_resources/images/msf/msf01432.
79. See Ashley Jackson, 'Winston Churchill, Oxfordshire, and Ditchley Park', *Finest Hour: The Journal of Winston Churchill* 165, 2014.
80. See Graham, *Oxfordshire at War*, p. 34.
81. PCA, PMB/J/1/68, Wartime requisition, 5/8/39–18/12/45, Hart-Synnot to bursars of four 'Halls for men', the St Catherine's Society, and the five women's colleges, 7/11/39, Compensation (Defence) Act 1939. Hart-Synnot to bursars of requisitioned colleges, 5/3/40. Sometimes referred to as the Committee on the Use of University and College Buildings in a National Emergency.

82. PCA, PMB/J/1/66, Wartime requisition, 12/4/40–30/1/47, Noel Dean, 'Report on Rental Values of Accommodation in Various University and College Buildings at Oxford Requisitioned by His Majesty's Government in the Exercise of Emergency Powers' (March 1940).

83. Harris Manchester College archives (hereafter HMCA), MS.3 World War II, Hart-Synott to bursar, 4/12/41.

84. Addison, 'Oxford and the Second World War', p. 170.

85. PCA, PMB/J/1/69 Wartime Requisition – Emergency Pool, 29/9/39–25/3/47, Registrar to HofHs, 29/9/39.

86. PCA, PMB/J/1/68, Wartime requisition, 5/8/39–18/12/45, memorandum, 12/9/39.

87. OUA, UR6/CQ/11/FD, file one, Veale to Francis Lys, Provost of Worcester, 5/7/39.

88. OUA, UR6/CQ/11, LC, file 1, Arthur Munro to Veale, 10/12/42.

89. OUA, UR6/CQ/11, 13, file 1, Memorandum of Hebdomadal Council committee on the use of University and college buildings in a national emergency, 12/9/39.

90. Christopher Tyerman (ed.), *New College* (London: Third Millennium, 2010), p. 119.

91. OUA, UR6/CQ/11/LC, file 1, Keith Murray to Veale, 15/5/45.

92. OUA, UR6/CQ/11/FD, file 1.

93. Peter Hennessy, *Whitehall* (London: Secker & Warburg, 1989), p. 115.

94. OUA, UR6/CQ/11/13, file 1, St John's ground floor plan and key.

95. Judith Curthoys, *The Cardinal's College: Christ Church, Chapter and Verse* (London: Profile Books, 2012), p. 314.

96. 'University College', in H.E. Salter and M. Lobel (eds), *A History of the County of Oxford*, Volume 3: *The University of Oxford* (London: Victoria County History, 1954).

97. Thomas Charles-Edwards and Julian Reid (eds), *Corpus Christi College Oxford: A History* (Oxford: Oxford University Press, 2017), p. 379.

98. Clare Hopkins, *Trinity: 450 Years of an Oxford College Community* (Oxford: Oxford University Press, 2005), p. 384.

99. Ibid.

100. Ibid., p. 387.

101. Catto (ed.), *Oriel*, p. 743. In Michaelmas 1942 Oriel had seventy-eight students, only twenty living in college.

102. Ibid., p. 692.

103. PCA, PMB J/1/68, wartime requisition.

104. SEHA, *St Edmund Hall Magazine*, 1939.

105. PCA, PMB J/1/68, wartime requisition.

106. Candida Lycett Green (ed.), *John Betjeman: Letters*, Volume 1: *1926–1951* (London: Methuen, 2006). He would cycle out for weekends at 'Colonel' Kolkhorst's home at Yarnton Manor. When the council offices moved to Blenheim late in the war, he would cycle through Bladon Woods and into the palace's grounds.

107. OUA, UR6/CQ/11/OC, file 1, Ministry of Works to Veale, 30/9/43.

108. L.W.B. Brockliss (ed.), *Magdalen College Oxford: A History* (Oxford: Magdalen College, 2008), pp. 739–40. The anecdote was offered up by a woman attending the Kellogg–Bletchley Park Week 2023.

109. OUA, UR6/CQ/11/MER, file 1, Newboult to Veale, 14/2/45.

110. G.H. Martin and J.R.L. Hughfield, *A History of Merton College* (Oxford: Oxford University Press, 1997), p. 340.

111. OUA, UR6/CQ/11/MER, file 1, Veale to Newboult, 25/9/42.
112. PCA, PMB J/1/6/8, Secretary of the Domestic Bursars' Committee, 21/11/41.

LIVING UNDER REQUISITION

1. Queen's College Archives (hereafter QCA), *The Queen's College Record*, vol. II, no. 7, 1939, 'The Provost's Letter'. Purists would have it 'The Queen's College', but 'Queen's' or 'Queen's College' is used here.
2. Ibid.
3. Ibid.
4. '"A Shadow of its Real Self": Brasenose during the World Wars', www.bnc.ox.ac.uk/about-brasenose/history/214-college-life/421-college-life-in-wartime.
5. Ann Thwaite (ed.), *My Oxford* (London: Robson Books, 1977), pp. 142–3.
6. BCA, W.T. Coxhill, 'BNC Under War Conditions, September 1939–September 1945'. Subtitled 'Some of the Minor Events Which Happened – Mainly from the Bursarial Point of View'. Coxhill was a clerk in the Bursary, later Keeper of the Archives.
7. Ibid.
8. Ibid.
9. Principal Stallybrass had apparently tried pulling strings in the Lord Chancellor's Office, probably to stop it being taken over by the military (as was to happen). J. Mordaunt Crook, *Brasenose: The Biography of an Oxford College* (Oxford: Oxford University Press, 2010), p. 370.
10. University Archive correspondence suggests that for the 'junior' requirement early in the war, activity in Brasenose came under the Liaison Wing at Sandhurst and also involved the Liaison School, Officer Cadet Training Unit, at Camberley.
11. Philip Notestine, '117th Cavalry Reconnaissance Squadron (Mecz) in World War II January 6, 1941–May 18, 1945 and Occupation' (2007), mcoecbamcoep-wprdo1.blob.core.usgovcloudapi.net/library/ABOLC_BA_2018/Research_Module_A/Montreval/117th_CRS_Ops.pdf.
12. OUA, UR6/CQ/11, 13, file 1, Veale to J.G. Cook, Rating of Government Property Department, October 1939.
13. P. Addison, 'Oxford and the Second World War', in Brian Harrison (ed.), *The History of the University of Oxford*, Volume 8: *The Twentieth Century* (Oxford: Oxford University Press, 1994), p. 170.
14. Mansfield College archives (hereafter MCA), *Mansfield College, Oxford Calendar, 1940–41*.
15. Ibid.
16. Ibid.
17. MCA, *Mansfield College Magazine* 116, 1940.
18. Wilson was a junior research fellow at Univ, and since 1938 had been helping William Beveridge in his research on employment patterns. He often attended chapel and Congregational Society meetings at Mansfield. Elaine Kaye, *Mansfield College Oxford: Its Origin, History, and Significance* (Oxford: Oxford University Press, 1996), p. 211n.
19. MCA, *Mansfield College Magazine* 118, 1941.
20. The National Archives (hereafter TNA), Kew, London, HW 40/262, Allied Codes and Cypers, Misc – Correspondence – OUP and Mansfield College, Production of codes and cyphers, Hok to D. G. Robertson, Treasury, 8/10/41. The expansion of its Mansfield operations would allow the unit to make 'a very much larger number of the smaller editions which besides being rapidly on the increase are beginning to clog our printers'. TNA, HW 40/260, Records: Allied

Codes and Cyphers: Miscellaneous correspondence: OUP and Mansfield College, Section 47B to E.W. Tavis, 2/1/41.

21. Ibid.

22. OUA, UR6/CQ/11/FD, file 1, Ministry of Works to Veale, 28/11/42.

23. Stephen Blundell and Michael Freeman (eds), *Mansfield: Portrait of an Oxford College* (London: Third Millennium, 2012), p. 51.

24. SHCA, *St Hugh's College Chronicle*, 1939–40.

25. Ibid.

26. SHCA, Ref File, P. Thomson (1940) memoir.

27. Ibid., 'Principal's Letter', *St Hugh's Chronicle*, 1940–41, p. 8.

28. Ibid.

29. Ibid.

30. 'History of the Intelligence Corps, www.89fss.com/int_corps.htm. By the end of the war the Corps numbered around 3,000 officers and 6,500 other ranks.

31. See Anthony Clayton, *Forearmed: A History of the Intelligence Corps* (London: Brassey's, 1995), and Nick van der Bijl, *Sharing the Secret: The History of the Intelligence Corps, 1940–2010* (Barnsley: Pen & Sword, 2013).

32. OUA, UR6/CQ/11/OC, file 1, Veale note, 3/12/40.

33. Anthony Leatherdale, 'Pembroke in World War II', *Pembroke College Record*, 1997–98.

34. Douglas Ross, 'A War Year: 1941–42 (Part 2)', *Pembroke College Record*, 1993.

35. James Cobban, 'The Secret War at Pembroke', *Pembroke College Record*, 1993.

36. *Pembroke College Record*, 1947. For an overview, see Brian Short, 'War in the Fields and Villages: The County War Agricultural Committees in England, 1939–45', *Rural History*, vol. 18, no. 2, 2007.

37. Margaret Rayner, *The Centenary History of St Hilda's College, Oxford* (London: Lindsay Ross Publishing, 1993), p. 79.

38. The Infirmary erected five huts in its grounds, each accommodating forty patients. OUA, UR6/CQ/11/3X, file 1, Oxford and District Hospitals Board, Hospital Organization Committee, 26/9/39.

39. Pauline Adams, 'Somerville and the "Isle of Man", 1939–1945', in *Somerville for Women: An Oxford College, 1879–1993* (Oxford: Oxford University Press, 1996), ch. 11.

40. OUA, UR6/CR/11/HMR, file 1.

41. HMCA, MS. 3 World War II, Ministry of Works to Nicol Cross, 17/10/41.

42. Ibid., Gimson to Nicol Cross, 23/2/43.

43. HMCA, House Committee minutes.

44. Ibid., Nicol Cross to A. Wynn Kendrick, 24/10/41.

45. Ibid., Bassett to Nicol Cross, 30/12/42.

46. Ibid., Bassett to Nicol Cross, 8/5/43.

47. Christopher Andrew, *The Defence of the Realm: The Authorized History of MI5* (London: Penguin, 2010), p. 231.

48. See Geoffrey Young's charming obituary for this man in the *Alpine Journal* 56, 1948, p. 279, www.alpinejournal.org.uk/Contents/Contents_1948_files/AJ56%201948%20264–284%20In%20Memoriam.pdf.

49. OUA, UR6/CQ/11/K, file 1, Heywood to Veale, 24/8/40.

50. Ibid.

51. Ibid., Veale to de Normann, 29/8/40.

52. Sometimes he had occasion to gently rebuke colleges for similarly discussing requisition matters directly with government departments rather than going through the agreed-upon 'proper channels'. Such a correspondence exists in this file, between Veale and Hart-Synnot of St John's. Of course, there was bound

NOTES 317

sometimes to be contact between a college and a department or other institution seeking Oxford accommodation and facilities. But the thing to do was to then involve Veale and the University authorities. This is just what the principal of LMH, Lynda Grier, did when her friend and former pupil, Geraldine 'Gem' Jebb, principal of Bedford College, London, approached her about the prospect of moving her college to LMH. Veale didn't discourage her, actually welcoming the idea, and stating categorically that the rumoured use of LMH as a 'hospital for shell-shock cases' would not take place. In the end, Bedford went to Girton College Cambridge. See OUA, UR6/CQ/11/LMH, file 1, Grier to Veale, 12/5/39.

53. Ibid.
54. Liddle Hart Centre for Military Archives, King's College London, Papers of Brigadier Vivian Street, Annette Street, 'Long Ago and Far Away', manuscript memoir.
55. Ibid.
56. Andrew, *The Defence of the Realm*.
57. Ibid., p. 234.
58. OUA, UR6/CQ/11/K, file 1, Heywood to Veale, 19/9/40.
59. Ibid., Heywood to Veale, 20/12/40.
60. Ibid.
61. Jeri Bapasola, *John Piper at Blenheim Palace* (Woodstock: Blenheim Palace, 2012), p. 6.
62. Jonathan Bate and Jessica Goodman, *Worcester: Portrait of an Oxford College* (London: Third Millennium, 2014), p. 72.
63. Hugo Jones, '1939: A Memory of Worcester', in ibid., p. 75.
64. Ken Coombe, 'Undergraduate 1945, Graduate 1981: An Adventure', *Worcester College Record*, 1982.
65. WCA, *Worcester College Record*, 1939–44. Lys's house in Pullen Lane, Headington, was occupied by the military.
66. WCA, *Worcester College Record*, 1943.
67. R.L.P. Milburn, 'The French Naval, Military and Air Force Missions, 1940', *Worcester College Record*, 1988.
68. Ibid.
69. SEHA, *St Edmund Hall Magazine*, 1943–48.
70. SEHA, *St Edmund Hall Magazine*, 1940.
71. OUA, UR6/CQ/11, 13, file 1, Veale to McWatters, 9/12/39.
72. OUA, UR6/CQ/11, 13, file 1.
73. Ibid., Veale to Landon, 30/11/39.
74. He was responsible for managing St John's extensive agricultural estate and the completion of its North Oxford urban estate, and schemes such as Oxford's first large block of flats, Belsyre Court, and the establishment of the Playhouse on Beaumont Street. See Malcolm Vale, 'The Bursarship: St John's and its Bursars', *TW: The Magazine of St John's College, Oxford*, 2021.
75. OUA, UR6/CQ/11, 13, file 1, Hart-Synnot to Veale, 18/11/39.
76. PCA, PMB/J/165, Wartime requisition, 30/10/39–10/7/46, Veale to Salt, 11/12/39.
77. PCA, PMB J/1/68, Wartime requisition, 5/8/39–18/12/45.
78. Ibid.
79. OUA, UR6/CQ/11/MER, file 1, Newboult to Veale, 1/3/41.
80. Ibid.
81. HMCA, MS.3 World War II, Principal to Office of Works, 28/6/43.
82. Ibid., exchange between Nicol Cross and Ministry of Works, June 1945.

83. Ibid., MS. 3 World War II, Gimson to Nicol Cross, 28/4/42.

84. Ibid., General Committee minutes, 28/9/42.

85. Andrew, *The Defence of the Realm*, p. 232.

86. Addison, 'Oxford and the Second World War', p. 170.

87. Ibid., p. 179.

88. Balliol College archives, 'Short Leave Courses at Balliol during World War Two'. See www.flickr.com/photos/balliolarchivist/albums/72157625279691367.

89. Alice Blackford Millea, *Oxford University: Stories from the Archives* (Oxford: Bodleian Library Publishing, 2022), p. 160.

90. OUA, UR6/CQ/11/II, file 1.

91. OUA, UR6/CQ/11/ES, file 1, Veale to Whitelocke, 9/9/39. This is how Whitelocke, an RAMC officer, styled himself on the requisition form. Oxford people writing at the time refer to the 16th General Hospital, which tallies with other material showing that this unit was at Oxford at the start of the war.

92. Ibid., Veale to Craster, 27/9/39.

93. Ibid., Major J.D.T. Evans to Veale, 30/10/40.

94. A.L. Rowse, *Oxford in the History of the Nation* (London: Weidenfeld & Nicolson, 1975), p. 260.

95. Ibid., pp. 260–61.

96. Giles Barber, 'Libraries', in Harrison (ed.), *The History of the University of Oxford*, vol. 8, p. 478.

97. SHCA, 'Report of the Annual Meeting of the Association, 1941', *St Hugh's College Chronicle*, 1941–42, p. 7.

98. Ibid., 'News of Senior Members who are engaged in war-work'.

99. During the transformation of the New Bodleian into the Weston Library (opened in 2015), builders discovered correspondence with POWs.

100. 'Weston Library Workers Discover Remnants of Wartime Book Service', www.bodleian.ox.ac.uk/bodley/news/2013/wartime-book-service.

101. W. Roger Louis, 'Reassessing the History of Oxford University Press, 1896–1970', in Louis (ed.), *The History of Oxford University Press*, Volume 3: *1896–1970* (Oxford: Oxford University Press, 2013), p. 24.

102. TNA, HW 40/271, GC&CS Records, Allied Codes and Cypers. Misc. – Correspondence – OUP and Mansfield College, A. Cadogan, 1/12/42.

103. TNA, HW 40/270 Allied Codes & Cyphers, Misc. Correspondence – OUP and Mansfield Coll; Accts.

104. R.A. Denniston, 'Publishing and Bookselling', in Harrison (ed.), *A History of the University of Oxford*, vol. 8, p. 462.

105. Elizabeth Longford, 'Margaret Godfrey', obituary, *Independent*, 1 November 1995.

106. Louis, 'Reassessing the History of Oxford University Press, 1896–1970', p. 5.

107. TNA, HW 40/261, Records: Allied Codes and Cypers: Miscellaneous correspondence: OUP and Mansfield College: Printing presses, undated and unsigned letter.

108. Brockliss claims that all but 5 per cent of its output was war work. W.B. Brockliss, *The University of Oxford: A History* (Oxford: Oxford University Press, 2016), p. 520.

109. Ibid.

110. Addison, 'Oxford and the Second World War', p. 169.

111. See Flora Thompson, 'Lark Rise to Candleford', Oxford University Press Archive, 2008.

112. Paul Sullivan, *The Little History of Oxfordshire* (Stroud: History Press, 2019), p. 201.

113. About a dozen new Biggles books appeared during the war.
114. Eric Waldram Kemp, *The Life and Letters of Kenneth Escott Kirk, Bishop of Oxford 1937–1954* (London: Hodder & Stoughton, 1959), p. 81. The incumbent considered Cuddesdon too distant from Oxford and not well connected by public transport, so in February 1938 he had moved to a house on Boars Hill, 'Sandridge', owned by the University.
115. PCA, PMB/J/1/58, Wartime requisition, 5/8/30—18/12/45, Whinney, Smith, and Whinney to chairs, Bursars' Committee N, 5/2/40.
116. L.W.B. Brockliss (ed.), *Magdalen College Oxford: A History* (Oxford: Magdalen College, 2008), p. 610. The Alfred, Bertie and Churchill lodges also met there. SEHA, *St Edmund Hall Magazine*, 1943–48. Apollo is the University lodge.
117. HMCA, MS.4 World War II, unsigned letter, 18/10/41.
118. Ibid., letter, 19/10/41.
119. Ibid., letter, 31/10/41.

THREAT, WORRY AND EVACUATION

1. P. Addison, 'Oxford and the Second World War', in Brian Harrison (ed.), *The History of the University of Oxford*, Volume 8: *The Twentieth Century* (Oxford: Oxford University Press, 1994). After spending the academic year 1939–40 at Oxford, Stokes left to join up, never returning to complete his studies. archive-cat.magd.ox.ac.uk/records/P398.
2. SHCA, Reference file, Francis Lloyd (1938) memoir.
3. Malcolm Graham, *Oxfordshire at War* (Stroud: Alan Sutton, 1994), p. 10.
4. Richard Ollard (ed.), *The Diaries of A.L. Rowse* (London: Penguin, 2004), p. 101.
5. SHCA, Reference file, Laura Clish (1938) memoir.
6. P. and R. Malcolmson (eds), *A Vicar's Wife in Oxford, 1938–1943: The Diary of Madge Martin* (Woodbridge: Oxfordshire Record Society/Boydell Press, 2018), p. 61.
7. Ibid., pp. 79–80.
8. Zachary Leader, *The Life of Kingsley Amis* (London: Vintage, 2007), p. 93.
9. Oxfordshire Historical Centre (hereafter OHC), Oxford, Weekly reports, from the County Controller (submitted to the principal officer at the Ministry of Home Security in Reading) and the Oxford Police Chief Constable (submitted to the under-secretary of state at the Police Duty Room HQ in Whitehall), reports from 25/11/40 and 10/5/41.
10. QCA, *Queen's College Record*, vol. II, no. 7, 1939.
11. Frances Cairncross and Hannah Parham (eds), *Exeter College: The First 700 Years* (London: Exeter College and Third Millennium, 2013), p. 90.
12. Jeremy Catto (ed.), *Oriel College: A History* (Oxford: Oxford University Press, 2013), p. 692.
13. G.H. Martin and J.R.L. Hughfield, *A History of Merton College* (Oxford: Oxford University Press, 1997), p. 341.
14. Clare Hopkins, *Trinity: 450 Years of an Oxford College Community* (Oxford: Oxford University Press, 2005), p. 390.
15. John Harper-Nelson, *Oxford at War: An Undergraduate Memoir, John Harper-Nelson, 1940–42* (Northbridge, Western Australia: Access Press, 1996), p. 28.
16. Margaret Rayner, *The Centenary History of St Hilda's College, Oxford* (London: Lindsay Ross Publishing, 1993), p. 80.
17. Judith Curthoys, *The Cardinal's College: Christ Church, Chapter and Verse* (London: Profile Books, 2012), p. 314.
18. Some of it enforced; Magdalen's stained glass received damage during the removal process.

19. Christopher Woodforde, *The Stained Glass of New College, Oxford* (London: Oxford University Press, 1951), p. 63. The misericords were also removed from the chapel.
20. Dorothy Erskine Muir, *Oxford* (London: Blackie, n.d. [*c.* 1951]), p. 47.
21. C.S.L. Davies and Jane Garnett, *Wadham College* (Oxford: Wadham College, 1994), p. 110.
22. Ibid., p. 76.
23. Eric Lax, *The Mould in Dr Florey's Coat: The Remarkable True Story of the Penicillin Miracle* (London: Abacus, 2005), p. 4.
24. Addison, 'Oxford and the Second World War', p. 174.
25. Reader Bullard, *The Camel Must Go: An Autobiography* (London: Faber & Faber, 1961), p. 225.
26. Christopher Hibbert (ed.), *The Encyclopaedia of Oxford* (London: Macmillan, 1988), p. 240.
27. Available at McMaster University Digital Archive, digitalarchive.mcmaster.ca/islandora/object/macrepo%3A66508.
28. Caroline Shenton, *National Treasures: Saving the Nation's Art in World War II* (London: John Murray, 2022), p. 208.
29. Norman Longmate, *If Britain Had Fallen* (London: BBC and Arrow Books, 1975), p. 143.
30. Ibid.
31. 'Our History', www.ouh.nhs.uk/hospitals/churchill/history.aspx.
32. Graham, *Oxfordshire at War*, p. 20.
33. Radley History Club, World War Two memories.
34. Loraine Calvert, 'My Life during World War II: Coventry Cathedral and Torpedo-Checking', BBC World War Two People's War oral history archive, A2047907. Her father was a chief inspector for torpedoes being made at the Cowley works and the Standard Motor Company in Coventry.
35. D. Ross, 'A War Year: 1941–42 (Part II)', *Pembroke College Record*, 1993.
36. Hopkins, *Trinity*, p. 390.
37. Malcolm Reeves, 'Childhood and Evacuation', BBC World War Two People's War oral history archive, A4456749.
38. SHCA, Alastair Robb-Smith to Principal, 7/7/95 and to Lady Meadow, 17/5/88. He was a former assistant director of pathology at the Infirmary, and wrote a history of it.
39. Jonathan Bate and Jessica Goodman, *Worcester: Portrait of an Oxford College* (London: Third Millennium, 2014), p. 72.
40. QCA, *Queen's College Record*, vol. II, no. 8, 1941.
41. HMCA, General Committee minutes, 10/2/41.
42. Imperial War Museum sound archive, Peggy Lecroat interview, IWM 26753. The house was destroyed by fire in 1972, and on the site of house and grounds now stands Rolfe Place. Documents refer to the Harberton House establishment variously as an 'RAF Distributing Centre' and the 'Air Ministry Code and Cipher School', part of the 'Oxford Clerk and Dispatch School'; also of an 'RAF Regional Control School' at Brasenose.
43. She was bringing an Airspeed Oxford south from RAF Squires Gate.
44. Nigel Fisher and Keith Kirby, *A Guide to Wytham Woods: The Natural Place for Science* (Oxford: Wytham Woods, 2022), pp. 58–60.
45. George Lambrick, *An Illustrated Guide to the Rollright Stones* (Oxford: The Rollright Trust, 2017), p. 18.
46. C.P. Stacey, *The Canadian Army, 1939–1945: An Official History Summary* (Ottawa: Minister of National Defence, 1948), p. 19.

47. Peter Fleming, *Invasion 1940: An Account of the German Preparations and the British Counter-Measures* (London: Rupert Hart-Davis, 1957), p. 58.
48. TNA, WO 197/88, Dynamo – Progress, Movement Control, War Office, Dynamo movement instruction, no. 1, 22/5/40.
49. Ibid.
50. J.E.H. Neville (ed.), *The Oxfordshire and Buckinghamshire Light Infantry Chronicle: The Record of the 43rd, 52nd, 4th, 5th, 6th, 7th, 70th, 1st and 2nd Buckinghamshire Battalions and Regimental Training Centre in the Second German War*, Volume 2: *June 1940–June 1942* (Aldershot: Gale & Polden, 1950), p. 92.
51. TNA, WO 199/2040, HQ Southern Command to HQ 5 Corps, 10/7/40.
52. Ibid., Reinforcement camps, from HQ Southern Command, 4/7/40.
53. Neville (ed.), *The Oxfordshire and Buckinghamshire Light Infantry Chronicle*, vol. 2, p. 95.
54. Peter Lester, 'War Time Memories of 1435021 AC Stanley Lester', BBC World War Two People's War oral history archive, A8867965, www.bbc.co.uk/history/ww2peopleswar/stories/65/a8867965.shtml.
55. SHCA, Reference file, Monica Melles (1939) memoir. Of course, having gone up in 1939, Monica's experience was already deeply affected by war because she was an exile from her requisitioned college.
56. Ibid., Mary Healey (1938) memoir.
57. TNA, WO 199/2040, HQ Southern Command to 5 Corps, 8 Corps, and 54th Division, 3/4/41.
58. TNA, WO 166/57, 'Stop Lines', from Southern Command HQ, 15/8/40.
59. Stacey, *The Canadian Army*, p. 18.
60. Andrew Stewart, 'Ten Days in Oxford: How Canadian Troops Defended Britain in 1940', part 2 (2017), www.swwresearch.com/post/ten-days-in-oxford-how-canadian-troops-defended-britain-in-1940–part-2.
61. Stacey, *The Canadian Army*, p. 18.
62. Ibid., p. 19.
63. Ibid.
64. Ibid. For tabular representations of the troops available for defence May–July 1940, see Edmund Ironside, *Ironside: The Authorised Biography of Field Marshal Lord Ironside* (Stroud: History Press, 2018), tables VII and VIII.
65. OCCA.
66. OCCA, weekly reports, 6/7/40.
67. P. and R. Malcolmson (eds), *A Vicar's Wife in Oxford*, p. 90.
68. The boundary markings turned out to relate to the country before Edward I's invasion.
69. Fleming, *Invasion 1940*, p. 101.
70. Ibid., p. 102.
71. Joshua Levine, *The Secret History of the Blitz: How We Behaved during Our Darkest Days and Created Modern Britain* (London: Simon & Schuster, 2015), location 2263–2293.
72. Alex Danchev and Daniel Todman (eds), *Field Marshal Lord Alanbrooke War Diaries, 1939–1945* (London: Phoenix, 2002), p. 91, diary entry 8/7/40.
73. Ibid., p. 109, diary entry 17/9/40, and p. 129, diary entry 20/12/40. Lieutenant General Sir Francis Nosworthy commanded IV Corps. Another notable visitor was Major General Adrian Carton de Wiart, who in October 1939 took over command of 61st Division, one of the units created to grow the army using territorials and regular volunteers. It was headquartered in Oxford, at Norham Gardens, its brigades and battalions scattered across the Southern Command region.

74. Stacey, *The Canadian Army*, p. 19.
75. TNA, WO 166/57, 15/8/40, Southern Command Operation Instruction No 23, 'Air Borne Attack'. Signed Auchinleck, Commanding in Chief, Southern Command.
76. Ibid.
77. Ibid.
78. Hibbert (ed.), *Encyclopaedia*, p. 240. Oxford, Bodleian Library, C17:70 Oxford (58).
79. Neville (ed.), *The Oxfordshire and Buckinghamshire Light Infantry Chronicle*, vol. 2, p. 101.
80. TNA, WO 166/57, Military assistance in case of heavy air raid damage, 3/12/40.
81. 'The Home Guard, Oxfordshire', in J.E.H. Neville (ed.), *The Oxfordshire and Buckinghamshire Light Infantry Chronicle*, vol. 4: *June 1944–December 1945* (Aldershot: Gale & Polden, 1954).
82. In late 1942 the Home Guard was instructed to form a rocket battery at Oxford, sited at Cowley Marsh, presumably to take over a 'Z Battery' established by the Royal Artillery.
83. Humphry Carpenter, *The Inklings: C.S. Lewis, J.R.R. Tolkien, Charles Williams and Their Friends* (London: HarperCollins, 1997), p. 69.
84. Ibid., p. 174.
85. Neville (ed.), *The Oxfordshire and Buckinghamshire Light Infantry Chronicle*, vol. 2, p. 97.
86. OCCA, weekly reports, 6/7/40.
87. Albert Thomas, *Wait & See* (London: Michael Joseph, 1944), p. 186.
88. Simon Bishop, 'The Spirit of Place: Paul Nash, a Painter in Wartime Oxford', *Oxford Art Journal*, vol. 1, no. 1, 1978, p. 41.
89. Ibid.
90. Ibid.
91. Ibid.
92. Levine, *The Secret History of the Blitz*, location 322.
93. Robin Darwall-Smith, 'Univ. during the Second World War', *University College Record*, 2005.
94. Levine, *The Secret History of the Blitz*, location 329.
95. Barry Webb, *Edmund Blunden: A Biography* (New Haven CT and London: Yale University Press, 1990), p. 226.
96. Ibid., p. 227.
97. Margaret Rayner, *The Centenary History of St Hilda's College, Oxford* (London: Lindsay Ross Publishing, 1993), p. 82.
98. Leslie Mitchell, *Maurice Bowra: A Life* (Oxford: Oxford University Press, 2010), p. 241.
99. MCA, *Mansfield College Magazine* 118, 1941.
100. Addison, 'Oxford and the Second World War', p. 172.
101. Beveridge/Wheare, entry in the SCR betting book, 8/10/40, B. Harrison, 'College Life, 1918–1939', in Harrison (ed.), *The History of the University of Oxford*, vol. 8, p. 87. The day after the declaration of war, running into Edmund Blunden as he walked into Christ Church, Wheare expressed the opinion that a negotiated settlement with Hitler was a possibility. Webb, *Edmund Blunden*, p. 219.
102. L.W.B. Brockliss (ed.), *Magdalen College Oxford: A History* (Oxford: Magdalen College, 2008), p. 608.
103. Webb, *Edmund Blunden*, p. 225.
104. A.L. Rowse, 'Oxford in War-Time', in Rowse, *The English Spirit: Essays in History and Literature* (London: Macmillan, 1944), p. 120.

105. Alan Hackney, *Private's Progress: A Novel* (London: Victor Gollancz, 1954), p. 7.
106. Albert Thomas, *Wait & See* (London: Michael Joseph, 1944), p. 182.
107. Philip Larkin, *Jill* (London: Faber & Faber, 2005), p. viii.
108. Ibid.
109. Leader, *The Life of Kingsley Amis*, pp. 93–4.
110. Thomas Charles-Edwards and Julian Reid (eds), *Corpus Christi College Oxford: A History* (Oxford: Oxford University Press, 2017), p. 38.
111. A. Grenville, 'Academic Refugees', in Sally Crawford, Katharina Ulmschneider and Jaś Elsner (eds), *Ark of Civilization: Refugee Scholars and Oxford University, 1930–1945* (Oxford: Oxford University Press, 2017), p. 56.
112. Ibid., p. 57.
113. Bojan Bujić, 'Shipwrecked on the Island of the Blessed: Egon Wellesz's New Beginnings in Wartime Oxford', in Crawford et al. (eds), *Ark of Civilization*, p. 317.
114. Quotation from Fran Lloyd chapter in Crawford et al. (eds), *Ark of Civilization*.
115. Addison, 'Oxford and the Second World War', p. 174.
116. Ibid.
117. Ibid., p. 175.
118. Larkin, *Jill*, p. xiv.
119. Christopher Tyerman (ed.), *New College* (London: Third Millennium, 2010), p. 119. Residents were prevailed upon to subscribe a shilling a piece for the purchase of a stirrup pump and three long-handled shovels.
120. Edmund Craster, *History of the Bodleian Library, 1845–1945* (Oxford: Clarendon Press, 1952), p. 342.
121. 'Jesus College', in H.E. Salter and Mary Lobel, *A History of the County of Oxford*, Volume 3: *The University of Oxford* (London: Victoria County History, 1954).
122. Ibid.
123. Rayner, *The Centenary History of St Hilda's College*, p. 82.
124. Pauline Adams, *Somerville for Women: An Oxford College, 1879–1993* (Oxford: Oxford University Press, 1996), p. 242.
125. QCA, *Queen's College Record*, vol. II, no. 9, 1942.
126. Ann Brown and Ruth Flanagan, 'The Ashmolean at War, Part Two, 1940–1946', *The Ashmolean* 20, 1991, p. 21.
127. Ibid., p. 18.
128. Ibid.
129. Eric Lax, *The Mould in Dr Florey's Coat: The Remarkable True Story of the Penicillin Miracle* (London: Abacus, 2005), p. 191.
130. Don Chapman, *Oxford Playhouse: High and Low Drama in a University City* (Hatfield: University of Hertfordshire Press, 2008), p. 125.
131. Addison, 'Oxford and the Second World War', p. 175.
132. Harper-Nelson, *Oxford at War*, p. 100. A rolling pin, one assumes.
133. Darwall-Smith, 'Univ. during the Second World War'.
134. Ibid.
135. Harper-Nelson, *Oxford at War*, p. 30.
136. Ibid.
137. Frances Cairncross and Hannah Parham (eds), *Exeter College: The First 700 Years* (London: Exeter College and Third Millennium Publishing, 2013), p. 91.
138. Ann Thwaite (ed.), *My Oxford* (London: Robson Books, 1977), p. 162.
139. Darwall-Smith, 'Univ. during the Second World War'.
140. SHCA, Reference file, Janet Gibbins (1942) memoir.
141. P. and R. Malcolmson (eds), *A Vicar's Wife in Oxford*, p. 210, diary entry 21/2/43.
142. Bletchley Park oral history project, interview with Coppock, May 2015.

143. P. and R. Malcolmson (eds), *A Vicar's Wife in Oxford*, p. 111.
144. See the picture in Malcolm Graham and Laurence Waters, *Oxford Yesterday and Today* (Stroud: Sutton, 2002), p. 99.
145. Brockliss, *Magdalen College*, p. 638.
146. Candida Lycett Green (ed.), *John Betjeman: Letters*, Volume 1: *1926–1951* (London: Methuen, 2006), p. 194.
147. Graham, *Oxfordshire at War*, p. 35.
148. Ibid., p. 40.
149. Judith Curthoys, *The Cardinal's College: Christ Church, Chapter and Verse* (London: Profile Books, 2012), p. 315.
150. Adams, *Somerville for Women*, p. 79.
151. P. and R. Malcolmson (eds), *A Vicar's Wife in Oxford*, p. 118, diary entry 21/10/40.
152. For the bomb damage to Amen House in 1942, see Randolph Schwabe's picture at www.fulltable.com/VTS/a/accident/SH341.jpg.
153. Graham, *Oxfordshire at War*, p. 38.
154. Ibid., p. 47.
155. Ibid., p. 39.
156. See Giles Barber, 'Libraries' in Harrison (ed.), *The History of the University of Oxford*, vol. 8; P.H.J. Gosden, *Education in the Second World War: A Study in Policy and Administration* (London: Methuen, 1976), p. 156; Gordon Huelin, *King's College London, 1828–1978* (London: University of London King's College, 1978).
157. Initial summary report, 9/12/46.
158. Arthur Mee, *Oxfordshire: County of Imperishable Fame* (London: Hodder & Stoughton, 1942), pp. 311–12. Closure afforded the opportunity to begin restoring Taharqa's Shrine, presented to the Museum in 1936. Ann Brown and Ruth Flanagan, 'The Ashmolean at War, Part One, 1939–1940', *The Ashmolean* 19, 1990–91, p. 19.
159. Caroline Shenton, *National Treasures: Saving the Nation's Art in World War II* (London: John Murray, 2022), p. 208.
160. J. Mabbott, *Oxford Memories* (Oxford: Thornton's, 1986), p. 114.
161. F. Dubber, 'War Deposits in the New Library, 1939–1945', as summarized in Robert Bruce, 'Deposits in the New Bodleian during the Second World War', *Bodleian Library Record*, vol. 26, no. 1, 2013.
162. Craster, *History of the Bodleian*, p. 144. 'Almost unnoticed', wrote Craster, 'the whole contents of the Bodleian, amounting to a million and a half of volumes, had been ranged in order in the new stack. Despite the staff's diminishing numbers, the work was complete by the summer of 1942.' Ibid., p. 341.
163. Initial summary report, 9/12/46.
164. Chips Channon, dispersing his valuables from his town and country houses, sent a tin box of *bibelots*, watches and Fabergé ornaments to the National Provincial Bank in Oxford. Simon Heffer (ed.), *Henry 'Chips' Channon: The Diaries, 1938–1943*, vol. 2 (London: Hutchinson, 2021), 4/11/40, location 442.
165. The Lewis Evans Collection opened as a museum in the old Ashmolean Building on Broad Street in 1924, renamed the University Museum of the History of Science in 1935. L.W.B. Brockliss, *The University of Oxford: A History* (Oxford: Oxford University Press, 2016), p. 488.
166. Duff Hart-Davis (ed.), *King's Counsellor: Abdication and War: The Diaries of Sir Alan 'Tommy' Lascelles* (London: Weidenfeld & Nicolson, 2020), p. 118, diary entry 28/3/43.
167. Craster, *History of the Bodleian*, p. 342.
168. Mary Clapinson, *A Brief History of the Bodleian Library* (Oxford: Bodleian Library Publishing, 2015), p. 146.

169. Nigel Nicolson (ed.), *Harold Nicolson: Diaries and Letters, 1939–1945* (London: Collins, 1968), p. 227, diary entry 5/6/42.

IN WARTIME OXFORD

1. Ann Rau Dawes, 'Milein Cosman at the Slade', in Sally Crawford, Katharina Ulmschneider and Jaś Elsner (eds), *Ark of Civilization: Refugee Scholars and Oxford University, 1930–1945* (Oxford: Oxford University Press, 2017), p. 280.
2. Angela Edward, 'Object Biographies – A Green Car Lamp in Oxford', British Archaeology at the Ashmolean Museum, britisharchaeology.ashmus.ox.ac.uk/east-oxford/ob-green-car-lamp.html.
3. Oxford Bus Museum, Long Hanborough, museum information board.
4. *Oxford Mail*, letter from Bette Martin, 5 April 2011. The king's surgeon, writing in the *British Medical Journal* in 1939, 'complained that by "frightening the nation into blackout regulations, the Luftwaffe was able to kill 600 British citizens a month without ever taking to the air"'. Gavin Thompson et al., *Olympic Britain: Social and Economic Change Since the 1908 and 1948 London Games* (London: UK Parliament, 2012). See 'Look Out in the Blackout: Road Traffic Accidents', p. 131.
5. Albert Thomas, *Wait & See* (London: Michael Joseph, 1944), p. 182.
6. Ann Thwaite (ed.), *My Oxford* (London: Robson Books, 1977), p. 155.
7. John Harper-Nelson, *Oxford at War: An Undergraduate Memoir, John Harper-Nelson, 1940–42* (Northbridge, Western Australia: Access Press, 1996), p. 3.
8. Bojan Bujić, 'Shipwrecked on the Island of the Blessed: Egon Wellesz's New Beginnings in Wartime Oxford', in Crawford et al. (eds), *Ark of Civilization*. p. 315.
9. SEHA, *St Edmund Magazine*, 1940 and 1941.
10. P. and R. Malcolmson (eds), *A Vicar's Wife in Oxford, 1938–1943: The Diary of Madge Martin* (Woodbridge: Oxfordshire Record Society/Boydell Press, 2018), p. 172. Many of these snippets come from Malcolm Graham, *Oxfordshire at War* (Stroud: Alan Sutton, 1994).
11. QCA, *Queen's College Record*, vol. II, no. 8, 1941.
12. SHCA, *St Hugh's Chronicle*, 1939–40, p. 11.
13. P. and R. Malcolmson (eds), *A Vicar's Wife in Oxford*, p. 155, diary entry 16/10/41. Visited by the Duchess of Kent, 22/10/41.
14. TNA, HW 40/271, GC&CS Records, Allied Codes and Cypers, Miscellaneous Correspondence, OUP and Mansfield College, Hok to Travis, 2/4/42. Commander Hok, responsible for the secret activities taking place in the college, wrote that the authorities needed to be careful so as to avoid this being the thin end of the wedge 'for further gatherings of German refugees'.
15. Graham, *Oxfordshire at War*, p. 163.
16. Harper-Nelson, *Oxford at War*, p. 100.
17. P. and R. Malcolmson (eds), *A Vicar's Wife in Oxford*, p. 200.
18. Eric Waldram Kemp, *The Life and Letters of Kenneth Escott Kirk, Bishop of Oxford 1937–1954* (London: Hodder & Stoughton, 1959), p. 85.
19. Christopher Hibbert (ed.), *The Encyclopaedia of Oxford* (London: Macmillan, 1988), p. 297.
20. 'History of Oxfam', www.oxfam.org.uk/about-us/history-oxfam.
21. Pauline Adams, *Somerville for Women: An Oxford College, 1879–1993* (Oxford: Oxford University Press, 1996), p. 244.
22. P. and R. Malcolmson (eds), *A Vicar's Wife in Oxford*, p. 122.
23. Leslie Mitchell, *Maurice Bowra: A Life* (Oxford: Oxford University Press, 2010), p. 243.

24. Harper-Nelson, *Oxford at War*, p. 171.
25. This calculation is based on final specific gravity figures of 1040 and 1034. Morrell's information from Brigid Allen, *Morrells of Oxford: The Family and Their Brewery, 1743–1993* (Oxford: Oxfordshire Books, 1994), p. 120. The dark and light Morrells brews had a uniform gravity of 1029. See Original Gravity to ABV list, ibid., p. 146. Morrells also managed to continue brewing 'small quantities' of one of its regulars, College Ale, a much stronger beer of about 7.5 per cent ABV; ibid., p. 121. The war put paid, however, to its oatmeal stout, introduced in the 1930s as a contribution to the craze for 'nourishing-seeming drinks' exemplified by the success of Ovaltine. Ibid., pp. 116–17.
26. Ibid., p. 121.
27. Information from the research of James Tobin, the brewery's resident historian. The brewery's record number of brews came in 1944, with over 140, up from under 100 in 1938.
28. Allen, *Morrells of Oxford*, p. 121.
29. Adams, *Somerville*, p. 80.
30. Jeremy Catto (ed.), *Oriel College: A History* (Oxford: Oxford University Press, 2013), p. 745.
31. Adams, *Somerville*, p. 241.
32. Stephen Blundell and Michael Freeman (eds), *Mansfield: Portrait of an Oxford College* (London: Third Millennium, 2012), p. 51.
33. HMCA, General Committee minutes, 23/9/40.
34. Harper-Nelson, *Oxford at War*, p. 169.
35. Reader Bullard, *Letters from Tehran: A British Ambassador in World War Two Persia*, ed. E.C. Hodgkin (London: I.B. Tauris, 1991), pp. 134, 253.
36. Judith Curthoys, *The Cardinal's College: Christ Church, Chapter and Verse* (London: Profile Books, 2012), p. 315.
37. Robin Darwall-Smith, 'Univ. during the Second World War, *University College Record*, 2005.
38. Margaret Rayner, *The Centenary History of St Hilda's College, Oxford* (London: Lindsay Ross Publishing, 1993), p. 80.
39. Ibid.
40. William Whyte, 'Oxford University Press, 1896–1945', in William Roger Louis, *Imperialism at Bay: The United States and the Decolonization of the British Empire 1941–45*, vol. 3 (New York: Oxford University Press, 1978), p. 92.
41. Figure from Edmund Craster, *History of the Bodleian Library, 1845–1945* (Oxford: Clarendon Press, 1952), p. 255.
42. Hibbert (ed.), *The Encyclopaedia of Oxford*, p. 375.
43. Harper-Nelson, *Oxford at War*, p. 14. By 'quad' one assumes he means the gravelled yard between the Bodleian quadrangle and the Clarendon Building.
44. OHC, weekly reports.
45. See Graham, *Oxfordshire at War*, for pictures.
46. L.W.B. Brockliss (ed.), *Magdalen College Oxford: A History* (Oxford: Magdalen College, 2008), pp. 739–40.
47. Graham, *Oxfordshire at War*, p. 73; Margaret Thatcher, *The Path to Power* (London: HarperCollins, 1995), p. 41.
48. 'Our History', www.ouh.nhs.uk/hospitals/churchill/history.aspx.
49. From the British Council's *Oxford* pamphlet, TNA, BW 2/286. The hotel was finally demolished in 1954, to make way for a new Woolworth's store – itself razed in the 1980s to make way for the Clarendon Shopping Centre. Savage's film shows the words 'American Red Cross Service Club' above the entrance to the Clarendon, its doorstep crowded with uniformed American servicemen.

NOTES   327

50. P. and R. Malcolmson (eds), *A Vicar's Wife in Oxford*, p. 232, diary entry 27/10/43.
51. St Margaret's Institute website, www.smi-oxford.org.uk/about-us.
52. See Old Road Camp (headington.org.uk) and 'Camp 43 – Harcourt Hill Camp, North Hinksey, Oxfordshire', www.ww2pow.uk/wp-content/uploads/2019/10/43Harcourt.docx.
53. See the picture in Graham, *Oxfordshire at War*.
54. P. and R. Malcolmson (eds), *A Vicar's Wife in Oxford*, p. 160.
55. Zachary Leader. *The Life of Kingsley Amis* (London: Vintage, 2007), p. 94.
56. OHC, CCC 1107, Woodstock town clerk to OCC clerk, 16/1/41.
57. Brockliss, *Magdalen College*, photograph, p. 740. For Watt, see R.G.M. Nisbet, 'William Smith Watt, 1913–2002', *Proceedings of the British Academy* 124, 2004, p. 364.
58. Bletchley Park oral history project.
59. P. and R. Malcolmson (eds), *A Vicar's Wife*, p. 148.
60. Ibid., p. 166.
61. Ibid., p. 210.
62. BCA, 'BNC Under War Conditions'.
63. Before rejoining the army in 1939 Howard had been in the Oxford City Police.
64. Thomas, *Wait & See*, p. 186.
65. Nicholas Ilett, 'Oxford History and the Civil Service', *The Brazen-Nose* 55, 2020–21.
66. Hibbert (ed.), *Encyclopaedia of Oxford*, p. 426.
67. Webb, *Edmund Blunden*, p. 227.
68. Ibid.
69. Douglas Ross, 'A War Year: 1941–42 (Part 2)', *Pembroke College Record*, 1993.
70. OHC archives, CCC 1135, 28/4/40.
71. Graham, *Oxfordshire at War*, p. 62.
72. P. and R. Malcolmson (eds), *A Vicar's Wife*, p. 207.
73. Adams, *Somerville*, p. 243.
74. Rayner, *The Centenary History of St Hilda's College*, p. 83.
75. P. and R. Malcolmson (eds), *A Vicar's Wife*, p. 207.
76. Ibid., p. 208.
77. OHC, CCC 136A Civil Defence exercises Controllers' copy notes.
78. P. and R. Malcolmson (eds), *A Vicar's Wife*, p. 203.
79. Phil Grinton's 258-page 'US Army/Army Air Force Units in the UK from ETOUSA [European Theater of Operations United States Army] Station List' (2004) is a definitive list of American units stationed in Britain in 1944–45. There are 176 entries for Oxfordshire. See thedodaystory.com/wp-content/uploads/2022/11/US-units-in-UK_44–05–D-Day-Story.docx.
80. See, for example, Richard Hunt, 'A Poker Game: American Soldiers in Chipping Norton', BBC World War Two People's War oral history archive, A2742860.
81. P. and R. Malcolmson (eds), *A Vicar's Wife*, p. 202.
82. Imperial War Museum, sound archive, IWM 18784, Amy Selina 'Pam' Dunnett, reels 2 and 3, interviewed 25 March 1999 by Lyn Smith. In France she served as part of 81st British General Hospital's 3rd Casualty Clearing Station, working close to the German lines, then in Arnhem, and even visiting the Bergen-Belsen concentration camp.
83. BCA, 'Oxford Blues', letter, newspaper cutting, October 1999.
84. Ibid.
85. See Robin Brooks, *Oxfordshire Airfields in the Second World War* (Newbury: Countryside Books, 2001).
86. Ibid., pp. 17, 13.

87. Graham, *Oxfordshire at War*, p. 55.
88. Ibid., p. 58.
89. Webb, *Edmund Blunden*, p. 228.
90. Douglas Ross, 'A War Year: 1941–42 (Part 2)', *Pembroke College Record*, 1993.
91. Candida Lycett Green (ed.), *John Betjeman: Letters*, Volume 1: *1926–1951* (London: Methuen, 2006), p. 323.
92. Ibid. Lycett Green writes that 'things could never be the same as they had been before the outbreak of war. A sadness hovered.'
93. Lord Berners, *Far from the Madding War* (London: Constable, 1941), pp. 2–3.
94. P. Addison, 'Oxford and the Second World War', in Brian Harrison (ed.), *The History of the University of Oxford*, Volume 8: *The Twentieth Century* (Oxford: Oxford University Press, 1994), p. 178.
95. Dacre Balsdon, *Oxford Life* (London: Eyre & Spottiswoode, 1957), p. 161.
96. Peter Conradi (ed.), *Iris Murdoch: A Writer at War, Letters and Diaries 1939–45* (London: Short Books, 2010), p. 186, letter 21/3/41.
97. A.L. Rowse, *The English Spirit: Essays in History and Literature* (London: Macmillan, 1944), p. 262.
98. OHC, weekly reports.
99. OHC, weekly reports.
100. Berners, *Far from the Madding War*, pp. 123–4. Giving up Buscot for war occupation, Berners was living in a well-appointed set of rooms on St Giles'.
101. Rowse, *The English Spirit*, p. 261.
102. MCA, *Mansfield College Magazine* 119, 1941.
103. TNA, HO 187/461, Cooperation with the military, second front operations, fire susceptibility of European towns.
104. Ann Rau Dawes, 'Milein Cosman at the Slade', in Crawford et al. (eds), *Ark of Civilization*, p. 282.
105. Ibid., p. 280.
106. Bujić, 'Shipwrecked on the Island of the Blessed'.
107. Ibid., p. 314.
108. Detail from F. Lloyd, 'Becoming Artists: Ernst Eisenmayer, Kurt Weller, and Refugee Support Networks in Oxford', in Crawford et al. (eds), *Ark of Civilization*.
109. Formed in 1934 through the merger of the Oxford City Technical School and the Oxford School of Art and headed by John Henry Brookes; it would later form the basis of Oxford Polytechnic, moved to Headington shortly after the war, and was renamed Oxford Brookes University in 1992.
110. The hostel remained empty until 9 August, when it was occupied by German refugee boys relocated from a school in Ipswich.
111. OHC, weekly reports, 19/1/40.
112. PCA, PMB/J/1/68, Wartime requisition, 5/8/39–18/12/45, Veale to Heads Houses, 30/10/40.
113. Webb, *Edmund Blunden*, p. 226.
114. Harper-Nelson, *Oxford at War*, p. 32.
115. Ibid., p. 199.
116. SHCA, *St Hugh's Chronicle*, 1939–40, p. 11.
117. Addison, 'Oxford and the Second World War', p. 171.
118. Catherine McIlwaine (ed.), *Tolkien: Maker of Middle-earth* (Oxford: Bodleian Library Publishing, 2018), p. 246.
119. SHCA, Clish memoir.
120. Harper-Nelson, *Oxford at War*, p. 169.
121. HMCA, MS.2 World War II, translation of unpublished memoir.

122. Ken Coombe, 'Undergraduate 1945, Graduate 1981: An Adventure', *Worcester College Record*, 1982.
123. MCA, *Mansfield College Magazine* 117, 1940.
124. SHCA, *St Hugh's Chronicle*, 1940–41.
125. Addison, 'Oxford and the Second World War', p. 171.
126. PCA, PMB/J/1/68, Wartime requisition, 5/8/39–18/12/45, letter to Austin Daft, 30/5/40.
127. Ibid., Austin Daft to estates bursars 3/6/40. Later in the war, there was a campaign to surrender rubber items such as old hot-water bottles, linked to Japan's conquest of Britain's rubber-producing colonial fief in South East Asia. Oxford's WVS put on a salvage display in mid-1943 focusing on rubber and its use in various manufactured items and intended to garner contributions. P. and R. Malcolmson (eds), *A Vicar's Wife*, p. 205.
128. Curthoys, *The Cardinal's College*, p. 312.
129. Graham, *Oxfordshire at War*, p. 134.
130. Thomas, *Wait & See*, p. 182.
131. P. and R. Malcolmson (eds), *A Vicar's Wife*, p. 91.
132. Ibid.
133. TNA, BW 2/75. Composed of the registrar, president of St John's, provost of Worcester, warden of Wadham, censor of St Catherine's, and Professor Goodhart and, for the Council, Sir Angus Gillan (director of (the Empire Division), Professor Entwistle, Mr Orton and Mrs Beck. University people were used by the Council for Empire and foreign cultural work, for example when they travelled during sabbaticals.
134. He described receiving a 'fantastic view of Oxford from 10,000 feet' while acting as rear gunner on a Wellington bomber test flight.
135. The Council had an office at 36 Beaumont Street. The booklet was very popular and was reprinted later in 1943. The Ministry of Information had asked the Council to prepare booklets on towns where American forces were to be based, Oxford being one of the first. British Council to Vice Chancellor, 15/12/42, TNA, BW 2/286. Reverend Martin was the author and was also asked to write a guide for places of interest outside of Oxford.
136. TNA, BW 2/286.
137. Rayner, *The Centenary History of St Hilda's*, p. 85.
138. P. and R. Malcolmson (eds), *A Vicar's Wife*, p. 232.
139. Graham, *Oxfordshire at War*, p. 74.
140. Ibid., p. 161.
141. Ibid., p. 163.
142. Ibid., p. 165.
143. Thomas, *Wait & See*, p. 185.
144. *Daily Express*, 13 July 1941.
145. John Reeks, 'Professor Charles M. MacInnes: The University of Bristol's Blind War Hero', historiansatbristol.blogs.bristol.ac.uk/archives/319.
146. Don Chapman, *Oxford Playhouse: High and Low Drama in a University City* (Hatfield: University of Hertfordshire Press, 2008), p. 5.
147. Lycett Green (ed.), *John Betjeman*, p. 199.
148. David Boyd Haycock, *A Crisis of Brilliance: Five Young Artists and the Great War* (London: Old Street, 2009), p. 328. The War Artists' committee also commissioned John Piper to record scenes around the country, including Coventry Cathedral and Blenheim Palace. See Jeri Bapasola, *John Piper at Blenheim Palace* (Woodstock: Blenheim Palace, 2012).

149. Now at the Victoria and Albert Museum. See collections.vam.ac.uk/item/ O596518/the-dome-of-queens-college-watercolour-bayes-walter.
150. F. Lloyd, 'Becoming Artists: Ernst Eisenmayer, Kurt Weller, and Refugee Support Networks in Oxford', in Crawford et al. (eds), *Ark of Civilization*, p. 256.
151. Ibid.
152. Ibid.
153. Chapman, *Oxford Playhouse*, p. 5.
154. Ann Brown and Ruth Flanagan, 'The Ashmolean at War, Part One, 1939–1940', *The Ashmolean* 19, 1990–91, p. 21.
155. Rowse, *The English Spirit*, p. 262.
156. Graham, *Oxfordshire at War*, p. 160.

UNDERGRADUATES AT WAR

1. SHCA, Reference file, Stella Grove (1939) memoir.
2. Roy Jenkins, *A Life at the Centre* (London: Papermac, 1994), p. 26.
3. Nina Bawden in Ann Thwaite (ed.), *My Oxford* (London: Robson Books, 1977), p. 160.
4. Thwaite (ed.), *My Oxford*, pp. 133–4. The quotation continued, deliciously: 'indeed, they were famous for nothing except being Oxford characters: once they left their natural habitat in Magdalen or the House they grew faint and dim and ended up down back corridors in Bush House or as announcers on Radio Monte Carlo.'
5. Ibid., p. 146.
6. John Harper-Nelson, *Oxford at War: An Undergraduate Memoir, John Harper-Nelson, 1940–42* (Northbridge, Western Australia: Access Press, 1996), p. 106.
7. Ibid., p. 56.
8. Jenkins, *A Life at the Centre*, p. 26.
9. SHCA, 'The Junior Common Room', *St Hugh's Chronicle*, 1945–46, p. 11.
10. Edmund Crispin, *The Case of the Gilded Fly* (London: HarperCollins, 2018), p. 32; written in two weeks during the Easter vacation. The age issue affected women's colleges too. Margaret Roberts and many of her contemporaries at Somerville were only 17 (normal matriculation age was 18), and the cohort's immaturity was notable – as was the temperature change in 1945 when ex-servicemen returned, and an air of maturity pervaded the University. Margaret Thatcher, *The Path to Power* (London: HarperCollins, 1995), p. 37.
11. L.W.B. Brockliss (ed.), *Magdalen College Oxford: A History* (Oxford: Magdalen College, 2008), p. 622.
12. QCA, *Queen's College Record*, 1943. 'Guides' because male staff attending students were called 'scouts'.
13. Robin Darwall-Smith, 'Univ. during the Second World War', *University College Record*, 2005. Nevertheless, the problems that afflicted some colleges were not as noticeable in Queen's, to begin with at least: 'We have enough senior men for College traditions to be passed on to the Freshmen', the *Record* noted in 1939.
14. A dozen Dutch naval cadets were entertained at St Edmund Hall during their Christmas leave in 1941. SEHA, *St Edmund Hall Magazine*, 1941.
15. Worcester's chaplain claimed that Beveridge gathered the new arrivals together in hall 'and addressed them at some length on the principles of western democracy, after which experience the women felt that the hazards of Whitechapel were preferable and returned home'. R.L.P. Milburn, 'The French Naval, Military, and Air Force Missions, 1940', *Worcester College Record*, 1988.

16. 'Then and Now: Evacuees at Univ', blog post 22 June 2022, www.univ.ox.ac.uk/news/then-and-now-evacuees-at-univ.

17. Eversley Belfield, 'Further Pembroke Recollections', *Pembroke College Record*, 1983.

18. Kristin Bluemel offers a fascinating reading of Hillary's life and career and the myths he embodied in 'The Making of a Londoner: Richard Hillary and the Myths of War', *Literary London: Interdisciplinary Studies in the Representation of London*, vol. 7, no. 1, 2009.

19. Richard Hillary, *The Last Enemy* (London: Macmillan, 1942), p. 85.

20. Ibid., p. 86.

21. Things picked up for Hillary when, despite the sign behind the bar and the tide of 'strange faces', he ran into a friend, Eric Dehn, also in uniform. They went for dinner at the George, then on to the Playhouse to find some women known to Dehn.

22. Jenkins, *A Life at the Centre*, p. 35.

23. Barry Webb, *Edmund Blunden: A Biography* (New Haven CT and London: Yale University Press, 1990), p. 228.

24. Judith Curthoys, *The Cardinal's College: Christ Church, Chapter and Verse* (London: Profile Books, 2012), p. 315.

25. Harper-Nelson, *Oxford in Wartime*, p. 169.

26. James Cobban, 'The Secret War at Pembroke' *Pembroke College Record*, 1993.

27. Peter Conradi (ed.), *Iris Murdoch: A Writer at War, Letters and Diaries 1939–45* (London: Short Books, 2010), pp. 13–14.

28. Ibid., p. 183, letter to David Hicks, 29/4/40.

29. Ibid., p. 186, letter 21/3/41.

30. QCA, *Queen's College Record*, vol. II, no. 7, 1939.

31. SHCA, Reference file, Stella Grove (1939) memoir.

32. Ibid., Mary Healey (1938) memoir.

33. Jenkins, *A Life at the Centre*, p. 26.

34. Douglas Ross, 'Pembroke Past: A War Year: 1941–42', *Pembroke College Record*, 1992.

35. Jeremy Catto (ed.), *Oriel College: A History* (Oxford: Oxford University Press, 2013), p. 746.

36. Ken Coombe, 'Undergraduate 1945, Graduate 1981: An Adventure', *Worcester College Record*, 1982.

37. SHCA, Reference file, Stella Grove.

38. Darwall-Smith, 'Univ. during the Second World War'.

39. Harper-Nelson, *Oxford in Wartime*, p. 196.

40. John Jones, *Balliol College: A History, 1263–1939* (Oxford: Oxford University Press, 1989), p. 385.

41. A.L. Rowse, *The English Spirit: Essays in History and Literature* (London: Macmillan, 1944), p. 264.

42. Ibid.

43. Roger Ainsworth and Clare Howell, *St Catherine's, Oxford: A Pen Portrait* (London: St Catherine's College Oxford and Third Millennium, 2012), p. 20.

44. P. Addison, 'Oxford and the Second World War', in Brian Harrison (ed.), *The History of the University of Oxford*, Volume 8: *The Twentieth Century* (Oxford: Oxford University Press, 1994), pp. 178–9.

45. St Hugh's College JCR Report 1941; E. Clare Friedman, *Strawberries and Nightingales with Buz: The Pioneering Mathematical Life of Ida Busbridge, 1908–1988* (self-published, 2014), p. 89.

46. SHCA, Reference file, Mary Healey memoir.

47. Ibid., J. Robinson (1943) memoir.
48. Ibid., Janet Gibbins (1942) memoir.
49. Ibid., Stella Grove (1939) memoir.
50. Thwaite (ed.), *My Oxford*, p. 161.
51. Ibid., p. 160.
52. Ibid., p. 243.
53. Margaret Rayner, *The Centenary History of St Hilda's College, Oxford* (London: Lindsay Ross Publishing, 1993), p. 82.
54. *Pembroke College Record*, 1947.
55. Darwall-Smith, 'Univ. during the Second World War'.
56. Harper-Nelson, *Oxford in Wartime*, p. 134.
57. '1943: Not a Blue Race', 'Hear the Boat Sing' (2014), heartheboatsing. com/2014/12/14/9398. Contains a link to Pathé News coverage of the 1943 race at Sandford-on-Thames.
58. 'A War Year: 1941–42 (Part 2)', *Pembroke College Record*, 1993.
59. Ibid.
60. MCA, MS.3 World War II, Translation of Norwegian Heidi Brønner.
61. Darwall-Smith, 'Univ. during the Second World War'.
62. John Platts, 'A Chorister's War', in Christopher Tyerman (ed.), *New College* (London: Third Millennium, 2010), p. 79.
63. Ibid.
64. Ibid.
65. Christopher Hollis, *The Oxford Union* (London: Evans Brothers, 1965), p. 202.
66. Ibid., p. 205.
67. Addison, 'Oxford and the Second World War', p. 180.
68. Hollis, *The Oxford Union*, p. 204.
69. Email exchange with Izzie Alexandrou and Meg Lintern, *Cherwell* editors, 16 April 2023.
70. Thwaite (ed.), *My Oxford*, p. 158.
71. Darwall-Smith, 'Univ. during the Second World War'.
72. Ross, 'A War Year: 1941–42 (Part 2)'.
73. Harper-Nelson, *Oxford in Wartime*, p. 103.
74. Rayner, *The Centenary History of St Hilda's*, p. 80.
75. Hollis, *The Oxford Union*, photograph.
76. BCA, undated paper cutting.
77. Brockliss, *Magdalen*, p. 646.
78. Ibid., pp. 645–6.
79. Pauline Adams, *Somerville for Women: An Oxford College, 1879–1993* (Oxford: Oxford University Press, 1996), p. 80.
80. HMCA, House Committee minutes.
81. Thwaite (ed.), *My Oxford*, p. 161.
82. Jonathan Bate and Jessica Goodman, *Worcester: Portrait of an Oxford College* (London: Third Millennium, 2014), p. 75.
83. Darwall-Smith, 'Univ. during the Second World War'.
84. SHCA, Laura Clish memoir.
85. Darwall-Smith, 'Univ. during the Second World War'.
86. Felicity Heal (ed.), *Jesus College Oxford of Queen Elizabethes Foundation: The First 450 Years* (London: Jesus College and Profile Editions, 2021), p. 68.
87. Adams, *Somerville*, p. 79.
88. Douglas Ross, 'Pembroke Past: A War Year: 1941–42', *Pembroke College Record*, 1992.
89. Zachary Leader, *The Life of Kingsley Amis* (London: Vintage, 2007), p. 92.

NOTES   333

90. Ibid., p. 94.

91. Ibid.

92. Ken Coombe, 'Undergraduate 1945, Graduate 1981: An Adventure', *Worcester College Record*, 1982.

93. Clare Hopkins, *Trinity: 450 Years of an Oxford College Community* (Oxford: Oxford University Press, 2005), p. 388.

94. Curthoys, *The Cardinal's College*, p. 315.

95. Coombe, 'Undergraduate 1945, Graduate 1981'.

96. Harper-Nelson, *Oxford in Wartime*, p. 170.

97. Albert Thomas, *Wait & See* (London: Michael Joseph, 1944), pp. 7–8. This unusual book, printed on obligatory 'wartime production standards' paper, chronicles the eventful life of the subject, mainly through his various positions before arriving at Brasenose later in life. He had been a soldier, lounge waiter, proprietor of a country pub, head waiter, farm hand, hotel page-boy, 'valet to a gentleman', 'footman to his grace', country house general factotum, club steward, steward for a block of flats, manager of a castle, tea-house owner, hotel manager, and supervisor at a holiday camp.

98. PCA, PMB/J/1/68, Wartime requisition, 5/8/39–18/12/45, Whinney, Smith, and Whinney to chair of Committee N, 5/2/40.

99. Ibid., Salt to Veale, 12/11/43.

100. Catto (ed.), *Oriel*, p. 745.

101. Ibid.

102. Roger du Boulay, 'Wartime New College', in Tyerman (ed.), *New College*, p. 123.

103. Heal (ed.), *Jesus*, p. 68.

104. Anthony Leatherdale, 'Pembroke in World War II', *Pembroke College Record*, 1997–98. James Oliver and Edward Gurden, who founded the company in 1919, were chefs at Keble.

105. Ross, 'Pembroke Past'.

106. Darwall-Smith, 'Univ. during the Second World War'.

107. Leader, *The Life of Kingsley Amis*, pp. 93–4.

108. Thomas, *Wait & See*, p. 182.

109. Thwaite (ed.), *My Oxford*, p. 167.

110. Larkin, *Jill*, p. vii.

111. Ibid., pp. vii–viii.

112. Ibid., p. viii.

113. Thwaite (ed.), *My Oxford*, p. 144.

114. See the descriptions of a couple of his acquaintances at Harper-Nelson, *Oxford in Wartime*, pp. 97–8.

115. Lord Longford, *Avowed Intent: An Autobiography of Lord Longford* (London: Little, Brown, 1994), p. 54.

116. Eversley Belfield, 'Further Pembroke Recollections', *Pembroke College Record*, 1983.

117. John Buxton, 'Reflections on an Undergraduate Diary', in John Buxton and Penry Williams (eds), *New College Oxford, 1379–1979* (Oxford: The Warden and Fellows of New College Oxford, 1979), p. 143. Visiting the college at the end of the war (he'd been captured in Norway in 1940 and spent the duration as a POW), the new warden, A.H. Smith, asked if he'd like to come back as a lecturer when he left the army. The thought of an academic career had never occurred to Buxton, but he agreed, and stayed at New College until retirement.

118. J. Mordaunt Crook, *Brasenose: The Biography of an Oxford College* (Oxford: Oxford University Press, 2010), p. 375.

119. Ibid., pp. 375–6.

120. G.H. Martin and J.R.L. Hughfield, *A History of Merton College* (Oxford: Oxford University Press, 1997), p. 340.
121. Conradi (ed.), *Iris Murdoch*, p. 196, letter 20/1/43.
122. Thomas Charles-Edwards and Julian Reid (eds), *Corpus Christi College Oxford: A History* (Oxford: Oxford University Press, 2017), p. 38.
123. Conradi (ed.), *Iris Murdoch*, p. 111.
124. Villages near the spot where he died were later collectively renamed 'Thompson' in his honour by the communist government.
125. Candida Lycett Green (ed.), *John Betjeman: Letters*, Volume 1: *1926–1951* (London: Methuen, 2006), p. 274.
126. Ibid.
127. Poem 'Myfanwy', inspired by Myfanwy Piper, wife of the artist John, was published in 1941 in *The Lincoln Imp*.
128. In William Bell (ed.), *Poetry from Oxford in Wartime* (London: The Fortune Press, 1945), p. 61.
129. J. Alan Thompson, *Only the Sun Remembers* (London: Andrew Dakers, 1950), p. 187.
130. Ibid., p. 191.

DONS AT WAR

1. John Mabbott, *Oxford Memories* (Oxford: Thornton's, 1986), p. 91.
2. See G.D.N. Worswick, 'Kalecki at Oxford, 1940–44', *Oxford Bulletin of Economics and Statistics*, vol. 39, no. 1, 1977.
3. Brian Harrison, 'Politics', in Harrison (ed.), *The History of the University of Oxford*, Volume 8: *The Twentieth Century* (Oxford: Oxford University Press, 1994), p. 388. Denis Healey was 'greatly irritated by the spectacle of lecturers who had played no part in the struggle to prevent the war, and were on their way to comfortable berths in the civil service, urging their students, most of whom had already volunteered, to fight and die for Britain'. Denis Healey, *The Time of My Life* (London: Michael Joseph, 1989), p. 45.
4. Ann Thwaite (ed.), *My Oxford* (London: Robson Books, 1977), p. 147. Mortimer might have been thinking of the head of his college, the lawyer Stallybrass, who died roughly in this fashion a couple of years *after* the war.
5. Alan Ryan, 'Herbert Fisher', *Dictionary of National Biography*.
6. Adam Sisman, *Hugh Trevor-Roper: The Biography* (London: Phoenix, 2011), pp. 77–8.
7. Nigel Nicolson (ed.), *Harold Nicolson: Diaries and Letters, 1939–1945* (London: Collins, 1968), pp. 33–4.
8. P. Addison, 'Oxford and the Second World War', in Harrison (ed.), *The History of the University of Oxford*, vol. 8, p. 181.
9. Christopher Tyerman (ed.), *New College* (London: Third Millennium, 2010), p. 119.
10. Willis Jackson, 'Professor E.B. Moullin', *Nature*, vol. 4905, no. 200, November 1963, p. 405.
11. Ibid.
12. See H.G. Nicholson, *Washington Dispatches, 1941–45: Weekly Political Reports from the British Embassy* (London: Weidenfeld & Nicolson, 1981).
13. Anthony Croft, *Oxford's Clarendon Laboratory* (Oxford: Department of Physics, 1986), p. 103.
14. G.R. Evans, *The University of Oxford: A New History* (London: I.B. Tauris, 2013), p. 45. The quotation is from Thomas Wilson, *Churchill and the Prof* (London: Cassell, 1995), p. 1, quoting in turn Lord Birkenhead, *The Prof in Two World Wars*

(London: Collins, 1961), p. 159. See Donald MacDougall, 'The Prime Minister's Statistical Section', in D.N. Chester (ed.), *Lessons of the British War Economy* (Cambridge: Cambridge University Press, 1951).

15. Information from 'A Handlist of the Papers of F.A. Lindemann, Viscount Cherwell of Oxford, 1886–1957' (2011), Nuffield College Oxford, CSAC 80/4/81.

16. Augustus John, 'Martin D'Arcy', *Dictionary of National Biography*.

17. He also served as treasurer of the Oxford Basque Children's Committee.

18. Barry Webb, *Edmund Blunden: A Biography* (New Haven CT and London: Yale University Press, 1990), p. 225.

19. Addison, 'Oxford and the Second World War', p. 173.

20. Leslie Mitchell, *Maurice Bowra: A Life* (Oxford: Oxford University Press, 2010), p. 244.

21. Ibid., p. 241.

22. C.S.L. Davies and Jane Garnett, *Wadham College* (Oxford: Wadham College, 1994), p. 76. For Lindemann, see Mitchell, *Maurice Bowra*, p. 241.

23. Jose Harris, *William Beveridge: A Biography* (Oxford: Oxford University Press, 1997), p. 354.

24. Ibid., p. 350.

25. Ibid., pp. 356–7. Churchill was nearly five years older than Beveridge.

26. Adam Sisman, *A.J.P. Taylor: A Biography* (London: Sinclair-Stevenson, 1994), p. 136.

27. UOA, UR6/QC/11/1, file 1, Hodgkin to Veale, 21/7/39.

28. Webb, *Edmund Blunden*, p. 231.

29. Robin Darwall-Smith, 'Univ. during the Second World War, *University College Record*, 2005.

30. L.W.B. Brockliss (ed.), *Magdalen College Oxford: A History* (Oxford: Magdalen College, 2008), p. 594.

31. Ibid.

32. Ibid., p. 595.

33. Clare Hopkins, *Trinity: 450 Years of an Oxford College Community* (Oxford: Oxford University Press, 2005), p. 386.

34. Brockliss, *Magdalen*, p. 622.

35. Catherine McIlwaine (ed.), *Tolkien: Maker of Middle-earth* (Oxford: Bodleian Library Publishing, 2018), p. 246.

36. Darwall-Smith, 'Univ. during the Second World War'.

37. Sisman, *A.J.P. Taylor*, p. 136.

38. Mitchell, *Maurice Bowra*, p. 243.

39. Ibid.

40. Thomas Charles-Edwards and Julian Reid (eds), *Corpus Christi College Oxford: A History* (Oxford: Oxford University Press, 2017), p. 379.

41. A.L. Rowse, *The English Spirit: Essays in History and Literature* (London: Macmillan, 1944), p. 261.

42. Mabbott, *Oxford Memories*, p. 92.

43. Rowse, *The English Spirit*, p. 261.

44. Philip Larkin, *Jill* (London: Faber & Faber, 2005), p. viii.

45. Darwall-Smith, 'Univ. during the Second World War'.

46. Jeremy Catto (ed.), *Oriel College: A History* (Oxford: Oxford University Press, 2013), p. 744.

47. Hertford College Oxford archives, GB 454 HC, X-HC/WW/2/2.

48. Ibid.

49. Charles-Edwards and Reid (eds), *Corpus*, p. 38.

50. Exeter College archives (hereafter ECA), EC/6/4/1 B and EC/6/4/4.
51. Frances Cairncross and Hannah Parham (eds), *Exeter College: The First 700 Years* (London: Exeter College and Third Milennium Publishing, 2013), p. 90.
52. Webb, *Edmund Blunden*, p. 233.
53. Sisman, *Hugh Trevor-Roper*, p. 119.
54. PCA, PMB/v/1/2/6, World War Two roll of service, general papers, 1940–45, Frost to Homes Dudden, 27/4/43.
55. WCA, *Worcester College Record*, 1939–44 and 1945.
56. BCA, Benefactor's Book. Thanks to Helen Sumping for this material.
57. Humphrey Carpenter, *The Inklings: C.S. Lewis, J.R.R. Tolkien, Charles Williams and Their Friends* (London: HarperCollins, 1997), p. 131.
58. Humphrey Carpenter, *J.R.R. Tolkien* (London: HarperCollins, 2016), p. 257. *Sir Orfeo* reference, ibid., p. 191.
59. Webb, *Edmund Blunden*, p. 227.
60. Sisman, *A.J.P. Taylor*, p. 137.
61. A.N. Wilson, *C.S. Lewis: A Biography* (London: Harper Perennial, 2005), p. 192.
62. Jennifer Thorp, 'The College at War', in Tyerman (ed.), *New College*, p. 118. Smith was confirmed in post in 1944 and served as warden until 1958.
63. Mitchell, *Maurice Bowra*, p. 242.
64. Lord Longford, *Avowed Intent: An Autobiography of Lord Longford* (London: Little, Brown, 1994), p. 91.
65. Ibid., p. 92.
66. Ibid.
67. Charles Carrington, *Chatham House: Its History and Inhabitants* (London: Royal Institute of International Affairs, 2004).
68. Lord Gladwyn, *The Memoirs of Lord Gladwyn* (London: Weidenfeld & Nicolson, 1972), p. 95.
69. John Harvey (ed.), *The War Diaries of Oliver Harvey, 1941–1945* (London: Collins, 1978), p. 49. On 13 October 1941 Harvey was pleased to record '[o]ur first meeting to-day in F.O. to discuss the future of the world. This was really the first fruits of my own efforts to get the F.O. to start planning the peace settlement'. Ibid., p. 52. Eden and others in the Foreign Office thought Churchill had been 'bowled a fast' one by Roosevelt in agreeing to the text of the Atlantic Charter, which was inconsistent with continued British imperial rule.
70. Ibid., p. 140.
71. Lord Berners, *Far from the Madding War* (London: Constable, 1941), p. 113.
72. J. Darwin, 'A World University', in Harrison (ed.), *The History of the University of Oxford*, vol. 8, p. 617.
73. Ibid.
74. Darwin writes that at the end of the war Perham's 'informal empire of books and bodies' was incarnated as the Institute of Colonial Studies at Oxford, which Queen Elizabeth House later became a part of. From 1945 Perham was the director of the new Oxford Institute of Colonial Studies.
75. SHCA, 'Principal's Letter', *St Hugh's Chronicle*, 1941–42.
76. Patricia Pugh, 'Margery Perham', *Dictionary of National Biography*.
77. TNA, DO 35/1204, Constitutional matters, Foreign Office proposals for consultation with Commonwealth governments.
78. Clive Whitehead, 'Christopher Cox', *Dictionary of National Biography*. Awarded a CMG in 1944, Cox remained an influential figure as the Labour government of 1945–51 set about reforming colonial policy.
79. Jose Harris, 'Political Ideas and the Debate on State Welfare, 1940–45', in

Harold Smith (ed.), *War and Social Change: British Society in the Second World War* (Manchester: Manchester University Press, 1986), p. 236.

80. Addison, 'Oxford and the Second World War', p. 185.
81. This draws on Harris's biography.
82. This produced results: Beveridge found that the military squandered specialists on general duties, largely through multiple points of recruitment (e.g. regiments). His recommendation for 'general enlistment' was taken up by the War Office in February 1942.
83. Ibid., p. 364.
84. Harris, 'Political Ideas and the Debate on State Welfare', p. 249.
85. Addison, 'Oxford and the Second World War', p. 186.
86. Daniel Ritschel, 'The Making of Consensus: The Nuffield College Conferences during the Second World War', *Twentieth Century British History*, vol. 6, no. 3, 1995, p. 267.
87. Marc Stears, 'George Cole', *Dictionary of National Biography*.
88. Barnett House Study Group, *London Children in War-Time Oxford: A Survey of Social and Educational Results of Evacuation* (London: Oxford University Press, 1947). Barnett House prepared students for the Diploma in Economic and Political Science and, from 1936, the Diploma in Public and Social Administration. 'History', Department of Social Policy and Intervention, www.spi.ox.ac.uk/about-us/history.html#collapse399951.
89. Adams also 'poached' Cole from Nuffield in 1944.
90. Addison, 'Oxford and the Second World War', p. 186.
91. Ibid., p. 183.
92. Sisman, *A.J.P. Taylor*, p. 138.
93. J. Harris, 'The Arts and Social Sciences, 1919–1939', in Harrison (ed.), *The History of the University of Oxford*, vol. 8, p. 221.
94. A.F. Thompson, 'Alan Taylor', *Dictionary of National Biography*.
95. Sisman, *A.J.P. Taylor*, p. 132.
96. Brockliss, *Magdalen*, p. 622.
97. Sisman, *A.J.P. Taylor*, p. 148.
98. Ibid., p. 136.
99. Richard Davenport-Hines, 'Hugh Trevor-Roper', *Dictionary of National Biography*.
100. Micklem had spent time in Germany before going up to read Classics at New College as a young man, and was fluent in German.
101. Elaine Kaye, 'Nathaniel Micklam', *Dictionary of National Biography*.
102. Elaine Kaye, *Mansfield College Oxford: Its Origin, History, and Significance* (Oxford: Oxford University Press, 1996).
103. George Garnsey, 'The Moral Theology of Kenneth Kirk, Bishop of Oxford: Studies in Its Development, Application, and Influence' (D.Phil. thesis, University of Oxford, 2012), p. 8.
104. Carpenter, *The Inklings*, p. 183. The book *Broadcast Talks* was published in 1942.
105. Alister McGrath, *C.S. Lewis: A Life* (London: Hodder & Stoughton, 2013), p. 205.
106. A.N. Wilson, *C.S. Lewis: A Biography* (London: Harper Perennial, 2005), p. 169.
107. A.L. Rowse, *Oxford in the History of the Nation* (London: Weidenfeld & Nicolson, 1975), p. 242.
108. F.M. Turner, 'Religion', in Harrison (ed.), *The History of the University of Oxford*, vol. 8, p. 310.
109. For some troll king poetry, see Brian Hutton, 'Elegy in the North', in William Bell (ed.), *Poetry from Oxford in Wartime* (London: The Fortune Press, 1945), pp. 50–52.
110. Carpenter, *J.R.R. Tolkien*, p. 200.

111. From 1945 Professor of English Language and Literature and fellow of Merton.
112. Carpenter, *The Inklings*, p. 123.
113. Carpenter, *J.R.R. Tolkien*, p. 222. Carpenter writes that in the years he ran a car, 1932 until the start of the war, Tolkien 'loved to explore the villages of Oxfordshire, particularly those in the east of the county'. Ibid., p. 169. Tolkien explained to his publisher that the character Tom Bombadil was intended to represent 'the spirit of the (vanishing) Oxford and Berkshire countryside'. Ibid., p. 217.
114. Ibid., p. 170.
115. Ibid., p. 212.
116. Ibid., p. 259. For the war's influence on *The Lord of the Rings*, see Janet Croft, '"The Young Perish and the Old Wither, Lingering": J.R.R. Tolkien and World War II', *Mythlore: A Journal of J.R.R. Tolkien, C.S. Lewis, and Charles Williams and Mythopoeic Literature*, vol. 24, no. 2, 2004.
117. Evelyn Waugh, 'Preface', *Brideshead Revisited* (London: Penguin Classics, 2000), p. 7.
118. G.R. Evans, *The University of Oxford: A New History* (London: I.B. Tauris, 2013), p. 38.
119. Waugh, 'Preface', *Brideshead Revisited*, pp. 7, 8. Waugh abandoned the novel *Work Suspended* because 'the world on which and for which it was designed had ceased to exist'. With the coming of war, 'an epoch, my epoch, came to an end'. Martin Stannard, '*Work Suspended*: Waugh's Climacteric', *Essays in Criticism*, vol. XXVIII, no. 4, 1978, p. 319. Bowra also was 'acutely aware that, in victory or defeat, the world of 1939 had been fatally undermined'. Mitchell, *Maurice Bowra*, p. 244. It was no coincidence that his published memoir stopped in 1939; 'He had no interest or motivation to write about the post-War world.' Ibid., p. 239. Powell wrote that one of the reasons for embarking on the *Dance to the Music of Time* sequence was 'to try and recapture the epoch that ended with the Second World War'. Michael Barber, *Anthony Powell: A Life* (London: Duckworth Overlook, 2005), p. xi.
120. Rowse, *The English Spirit*, p. 263.
121. W.R. Louis, *Imperialism at Bay: The United States and the Decolonization of the British Empire 1941–45* (New York: Oxford University Press, 1978), p. 252.
122. Simon Heffer (ed.), *Henry 'Chips' Channon: The Diaries, 1938–1943*, vol. 2 (London: Hutchinson, 2021), locations 256 and 962.
123. Kent Fedorowich and Jayne Gifford (eds), *Sir Earle Page's British War Cabinet Diary, 1941–1942* (Cambridge: Cambridge University Press for the Royal Historical Society, 2021), p. 160.
124. Ibid., p. 133.
125. Ibid., p. 162.
126. Heffer (ed.), *Henry 'Chips' Channon*, location 1019–21.
127. Herbert Morrison, *Herbert Morrison: An Autobiography* (London: Odhams, 1960), p. 191.
128. His responsibilities including the compilation of the honours list.
129. See John Martin, *Downing Street: The War Years* (London: Bloomsbury, 1991), and Michael Jackson, *A Scottish Life: Sir John Martin, Churchill and Empire*, ed. Janet Jackson (London: Radcliffe Press, 1999).
130. Halifax Papers, Halifax Diary, 14/9/43, A7:8:13, p. 895. This was urgent academic business given the evolving relationship between Britain and the dominions, and political progress in India now that the prospect of full internal self-government, even outright independence, had been rendered more likely by the extraordinary circumstances of war. There were concerns about the

'fossilization' of the Indian Institute and the failure of Oxford to adequately concern itself with the history of India and its people, as opposed to the history of Britain's administration of the subcontinent. Contemptuous of the Indian Institute and the Oriental Faculty, Edward Thompson told Godfrey Elton in 1942 that 'nearly all of them are ICS [Indian Civil Service] ... this criminal tribe ... as long as North Oxford remains unbombed the wicked will continue to prosper and to earn their ill-gotten pensions'. Richard Symonds, *Oxford and Empire: The Last Lost Cause?* (Oxford: Oxford University Press, 1986), p. 119. There were other self-reflective debates about the impact of Oxford scholarship on world affairs; Jose Harris writes that the publication of R.G. Collingwood's *An Autobiography* (1939) and *New Leviathan* (1942) provoked heated debate about whether the moral collapse of the 1930s had been fostered by the 'realism' and logical positivism espoused by Oxford philosophers.

131. Halifax Diary, 14/9/43, A7:8:13, p. 895. Halifax Papers. In the afternoon Halifax talked at length with Vice Chancellor Ross, who then took him out to Wytham, to show him the house and estate that the University had just bought; 'a lovely thing and a great possession. We motored to the top of the Park in imminent danger of breaking the springs, and looked out all across the Thames valley to the Cotswolds and Berkshire downs, and everything was perfect except that old ffennell, the present owner, was unkind to two people picking blackberries, which shocked me when, thanks to his own neglect, his Park is so largely brambles! ... After dinner to Little Compton for Sunday, which was peaceful and pleasant. Babs [who?] took me to evensong at Chastleton, where they sang four of the longest hymns and the highest tunes in Ancient and Modern.'

132. Ben Pimlott (ed.), *The Second World War Diary of Hugh Dalton, 1940–45* (London: Jonathan Cape, 1986), p. 77, diary entry 24/8/40.

133. Ibid., p. 721.

134. Ibid., pp. 762–3.

135. Ibid., p. 654, diary entry 19/10/43.

136. Longford, *Avowed Intent*, p. 94.

137. Pimlott (ed.), *The Second World War*, p. 609, diary entry 28/6/43.

138. Nigel Nicolson (ed.), *Harold Nicolson: Diaries and Letters, 1939–1945* (London: Collins, 1968), p. 432, letter 26/1/45. Sparrow did return to the Bar, and became warden of All Souls in 1952. Bernays, a Worcester College graduate and former president of the Oxford Union, was confirmed dead, killed in a plane crash in the Adriatic.

139. Ibid., p. 411, letter 8/11/44. After walking home one night with Vincent Massey and Ridley, Lascelles wrote that they had 'plunged themselves into a proper hornets' nest by intimating to Lindsay, master of Balliol, that they and other old Balliol men are dissatisfied with his conduct of the college'. Duff Hart-Davis (ed.), *King's Counsellor: Abdication and War: The Diaries of Sir Alan 'Tommy' Lascelles* (London: Weidenfeld & Nicolson, 2020), p. 302, diary entry 12/3/45.

140. Hart-Davis (ed.), *King's Counsellor*, p. 296, diary entry 19/2/45.

INTELLIGENCE, SCIENCE AND MEDICINE

1. David Kenyon, '"Nice Girls" and "Professor-Types": Graduate Recruitment Practices of the Government Code and Cypher School, 1919–1945', Kellogg College Oxford, 22 February 2023.

2. Paul Addison, 'Oxford and the Second World War', in Brian Harrison (ed.), *The History of the University of Oxford*, Volume 8: *The Twentieth Century* (Oxford: Oxford University Press, 1994), p. 181.

3. TNA, 40/259, HW Records: Allied Codes and Cyphers: Miscellaneous

correspondence: OUP and Mansfield College, personnel, Hok to Regional Controller, Ministry of Labour and National Service, 9/4/42.

4. R.G.M. Nisbet, 'William Smith Watt, 1913–2002', *Proceedings of the British Academy* 124, 2004, p. 363.

5. This preliminary list of two dozen Oxford graduates working at Bletchley Park is based on the British Academy's 'Humanities Scholars Who Worked in Military Intelligence in the Second World War', www.thebritishacademy.ac.uk/publishing/memoirs/humanities-scholars-who-worked-military-intelligence-second-world-war. For the need for translation, see Nigel Vincent and Helen Wallace, 'Lost Without Translation: Why Codebreaking Is Not Just a Numbers Game', *British Academy Review* 25, 2015.

6. See Martin Sugarman, 'Breaking the Codes: Jewish Personnel at Bletchley Park', *Jewish Historical Studies* 40, 2005, p. 210.

7. Ibid., p. 215.

8. Ibid., p. 204.

9. SHCA, 'St Hugh's and Bletchley Park', undated presentation.

10. Adam Sisman, *Hugh Trevor-Roper: The Biography* (London: Phoenix, 2011), p. 78.

11. R. Davenport-Hines, 'Hugh Trevor-Roper', *Dictionary of National Biography*.

12. Mark Allen, 'Daphne Park', *Dictionary of National Biography*.

13. The organization's title is often rendered in different ways. This was the case during the war as well as among subsequent historians. Official documents specifically on ISTD could render it incorrectly – for example, 'History of the Geological Section Inter-Services Topographical Department, October 1943–June 1946', TNA WO 402/378. In this book the spelling is taken from the organization's leader, Colonel Sam Bassett. His headed notepaper read: 'From the Superintendent, Inter-Service Topographical Department, Manchester College, Mansfield Road, Oxford.' Taken from HMCA, MS. 3 World War II, 1942 letters.

14. Hugh Clout and Cyril Gosme, 'The Naval Intelligence Handbooks: A Monument in Geographical Writing', *Progress in Human Geography*, vol. 27, no. 2, 2003, p. 153.

15. W.G.V. Balchin, 'United Kingdom Geographers in the Second World War: A Report', *Geographical Journal*, vol. 153, no. 2, 1987, p. 165.

16. Ibid., p. 159.

17. Ibid., p. 160.

18. See Tom Harrisson, *World Within: A Borneo Story* (London: Cresset Press, 1959), and Ooi Keat Gin, 'Prelude to Invasion: Covert Operations before the Re-Occupation of Northwest Borneo, 1944–45', *Journal of the Australian War Memorial* 37, 2002.

19. See Stephen Haddesley with Alan Carroll, *Operation Tabarin: Britain's Secret Wartime Expedition to Antarctica, 1944–46* (Stroud: History Press, 2014).

20. Sam Bassett, *Royal Marine: The Autobiography of Colonel Sam Bassett, CBE, RM* (London: Peter Davies, 1962), p. 180.

21. The work of the Inter-Service Topographical Department has been examined in several excellent articles in geographical, cartographical, engineering and military journals, a prominent name in the field being Edward Rose. For the history of the Naval Intelligence Department, see Anthony Wells, 'Studies in British Naval Intelligence, 1880–1945' (Ph.D. thesis, King's College London, 1972), and John Godfrey, 'The Naval Memoirs of Admiral J.H. Godfrey', unpublished manuscript (copies held in the library of the Joint Service Command and Staff College, Defence Academy of the United Kingdom, Imperial War Museums and the National Maritime Museum).

22. Edward Rose and Jonathan Clatworthy, 'Specialist Maps of the Geological Section, Inter-Service Topographical Department: Aids to British Military Planning during World War II', *Cartographic Journal*, vol. 44, no. 1, 2007, p. 13.

23. TNA, ADM 223/90, Bassett and Wells, 'Inter-Service Topographical Department' (1946).

24. Bassett, *Royal Marine*, p. 186.

25. Collected by and on behalf of ISTD, the collection was held in the Bodleian until the end of the war and then moved to the Joint Intelligence Library Bureau in what became the Ministry of Defence. It is now at the IWM (catalogue number PC 1878), and runs to 3,471 cardboard boxes. Bill Donovan, OSS, realized the value of this intelligence, and sent fifty American servicemen to help out.

26. TNA, HO 187/461,'Creation and Mandate of the ISTD May 1940', in a topographical intelligence document produced by ISTD, November 1944.

27. Bassett, *Royal Marine*, p. 207.

28. TNA, HO 187/462, Cooperation with the military, second front operations, fire susceptibility of European towns, establishment for section of ISTD Oxford. 'Preparation of Folders giving essential Fire Defence for CA Fire Officers'.

29. HMCA, MS. 4 World War II, Pam Braham, 'Recollections of the Wartime World in Manchester College Oxford'.

30. Clowser is listed as being in the Royal Navy Reserve (Special Branch). Finn would cycle to visit Roald's mother – his aunt – at Great Missenden.

31. HMCA, MS. 4 World War II, Eleonore Fredrikke Knudtzon, 'Recollections of the Wartime World in Manchester College Oxford'.

32. HMCA, MS. 4 World War II, translation of Heidi Brønner's memoir. The population of the settlement there was evacuated by the Royal Navy in 1941.

33. Edward Rose, Jonathan Clatworthy and Paul Nathanail, 'Specialist Maps Prepared by British Military Geologists for the D-Day Landings and Operations in Normandy, 1944', *Cartographic Journal*, vol. 43, no. 2, 2006.

34. Bassett, *Royal Marine*, p. 207.

35. Ibid., p. 214.

36. It had its own social club in the School of Geography, and an amusing 'mock armorial' coat of arms. This showed, among other things, a bottle of gin and a pet dog, blinded in the Blitz, which would apparently hold up a paw in a Hitler-style salute on the kerb when he wanted to cross Mansfield Road as he moved from the School of Geography to Manchester.

37. Listen to the Bletchley Park podcast episode dealing with code-making and Mansfield's role, featuring Bletchley historians Thomas Cheetham and David Kenyon. E135 'Two Way Traffic' (March 2022), at bletchleypark.org.uk/our-story/e135–two-way-traffic.

38. Ibid.

39. TNA, HW 40/259, 'Staff employed on analysis of Naval Signals traffic – Transfer from London to Oxford', 29/3/42, NID 10.

40. Ibid.

41. Bletchley Park oral history project, interview with Coppock, May 2015.

42. Ibid., interview with Roxby.

43. TNA, HW 40/262, Allied Codes and Cypers. Misc – Correspondence – OUP and Mansfield College, Production of codes and cyphers, 1941 Annual Report 4B, 6/1/42. Fifty more were required for the expansion programme then ongoing.

44. TNA, HW 40/261, Records: Allied Codes and Cyphers: Miscellaneous correspondence: OUP and Mansfield College: Printing presses, Hok to Travis, 12/11/41.

45. For specimens, see TNA, HW 40/273, Records: Allied Codes and Cyphers: Miscellaneous correspondence: OUP and Mansfield College.
46. TNA, HW 40/272, Records: Allied Codes and Cyphers: Miscellaneous correspondence: OUP and Mansfield College: Specimen BP forms.
47. TNA, HW 40/267, Records: Allied Codes and Cyphers: Miscellaneous correspondence: OUP and Mansfield College: Orders for RT and IPI pads.
48. TNA, HW 40/261, Allied Codes and Cypers, Misc correspondence – OUP and MC: Printing Presses, Hok to Travis, 12/11/41.
49. TNA, HW 40/262, Allied Codes and Cyphers, miscellaneous, correspondence, OUP and Mansfield College, production of codes and cyphers, Hok to Wing Commander K. Johnston, Air Ministry, 10/7/42.
50. Ibid., production of codes and cyphers, NID to Travis 2/5/42.
51. Ibid., to Godfrey, 22/5/42.
52. Addison, 'Oxford and the Second World War', p. 181.
53. J. Harris, 'The Arts and Social Sciences', in Harrison (ed.), *The History of the University of Oxford*, vol. 8, p. 220.
54. Jack Morrell, 'Research in Physics at the Clarendon Laboratory, 1919–1939', *Historical Studies in the Physical and Biological Sciences*, vol. 22, no. 2, 1992, p. 307.
55. J. Darwin, 'A World University', in Harrison (ed.), *The History of the University of Oxford*, vol. 8, p. 622.
56. E. Clare Friedman, *Strawberries and Nightingales with Buz: The Pioneering Mathematical Life of Ida Busbridge, 1908–1988* (self-published, 2014), p. 87.
57. Enormous features of the work of people such as Florey and Lindemann.
58. J. Roche, 'The Non-Medical Sciences', in Harrison (ed.), *The History of the University of Oxford*, vol. 8, p. 251.
59. Charles Webster, 'Medicine', in Harrison (ed.), *The History of the University of Oxford*, vol. 8, p. 332.
60. G.J. Piller, 'Henry Tizard', *Dictionary of National Biography*.
61. J.S. Rowlinson, 'The Wartime Work of Hinshelwood and His Colleagues', *Notes and Records of the Royal Society of London*, vol. 58, no. 2, 2004, p. 161.
62. SEHA, *St Edmund Hall Magazine*, 1943–48.
63. Rowlinson, 'The Wartime Work', p. 168.
64. Anthony Croft, 'Oxford's Clarendon Laboratory' (Oxford: Department of Physics, 1986), p. 97.
65. Robert Fox and Graeme Gooday, 'Epilogue', in Fox and Gooday (eds), *Physics in Oxford, 1839–1939: Laboratories, Learning and College Life* (Oxford: Oxford University Press, 2010), p. 303.
66. 'Physics at the University of Oxford', www.physics.ox.ac.uk/history.asp?page=historylong.
67. Roche, 'The Non-Medical Sciences', p. 252.
68. Croft, 'Oxford's Clarendon Laboratory', p. 101.
69. Ibid., p. 103.
70. Ibid.
71. Croft, 'Oxford's Clarendon Laboratory', p. 77.
72. The assessment belongs to Rowse, *Oxford in the History of the Nation*, p. 222.
73. J. Morrell, 'The Lindemann Era', in Fox and Gooday (eds), *Physics in Oxford*, p. 260.
74. Webster, 'Medicine', p. 320.
75. Ibid.
76. Ibid.
77. Ibid., p. 332.

78. Jemma Houghton, '"Digging for Drugs": The Medical Plant Collection Scheme of the Second World War', *Pharmaceutical Historian*, vol. 5, no. 2/3, 2022, p. 65.
79. Ibid.
80. Ibid., p. 68.
81. Ibid., p. 70.
82. He was also sent by the Colonial Office during the war to investigate an epidemic of polio in Malta and an outbreak in Mauritius.
83. Keith Sykes, 'Robert Macintosh', *Dictionary of National Biography*.
84. Ibid.
85. Katherine Venables, 'Surgery on the Battlefield: Mobile Surgical Units in the Second World War and the Memoirs They Produced', *Journal of Medical Biography*, 2010, p. 2.
86. R.B. Duthie, 'Josep Trueta', *Dictionary of National Biography*, 2004.
87. Rachel Huxley, B.B. Lloyd, M. Goldacre and H.A.W. Neil, 'Nutritional Research in World War 2: The Oxford Nutrition Survey and its Research Potential 50 Years Later', *British Journal of Nutrition* 84, 2000, p. 247.
88. Ibid.
89. Susan Aldridge et al., *The Discovery and Development of Penicillin, 1928–1945* (London: American Chemical Society/Royal Society of Chemistry, 1999), p. 3.
90. Eric Lax, *The Mould in Dr Florey's Coat: The Remarkable True Story of the Penicillin Miracle* (London: Abacus, 2005), p. 78.
91. L.W.B. Brockliss, *The University of Oxford: A History* (Oxford: Oxford University Press, 2016), p. 521.
92. Howard Florey and Edward Abraham, 'The Work on Penicillin at Oxford', *Journal of the History of Medicine and Applied Sciences*, vol. 6, no. 3, 1951.
93. Ibid., p. 304.
94. Jonathan Wood, Oxford Science blog, 16 October 2010.
95. Florey and Abraham, 'The Work on Penicillin', p. 308.
96. Charles Fletcher, 'First Clinical Use of Penicillin', *British Medical Journal* 289, 1984, p. 1721. Fletcher had just completed six months as a house physician under Witts in the Department of Medicine, and was now a Nuffield research fellow.
97. Ibid., p. 1723.
98. An alternative explanation has Alexander seconded for duty to Southampton, where he was wounded in an air raid. See Jonathan Wood, 'Penicillin: The Oxford Story', Oxford Science blog, 16 July 2010, www.ox.ac.uk/news/science-blog/penicillin-oxford-story#:~:text=The%20first%20patient%20Albert%20Alexander,and%20the%20infection%20had%2c spread.
99. Ibid.
100. Roche, 'The Non-Medical Sciences', p. 253.
101. Christopher Hibbert (ed.), *The Encyclopaedia of Oxford* (London: Macmillan, 1988), p. 353.
102. Aldridge et al., *The Discovery and Development of Penicillin*, p. 3.
103. Lax, *The Mould*, p. 236.
104. Florey mentions making a film in Tripoli of treatment.
105. Lax, *The Mould*, p. 282.
106. Roche, 'The Non-Medical Sciences', p. 283.
107. Ibid. Hodgkin also published the first structure of a steroid in 1945.
108. James Stone, 'Sir Hugh Cairns and World War II British Advances in Head Injury Management, Diffuse Brain Injury, and Concussion: An Oxford Tale', *Journal of Neurosurgery* 125, 2016, p. 1303.
109. The family allowed him to perform the autopsy and keep the brain. He was later

flown to attend American General George Patton following his motor accident in Germany in December 1945, a measure of the reputation the war had earned him in military circles.

110. Geoffrey Jefferson, 'Memories of Hugh Cairns', *Journal of Neurosurgical Psychiatry*, vol. 22, no. 155, 1959, p. 160.
111. Ibid., p. 162.
112. Stone, 'Sir Hugh Cairns and World War II', p. 1304.
113. SHCA, T.J. Hughes, 'Combined Services Hospital for Head Injuries, St Hugh's College, Oxford', unpublished typescript (August 2009).
114. SHCA, Reference file, 'St Hugh's in Wartime', notes for summer school talk (2004).
115. 'Sir Hugh Cairns', Nuffield Department of Surgical Sciences, www.nds.ox.ac. uk/about-us/our-history/sir-hugh-cairns.
116. SHCA, Reference file, John Potter, 'St Hugh's on D-Day and Later', manuscript (1992).
117. Ibid.
118. Ibid., Philippa Hesketh-Williams (1933) memoir.
119. Ibid., John Potter, 'St Hugh's on D-Day and Later'.
120. TNA AIR 2/3948, letter from Symonds, 13/4/42. Group Captain Symonds, a neurology consultant, spent time at St Hugh's in April 1942, observing the work of the hospital with special reference to RAF personnel.
121. 'Memorial to Sir Hugh Cairns, St Hugh's College, Oxford', Wellcome Collection, wellcomecollection.org/works/cuhw56k9.
122. Jefferson, 'Memories of Hugh Cairns', p. 162.
123. Ibid. See also Edward Attwood et al., 'Sir Hugh Cairns: A Pioneering Collaborator', *Acta Neurochirurgica*, vol. 161, no. 1491–1495, 2019.
124. Peter Schurr, 'The Evolution of Field Neurosurgery in the British Army', *Journal of the Royal Society of Medicine* 98, 2005, p. 423.
125. SHCA, Reference file, T.J. Hughes typescript, 'Combined Services Hospital for Head Injuries, St Hugh's College, Oxford' (August 2009).
126. SHCA, HHA/6/6/3, for a photograph, sketch and floor plan.
127. Peter Schurr, 'The Evolution of Field Neurosurgery in the British Army', *Journal of the Royal Society of Medicine* 98, 2005, p. 424.
128. SHCA, HHA/6/6/9.
129. Schurr, 'The Evolution of Field Neurosurgery', p. 426.
130. SHCA, HA/6/6/9.
131. SHCA, Reference file, Philippa Hesketh-Williams.
132. Text of Cairns and Florey's October 1943 report to the War Office, 'A Preliminary Report on the Treatment of Head Wounds with Penicillin', reproduced in 'A Review of the Florey and Cairns Report on the Use of Penicillin in War Wounds', *Journal of Neurosurgery*, vol. 1, no. 3, 1944.
133. Jefferson, 'Memories', p. 163.
134. Dawn Griffis, *Headington Hill Hall: The Forgotten Years, 1939 to 1958*, Lulu.com, 2012, p. 9.
135. John Kennedy, 'The Work of the Red Cross in War', *Journal of the Royal Society of Arts*, vol. 89, no. 4590, 1941, p. 489.
136. SHCA, Reference file, Nurse Joan Staniforth letter, 10 July 2002.
137. Schurr, 'The Evolution of Field Neurosurgery', p. 423.
138. Under auspices of the Brain Injuries Committee of the Medical Research Council the case records have been filed and indexed for research purposes.
139. Jefferson, 'Memories', p. 162.
140. John Silver, 'A History of Stoke Mandeville Hospital and the National Spinal

Injuries Hospital', *Journal of the Royal College of Physicians of Edinburgh*, vol. 49, no. 4, 2019, p. 331.

141. Stone, 'Sir Hugh Cairns and World War II', p. 1303.
142. J.T. Hughes, 'Hugh Cairns (1896–1952) and the Mobile Neurosurgical Units of World War II', *Journal of Medical Biography* 12, 2004, p. 18.
143. SHCA, 'St Hugh's College 1939–45: Military Hospital (Head Injuries), Oxford'.

THE POST-WAR WORLD

1. Albert Thomas, *Wait & See* (London: Michael Joseph, 1944), p. 186.
2. Christopher Andrew, *The Defence of the Realm: The Authorized History of MI5* (London: Penguin, 2010), p. 317.
3. P. and R. Malcolmson (eds), *A Vicar's Wife in Oxford, 1938–1943: The Diary of Madge Martin* (Woodbridge: Oxfordshire Record Society/Boydell Press, 2018), p. 242.
4. Ibid.
5. SHCA, Reference file, JT Quirk, Sgt, REME, 79th Armoured Assault Division, 'A patient on VE Day', letter, 8 May 1994.
6. Ibid., 'A Student on VE Day'.
7. Malcolm Graham, *Oxfordshire at War* (Stroud: Alan Sutton, 1994), p. 169.
8. SHCA, 'A Student on VE Day'.
9. SHCA, *St Hugh's Chronicle*, 1945–6.
10. Bletchley Park oral history project.
11. Ann Brown and Ruth Flanagan, 'The Ashmolean at War, Part One, 1939–1940', *The Ashmolean* 19, 1990–91, pp. 20–21.
12. MCA, *Mansfield College Magazine* 127, 1945.
13. Graham, *Oxfordshire at War*, p. 170. Picture of Glanville Road bonfire and conga, p. 171.
14. Letter to the editor, *Oxford Mail*, 8 May 2020.
15. Radley Historical Committee.
16. Martin Gilbert, *The Day the War Ended: VE Day 1945 in Europe and around the World* (London: HarperCollins, 1995), p. xx.
17. Bevis Hillier, *John Betjeman: The Biography* (London: John Murray, 2007), p. 271. Corroborated in Adam Sisman, *A.J.P. Taylor: A Biography* (London: Sinclair-Stevenson, 1994), p. 157.
18. Ibid.
19. Christopher Tyerman (ed.), *New College* (London Third Millennium, 2010), p. 119.
20. Graham, *Oxfordshire at War*, p. 170.
21. Ann Thwaite (ed.), *My Oxford* (London: Robson Books, 1977), pp. 162–3.
22. QCA, *Queen's College Record*. Thwaite (ed.), *My Oxford*, 194–5.
23. Ibid.
24. Humphrey Carpenter, *The Inklings: C.S. Lewis, J.R.R. Tolkien, Charles Williams and Their Friends* (London: HarperCollins, 1997), p. 199.
25. Eric Waldram Kemp, *The Life and Letters of Kenneth Escott Kirk, Bishop of Oxford 1937–1954* (London: Hodder & Stoughton, 1959), p. 86.
26. PCA, PMB/J/1/69 Wartime Requisition – Emergency Pool, 29/9/39–25/3/47, A.H. Murray to Secretary, University Chest, 7/11/45.
27. Ibid., 17/1/46.
28. Ibid., 6/12/45.
29. Ibid., 8/12/45 (Queen's) and 11/12/45 (Somerville).
30. Ibid., 11/12/45.
31. Ibid., 8/11/45.
32. Ibid., 16/12/45.

33. Ibid., 29/11/45.
34. Ibid.
35. PMB/J/1/68, Wartime requisition, 5/8/39–18/12/45, Salt to Hart-Synnot, 30/5/41.
36. PMB/J/1/69 Wartime Requisition – Emergency Pool, 29/9/39–25/3/47, Hardship Pool, Homes Dudden to Secretary, University Chest, 10/11/45.
37. Ibid., Memorandum to the Bursars' Committee from the Bursars of New College and Magdalen upon the Policy to be pursued with reference to the hardship pool.
38. Ibid., 21/11/45.
39. Ibid., 8/11/45.
40. PCA, PMB/J/1/8, Wartime requisitions, 5/8/39–18/12/45, Salt to Veale, 18/12/45.
41. OUA, UR6/CQ/11/LC, file 1, Veale to Rector, 15/6/45.
42. Ibid., Keith Murray to UGC, 11/6/45.
43. Ibid., Murray to Veale, 15/5/45.
44. OUA, UR6/CQ/11/MER, file 1, Warden to Veale, 1/10/45 and 7/10/45.
45. Ibid., W. Holland-Hibbert to Ministry of Works, 26/6/45.
46. MCA, MS.4 World War II.
47. Ibid., Principal to Noel Dean, 22/3/47.
48. MCA, Cupd. 24 Second World War folder, Wilson to Marsh, 18/6/46. See also bletchleypark.org.uk/our-story/bletchley-parks-eastcote-outstation.
49. MCA, *Mansfield College, Oxford Calendar*, 1946–7.
50. Ibid.
51. MCA, *Mansfield College, Oxford Calendar*, 1947–8.
52. SHCA, *St Hugh's Chronicle*, 1945–46, p. 8. 'Our "treasures", deposited under the wing of Bodley's Librarian in some secret fastness, have safely returned.'
53. SHCA, Reference file, Margaret Jacobs (1942) memoir.
54. Ibid.
55. Ibid., Merrill Brady (1945) memoir.
56. SHCA, *St Hugh's College Chronicle*, 1946–47.
57. Ibid.
58. SHCA, *St Hugh's Chronicle*, 1947–48.
59. SHCA, *St Hugh's Chronicle*, 1951–52.
60. P.H.J. Gosden, *Education in the Second World War: A Study in Policy and Administration* (London: Methuen, 1976), p. 3. Preparations for an education volume in the war histories series began in September 1939 within the Board of Education. In 1941 the Cabinet Office appointed Sir Keith Hancock as editor-in-chief for the series and in 1945 Dr Sophia Weizman was appointed to write the education volume. It was incomplete when she died in 1969, and the Department of Education and Science was not prepared to appoint a successor. Gosden's book results from this situation, and the initiative of the Social Science Research Council which invited him to write the overdue volume.
61. It was written on the flyleaf of a reprint of Betjeman's *An Oxford University Chest* and sent to the person it was written to, Monica, who had been at Oxford (St Hugh's) at the same time without knowing Larkin. They became an item after meeting in September 1946. Philip Larkin, *The Complete Poems*, ed. Archie Burnett (London: Faber & Faber, 2012), p. 1325.
62. Personal communication from Robin Darwall-Smith, August 2023.
63. ECA, EC/6/4/1 B. Personal communication with Victoria Northridge, August 2023.
64. P. Addison, 'Oxford and the Second World War', in Brian Harrison (ed.), *The*

NOTES   347

History of the University of Oxford, Volume 8: *The Twentieth Century* (Oxford: Oxford University Press, 1994), p. 181. Brockliss cites this figure.

65. *Pembroke College Record*, 1947.

66. J. Mordaunt Crook, *Brasenose: The Biography of an Oxford College* (Oxford: Oxford University Press, 2010), p. 370.

67. Felicity Heal (ed.), *Jesus College Oxford of Queen Elizabethes Foundation: The First 450 Years* (London: Jesus College and Profile Editions, 2021); Frances Cairncross and Hannah Parham (eds), *Exeter College: The First 700 Years* (London: Exeter College and Third Millennium, 2013), p. 90; and G.H. Martin and J.R.L. Hughfield, *A History of Merton College* (Oxford: Oxford University Press, 1997), p. 340.

68. Jeremy Catto (ed.), *Oriel College: A History* (Oxford: Oxford University Press, 2013), p. 746.

69. Robin Darwall-Smith, 'Univ. during the Second World War, *University College Record*, 2005.

70. Clare Hopkins, *Trinity: 450 Years of an Oxford College Community* (Oxford: Oxford University Press, 2005), p. 396.

71. L.W.B. Brockliss, *The University of Oxford: A History* (Oxford: Oxford University Press, 2016), p. 436. On this sombre note, it is interesting to reflect on students in other parts of the world called to duty and possessed of useful skills and aptitudes. Of the 769 Japanese officers who died as kamikazes, 638 were students. The kamikaze was not a fanatic, writes Ben-Ami Shillony, 'most being well-educated, idealistic youth with little personal hatred for the American enemy'. He was driven by 'a sense of duty and a wish to prove himself in the social milieu of his peers'. Students were looked to for these 'gruesome missions' because they demanded 'self-confidence and some technical competence, found in students'. Ben-Ami Shillony, 'Universities and Students in Wartime Japan', *Journal of Asian Studies*, vol. 45, no. 4, 1986, p. 783.

72. Addison, 'Oxford and the Second World War', p. 181.

73. Darwall-Smith, 'Univ. during the Second World War'.

74. David Walter, *The Oxford Union: Playground of Power* (London: Macdonald, 1984), p. 119.

75. Eversley Belfield, 'Further Pembroke Recollections', *Pembroke College Record*, 1983.

76. C.S.L. Davies and Jane Garnett, *Wadham College* (Oxford: Wadham College, 1994), p. 77.

77. Alan Hackney, *Private's Progress* (London: Gollancz, 1954), p. 217.

78. Catto (ed.), *Oriel*, p. 746.

79. Leslie Mitchell, *Maurice Bowra: A Life* (Oxford: Oxford University Press, 2010), p. 239.

80. K. Thomas, 'College Life, 1945–1970', in Harrison (ed.), *The History of the University of Oxford*, vol. 8, p. 201.

81. Diane Kaye, 'Architecture', in Harrison (ed.), *The History of the University of Oxford*, vol. 8, p. 548.

82. John Harper-Nelson, *Oxford at War: An Undergraduate Memoir, John Harper-Nelson, 1940–42* (Northbridge, Western Australia: Access Press, 1996), p. 207.

83. Ibid.

84. Darwall-Smith, 'Univ. during the Second World War'.

85. Thomas, 'College Life, 1945–1970', p. 208.

86. J. Harris, 'The Arts and Social Sciences, 1919–1939', in Harrison (ed.), *The History of the University of Oxford*, vol. 8, p. 223.

87. Thwaite (ed.), *My Oxford*, pp. 166–7.

88. See – including Pathé news footage – 'When the King Broke the Key to the New

Bodleian', bodleianlibs.tumblr.com/post/173796191180/when-the-king-broke-the-key-to-the-new-bodleian.

89. Robert Bruce, 'Deposits in the New Bodleian during the Second World War', *Bodleian Library Record*, vol. 26, no. 1, 2013.

90. TNA, HW 40/271, GC&CS Records, Allied Codes and Cypers. Misc – Correspondence – OUP and Mansfield College, A. Cadogan, 1/12/42.

91. 'The Nobel Prize in Physiology or Medicine 1945', www.nobelprize.org/prizes/medicine/1945/summary. Reflecting his roots as well as the place where he made his name, when ennobled as a life peer in 1965 he chose to become Baron Florey of Adelaide and Marston, linking his place of birth to the village, then on Oxford's outskirts, where he spent his final years.

92. Gosden, *Education in the Second World War:*, pp. 157, 150.

93. Ibid., p. 159.

94. Ibid., p. 157.

95. Ibid., p. 159.

96. A.H. Halsey, 'Oxford and the British Universities', in Harrison (ed.), *The History of the University of Oxford*, vol. 8, pp. 581–2.

97. Gosden, *Education in the Second World War*, p. 160.

98. Robert Anderson, *Universities and Elites in Britain Since 1800* (Cambridge: Cambridge University Press, 1992), p. 16.

99. Heal (ed.), *Jesus*, p. 68; and Catto (ed.), *Oriel*, p. 748.

100. Thomas, 'College Life, 1945–1970', p. 189.

101. Angela Edward, 'Object Biographies – A Green Car Lamp in Oxford', British Archaeology at the Ashmolean Museum, britisharchaeology.ashmus.ox.ac.uk/east-oxford/ob-green-car-lamp.html. The kennels belonged to Christ Church. Following the war there was a dispute over who owned the beagles. Correspondence with Honorary Secretary, Christ Church and Farley Hill Beagles, May 2023.

102. Addison, 'Oxford and the Second World War', p. 187.

103. Ibid., p. 177.

104. Ibid., p. 179.

105. Edmund Crispin, *The Moving Toyshop* (London: Victor Gollancz, 1946); Dorothy L. Sayers, *Gaudy Night* (London: Gollancz, 1935); Mavis Doriel Hay, *Death on the Cherwell* (London: Skeffington, 1935); J.C. Masterman, *An Oxford Tragedy* (London: Gollancz, 1933).

106. J.C. Masterman, *To Teach the Senators Wisdom or An Oxford Guide-Book* (London: Hodder & Stoughton, 1952); Dacre Balsdon, *Oxford Life* (London: Eyre & Spottiswoode, 1957).

107. Philip Larkin, *Jill* (London: Faber & Faber, 2005), p. viii.

108. Paul Johnson, *Intellectuals* (London: Weidenfeld & Nicolson, 1988), p. 324.

109. Sisman, *A.J.P. Taylor*, p. 134.

110. J. Mabbott, *Oxford Memories* (Oxford: Thornton's, 1986), p. 115.

111. Mitchell, *Maurice Bowra*, p. 254.

112. Addison, 'Oxford and the Second World War', p. 188.

113. D. Greenstein, 'The Junior Members', in Harrison (ed.), *The History of the University of Oxford*, vol. 8, p. 54.

114. Ibid., p. 57.

115. Addison, 'Oxford and the Second World War', pp. 186–7.

116. Greenstein, 'The Junior Members', p. 49.

117. Addison, 'Oxford and the Second World War', p. 187.

118. Thomas, 'College Life, 1945–1970', p. 190.

119. SEHA, *St Edmund Hall Magazine*, 1943–48.

120. Ibid.

121. Gervase Jackson-Stops, 'Restoration and Expansion: The Buildings Since 1750', in John Buxton and Penry Williams (eds), *New College Oxford, 1379–1979* (Oxford: The Warden and Fellows of New College Oxford, 1979) p. 258.
122. Davies and Garnett, *Wadham*, p. 76. Wadham was up to 350 undergraduates by Michaelmas 1947.
123. OUA, UR6/CQ/11/OC, file 1, extract from *Acts*, volume 192, Michaelmas 1945, p. vi.
124. Ibid.
125. See the photograph in Tyerman (ed.), *New College*, p. 123.
126. Mabbott, *Oxford Memories*, p. 110.
127. Ibid.
128. OUA, UR6/CQ/11/ES, file 1.
129. PCA, PMB/J/1/8, Wartime requisitions, 5/8/39–18/12/45, letter 25/9/45.
130. J. Darwin, 'A World University', in Harrison (ed.), *The History of the University of Oxford*, vol. 8, p. 623.
131. Hibbert contends that the war had 'a profound effect' on the Radcliffe Infirmary. By the end of the war it had 630 beds, including those in the four prefabricated wards. In preparing for large numbers of casualties it had developed a range of specialist services, such as for the treatment of burns. Christopher Hibbert (ed.), *The Encyclopaedia of Oxford* (London: Macmillan, 1988), p. 353.
132. David Edgerton, *The Rise and Fall of the British Nation: A Twentieth-Century History* (London: Penguin, 2019), p. 341. Edgerton also points out that the 'warfare state helped maintain the highly masculinized university that had emerged in the 1930s'.
133. J. Roche, 'The Non-Medical Sciences', in Harrison (ed.), *The History of the University of Oxford*, vol. 8, p. 287.
134. Darwin, 'A World University', p. 625.
135. Graeme Gooday, Tony Simcock and Robert Fox, 'Physics in Oxford: Problems and Perspectives', in Gooday and Fox (eds), *Physics in Oxford, 1839–1939: Laboratories, Learning and College Life* (Oxford: Oxford University Press, 2010), p. 4.
136. Roche, 'The Non-Medical Sciences', p. 255.
137. Ibid., p. 259. Culham became a major site of United Kingdom Atomic Energy Authority research in 1965.
138. Ibid.
139. Ibid.
140. Ibid.
141. Harris, 'The Arts and Social Sciences, 1919–1939', p. 233.
142. Ibid., p. 235.
143. The war was something of a 'scholar's war', proclaimed one optimistic Classics don: 'now Greece is at war with Rome, and British scholarship finds itself mercifully allied on the side on which its sympathies would naturally lie. The Classical Atlas has become a war map ... Classical education has become a national asset overnight; a year spent in the British School in Athens is worth three months in an OCTU'. Ibid., p. 221.
144. Harris, ''The Arts and Social Sciences, 1919–1939', p. 221.
145. A. Ryan, 'H.A.L. Fisher', *Dictionary of National Biography*.
146. W.F. Oakeshott (ed.), *Oxford Stone Restored: The Work of the Oxford Historic Buildings Fund, 1957–1974* (Oxford: The Trustees of the Oxford Historic Buildings Fund, 1975), p. 5.
147. See Thomas Sharp, *Oxford Replanned* (London: Architectural Press, 1948), and Lawrence Dale, *Towards a Plan for Oxford City* (London: Faber & Faber, 1944). The plans are the subject of a Bodleian Map Room blog article, 'Further Outlook

Stormy', http://blogs.bodleian.ox.ac.uk/maps/2017/04/21/further-outlook-stormy.

148. Peter Collison, *Oxford Town and Gown* (Stroud: Amberley, 2011), p. 107.

149. R. Whiting, 'University and Locality', in Harrison (ed.), *The History of the University of Oxford*, vol. 8, p. 575.

150. A plaque placed by the window in 2016 recounts the story of the tree planted in 1973 in South Park for Oxfordshire Far East POWs who had died. It was later damaged and removed, and the memorial in St Michael's grew from this earlier effort.

151. Bodleian Library *Great Medical Discoveries* exhibition, 'Penicillin', www.bodleian.ox.ac.uk/whatson/whats-on/online/great-medical-discoveries/penicillin.

152. Addison, 'Oxford and the Second World War', p. 177.

153. See John Connelly and Michael Grüttner (eds), *Universities Under Dictatorship* (University Park PA: Pennsylvania State University Press, 2005).

154. Christopher Brooke, *A History of the University of Cambridge*, Volume 4: *1870–1990* (Cambridge: Cambridge University Press, 2004), p. 177.

NOTES   351

BIBLIOGRAPHY

'A Review of the Florey and Cairns Report on the Use of Penicillin in War Wounds', *Journal of Neurosurgery*, vol. 1, no. 3, 1944.

'"A Shadow of its Real Self": Brasenose during the World Wars', www.bnc.ox.ac.uk/about-brasenose/history/214-college-life/421-college-life-in-wartime.

Adams, Pauline, *Somerville for Women: An Oxford College, 1879–1993* (Oxford: Oxford University Press, 1996).

Ainsworth, Roger, and Clare Howell, *St Catherine's, Oxford: A Pen Portrait* (London: St Catherine's College Oxford and Third Millennium, 2012).

Alden's Guide to Oxford (Oxford: Alden and Company, 1938).

Allen, Brigid, *Morrells of Oxford: The Family and Their Brewery, 1743–1993* (Oxford: Oxfordshire Books, 1994).

Allen, Charles (ed.), *Tales from the Dark Continent: Images of British Colonial Africa in the Twentieth Century* (London: André Deutsch/BBC, 1979).

Allen, Dorothy, *Sunlight and Shadow* (London: Oxford University Press, 1960).

Anderson, Robert, *Universities and Elites in Britain Since 1800* (Cambridge: Cambridge University Press, 1992).

Andrew, Christopher, *The Defence of the Realm: The Authorized History of MI5* (London: Penguin, 2010).

Annan, Noel, *Our Age: The Generation that Made Post-War Britain* (London: Weidenfeld & Nicolson, 1990).

Archer, Ian, and Averil Cameron, *Keble Past and Present* (London: Third Millennium, 2008).

Attwood, Edward, et al., 'Sir Hugh Cairns: A Pioneering Collaborator', *Acta Neurochirurgica*, vol.161, no. 1491–1495, 2019.

Ayer, A.J., *Part of My Life* (London: Collins, 1977).

Balchin, W.G.V., 'United Kingdom Geographers in the Second World War: A Report', *The Geographical Journal*, vol. 153, no. 2, 1987.

Balsdon, Dacre, *Oxford Life* (London: Eyre & Spottiswoode, 1957).

Bapasola, Jeri, *John Piper at Blenheim Palace* (Woodstock: Blenheim Palace, 2012).

Barber, Michael, *Anthony Powell: A Life* (London: Duckworth Overlook, 2005).

Barnes, Sarah, 'England's Civic Universities and the Triumph of the Oxbridge Ideal', *History of Education Quarterly*, vol. 36, no. 3, 1996.

Barnett House Study Group, *London Children in War-Time Oxford: A Survey of Social and Educational Results of Evacuation* (London: Oxford University Press, 1947).

Bassett, Sam, *Royal Marine: The Autobiography of Colonel Sam Bassett, CBE, RM* (London: Peter Davies, 1962).

Bate, Jonathan, and Jessica Goodman, *Worcester: Portrait of an Oxford College* (London: Third Millennium, 2014).

Belfield, Eversley, 'Further Pembroke Recollections', *Pembroke College Record*, 1983.

Berners, Lord, *Far from the Madding War* (London: Constable, 1941).

Betjeman, John, *An Oxford University Chest* (Oxford: Oxford University Press, 1979).

Bishop, Simon, 'The Spirit of Place: Paul Nash, a Painter in Wartime Oxford', *Oxford Art Journal*, vol. 1, no. 1, 1978.

Black, Alistair, 'Information, Topography and War: Information Management in Britain's Inter-Service Topographical Department (ISTD) in the Second World War', in Toni Weller, Alistair Black, Bonnie Mak and Laura Skouvig (eds), *Routledge Handbook of Information History* (Abingdon: Routledge, 2024).

Bluemel, Kristin, 'The Making of a Londoner: Richard Hillary and the Myths of War', *Literary London: Interdisciplinary Studies in the Representation of London*, vol. 7, no. 1, 2009.

Blundell, Stephen, and Michael Freeman (eds), *Mansfield: Portrait of an Oxford College* (London: Third Millennium, 2012).

Bowra, C.M., *Memories, 1898–1939* (London: Weidenfeld & Nicolson, 1966).

Brockliss, L.W.B. (ed.), *Magdalen College Oxford: A History* (Oxford: Magdalen College, 2008).

————, *The University of Oxford: A History* (Oxford: Oxford University Press, 2016).

Brooke, Christopher, *A History of the University of Cambridge*, Volume 4: *1870–1990* (Cambridge: Cambridge University Press, 2004).

Brooks, Robin, *Oxfordshire Airfields in the Second World War* (Newbury: Countryside Books, 2001).

Brown, Ann, and Ruth Flanagan, 'The Ashmolean at War, Part One, 1939–1940', *The Ashmolean* 19, 1990–91.

————, 'The Ashmolean at War, Part Two, 1940–1946', *The Ashmolean* 20, 1991.

Bruce, Robert, 'Deposits in the New Bodleian during the Second World War', *Bodleian Library Record*, vol. 26, no. 1, 2013.

Bryson, Bill, *Notes from a Small Island* (London: Black Swan, 1995).

Burley, Jeffery, Roger Mills, Robert Plumptre, Peter Savill, Peter Wood and Howard Wright, 'A History of Forestry at Oxford University', *British Scholar*, vol. 1, no. 2, 2009.

Buxton, John, and Penry Williams (eds), *New College Oxford, 1379–1979* (Oxford: The Warden and Fellows of New College Oxford, 1979).

Cairncross, Frances, and Hannah Parham (eds), *Exeter College: The First 700 Years* (London: Exeter College and Third Milennium Publishing, 2013).

'Camp 43 – Harcourt Hill Camp, North Hinksey, Oxfordshire', www.ww2pow.uk/wp-content/uploads/2019/10/43Harcourt.docx.

Campbell, John, *Margaret Thatcher*, Volume 1: *The Grocer's Daughter* (London: Vintage, 2007).

Cannan, Joanna, *Oxfordshire* (London: Robert Hale, n.d. [c. 1952]).

Carpenter, Humphrey, *OUDS: A Centennial History of the Oxford University Dramatic Society, 1885–1985* (Oxford: Oxford University Press, 1985).

BIBLIOGRAPHY 353

————, *The Inklings: C.S. Lewis, J.R.R. Tolkien, Charles Williams and Their Friends* (London: HarperCollins, 1997).

————, *J.R.R. Tolkien* (London: HarperCollins, 2016).

Carrington, Charles, *Chatham House: Its History and Inhabitants* (London: Royal Institute of International Affairs, 2004).

Catto, Jeremy (ed.), *Oriel College: A History* (Oxford: Oxford University Press, 2013).

Ceadel, Martin, 'The "King and Country" Debate, 1933: Student Politics, Pacifism, and the Dictators', *Historical Journal*, vol. 22, no. 2, 1979.

Chapman, Don, *Oxford Playhouse: High and Low Drama in a University City* (Hatfield: University of Hertfordshire Press, 2008).

Charles-Edwards, Thomas, and Julian Reid (eds), *Corpus Christi College Oxford: A History* (Oxford: Oxford University Press, 2017).

Chisholm, Anne, and Michael Davis, *Beaverbrook: A Life* (London: Hutchinson, 1992).

Clapinson, Mary, *A Brief History of the Bodleian Library* (Oxford: Bodleian Library Publishing, 2015).

Clayton, Anthony, *Forearmed: A History of the Intelligence Corps* (London: Brassey's, 1995).

Clout, Hugh, and Cyril Gosme, 'The Naval Intelligence Handbooks: A Monument in Geographical Writing', *Progress in Human Geography*, vol. 27, no. 2, 2003.

Cobban, James, 'The Secret War at Pembroke', *Pembroke College Record*, 1993.

Collison, Peter, *Oxford Town and Gown* (Stroud: Amberley, 2011).

Connelly, John, and Michael Grüttner (eds), *Universities Under Dictatorship* (Pennsylvania PA: Penn State University Press, 2005).

Conradi, Peter (ed.), *Iris Murdoch: A Writer at War, Letters and Diaries 1939–45* (London: Short Books, 2010).

Coombe, Ken, 'Undergraduate 1945, Graduate 1981: An Adventure', *Worcester College Record*, 1982.

Craster, Edmund, *History of the Bodleian Library, 1845–1945* (Oxford: Clarendon Press, 1952).

Crawford, Sally, Katharina Ulmschneider and Jaś Elsner (eds), *Ark of Civilization: Refugee Scholars and Oxford University, 1930–1945* (Oxford: Oxford University Press, 2017).

Crispin, Edmund, *The Case of the Gilded Fly* (London: Gollancz, 1944).

————, *The Moving Toyshop* (London: Victor Gollancz, 1946).

Croft, Anthony, 'Oxford's Clarendon Laboratory' (Oxford: Department of Physics, 1986).

Croft, Janet, '"The Young Perish and the Old Wither, Lingering": J.R.R. Tolkien and World War II', *Mythlore: A Journal of J.R.R. Tolkien, C.S. Lewis, and Charles Williams and Mythopoeic Literature*, vol. 24, no. 2, 2004.

Crook, J. Mordaunt, *Brasenose: The Biography of an Oxford College* (Oxford: Oxford University Press, 2010).

Crossley, Alan, and C.R. Elrington (eds), *A History of the County of Oxford*, Volume 4: *The City of Oxford* (London: Victoria County History, 1979).

Curthoys, Judith, *The Cardinal's College: Christ Church, Chapter and Verse* (London: Profile Books, 2012).

Danchev, Alex, and Daniel Todman (eds.), *Field Marshal Lord Alanbrooke War Diaries, 1939–1945* (London: Phoenix, 2002).

Darwall-Smith, Robin, 'Univ. and the Second World War, *University College Record*, 2005.

———, *A History of University College, Oxford* (Oxford: Oxford University Press, 2008).

———, 'Univ: Plague and War, Part 3', blog post (2020), www.univ.ox.ac.uk/news/univ-plague-war-part-3.

Davies, C.S.L., and Jane Garnett, *Wadham College* (Oxford: Wadham College, 1994).

Dawe, Nigel, *Tubney Wood at War: The Hush-Hush Factory* (Kingston Bagpuize: Thematic Trails, 2014).

Duncan, Celia, *Oxford in War Time* (Oxford: Oxford Society, vol. 49, no. 1, 1997; vol. 41, no. 2, 1989).

Dunn, Daisy, *Not Far from Brideshead: Oxford Between the Wars* (London: Weidenfeld & Nicolson, 2022).

Edgerton, David, *The Rise and Fall of the British Nation: A Twentieth-Century History* (London: Penguin, 2019).

Edward, Angela, 'Object Biographies – A Green Car Lamp in Oxford', British Archaeology at the Ashmolean Museum, britisharchaeology.ashmus.ox.ac.uk/east-oxford/ob-green-car-lamp.html.

Elton, Lord (ed.), *The First Fifty Years of the Rhodes Trust and the Rhodes Scholarships, 1903–1953* (Oxford: Blackwell, 1955).

Evans, G.R., *The University of Oxford: A New History* (London: I.B. Tauris, 2013).

Faiz, A.S., 'A Flight from Self, to Self', *Worcester College Record*, 1992.

Farman, Chris, Valery Rose and Liz Woolley, *No Other Way: Oxfordshire and the Spanish Civil War, 1936–39* (Oxford: Oxford International Brigade Memorial Committee, 2015).

Fasnacht, Ruth, *A History of the City of Oxford* (Oxford: Basil Blackwell, 1954).

Fedorowich, Kent, and Jayne Gifford (eds), *Sir Earle Page's British War Cabinet Diary, 1941–1942* (Cambridge: Cambridge University Press for the Royal Historical Society, 2021).

Fenby, Charles, *The Other Oxford: The Life and Times of Frank Gray* (London: Lund Humphries, 1970).

Fisher, Nigel, and Keith Kirby, *A Guide to Wytham Woods: The Natural Place for Science* (Oxford: Wytham Woods, 2022).

Fleming, Peter, *Invasion 1940: An Account of the German Preparations and the British Counter-Measures* (London: Rupert Hart-Davis, 1957).

Fletcher, Charles, 'First Clinical Use of Penicillin', *British Medical Journal* 289, 1984.

Florey, Howard, and Edward Abraham, 'The Work on Penicillin at Oxford', *Journal of the History of Medicine and Applied Sciences*, vol. 6, no. 3, 1951.

Fox, Robert, and Graeme Gooday (eds), *Physics in Oxford, 1839–1939: Laboratories, Learning and College Life* (Oxford: Oxford University Press, 2010).

Freeman, Richard, Michael Foot, Frank Hardie and Keith Steel-Maitland, *Young Oxford and War* (London: Selwyn & Blount, 1934).

Friedman, E. Clare, *Strawberries and Nightingales with Buz: The Pioneering Mathematical Life of Ida Busbridge, 1908–1988* (self-published, 2014).

Garnsey, George, 'The Moral Theology of Kenneth Kirk, Bishop of Oxford: Studies in its Development, Application, and Influence', D.Phil. thesis, University of Oxford, 2012.

Gilbert, Martin, *The Day the War Ended: VE Day 1945 in Europe and Around the World* (London: HarperCollins, 1995),

Gordon, Mary, *The Life of G.S. Gordon, 1881–1942* (London: Oxford University Press, 1945).

BIBLIOGRAPHY 355

Gosden, P.H.J., *Education in the Second World War: A Study in Policy and Administration* (London: Methuen, 1976).

Graham, Malcolm, *Oxfordshire at War* (Stroud: Alan Sutton, 1994).

————, and Laurence Waters, *Oxford Yesterday and Today* (Stroud: Sutton, 2002).

Grenville, Anthony, *Encounters with Albion: Britain and the British in Texts by Jewish Refugees from Nazism* (Cambridge: Modern Humanities Research Association, 2018).

————, 'The Jewish Scholars Who Found Safety among the Spires', *Jewish Renaissance*, October 2019.

Griffis, Dawn, *Headington Hill Hall: The Forgotten Years, 1939 to 1958* (Lulu.com, 2012).

Grinton, Phil, 'US Army/Army Air Force Units in the UK from ETOUSA Station List' (2004), theddaystory.com/wp-content/uploads/2022/11/US-units-in-UK_44-05-D-Day-Story.docx.

Hackney, Alan, *Private's Progress* (London: Gollancz, 1954).

Haddesley, Stephen, with Alan Carroll, *Operation Tabarin: Britain's Secret Wartime Expedition to Antarctica, 1944–46* (Stroud: History Press, 2014).

Handbook to the University of Oxford (Oxford: Clarendon Press, 1932).

Harper-Nelson, John, *Oxford at War: An Undergraduate Memoir, John Harper-Nelson, 1940–42* (Northbridge, Western Australia: Access Press, 1996).

Harris, Jose, 'Political Ideas and the Debate on State Welfare, 1940–45', in Harold Smith (ed.), *War and Social Change: British Society in the Second World War* (Manchester: Manchester University Press, 1986).

————, *William Beveridge: A Biography* (Oxford: Oxford University Press, 1997).

Harrison, Brian (ed.), *The History of the University of Oxford*, Volume 8: *The Twentieth Century* (Oxford: Oxford University Press, 1994).

Harrisson, Tom, *Letter to Oxford* (Wyck: Hate Press, 1933).

Hart-Davis, Duff (ed.), *King's Counsellor: Abdication and War: The Diaries of Sir Alan 'Tommy' Lascelles* (London: Weidenfeld & Nicolson, 2020).

Harvey, John (ed.), *The War Diaries of Oliver Harvey, 1941–1945* (London: Collins, 1978).

Hay, Mavis Doriel, *Death on the Cherwell* (London: Skeffington, 1935).

Haycock, David Boyd, *A Crisis of Brilliance: Five Young Artists and the Great War* (London: Old Street, 2009).

Heal, Felicity (ed.), *Jesus College Oxford of Queen Elizabethes Foundation: The First 450 Years* (London: Jesus College and Profile Editions, 2021).

Healey, Denis, *The Time of My Life* (London: Michael Joseph, 1989).

Heath, Edward, *The Course of My Life: My Autobiography* (London: Hodder & Stoughton, 1998).

Heffer, Simon (ed.), *Henry 'Chips' Channon: The Diaries, 1938–1943*, vol. 2 (London: Hutchinson, 2021).

Heffernan, Michael, and Heike Jöns, 'Degrees of Influence: The Politics of Honorary Degrees in the Universities of Oxford and Cambridge, 1900–2000', *Minerva*, vol. 45, no. 4, 2007.

Hennessy, Peter, *Whitehall* (London: Secker & Warburg, 1989).

Hertford College archives, 'Memories of 1939: Lieutenant Tom Roberts' (November 2021), sites.hertford.ox.ac.uk/library-archives/tag/world-war-2.

Hibbert, Christopher (ed.), *The Encyclopaedia of Oxford* (London: Macmillan, 1988).

Hillary, Richard, *The Last Enemy* (London: Macmillan, 1942).

Hillier, Bevis, *John Betjeman: The Biography* (London: John Murray, 2007).

Historic Urban Character Assessment, 'Wester Suburb: Castle Mill Stream and Fisher Row', Historic Urban Character Area 7, 2013.

Hobhouse, Christopher, *Oxford: As It Was and As It Is To-day* (London: Batsford, 1941–42).

Hodgkin, E.C. (ed.), Reader Bullard, *Letters from Tehran: A British Ambassador in World War Two Persia* (London: I.B. Tauris, 1991).

Hollinghurst, Alan, *The Sparsholt Affair* (London: Picador, 2017).

Hollis, Christopher, *The Oxford Union* (London: Evans Brothers, 1965).

Hopkins, Clare, *Trinity: 450 Years of an Oxford College Community* (Oxford: Oxford University Press, 2005).

Houghton, Jemma, '"Digging for Drugs": The Medical Plant Collection Scheme of the Second World War', *Pharmaceutical Historian*, vol. 52, no. 3, 2022.

Howarth, T.E.B., *Cambridge Between Two Wars* (London: Collins, 1978).

Huelin, Gordon, *King's College London, 1828–1978* (London: University of London King's College, 1978).

Hughes, J.T., 'Hugh Cairns (1896–1952) and the Mobile Neurosurgical Units of World War II', *Journal of Medical Biography* 12, 2004.

Hutchins, Roger, and Richard Sheppard, *The Undone Years: Magdalen College Roll of Honour 1939–1945* (Oxford: Magdalen Society for Magdalen College, 2004).

Huxley, Rachel, B.B. Lloyd, M. Goldacre and H.A.W. Neil, 'Nutritional Research in World War 2: The Oxford Nutrition Survey and its Research Potential 50 Years Later', *British Journal of Nutrition* 84, 2000.

Ilett, Nicholas, 'Oxford History and the Civil Service', *The Brazen-Nose* 55, 2020–21.

Ironside, Edmund, *Ironside: The Authorised Biography of Field Marshal Lord Ironside* (Stroud: History Press, 2018).

Jackson, Ashley, 'Winston Churchill, Oxfordshire, and Ditchley Park', *Finest Hour: The Journal of Winston Churchill* 165, 2014.

Jackson, Michael, *A Scottish Life: Sir John Martin, Churchill and Empire*, ed. Janet Jackson (London: Radcliffe Press, 1999).

Jackson, Willis, 'Professor E.B. Moullin', *Nature*, vol. 4905, no. 200, November 1963.

Jefferson, Geoffrey, 'Memories of Hugh Cairns', *Journal of Neurosurgical Psychiatry*, vol. 22, no. 155, 1959.

Jenkins, Roy, *A Life at the Centre* (London: Papermac, 1994).

Johnson, Paul, *Intellectuals* (London: Weidenfeld & Nicolson, 1988).

Jones, John, *Balliol College: A History, 1263–1939* (Oxford: Oxford University Press, 1989).

Jump, Meirian, 'The Basque Refugee Children in Oxfordshire during the Spanish Civil War: Politically Charged Project or Humanitarian Endeavour?', *Oxoniensia*, 2007.

Kaye, Elaine, *Mansfield College Oxford: Its Origin, History, and Significance* (Oxford: Oxford University Press, 1996).

Keat Gin, Ooi, 'Prelude to Invasion: Covert Operations before the Re-Occupation of Northwest Borneo, 1944–45', *Journal of the Australian War Memorial* 37, 2002.

Kemp, Eric Waldram, *The Life and Letters of Kenneth Escott Kirk, Bishop of Oxford 1937–1954* (London: Hodder & Stoughton, 1959).

Kennedy, John, 'The Work of the Red Cross in War', *Journal of the Royal Society of Arts*, vol. 89, no. 4590, 1941.

Lambrick, George, *An Illustrated Guide to the Rollright Stones* (Oxford: The Rollright Trust, 2017).

Larkin, Philip, *Jill* (London: Faber & Faber, 2005).

———, *The Complete Poems*, ed. Archie Burnett (London: Faber & Faber, 2012).

Lax, Eric, *The Mould in Dr Florey's Coat: The Remarkable True Story of the Penicillin Miracle* (London: Abacus, 2005).

Leader, Zachary, *The Life of Kingsley Amis* (London: Vintage, 2007).

Leatherdale, Anthony, 'Pembroke in World War II', *Pembroke College Record*, 1997–98.

Levine, Joshua, *The Secret History of the Blitz: How We Behaved during Our Darkest Days and Created Modern Britain* (London: Simon & Schuster, 2015).

Liber Vitae Reginensium Qui Pro Patria Morten Obierunt, MCMXXXIX–MCMXLV, 1951.

'Liquid Legacies: Beer and Brewing at the Queen's College', www.queens.ox.ac.uk/liquid-legacies-beer-and-brewing-queens-college.

Longford, Lord, *Avowed Intent: An Autobiography of Lord Longford* (London: Little, Brown, 1994).

Longmate, Norman, *If Britain Had Fallen* (London: BBC and Arrow Books, 1975).

Louis, William Roger, *Imperialism at Bay: The United States and the Decolonization of the British Empire 1941–45* (New York: Oxford University Press, 1978).

——— (ed.), *The History of Oxford University Press*, Volume 3: *1896–1970* (Oxford: Oxford University Press, 2013).

Lycett Green, Candida (ed.), *John Betjeman: Letters*, Volume 1: *1926–1951* (London: Methuen, 2006).

McGrath, Alister, *C.S. Lewis: A Life* (London: Hodder & Stoughton, 2013).

McIlwaine, Catherine (ed.), *Tolkien: Maker of Middle-earth* (Oxford: Bodleian Library Publishing, 2018).

Madden, Frederick, and D.K. Fieldhouse (eds), *Oxford and the Idea of Commonwealth: Essays Presented to Sir Edgar Williams* (London: Croom Helm, 1982).

Malcolmson, Patricia and Robert (eds), *A Vicar's Wife in Oxford, 1938–1943: The Diary of Madge Martin* (Woodbridge: Oxfordshire Record Society/Boydell Press, 2018).

Martin, G.H. and J.R.L. Hughfield, *A History of Merton College* (Oxford: Oxford University Press, 1997).

Martin, John, *Downing Street: The War Years* (London: Bloomsbury, 1991).

Masterman, J.C., *An Oxford Tragedy* (London: Gollancz, 1933).

———, *To Teach the Senators Wisdom or An Oxford Guide-Book* (London: Hodder & Stoughton, 1952).

Medawar, J., and D. Pyke, *Hitler's Gift: Scientists Who Fled Nazi Germany* (London: Richard Cohen Books, 2000).

Milburn, R.L.P., 'The French Naval, Military and Air Force Missions, 1940', *Worcester College Record*, 1988.

Millea, Alice Blackford, *Oxford University: Stories from the Archives* (Oxford: Bodleian Library Publishing, 2022).

Morrell, Jack, 'Research in Physics at the Clarendon Laboratory, 1919–1939', *Historical Studies in the Physical and Biological Sciences*, vol. 22, no. 2, 1992.

Morris, Jan, *The Oxford Book of Oxford* (Oxford: Oxford University Press, 1984).

Morrison, Herbert, *Herbert Morrison: An Autobiography* (London: Odhams, 1960).

Muir, Dorothy Erskine, *Oxford* (London: Blackie, n.d. [c. 1951]).

Neville, J.E.H. (ed.), *The Oxfordshire and Buckinghamshire Light Infantry Chronicle: The Record of the 43rd, 52nd, 4th, 5th, 6th, 7th, 70th, 1st and 2nd Buckinghamshire*

Battalions and Regimental Training Centre in the Second German War, Volume 2: *June 1940–June 1942* (Aldershot: Gale & Polden, 1950).

———, *The Oxfordshire and Buckinghamshire Light Infantry Chronicle: The Record of the 43rd, 52nd, 4th, 5th, 6th, 7th, 70th, 1st and 2nd Buckinghamshire Battalions and Regimental Training Centre in the Second German War*, Volume 4: *June 1944–December 1945* (Aldershot: Gale & Polden, 1954).

Nicolson, Nigel (ed.), *Harold Nicolson: Diaries and Letters, 1939–1945* (London: Collins, 1968).

Nisbet, R.G.M., 'William Smith Watt, 1913–2002', *Proceedings of the British Academy* 124, 2004.

Notestine, Philip, '117th Cavalry Reconnaissance Squadron (Mecz) in World War II Janury 6, 1941–May 18, 1945 and Occupation' (2007), mcoecbamcoepwprd01. blob.core.usgovcloudapi.net/library/ABOLC_BA_2018/Research_Module_A/ Montreval/117th_CRS_Ops.pdf.

Nutting, Willis, 'The British Case', *The Review of Politics*, vol. 2, no. 2, 1940.

Oakeshott, W.F. (ed.), *Oxford Stone Restored: The Work of the Oxford Historic Buildings Fund, 1957–1974* (Oxford: The Trustees of the Oxford Historic Buildings Fund, 1975).

Ollard, Richard (ed.), *The Diaries of A.L. Rowse* (London: Penguin, 2004).

Oxford and District Illustrated Guide Book (London: Ward, Lock, 1938).

Oxfordshire County Council, *The Story of Oxford* (Stroud: Alan Sutton, 1992).

Pimlott, Ben (ed.), *The Second World War Diary of Hugh Dalton, 1940–1945* (London: Jonathan Cape, 1986).

Platt, John, 'H.L. Drake and the Pembroke War Dead', *Pembroke College Record*, 2009–10.

Rayner, Margaret, *The Centenary History of St Hilda's College, Oxford* (London: Lindsay Ross Publishing, 1993).

Reader, Bullard, *The Camel Must Go: An Autobiography* (London: Faber & Faber, 1961).

Reeks, John, 'Professor Charles M. MacInnes: The University of Bristol's Blind War Hero', historiansatbristol.blogs.bristol.ac.uk/archives/319.

Reeves, Marjorie, *St Anne's College Oxford: An Informal History* (Oxford: St Anne's College, 1979).

Ritschel, Daniel, 'The Making of Consensus: The Nuffield College Conferences during the Second World War', *Twentieth Century British History*, vol. 6, no. 3, 1995.

Robins, N., Edward Rose and Jonathan Clatworthy, 'Water Supply Maps for Northern France Created by British Military Geologists during World War II: Precursors of Modern Groundwater Development Potential Maps', *Quarterly Journal of Engineering Geology and Hydrogeology* 40, 2007.

Robinson, John Martin, *Requisitioned: The British Country House in the Second World War* (London: Aurum Press, 2014).

Rose, Edward, '"Secret Sappers": Terrain Intelligence by the Geological Section ISTD during World War II', *Royal Engineers Journal*, 2008.

———, and Jonathan Clatworthy, 'Specialist Maps of the Geological Section, Inter-Service Topographical Department: Aids to British Military Planning during World War II', *The Cartographic Journal*, vol. 44, no. 1, 2007.

———, and Jonathan Clatworthy, '"Secret" British Reports and Specialist Maps Generated by the Geological Section, Inter-Service Topographical Department', *Quarterly Journal of Engineering Geology and Hydrogeology* 42, 2009.

———, Jonathan Clatworthy and Paul Nathanail, 'Specialist Maps Prepared by

British Military Geologists for the D-Day Landings and Operations in Normandy, 1944', *Cartographic Journal*, vol. 43, no. 2, 2006.

Ross, Douglas, 'Pembroke Past: A War Year: 1941–42', *Pembroke College Record*, 1992.

———, 'A War Year: 1941–42 (Part 2)', *Pembroke College Record*, 1993.

Rowlinson, J.S., 'The Wartime Work of Hinshelwood and His Colleagues', *Notes and Records of the Royal Society of London*, vol. 58, no. 2, 2004.

Rowse, A.L., 'Oxford in War-Time', in Rowse, *The English Spirit: Essays in History and Literature* (London: Macmillan, 1944).

———, *Oxford in the History of the Nation* (London: Weidenfeld & Nicolson, 1975).

Rubenstein, W.D., 'Education and the Social Origins of British Elites, 1880–1970', *Past and Present*, vol. 112, no. 1, 1986.

Salter, H.E., and Mary Lobel, *A History of the County of Oxford*, Volume 3: *The University of Oxford* (London: Victoria County History, 1954).

Sayers, Dorothy L., *Gaudy Night* (London: Gollancz, 1935).

Schurr, Peter, 'The Evolution of Field Neurosurgery in the British Army', *Journal of the Royal Society of Medicine* 98, 2005.

Sharp, Thomas, *Oxford Replanned* (London: Architectural Press, 1948).

Shenton, Caroline, *National Treasures: Saving the Nation's Art in World War II* (London: John Murray, 2022).

Sherriff, Clare, *The Oxford College Barges* (London: Unicorn Press, 2003).

Shillony, Ben-Ami, 'Universities and Students in Wartime Japan', *Journal of Asian Studies*, vol. 45, no. 4, 1986.

Short, Brian, 'War in the Fields and Villages: The County War Agricultural Committees in England, 1939–45', *Rural History*, vol. 18, no. 2, 2007.

Silver, John, 'A History of Stoke Mandeville Hospital and the National Spinal Injuries Hospital', *Journal of the Royal College of Physicians of Edinburgh*, vol. 49, no. 4, 2019.

Simon, Vicky, and Richard Pollard, 'Oxford Central (City and University) Conservation Area Boundary Review Consultation Report', appendix report (London: Alan Baxter, 2019).

Sisman, Adam, *A.J.P. Taylor: A Biography* (London: Sinclair-Stevenson, 1994).

———, *Hugh Trevor-Roper: The Biography* (London: Phoenix, 2011).

Smith, Eric, *St Peter's: The Founding of an Oxford College* (Gerrards Cross: Colin Smythe, 1978).

Smith,, Harold (ed.), *War and Social Change: British Society in the Second World War* (Manchester: Manchester University Press, 1986).

Stacey, C.P., *The Canadian Army, 1939–1945: An Official History Summary* (Ottawa: Minister of National Defence, 1948).

Stannard, Martin, '*Work Suspended*: Waugh's Climacteric', *Essays in Criticism*, vol. XXVIII, no. 4, 1978.

Stazicker, Nathan, 'Memories of 1939: Lieutenant Tom Roberts', *Hertford College Library & Archives Blog*, 10 November 2021.

Stephens Curl, James, *The Erosion of Oxford* (Oxford: Oxford Illustrated Press, 1977).

Stewart, Andrew, 'Ten Days in Oxford: How Canadians Troops Defended Britain', King's College London Second World War Research Group blog, 27 March 2017, www.swwresearch.com/post/ten-days-in-oxford-how-canadian-troops-defended-britain-in-1940-part-1.

Stone, James, 'Sir Hugh Cairns and World War II British Advances in Head Injury Management, Diffuse Brain Injury, and Concussion: An Oxford Tale', *Journal of Neurosurgery* 125, 2016.

Sullivan, Paul, *The Little History of Oxfordshire* (Stroud: History Press, 2019).

Summers, Julie, *Our Uninvited Guests: The Secret Lives of Britain's Country Houses, 1939–45* (London: Simon & Schuster, 2018).

Symonds, A.S., *Havens Across the Sea* (Oxford, Robert Boyd Publications, 1990).

Symonds, Richard, *Oxford and Empire: The Last Lost Cause?* (Oxford: Oxford University Press, 1986).

Tanner, Graham, and Laurence Chandy, *The History of the Oxford University Athletic Club* (Oxford: OUAC, 2010).

Taylor, A.J.P., *A Personal History* (London: Hamish Hamilton, 1983).

Thatcher, Margaret, *The Path to Power* (London: HarperCollins, 1995).

'The Ashmolean Museum Conservation Plan' (Oxford: University of Oxford Estates Services, 2012).

Thom, Deborah, 'The 1944 Education Act: The 'art of the possible'?', in Harold Smith (ed.), *War and Social Change: British Society in the Second World War* (Manchester: Manchester University Press, 1986).

Thomas, Albert, *Wait & See* (London: Michael Joseph, 1944).

Thompson, Flora, 'Lark Rise to Candleford', Oxford University Press Archive, 2008. 'Lark Rise to Candleford', Oxford University Press Archive (2008), global.oup.com/uk/archives/2/2_11.html.

Thomson, G.P., 'Frederick Alexander Lindemann, Viscount Cherwell, 1886–1957', *Biographical Memoirs of Fellows of the Royal Society* 4, 1958.

Thompson, Gavin, et al., *Olympic Britain: Social and Economic Change Since the 1908 and 1948 London Games* (London: UK Parliament, 2012).

Theakston, Kevin, 'Edward Bridges', in Theakston, *Leadership in Whitehall* (London: Macmillan, 1999).

Thompson, J. Alan, *Only the Sun Remembers* (London: Andrew Dakers, 1950).

Thompson, Joe, 'Atonement, Scapegoats, and the Oxford Debating Society', *Kentucky Review*, vol. 5, no. 2, 1984.

Thwaite, Ann (ed.), *My Oxford* (London: Robson Books, 1977).

Tinniswood, Adrian, *The Long Weekend: Life in the English Country House between the Wars* (London: Jonathan Cape, 2016).

Tobin, James, 'Hook Norton Brewery: A Brief History, 1849–2019', unpublished paper, 2019.

Tyerman, Christopher (ed.), *New College* (London: Third Millennium, 2010).

Utechin, Patricia, *Sons of This Place: Commemoration of the War Dead in Oxford Colleges and Institutions* (Oxford: Robert Dugdale, 1998).

Vale, Malcolm, 'The Bursarship: St John's and its Bursars', *TW: The Magazine of St John's College, Oxford*, 2021.

Van der Bijl, Nick, *Sharing the Secret: The History of the Intelligence Corps, 1940–2010* (Barnsley: Pen and Sword, 2013).

Venables, Katherine, 'Surgery on the Battlefield: Mobile Surgical Units in the Second World War and the Memoirs They Produced', *Journal of Medical Biography*, 2010.

Vernon, Keith, *Universities and the State in England, 1850–1939* (Abingdon: Routledge/Falmer, 2004).

Vincent, Nigel, and Helen Wallace, 'Lost Without Translation: Why Codebreaking is Not Just a Numbers Game', *British Academy Review* 25, 2015.

Wain, J.B., *Sprightly Running: Part of an Autobiography* (London: St Martin's Press, 1962).

Walter, David, *The Oxford Union: Playground of Power* (London: Macdonald, 1984).

Waugh, Evelyn, *Brideshead Revisited* (London: Penguin Classics, 2000).

Webb, Barry, *Edmund Blunden: A Biography* (New Haven CT and London: Yale University Press, 1990).

Wells, Anthony, 'Studies in British Naval Intelligence, 1880–1945', Ph.D. thesis, King's College London, 1972.

Weston, Timothy, *From Appointments to Careers: A History of the Oxford University Careers Service, 1892–1992* (Oxford: Oxford University Careers Service, 1994).

Whiting, R.C., *The View from Cowley: The Impact of Industrialization upon Oxford, 1919–1939* (Oxford: Clarendon Press, 1983).

Whyte, William, *Redbrick: A Social and Architectural History of Britain's Civic Universities* (Oxford: Oxford University Press, 2016).

Williams, Ethel Carleton, *Companion into Oxfordshire* (London: Methuen, 1935).

Wilson, A.N., *C.S. Lewis: A Biography* (London: Harper Perennial, 2005).

Wilson, Thomas *Churchill and the Prof* (London: Cassell, 1995).

Winnifrith, John, 'Edward Ettingdean Bridges – Baron Bridges, 1892–1969', *Biographical Memoirs of Fellows of the Royal Society* 16, 1970.

Wootton, Christine (ed.), 'World War Two Memories', online publication (Radley: Oxfordshire, Radley History Club, 2020).

Worswick, G.D.N., 'Cole and Oxford, 1938–1958', in Asa Briggs and John Saville (eds), *Essays in Labour History in Memory of G.D.H. Cole* (London: Macmillan, 1960).

———, 'Kalecki at Oxford, 1940–44', *Oxford Bulletin of Economics and Statistics*, vol. 39, no. 1, 1977.

ACKNOWLEDGEMENTS

As a research fellow at Mansfield College in the 1990s, I often asked myself what the thick black line above the window of the library was, shown on a relatively recent postcard photograph. It being the pre-email age, I fired off several messages a day via the University's pigeon post messenger service, using said postcards and thus having frequent occasion to ponder the question. A chance conversation with the college Archivist and Librarian, Alma Jenner, eventually provided an answer. The 'black line' was in fact a pelmet, put in place to house a blackout curtain. She told me that Mansfield had been 'taken over by the Admiralty' during the war, and that the pelmet had remained in place for decades after. The next question was inevitable: what had the Admiralty wanted the college for? It has taken me the best part of three decades to get around to doing the research necessary to provide an answer, which turns out to be just one part of the intriguing story of Oxford's experience of the Second World War.

My thanks are due to the anonymous manuscript reviewer, and:

Dr Silke Ackermann, Director, History of Science Museum, Oxford
Kate Alderson-Smith, Fellow Librarian, Harris Manchester College, Oxford
Izzie Alexandrou, Balliol College, Oxford, and Co-editor of *Cherwell* (2023)
Dr Ian Archer, Keble College, Oxford
Dr Suzanne Bardgett, former Head of Research and Academic Partnerships, Imperial War Museums
Professor Sir John Boardman, former Assistant Keeper, Ashmolean Museum, Emeritus Lincoln Professor of Classical Archaeology and Art, University of Oxford
Julia Boardman
Dr Thomas Cheetham, Research Officer, Bletchley Park
Tom Cosgrove, Oxford Brookes University
Judith Curthoys, Archivist and Data Protection Compliance Manager, Christ Church, Oxford
Dr Robin Darwall-Smith, Archivist, Jesus College, Oxford, and University College, Oxford

Dr Amy Ebrey, Assistant Archivist, The Queen's College, Oxford
Dr Samuel Fanous, Head of Publishing, Bodleian Library Publishing
Professor David French, University College London
Liz Gardner, PhD research student, King's College London
Emma Goodrum, Archivist and Records Manager, Worcester College, Oxford
Bethany Hall, Assistant Archivist, Corpus Christi College, Oxford
Dr David Ian Hall, King's College London
Nick Hawkins, PhD research student, King's College London
The Honorary Secretaries, Christ Church and Farley Hill Beagles
Dr Tim Horder, Co-editor, *Oxford Magazine*
Amanda Ingram, Archivist, Pembroke College, Oxford, and St Hugh's College, Oxford
David Innes, Soldiers of Oxfordshire Museum
Dr Emily Jennings, Assistant Archivist and Records Manager, Magdalen College, Oxford
Sally Jones, Librarian and Archivist, Mansfield College, Oxford
Dr David Jordan, King's College London
Clare Kavanagh, Librarian and Archivist, Mansfield College, Oxford
Dr Saul Kelly, King's College London
Dr David Kenyon, Historian, Bletchley Park
Julie Anne Lambert, Librarian of the John Johnson Collection of Printed Ephemera, Bodleian Libraries, Oxford
Meg Lintern, St Catherine's College, Oxford, and Co-editor of *Cherwell* (2023)
Alice Millea, Assistant Keeper of the University Archives, Bodleian Libraries, Oxford
Nick Millea, Map Librarian, Bodleian Libraries, Oxford
Peter Monteith, Archivist and Information Compliance Manager, Keble College, Oxford
Tony Morris, historian and keeper of the 'Morris Oxford' website
Lucy Morton, book designer
Victoria Northridge, Archivist and Records Manager, Exeter College, Oxford
Kate O'Donnell, Assistant Archivist and Records Manager, Somerville College, Oxford
The Oxford Union
Verity Parkinson, Resource Services and Support Librarian, Merton College, Oxford
Rob Petre, Archivist, St Edmund Hall, Oxford
Janet Phillips, Editor, Bodleian Library Publishing
Michael Riordan, Archivist, The Queen's College and St John's College, Oxford
Leanda Shrimpton, Picture Editor, Bodleian Library Publishing
Professor Andrew Stewart, Head of Conflict Research, Centre for Historical Analysis and Conflict Research, Camberley
Helen Sumping, Archivist, Brasenose College, Oxford
Stewart Tiley, Librarian, Balliol College, Oxford
James Tobin, historian, Hook Norton Brewery
Colonel Dr Martin Todd, Director Plans, Land Command and Staff College
David Tomkins, Research Data Curation Specialist, Bodleian Libraries, Oxford
Stephen Witkowski, British Council

PICTURE CREDITS

1 Bodleian Library, C17:49 (55)
2 Bodleian Library, OUA UR6/CQ/11/1 file 1
3 Author's collection
4 Bodleian Library, OUA UR6/CQ/11/13 file 1
5 Harris Manchester College Archive. Reproduced with permission of the Principal and Fellows of Harris Manchester College, Oxford, MS. 3 World War II
6 Reproduced courtesy of Mansfield College, Oxford
7 The Principal and Fellows of Brasenose College, Oxford, B1240-1, p.1
8 Oxfordshire County Council – Oxfordshire History Centre, POX0081384
9 Oxfordshire County Council – Oxfordshire History Centre, POX0135195
10 Author's collection
11 The Provost and Fellows, Worcester College, Oxford, Accession no. 256
12 Author's collection
13 © Tate N05717
14 Imperial War Museum, London, Art.IWM ART LD 6009
15 Ashmolean Museum, University of Oxford, WA2011.71 / © Estate of Milein Cosman
16 Oxfordshire County Council – Oxfordshire History Centre, POX0137273
17 Oxfordshire County Council – Oxfordshire History Centre, POX0082280
18 Oxfordshire County Council – Oxfordshire History Centre, POX0130208
19 Oxfordshire County Council – Oxfordshire History Centre, POX0130285
20 Bodleian Library, d. 1866
21 Bodleian Library, MS. Minn 60/3
22 Imperial War Museum, London, D 19141
23 Reproduced by kind permission of the copyright holders and the Master and Fellows of Balliol College, Oxford, Catalogue number 59
24 Bodleian Library, OUA AM 28/10
25 Reproduced courtesy of St Hilda's College, Oxford
26 Author's collection
27 Oxfordshire County Council – Oxfordshire History Centre, POX0131594
28 Harris Manchester College Archive. Reproduced with permission of the Principal and Fellows of Harris Manchester College, Oxford, MS. Bradford 1
29 Harris Manchester College Archive. Reproduced with permission of the Principal and Fellows of Harris Manchester College, Oxford, MS. Bradford 1
30 Bodleian Library, 20503 e.143
31 By kind permission of the Principal and Fellows of St Hugh's College, Oxford, SHC HHA-6-1-19
32 By kind permission of the Principal and Fellows of St Hugh's College, Oxford, SHC HHA-6-2-5
33 Library of Congress
34 © The Estate of John Harvey. By kind permission of the Master, Fellows and Scholars of Pembroke College, Oxford/The Pembroke College JCR Art Collection WMR-60036

INDEX

Addison, Paul 190, 226, 273
Air Raid Precaution (ARP) 1, 2, 11, 57–60, 63, 67, 79, 85, 92, 123, 137, 139, 140, 149, 151, 156, 161, 204, 209, 245, 269
Alington, Giles 108
Allen, Carleton Kemp 36
All Saints Church 2, 39, 272
All Souls College 5, 40, 45, 78, 79, 84, 87, 106, 113, 136, 148, 196, 199–200, 213, 216–17, 222, 224, 227
Amis, Kingsley 9, 135, 158, 187, 188
Anderson, Sir John 56, 78
Andrews, Herbert 184, 185
Anstey, Peter 180, 190, 206, 275
Apollo University Masonic Lodge 12, 114, 282
Apostles club 43
Arnold, Matthew 8, 36
Ashmolean Museum 2, 15, 22, 58, 62, 94, 98, 109, 118–19, 138, 143–5, 167, 170, 173–4, 209, 230, 263
Austin, J.L. 204
Ayer, A.J. 199

Baedeker air raids 2, 148
Baker, Herbert 14, 19
Balliol College 4, 9, 14, 22, 23, 25, 26, 29, 35, 44, 49, 53, 57, 67, 72, 79, 83, 84, 86, 95, 98, 108, 111, 139, 140, 145, 148, 151, 158, 167, 168, 178,
179, 184, 201, 209, 211, 213, 214, 222, 223, 225, 226, 228, 230, 254, 255, 268, 273, 282
Bassett, Colonel Sam 100, 232, 234, 237, 238, 239, 277
Battle of Britain 2, 69, 123, 151
Bawden, Nina 26, 140, 150, 175, 182, 186, 188, 191–2, 264, 276
Bayes, Walter 173
Belfield, Eversley 72–3, 177, 194, 274
Benner, Patrick 181
Berlin, Isaiah 122, 200
Berners, Lord, *Far from the Madding War*, 164–6
Betjeman, John 10, 19, 20, 31, 37, 87, 133, 161, 164, 195, 264
Summoned by Bells 195
Beveridge, Sir William 4, 53, 133–4, 177, 201–5, 214–16, 224
Bevin, Ernest 215
Blackwell's Bookshop 9, 111
Blenheim Palace 37, 47, 82, 101–3, 127, 178, 222, 261, 264, 288
Bletchley Park, Government Code and Cypher School 4, 5, 61, 94–5, 98, 112, 141, 167, 198, 202, 210, 226–30, 239, 241, 243
Blitz, the 97, 100, 137, 145, 150, 154, 180, 221
Blunden, Edmund 36, 65, 133, 134, 160, 158, 195, 202–3, 208, 209

Blyth, Cora 44
Bodleian Library 18, 58–9, 155
  Clarendon Building 18, 64, 66, 88
  Duke Humfrey's 144
  New Bodleian 1, 15, 18, 19, 58–9,
    67, 74, 98–9, 109–11, 118, 141,
    143–8, 183, 226, 230, 234, 236,
    238–9, 247, 276, 277
  Old Bodleian 59, 110
  Radcliffe Camera 59, 144, 169, 276
  Radcliffe Science Library 15, 27, 169
  Taylorian 110
Bodley's Librarian 59, 110, 137, 224,
  276
Botanic Garden, Oxford 14, 170
Boulay, Roger du 26, 191
Bowen, K.C. 29, 35
Bowra, Maurice 3, 19, 25–6, 38–9, 41,
  45, 49, 52, 61–2, 79, 134, 153, 164,
  194, 202–3, 205–6, 208, 210, 275,
  280
Braham, Pam 236
Brasenose College 2, 26, 32, 34, 84, 86,
  87, 91, 92, 106, 109, 114, 125, 132,
  140, 145, 159, 163, 169, 178, 183,
  184, 187, 190, 194, 208, 209, 227,
  261, 266, 273
Brierly, James 45, 113, 167, 203
British Library, London 1, 148
British Museum, London 143, 146, 211
Brittain, Vera 120
Brockliss, Laurence 33, 53, 273
Brønner, Heidi 169, 184, 237
Brooke, General Sir Alan 129
Buchan, John, Lord Tweedsmuir 53, 54
Bujić, Bojan 150, 167
Bullard, Sir Reader 120, 154
Butler, R.A. 81, 217, 222, 277
Buxton, John 194

Cairns, Hugh 253–60, 277
Calvert, Loraine 122
Campion Hall 14, 183, 201
Carpenter, H.J. 266
Cary, Joyce 209
Cecil, Lord David 26, 109
Chain, Ernst 251, 277

Chamberlain, Neville 47–9, 56
Chatham House, Royal Institute of
  International Affairs 4, 78–9, 83,
  86, 108, 201, 203, 209, 211–12, 218,
  219, 243
Cherwell newspaper 186
Chetwode, Penelope, Lady Betjeman
  141, 164
Christ Church 3, 4, 8, 13, 14, 18, 32,
  40, 47, 48, 52, 54, 63, 73, 74, 83,
  85, 86, 91, 92, 97, 116, 118, 130, 133,
  138, 142, 144, 154, 155, 166, 170,
  178, 181, 183, 184, 189, 199, 200,
  201, 218, 223, 227, 229, 264, 265,
  273, 278, 286
Christ Church Meadow 3, 8, 14, 50,
  181, 286
Churchill Hospital 3, 60, 121, 157, 174,
  284
Churchill, Randolph 41
Churchill, Sir Winston 47, 134, 198,
  201, 203, 223, 224, 232, 245, 264
Civilian Repair Organization (CRO)
  68–9, 88, 107
Clarendon Hotel 11, 63, 157, 282
Clarendon Laboratory 4, 77, 78, 109,
  201, 247
Clark, Sir Kenneth 173
Clay, Sir Charles Travis 59
Clish, Lorna 117, 169, 188, 191
Cobban, James 97, 178, 179
Cole, G.D.H. 40, 213, 215, 216
Collison, Peter 24, 38
Colvin, Howard 18
Cooke, Arthur 246, 277
Coombe, Ken 76, 140, 169, 180, 189
Cooper, Stephen 181
Coppock, June 141, 158, 240, 263
Corpus Christi College 44, 53, 58, 83,
  85, 86, 122, 136, 145, 205, 228, 273
Cosman, Milein 167, 173
Coupland, Sir Reginald 213, 223
Cowley works 1, 17, 18, 19, 68–9, 88,
  120–22, 182, 250, 287–8
Cox, Christopher 214
Craster, Edmund 59, 67, 137, 145–6,
  155

INDEX 367

Crispin, Edmund 279
Crossman, Richard 48, 224
Curtis, Lionel 79, 222
Cutteslowe Park 3, 154, 172

D-Day preparations 1, 3, 37, 159–63,
    235, 237, 239, 247, 254, 260, 287
Daft, W. Austin 170
Daily Express 46
Daily Mail 51
Daily Mirror 153
Dalton, Hugh 40, 202, 224
Darbishire, Helen 53, 161
Darwall-Smith, Robin 273
Darwin, John 51
Davis, C. Noel 114–15
Denniston, Alastair 78
Department of Scientific and Industrial
    Research (DSIR) 244–8
Douglas, Keith 37, 208
Driver, Godfrey 204
Dubber, Frank 58, 144, 277
Dudden, Homes 144, 169, 178, 283
Dummett, Michael 227
Dunkirk 2, 116, 123, 124, 125, 126,
    129, 131, 157, 159, 168, 200, 208
Dunnett, Pam 162
Dyson, Hugo 63

Eden, Anthony 74, 211
Einstein, Albert 51, 54
Eisenhower, Dwight D. 111, 204, 237,
    238, 239
Eisenmayer, Ernst 167–8
Emden, Alfred 105, 199
Evelyn, John 146
Examination Schools 5, 12, 29, 58, 67,
    85, 92, 109, 110, 144, 154, 283
Exeter College 64, 84, 93, 118, 140,
    208, 272
Eynsham Hall 127, 164

Faiz, A.S. 24
Fasnacht, Ruth 20
Ferrar, Dr W.L. 207
Fisher, H.A.L. 198, 209, 217, 286
Flatter, Otto 174

Fleming, Ian 230
Fletcher, Tom 61
Florey, Howard 4, 50, 119, 128, 251–4,
    258, 277, 288
Florey, James 128
Florey, Mary 252
Foot, Michael 47
Fox, Charles 59, 128, 136, 145, 172
Franco, General Francisco 43, 50, 148,
    250
Freeman, Richard 47
Fulljames, John 133
Fulton, J.F. 116

Gibbins, Janet 140, 182
Gilbert, Martin 264
Gill, Walter 199
Gimson, Herbert 107
Godfrey, Rear Admiral John 113, 230,
    234
Godfrey, Margaret 112
Goldsmiths College, London 146
Gollancz, Victor 185
    see also Left Book Club
Goodhart, Arthur 108, 223
Gordon, George 48–9, 53, 57, 70–71,
    79, 146, 209
Government Code and Cypher School
    (GCCS) 61, 78, 226, 227
    see also Bletchley Park
Government Communications
    Headquarters (GCHQ) *see*
    Government Code and Cypher
    School; Bletchley Park
Greene, Graham 55
Grenville, Anthony 51
Grove, Stella 175, 179, 180, 182
Gunther, Dr Robert 67, 147–8
Gwyer, Barbara 49, 58, 95, 262

Hackney, Alan, *Private's Progress* 135,
    274
Hadow, Grace 169
Haldane, Charlotte 50
Hampshire, Stuart 227
Hardie, Frank 47
Hardy, Thomas, *Jude the Obscure* 19, 38

Harper-Nelson, John 10, 25, 27, 29, 32–5, 73, 118, 139, 150, 156, 175, 181, 186, 189, 191, 193, 275
Harris, Jose 26
Harrisson, Tom 28
Hart-Synnot, Ronald 83, 106
Harvard, Robert 63
Hastings, Selina 37
Hayter, William 43
Headington Hill Hall 66, 91, 125, 259
Healey, Denis 38, 40, 43, 44, 45, 72
Healey, Mary 126, 179
Heath, Edward 40, 45, 47–8, 72
Heatley, Norman 119, 252–3
Herdman, Ethel 111–12
Hertford College 14, 74, 84, 86, 206–7, 273
Hesketh-Williams, Philippa 258
Heywood, Major Marcus 100–102, 108
Hibbert, Christopher 120
Hicks, David 195
Hill, Sir Arthur 145
Hillary, Richard 73, 177–8
Hitler, Adolf 2, 9, 41, 45, 46, 49, 51, 52, 60, 63, 82, 119, 120, 121, 131, 134, 148, 180, 184, 187, 218, 219, 239, 247, 251, 261, 263, 264, 285, 288
Hobhouse, Christopher 18, 28, 31, 46
Hodgkin, Dr Dorothy 254
Hodgkin, Robert 'Robin' 90, 203
Hogg, Quintin 49, 224
Hok, Edward 94, 227, 240, 242
Holdsworth, Richard 79, 200, 203
Hollinghurst, Alan, *The Sparsholt Affair* 139
Hollis, Christopher 185
Holst, Gustav 146
Holyoake Hall 142
Home Guard 1, 2, 3, 88, 115, 119, 123, 130, 131, 156, 158, 161, 171, 209, 210, 244
Hook Norton Brewery 66, 153, 155, 162

Indian Institute 12, 109, 110, 145
Inklings 10, 39, 142, 220, 265
    see also C.S. Lewis, J.R.R. Tolkien,

Charles Williams
Intelligence Corps 87, 96–7, 178, 200, 227–8
Inter-Service Topographical Department (ISTD) 112, 230–43, 277
Ironside, General Sir Edmund 128
Isis magazine 31, 40

James, J.D. 196
James, Dr W.O. 248–9
Jenkins, Roy 40, 67, 175, 176
Jesus College 44, 58, 64, 84, 86, 137, 141, 191, 272
Johns, Captain W.E., *Biggles* 22, 114
Johnson, John 113, 238, 242, 276
Joint Intelligence Committee (JIC) 232–3

Kantorowicz, Ernst 45, 49
Keble College 13, 67, 86, 100–102, 107, 170, 266, 273
Kelmscott Manor 146
Keynes, J.M. 202
King's College, London 143
Knudtzon, Eleonore Fredrikke 236
Kuhn, Heinrich 52, 247, 248

Lady Margaret Hall (LMH) 13, 14, 78, 97, 173, 228
Lamborn, Edmund Greening 13
Landon, Philip 118, 189
Lang, Cosmo 46
Larkin, Philip 10, 13, 32, 71, 75, 135, 149, 192, 193, 206, 272, 279
    Jill 10, 13, 149
Laurel and Hardy, *A Chump at Oxford* 42
Lawrence, T.E. 254, 260
Lazarus, Abe 44
Leatherdale, Anthony 97, 191
Leeds, Dr Edward 62
Lees-Milne, J. 37
Left Book Club 47, 176
Lester, Stanley 125, 171
Lewis, C.S. 2, 10, 63, 66, 111, 131, 142, 195, 205, 209, 219–20
    The Problem of Pain 219
Lewis, Warnie 2, 63

INDEX 369

Lincoln College 15, 33, 85, 106, 187, 265

Lindemann, Sir Frederick 4, 15, 45, 47, 52, 134, 198, 201–2, 223, 244, 246–7

Lindsay, A.D. 'Sandie' 44, 49, 50, 53, 64, 71, 254

Livingstone, Sir Richard 171

Lloyd, Francis 116

Local Defence Volunteers see Home Guard

Longmate, Norman 121

Luke, Sir Harry 114

Lutyens, Edwin 14

Mabbott, John 198, 205, 209, 211, 279, 282

McCallum, Neta 163

McFarlane, Bruce 176, 204, 218

MacInnes, Charles 172

Macintosh, Robert 249, 250

McNaughton, General Andrew 127

Magdalen College 1, 2, 3, 4, 5, 9, 11, 14, 16, 31, 33, 36, 52, 53, 66, 84, 87, 88, 114, 116, 134, 140, 141, 150, 151, 154, 157, 158, 161, 166, 169, 172, 176, 177, 184, 187, 188, 195, 200, 204, 209, 218, 223, 245, 262, 263, 264, 265, 267, 273, 279, 283, 287

Majestic Cinema 60, 142, 158

Manchester College 57, 85, 96, 98, 99, 100, 107, 111, 112, 114, 115, 118, 123, 154, 167, 169, 187, 201, 230, 232, 237, 239, 262

Mansfield College 12, 13, 46, 52, 61, 64, 84, 93, 94, 95, 98, 106, 112, 118, 134, 141, 145, 151, 154, 156, 166, 167, 169, 219, 226, 227, 230, 239–42, 263, 270, 287

Martin, John 223

Martin, Kingsley 221

Martin, Madge 39, 49, 63–4, 66, 117, 128, 141, 153, 158–9, 161, 162, 171–2, 262, 265

Marx, Enid, *Bulgy the Barrage Balloon* 114

Mason, Kenneth 230–31

Masterman, John Cecil 40, 229, 279

Mee, Arthur 20, 21

Melles, Monica 125

Mendelssohn, Kurt 52, 247

Merton College 1, 14, 36, 37, 45, 57, 61, 63, 73, 84, 86, 88, 107, 118, 134, 137, 144, 145, 177, 184, 199, 208, 262, 265, 268, 269, 273, 286

Micklem, Nathaniel 'Nat' 46, 93, 94, 95, 134, 151, 219

Milburn, R.L.P. 'Bobby' 87, 104

Miles, Sir John 134, 269

Milman, Octavius 107

Milne, Edward 244

Ministry of Food 1, 5, 55, 85, 192, 193, 288

Ministry of Works 57, 59, 60, 83, 85, 87, 90, 98, 99, 101, 102, 105, 107, 114, 238, 268, 269, 270

Mitchell, Leslie 40

Montgomery, Bruce 10, 32, 137, 176

Moore, Janie King 131

Morley, Thomas 140

Morrell, Jack 243

Morrell, Jimmy 30

Morrells Brewery 30, 66, 153, 259

Morris Motors 18, 66, 68

see also Cowley works

Morris, William, Baron Nuffield 14, 17, 19, 68–9, 248, 255, 284

Mortimer, John 25, 34, 91, 175, 193, 198

Mosley, Oswald 47–8

Moullin, Eric 200

Muir, Dorothy Erskine 13, 20

Murdoch, Iris 50, 61–2, 165, 179, 195

Murray, Gilbert 53, 136, 152

Museum of the History of Science 58, 67, 247–8, 287

Mussolini, Benito 41, 46, 264

Nash, Paul 69, 132, 133, 149, 164, 173

Battle of Britain 173

Oxford during the War 167, PLATE 11

Totes Meer 69, 173, PLATE 13

National Library of Wales 118

Naval Intelligence Division (NID) 98, 100, 111–12, 169, 230–34, 240–43
Newboult, Harold 107
New College 1, 2, 12, 13, 15, 23, 26, 27, 36, 48, 50, 84, 85, 86, 91, 94, 95, 97, 98, 119, 129, 137, 144, 151, 181, 184, 185, 191, 193, 194, 195, 198, 200, 209, 214, 230, 246, 262, 264, 267, 270, 273, 278, 282, 286
New Theatre 10, 17, 172, 262, 277
Nicol Cross, Robert 98, 100, 107
Nicolson, Harold 148, 199, 224
Nicolson, Nigel 25, 35, 37, 225
Norwood, Cyril 144, 217, 268
Nuffield College 16, 109, 213, 286
Nuneham Park 60
Nutting, Willis 51

Oriel College 3, 23, 24, 45, 58, 66, 79, 84, 86, 87, 96, 97, 100, 118, 136, 145, 154, 157, 172, 190, 206, 223, 226, 273, 275
Oxford Famine Relief Committee (Oxfam) 152
Oxford Labour Club 36, 40, 43, 47, 50
Oxford Magazine 80, 134, 186, 273, 285
Oxford Mail 64, 142, 172
Oxford Playhouse 17
Oxfordshire and Buckinghamshire Light Infantry (OBLI) 13, 66, 124, 130, 159
Oxford Town Hall 2, 17, 44, 48, 59, 72, 142, 151, 157, 158, 159
Oxford Union 13, 40, 41, 51, 145, 185, 222
Oxford University Press (OUP) 22, 39, 51, 54, 61, 63, 98, 109, 112–14, 121, 138, 155, 219, 226, 230, 238, 239–42, 276
Clarendon Press 113, 145
see also John Johnson

Pakenham, Frank (Baron Pakenham of Cowley) 3, 48, 50, 63
Palmer, Thomas 21
Palmer, Tony 186
Paolozzi, Eduardo 138, 173
Park, Daphne 229

Parker, Ruth 138
Parry, Glenys 160
Pembroke College 11, 25, 32, 73, 84, 86, 87, 96, 97, 106, 107, 130, 140, 144, 164, 169, 177, 178, 180, 183, 184, 186, 188, 190, 191, 194, 208, 220, 226, 267, 268, 272, 273, 274, 283
People's Bookshop 47
Perham, Margery 213
Phelps, Tony 139
Philpot, Oliver 32
Picasso, Pablo, *Guernica* 45
Piper, John 103
Platts, John 185
Playhouse theatre 17, 49, 138, 173
Pliatzky, Leo 195, 207
Plumer, Eleanor 156, 182
Political Warfare Executive (PWE) 217–18, 224, 243
Portillo, Luis 45
Portillo, Michael 45
Port Meadow 3, 8, 65, 125, 154, 158, 182
Potter, John 256
Powell, Anthony 38, 41
Powicke, Maurice 54
Priestley, J.B. 61
Prieto, Gregorio 173
Prior, Christopher 264
pubs 10, 13, 19, 30, 31, 32, 153, 169, 172, 220, 275
Eagle and Child 10, 173, 220
Grapes 3
King's Arms 10, 275
Lamb and Flag 10
Mitre Hotel 10, 11, 223
Turf Tavern 10
White Horse 10, 275
Pullman, Philip, *His Dark Materials* 7
Pusey House 1

Queen's College, The 3, 5, 23, 30, 32, 84, 85, 90, 91, 118, 123, 138, 142, 151, 154, 155, 171, 173, 176, 179, 183, 190, 203, 209, 227, 265, 266, 273

Quirk, J.T. 262

Radcliffe Infirmary 4, 17, 60, 97, 111,
115, 123, 138, 172, 182–3, 248,
250–52, 255, 260, 284
Radcliffe Square 1, 16, 159, 168
Randolph Hotel 10, 11, 45, 127, 137,
139, 148, 152, 177
Rayner, Margaret 33
Regent's Park College 15
Reynolds, Joshua 119
Rhodes House 3, 14, 18, 36, 59, 95,
109, 142, 162, 187, 209
Richards, J.M. 18
Roberts, Tom 74
Robertson, Grant 116
Roche, John 285
Rollright Stones 123
Roosevelt, Franklin D. 46, 82, 211, 223
Ross, Douglas 25, 72, 97, 122, 140, 160,
164, 180, 184, 188
Rowse, A.L. 18, 19, 36, 53, 68, 75, 110,
135, 165–6, 174, 181, 205, 206, 222
Roxby, Barbara 241
Royal Botanic Gardens, Kew 1, 145
Royal Holloway College, London 96
Rubinstein, Nicolai 54
Ruskin College 5, 61, 224, 251
Ruskin School of Art 138
Rutter, David 73
Ryle, Gilbert 227

St Anne's College 14, 23, 182
St Catherine's College 23
St Edmund Hall 5, 32, 35, 85, 87, 105,
150, 183, 188, 199, 245, 266, 281,
282
St Hilda's College 2, 9, 13, 25, 33, 37,
44, 66, 95, 97, 118, 134, 137, 142,
154, 155, 161, 172, 183, 186, 187,
188, 191
St Hugh's College 5, 14, 33, 49, 58, 67,
84, 95, 96, 106, 111, 116, 117, 123,
125, 126, 140, 151, 169, 175, 176,
179, 182, 184, 188, 191, 203, 209,
228, 229, 254–65, 266, 270, 271,
272, 274, 282

St Michael's Church 1, 39, 45, 64
St John's College 2, 5, 9, 10, 32, 57, 72,
78, 83, 84, 85, 103, 106, 137, 140,
144, 170, 186, 188, 198, 211, 217,
262, 267, 268, 279, 282, 283, 287
St Peter's College 23, 67, 86. 178, 266
St Peter-in-the-East 3
Salter's Boatyard 3, 63
Sayers, Dorothy L. 279
Scala Cinema 17
Schrödinger, Erwin 52
Science Museum, London 146
Scott, Sir Giles Gilbert 14, 18, 19, 144
Security Service (MI5) 5, 100–103,
107–8, 128, 229, 261
Seddon, Herbert 249
Sheldonian Theatre 18, 58, 71, 110, 113,
165, 170, 184, 207
Shenton, Caroline 121
Sherwood Taylor, Frank 147–8
Sisman, Adam 39
Slade School of Art 138
Smith, Alic 137, 209, 282
Smith, H. Tyson 272
Somerville College 3, 11, 13, 14, 24,
26, 34, 36, 50, 52, 53, 60, 84, 95,
97, 120, 138, 140, 152, 154, 161, 175,
177, 182, 183, 184, 187, 229, 249,
254, 265, 266
Southwell, Richard 78
Spanish Civil War 2, 43, 61, 176,
249–50
Sparrow, John 199, 224
Stallybrass, William 26, 29, 91–2, 194,
208, 266
Standen, Denis 122
Steel-Maitland, Keith 47
Stokes, John 116
Strawbridge, David 192
Street, Annette 101
Swinton, Sir Ernest 79
Symonds, Richard 45

Tawney, R.H. 214
Taylor, A.J.P. 3, 39, 64–5, 134, 154,
203, 212, 217, 264
Taylor, Margaret 151

Thatcher, Margaret (née Roberts) 24,
40, 157, 184, 191
Thomas, Albert 132, 135, 150, 159, 170,
172, 190, 192, 261
Thompson, E.P. 50
Thompson, Edward 79
Thompson, Flora 114
Thompson, Frank 50, 195
Thompson, James, *Only the Sun
Remembers* 33, 196
Thomson, Ian 206
Thwaite, Ann 37
Tizard, Sir Henry 4, 52, 114, 244, 277
Tolkien, Edith 39
Tolkien, J.R.R. 10, 39, 149, 154, 169,
202, 204, 209, 220–21, 265
The Hobbit 221
The Lord of the Rings 204, 220
Townshend, Sir John 77
Toynbee, Arnold 211
Trevor-Roper, Hugh 25, 36, 45, 48, 57,
63, 199, 208, 218, 229
Trinity College 2, 10, 29, 30, 32, 33,
34, 35, 67, 73, 76, 78, 84, 86, 110,
116, 118, 122, 134, 139, 140, 145,
150, 153, 154, 156, 166, 168, 169,
177, 178, 183, 184, 186, 187, 189,
204, 265, 273, 275
Trueta, Josep 250
Turing, Alan 228
Turrill, Dr William 111, 145
Tynan, Kenneth 279

University Archives 145
University College 4, 21, 62, 79, 85, 93,
108, 112, 130, 133, 134, 139, 140,
145, 155, 176, 177, 181, 184, 186,
187, 188, 200, 202, 204, 206, 215,
273, 274, 276
University College, London 21, 143
Senate House Library 146
University Museum 13, 45, 140, 244
University Officers' Training Corps
(UOTC) 72, 73, 76, 104

University Parks 1, 3, 8, 15, 135, 141,
151, 154, 162
Upper Thames Patrol 2

Vaughan, Dr Janet 249
Vaughan Williams, Ralph 8, 136
An Oxford Elegy 8
Veale, Dr Douglas 60, 83, 85, 93–6,
100–107, 136, 143, 147, 168, 209,
238, 254, 268–9, 276
Victoria and Albert Museum 145

Wadham College 1, 3, 4, 12, 19, 23, 26,
33, 49, 62, 67, 76, 98, 119, 153, 154,
208, 210, 244, 275, 282
Holywell Music Room 98
Wain, John 72
Walker, Patrick Gordon 48, 49
Watt, Bill 158, 201
Waugh, Evelyn 37, 38, 193, 221, 279
Brideshead Revisited 7, 38, 221
Wellington Square 1, 11, 137
Wells, Frederick 204, 232, 234
Westfield College, London 67, 87
Wheare, Kenneth 32, 134
Whittal, C.E. 125
Wild, John 133, 204, 205
Wilkinson, Cyril 72, 104, 209
Williams, Charles 39, 142, 220, 265
Williams, Emlyn 38
Williams, Penry 26
Wilson, Harold 94, 215, 270
Wingfield-Morris hospital 111, 115,
248–9
Women's Auxiliary Air Force (WAAF)
11, 25, 88
Worcester College 3, 12, 14, 16, 24,
32, 72, 76, 85, 87, 103, 104, 122,
151, 169, 179, 188, 189, 208, 229,
249, 273
Wren, Christopher 18

Zimmern, Alfred 51, 113